CONTENTS

ACKNOWLEDGEMENTS

The author would like to express his sincere gratitude to Mr Chris Gale for his thoughts at the proofs stage of this work, Mr Chris Turner and Ms Jacqueline Martin for their suggestions in improving the presentation of the materials, and Ms Alexia Chan and the staff at Hodder Arnold for their enormous patience and assistance in the completion of this book.

This book is dedicated to my late mother.

PREFACE

The *Unlocking the Law* series is an entirely new style of undergraduate law textbook. Many student texts are very prose dense and have little in the way of interactive materials to help a student feel his or her way through the course of study on a given module.

The purpose of this series, then, is to try to make learning each subject area more accessible by focusing on actual learning needs, and by providing a range of different supporting materials and features.

All topic areas are broken up into 'bite-size' sections, with a logical progression and extensive use of headings and numerous sub-headings. Each book in the series will also contain a variety of charts, diagrams and key facts summaries to reinforce the information in the body of the text. Diagrams and flow charts are particularly useful because they can provide a quick and easy understanding of the key points, especially when revising for examinations. Key facts charts not only provide a quick visual guide through the subject but are useful for revision purposes also.

The books have a number of common features in the style of text layout. Important cases are separated out for easy access and have full citation in the text as well as in the table of cases, for ease of reference. The emphasis of the series is on depth of understanding much more than breadth. For this reason, each text also includes key extracts from judgments, where appropriate. Extracts from academic comment from journal articles and leading texts are also included to give some insight into the academic debate on complex or controversial areas. In both cases these are indented to make them clear from the body of the text.

Finally, the books also include much formative 'self-testing', with a variety of activities ranging through subject-specific comprehension, application of the law, and a range of other activities to help the student gain a good idea of his or her progress in the course.

Symbols used in this series:

 This is a small extract from a judgment in a case. It may follow a case example or the case may be identified immediately above.

 This is a section from an Act.

 This is an Article of the EC Treaty or of the European Convention on Human Rights.

This is a clause from a draft Bill or Code.

 This is a quote from a government paper, Royal commission report or similar.

Where a paragraph is indented, this is an extract from an academic source such as an article or a leading textbook.

Note also that for all incidental references to 'he', 'him', 'his', we invoke the Interpretation Act 1978 and its provisions that 'he' includes 'she' etc.

The law of trusts has developed over the centuries as essentially a case law subject tempered occasionally by statutory intervention. This process of development continues in modern society as new situations arise. The principal objectives in writing this book are to produce a text that has the right balance in terms of exposition of the law in a clear, concise and simple style, and presentation of the subject in a structured and accessible manner. Chapters 1 and 2 introduce the reader to the subject, Chapters 3 to 12 (inclusive) analyse the various types of trusts in existence and Chapters 13 to 16 examine the principles involved in the administration of trusts.

This book is designed to assist undergraduate law students and those reading for professional and postgraduate qualifications.

The law is stated as I believe it to be on 28th February 2005.

M. Ramjohn

TABLE OF CASES ■

TABLE OF STATUTES
AND OTHER INSTRUMENTS

LIST OF FIGURES ◾

chapter 1 HISTORICAL OUTLINES OF EQUITY ■

1.1 Introduction to equity

'Equity is the branch of law, which, before the Judicature Acts 1873 and 1875 was applied and administered by the Court of Chancery.'

(Maitland, *Equity*, 2nd edn, (Brunyate ed))

The system of equity includes that portion of natural justice which is judicially enforceable but which for various reasons was not enforced by the courts of common law.

Equity, unlike the common law, was not an independent system of legal rules. It did not stand alone. It presupposed the existence of the common law, which it supplemented and modified. The rules of equity were originally based on conscience and were applied on a case-by-case basis. Although the rules of equity did not directly contradict the common law, the application of equitable rules could produce an effect different from the common law solution. The two systems of rules were complementary to each other.

1.1.1 Terminology

Originally, the expressions 'equity' or 'rules of equity' were synonymous with rules of justice and conscience. Individual Lord Chancellors did not consciously set out to develop a system of rules, but attempted in individual cases to achieve fairness and justice *ad hoc*. Accordingly, the principles originally applied by Lord Chancellors to determine disputes were based on rules of natural justice or conscience. These principles became known as equity.

Today, it would not be accurate to correlate 'equity' with 'justice', for rules of equity have become settled in much the same way as the common law.

1.1.2 Petitions to the Lord Chancellor

In the thirteenth century, the available writs covered a narrow ground of claims – even if a claim came within the scope of an existing writ, the claimant might not achieve justice before a common law court, for example in an action commenced by the writs of debt and detinue, the defendant was entitled to wage his law. This was a process whereby the defendant discharged himself from a claim by denying the claim on oath and calling 11 persons from his neighbourhood to swear that his denial was true. In addition, a great deal of unnecessary intricacies were attendant on the pleadings. The pleadings were drafted by experts and the rule at this time was that an incorrect pleading invariably led to the loss of the claim. Moreover, damages was the only remedy available at law. There were numerous occasions when this remedy proved inadequate.

An aggrieved claimant was entitled to petition the King in Council, praying for relief. These petitions were dealt with by the Lord Chancellor, who was an ecclesiastic well versed in the law. Later on, the petitions were addressed directly to the Lord Chancellor, who dealt personally with the more important cases. Eventually the Chancellor and staff formed a court called the Court of Chancery.

1.1.3 Procedure in Chancery

The petition was presented by way of a bill filed by the claimant. Since proceedings were not commenced by writ as in the common law courts, there was never any strict procedure to be followed. The intervention by the Lord Chancellor (creating new rights and remedies) did not need validation by the pretence adopted by the common law courts in declaring the law from time immemorial, but the Chancellor did not abandon his responsibility in deciding on the justice and merits of individual cases.

In appropriate cases a *subpoena* would be served on the defendant to compel his appearance to attend and answer the petition. The defendant was required to draft his answers on oath called 'interrogatories'.

Usually the evidence was given on affidavit so that proceedings were confined to hearing legal arguments on both sides, but occasionally when the testimony of a witness (including the parties) was required to be received in the court, the witness would testify on oath and be subject to cross-examination by the Chancellor and the opposing party.

The relevant decree of the court was issued in the name of the Chancellor and acted '*in personam*' on the defendant.

1.1.4 The trust – a product of equity

One of the most important contributions of equity was in the field of the 'use' (the predecessor to the 'trust'). The 'use' was a mode of transferring property to another (eg B) to hold to the 'use' or for the benefit of another or others (eg C or D and E)

The 'use' was created in the thirteenth and fourteenth centuries, for a variety of reasons:

(a) Crusades – a landowner who went on the crusades and, fearing for his life and the consequences of a succession of his wealth, might convey land to another (B) during the crusade. Before the Wills Act 1540, wills were not recognised at common law.

(b) Ownership by Franciscan monks – as a result of their vow of poverty, a community of Franciscan monks might transfer land to B, C and D to their use.

(c) Avoidance of feudal incidents.

By far the most important reason for the creation of a use was to avoid the feudal incidents inherent in land ownership such as wardship and escheat (no heir). These burdens were avoided if the land was vested in a number of feoffees to use (trustees). The feoffees were unlikely to die together or without heir. Those who died could be replaced. The feoffees to use were required to hold the land for the benefit of the *cestui que trust* (or beneficiary).

Thus, a tenant, A, might transfer his land by the appropriate common law conveyance to B, who undertook to hold it for the benefit of (or to the 'use' of) A and his heirs. The common law courts did not recognise A's interest (nor his heirs). The legal owner, or feoffee, B was everything. If B refused to account to his *cestuis que use*, A and his heirs, for the profits, or wrongfully conveyed the estate to another, this was treated merely as a breach of confidence on the part of B. The common law did not provide any redress, nor did the law acknowledge any right in A and his heirs to the enjoyment of the land.

1.1.5 The Chancellor's intervention

The non-recognition of the right of enjoyment of the land on the part of A and his heirs had the potential of stultifying the practice of putting lands in use, had there been no alternative means of protecting the *cestui que use*. From about 1400 the Lord Chancellor stepped in and interceded on behalf of the *cestui que use*. He did not interfere with the jurisdiction of the common law courts because the legal title was vested in the feoffees and this title was recognised and given effect by the common law courts. The Chancellor regarded his role as that of ensuring that the feoffee acted honestly and with morality. In accordance with the principle that equity acts *in personam* (against the wrongdoer personally), he proceeded against feoffees who disregarded the moral rights of the *cestui que use*. In other words, the wrong that a rogue feoffee committed was a breach of contract or understanding, but it was a breach for which, at that time, no remedy existed in the common law courts. The enforceability of contracts was still undeveloped and, in any event, the rules of privity of contract would have precluded a remedy to the *cestui que use*.

1.1.6 Duality of ownership

The Chancellor's intervention in the context of the 'use' created the notion of duality of land ownership, which in turn led to duality of ownership of all property. The method adopted by the Chancellor was to insist upon the feoffee scrupulously observing the directions imposed upon him. In other words, the Chancellor, like the common law courts, acknowledged that the feoffee was the owner of the property but the *cestui que use* was regarded as the true owner in equity. The former had the legal title but the latter acquired the equitable ownership in the same property.

Position of the feoffee

At law, the feoffee was regarded as the absolute owner of the property and liable to the incidents of tenure, ie the common law did not recognise the interest of the *cestui que trust*. But in Chancery the feoffee was compelled to carry out the obligations created by the use, ie to recognise the interest and act for the benefit of the *cestui que trust*. Moreover, the Chancery developed the rule that any third parties who took the land from the feoffee with knowledge of the existence of the use was bound by the use. Hence the rule which subsists today that the use (or trust) is valid against the world except a *bona fide* transferee of the legal estate for value without notice.

Position of the *cestui que use*

This individual's interest was not recognised at law but was granted recognition in equity and thus acquired an equitable interest. He was entitled to petition the Court of Chancery to have his interest and rights protected against the feoffee and the world.

1.1.7 Statute of Uses 1535

The principal objection to the use was the loss to the king of revenue arising from the incidents of tenure. The king needed all the revenue he could muster during the sixteenth century and the growth of the use hindered this process. Ultimately, the Statute of Uses 1535 was passed to reduce the scope of the use.

The statute provided that:

> **S** 'where any person(s) shall be seised of any lands or other hereditaments to the use, confidence or trust of any person(s), in every such case such person(s) that shall have any such use, confidence or trust in fee simple, fee tail, term of life or for years or otherwise shall stand and be seised, deemed and adjudged in lawful seisin, estate and possession of and in the same lands in such like estates as they had or shall have in the use.'

The statute did not suppress all uses. It only applied where the feoffee was seised to the use of another – if the feoffee held only for a term of years, he would not be seised and the statute would not apply. In addition, where the feoffee had active duties to perform, the statute did not apply because the *cestui que use* acquired property only after the feoffee had collected the rents and profits or performed his duties. In any event the statute did not execute uses in respect of personal property.

1.1.8 Use upon a use

The effect of the Statute of Uses was not to abolish uses *per se*, but to execute the use, whereby the *cestui que use* became the legal owner, and the feudal dues were collected from him. Where, for example, A (feoffee) held land to the use of B (*cestui que use*), B became the legal (and beneficial) owner.

A technique was adopted in order to create 'a use upon a use', in the hope that the first use would be executed and the second use rendered effective, ie 'to A to the use of B to the use of C'. The effect of this technique was that B held the property to the use of C.

This device did not find favour with the courts at law. The method adopted for defeating this avoidance practice was to treat the second use as repugnant to the first use, and thus void.

CASE EXAMPLE

Jane Tyrrel's Case (1557) Dyer 155

Jane Tyrrel settled land upon herself for life, remainder to her son with a gift over ('to the use of Jane Tyrrel for life remainder to her son with a gift over to the heirs of Jane Tyrrel'). The court held that the second use was repugnant and void and the son took absolutely.

The Court of Chancery at first did not disagree with this result, even though B was never intended to be the beneficial owner. By the seventeenth century the decline in the value of money had diminished the significance of feudal dues. This motivated the Chancellor to give effect to the intention of the creator of the use (settlor). All that was necessary was to add a second use and make the conveyance run 'to the use of B upon trust for C'. The effect was that B was called a trustee, who held the legal title, and C, a beneficiary or *cestui que trust*, who held the equitable title.

1.1.9 Struggle over injunctions

The Court of Chancery had adopted the strategy of issuing a 'common injunction' against the litigant who had obtained a common law remedy unjustly or indeed to prevent him resorting to the common law to obtain a remedy. The use of the common injunction had the effect of sterilising the common law order and was viewed with great dissatisfaction by common law judges.

CASE EXAMPLE

Earl of Oxford's Case (1615) 1 Rep Ch 1

An action was brought in respect of a lease. Judgment in default was entered in favour of the original plaintiff at common law. The defendant (petitioner) instituted a suit in the Chancery Court which issued a common injunction against the original plaintiff, who was served with a subpoena to appear in the Chancery Court.

The Court of Chancery held that the defendant was entitled to relief.

> J 'The office of the Chancellor is to correct man's consciences for frauds, breach of trusts, wrongs and oppressions of whatsoever nature and to soften and mollify the extremity of the law … When judgment is obtained by oppression, wrong and a hard conscience, the Chancellor will frustrate and set it aside, not for any error or defect in the judgment but for the hard conscience of the party.'
>
> (Per Lord Ellesmere LC)

The controversy was eventually resolved by James I in the seventeenth century. He referred the matter to Bacon, the Attorney-General and others learned in the law. They decided in favour of the Court of Chancery. Thereafter, by and large the principles of common law and equity were treated as parts of a complete body of law. This prompted Maitland to write: 'Equity came not to destroy the law but to fulfil it.'

1.2 Contributions of equity

The contributions of equity in the development of the law may be classified into three categories:

- <u>Exclusive jurisdiction (new rights)</u>. This category refers to the rights which the Court of Chancery had created and which the common law courts failed to enforce, for example trusts, mortgages, partnerships, administration of estates, bankruptcy, company law etc.

- <u>Concurrent jurisdiction (new remedies)</u>. Equity developed a wide range of remedies for the enforcement of rights, both at law and in equity. At common law the characteristic remedy was, and still is, damages – a monetary award for the loss suffered which is claimable as of right. However, equitable remedies were more varied and imaginative but were, and still are, discretionary. Accordingly, the court of equity will not grant an equitable remedy if a legal remedy would be adequate.

  Examples of equitable remedies are:

  - *specific performance* – an order to force the defendant to fulfil his bargain
  - *injunctions* – an order to restrain a party from committing a wrong
  - *rectification* – an order of the court requiring the defendant to modify a document to reflect the agreement made with the plaintiff
  - *account* – an order requiring a party who has control of money belonging to the plaintiff to report on the way in which the funds have been spent.

- <u>Auxiliary jurisdiction (new procedures)</u>. Procedural rules created by the Court of Chancery are discovery of documents, testimony on oath, *subpoena* of witnesses and interrogatories.

1.2.1 Court of Appeal in Chancery

The eighteenth and nineteenth centuries witnessed great advances in the development of equity. However, the personnel in the Court of Chancery proved to be corrupt: frequently such personnel were bribed in order to issue a common injunction. In addition, the Court became overloaded with petitions which resulted in delays. Until 1813 there were only two judges in the Court of Chancery: the Lord Chancellor and the Master of the Rolls. They were unhurried in arriving at their decisions.

In 1813 a Vice-Chancellor was appointed. In 1841 two more Vice-Chancellors were appointed. In 1851 two Lords Justices of Appeal in Chancery were appointed. By the early nineteenth century the Lord Chancellor had ceased to hear petitions at first instance. In 1851 the Court of Appeal in Chancery was created to hear appeals from decisions of Vice-Chancellors and the Master of the Rolls. This court consisted of the Lord Chancellor and two Lords Justices of Appeal. There was a further appeal to the House of Lords.

1.3 Nineteenth-century reforms

Before Parliament intervened, the Court of Chancery was capable of granting only equitable remedies. Likewise, common law courts could grant only the legal remedy of damages. This inconvenience was overcome by two statutory provisions:

- the Common Law Procedure Act 1854: this Act permitted the common law courts to grant equitable remedies

- the Chancery Amendment Act 1858 (Lord Cairns' Act): this Act gave the Court of Chancery power to award damages in addition to or in substitution for an injunction or specific performance.

However, what was needed was a more radical change which would fuse the administration of law and equity. It was an unnecessary waste of time and resources to require claimants entitled to common law and equitable rights or remedies to go to the respective court to redress their wrongs.

This change was effected by the Judicature Acts of 1873 and 1875, which adopted the following policies:

- The abolition of the separate Courts of Queen's Bench, Exchequer, Common Pleas, Chancery, Probate, the Divorce Court and the Court of Admiralty. In their place, the Supreme Court of Judicature was created. The High Court was divided into Divisions, known as the Queen's Bench, Chancery and Probate, Divorce and Admiralty. (The latter was renamed the Family Division, the Admiralty jurisdiction was transferred to the Queen's Bench Division and the probate business was transferred to the Chancery Division under the Administration of Justice Act 1970.)

- Each Division of the High Court exercises both legal and equitable jurisdiction. Thus, any point of law or equity may be raised and determined by any Division.

- It was foreseen that a court which applied rules of common law and equity would face a conflict where the common law rules produce one result and equity rules another. For example, s 4 of the Statute of Frauds 1677 (now repealed) enacted that contracts for the sale or other disposition of land must be evidenced in writing. The strict common law rule was rigidly adhered to, whether this produced unjust results or not. Equity adopted a notion of part performance which entitled the court to intervene in order to prevent fraud even though all the terms of the contract were not in writing.

Section 25(11) of the Judicature Act 1873 provides:

'25(11) Generally, in all matters not hereinbefore mentioned in which there is any conflict or variance between the rules of equity and the rules of common law with reference to the same matter, the rules of equity shall prevail.'

Thus, rules of equity are treated as paramount in the event of a conflict of rules of law and equity.

The effect of the Act is therefore procedural in the sense that the administration of law and equity has been fused, as distinct from the fusion of the rules of law and equity.

1.4 Maxims of equity

The intervention of the court of equity over the centuries may be reduced into the following maxims. The importance of the maxims ought not to be overstated: they are far from being rigid principles, but exist as terse sentences which illustrate the policy underlying specific principles.

Equity will not suffer a wrong to be without a remedy

This maxim illustrates the intervention of the Court of Chancery to provide a remedy if none was obtainable at common law. At the same time it must not be supposed that every infringement of a right was capable of being remedied. The 'wrongs' which equity was prepared to invent new remedies to redress were those subject to judicial enforcement in the first place.

Equity follows the law

The view originally taken by the Court of Equity was that deliberate and carefully considered rules of common law would be followed. Equity only intervened when some important factor became ignored by the law. Thus, in the early stages of the development of the law of trusts, the Lord Chancellor and, subsequently, the Court of Chancery acknowledged the valid existence of the legal title to property in the hands of the feoffee (or trustee). The acquisition of this title by the feoffee was dependent on compliance with the appropriate legal requirements for the transfer of the property.

Where there is equal equity, the law prevails

Equity did not intervene when, according to equitable principles, no injustice resulted in adopting the solution imposed by law. Thus, the *bona fide* purchaser of the legal estate for value without notice is capable of acquiring an equitable interest both at law and in equity.

Where the equities are equal, the first in time prevails

Where two persons have conflicting interests in the same property, the rule is that the first in time has priority at law and in equity: *qui prior est tempore potior est jure*.

He who seeks equity must do equity

A party claiming equitable relief is required to act fairly towards his opponent. For example, a tracing order would not be obtained in equity if the effect would be to promote injustice.

He who comes to equity must come with clean hands

The assumption here is that the party claiming an equitable relief must demonstrate that he has not acted with impropriety in respect of the claim.

Delay defeats equity (equity aids the vigilant and not the indolent)

Where a party has slept on his rights and has given the defendant the impression that he has waived his rights, the court of equity may refuse its assistance to the claimant. This is known as the doctrine of laches.

Equality is equity

Where two or more parties have an interest in the same property but their respective interests have not been quantified, equity as a last resort may divide the interest equally.

Equity looks at the intent rather than the form

The court looks at the substance of an arrangement rather than its appearance in order to ascertain the intention of the parties. For example, a deed is not treated in equity as a substitute for consideration.

Equity imputes an intention to fulfil an obligation

The principle here is based on the premise that if a party is under an obligation to perform an act and he performs an alternative but similar act, equity assumes that the second act was done with the intention of fulfilling the obligation.

Equity regards as done that which ought to be done

If a person is under an obligation to perform an act which is specifically enforceable, the parties acquire the same rights and liabilities in equity as though the act had been performed.

Equity acts *in personam*

Originally, equitable orders were enforced against the person of the defendant, with the ultimate sanction of imprisonment. A later equitable invention permitted an order to be attached to the defendant's property, ie *in rem*. Today this maxim has lost much of its importance.

KEY FACTS

Development of equity
- Defects in common law writ system and inadequate remedies
- Petitioning of king for fair solution as 'fountain of justice'
- Delegation of task to Lord Chancellor
- Creation of separate Court of Chancery – staffed by clerics
- Solutions based on discretion of court
- Conflict in *Earl of Oxford's Case* (1615) – in conflict, equity prevails
- Merged with common law in Judicature Acts 1873 and 1875
- Equitable remedies
- Injunctions – to prevent occurrences such as a breach of trust
- Specific performance – to ensure a contract is carried out
- Rectification – to change a document to reflect an actual agreement
- Account – report on ways in which funds have been used

Equitable maxims
- Equity will not suffer a wrong to be without a remedy
- Equity follows the law
- Where there is equal equity, the law prevails
- Where the equities are equal, the first in time prevails
- He who seeks equity must do equity
- He who comes to equity must come with clean hands
- Delay defeats equity
- Equity is equality
- Equity looks to intention not the form
- Equity imputes an intention to fulfil an obligation
- Equity regards that which should be done as being done
- Equity is equality
- Equity acts *in personam*

ACTIVITY

1. Was equity regarded as an independent system of rules?

2. What is the significance of the equitable maxims today?

3. What is the importance of the Judicature Acts 1873 and 1875?

Further reading

Winder, W, 'Precedent in equity' (1941) 57 LQR 245.

Mason, A, 'The place of equity and equitable remedies in contemporary society' (1994) 110 LQR 238.

chapter 2 INTRODUCTION TO TRUSTS ■

2.1 Introduction

Producing a comprehensive definition of a trust is extremely difficult, for a variety of trusts exist, and some of these do not fit into any of the traditional definitions. It is much simpler to describe a trust. In essence, the mechanism of the trust is an equitable device by which property is controlled by trustees for the benefit of others, called beneficiaries. These beneficiaries, subject to a few exceptions, are entitled to enforce the trust. For a variety of reasons, it may be prudent to prevent the entire ownership of property (legal and equitable) being vested and enjoyed by one person. A trust may be set up in order to advance this objective.

2.2 Trust concept

By origin, the trust was the exclusive product of the now defunct Court of Chancery, but since the Judicature Acts 1873 and 1875, trusts may be enforced in any court of law.

2.2.1 Underhill's definition

The classic definition of a trust was stated by Underhill as follows:

> 'A trust is an equitable obligation, binding a person (called a trustee) to deal with property over which he has control (which is called the trust property) for the benefit of persons (who are called the beneficiaries or *cestuis que trust*) of whom he may himself be one, and any one of whom may enforce the obligation.'

(Underhill, A and Hayton, D, Law of Trusts and Trustees (16th edn, Butterworths, 2002), p 1)

This definition does not include charitable and public purpose trusts. But Underhill was merely defining private trusts. Charitable trusts are distinct from private trusts in many ways (see later), and the Attorney-General is empowered to enforce such trusts on behalf of the public. Private purpose trust (or trusts for imperfect obligations) in any event are considered anomalous and are exceptionally treated as valid. Underhill's definition of a trust refers to an 'equitable obligation' in that originally the Lord Chancellor and later the Court of Chancery enforced moral obligations undertaken by trustees (feoffees) in the interests of natural justice and conscience. The definition refers to property under the 'control' of trustees. It is evident that the trustees have the legal title to property but the essence of a trust is that they are required to hold the property for the benefit of the beneficiaries. It is because of the fiduciary position of the trustees and the temptation to abuse their position that a number of duties are imposed on the trustees. Finally, the beneficiaries, by definition, are the persons who are entitled to enjoy the benefit of the trust property and who are given a *locus standi* to enforce the trust and to ensure that the trust property is properly administered.

2.2.2 Recognition of Trusts Act 1987

Section 1 of the Recognition of Trusts Act 1987 declares that the term 'trust' possesses the characteristics detailed in Art 2 of the Hague Convention on the Recognition of Trusts, referred to in the Schedule to the Act:

S

'For the purposes of this Convention, the term "trust" refers to the legal relationship created – *inter vivos* or on death – by a person, the settlor, when assets have been placed under the control of a trustee for the benefit of a beneficiary or for a specified purpose.

A trust has the following characteristics:

(a) the assets constitute a separate fund and are not a part of the trustee's own estate;

(b) title to the trust assets stands in the name of another person on behalf of the trustee;

(c) the trustee has the power and the duty, in respect of which he is accountable, to manage, employ or dispose of the assets in accordance with the terms of the trust and the special duties imposed upon him by law.

The reservation by the settlor of certain rights and powers and the fact that the trustee may himself have rights as a beneficiary, are not necessarily inconsistent with the existence of a trust.'

This description of a trust has been formulated by reference to the characteristics of a trust (these are discussed below).

2.2.3 Lord Browne-Wilkinson's essential characteristics of a trust

In *Westdeutsche Landesbank Girozentrale v Islington BC* [1996] AC 669, HL (for facts, see later), Lord Browne-Wilkinson identified four fundamental principles of trusts law the existence of which he considered uncontroversial.

J

'(i) Equity operates on the conscience of the owner of the legal interest. In the case of a trust, the conscience of the legal owner requires him to carry out the purposes for which the property was vested in him (express or implied trust) or which the law imposes on him by reason of his unconscionable conduct (constructive trust).

CONTINUED ▸

J

(ii) Since the equitable jurisdiction to enforce trusts depends upon the conscience of the holder of the legal interest being affected, he cannot be a trustee of the property if and so long as he is ignorant of the facts alleged to affect his conscience, ie until he is aware that he is intended to hold the property for the benefit of others in the case of an express or implied trust, or, in the case of a constructive trust, of the factors which are alleged to affect his conscience.

(iii) In order to establish a trust there must be identifiable trust property. The only apparent exception to this rule is a constructive trust imposed on a person who dishonestly assists in a breach of trust who may come under fiduciary duties even if he does not receive identifiable trust property.

(iv) Once a trust is established, as from the date of its establishment the beneficiary has, in equity, a proprietary interest in the trust property, which proprietary interest will be enforceable in equity against any subsequent holder of the property (whether the original property or substituted property into which it can be traced) other than a purchaser for value of the legal estate without notice.

These propositions are fundamental to the law of trusts and I would have thought uncontroversial.'

The reference to the 'conscience' of the trustee concerns the original assumption of jurisdiction by the Lord Chancellor for enforcing trusts. The trustee is treated as a fiduciary with special duties imposed on him. If they abuse their position as fiduciaries by receiving unauthorised profits they become trustees of those profits. This notion of conscience requires the trustees to be aware that they are acting with impropriety. It is evident that the trust is required to attach to identifiable property, except with regard to the liability to account as an accessory. Finally, Lord Browne-Wilkinson declares that a beneficiary under a trust acquires a proprietary interest in the trust property (ie a right *in rem*). The effect is that the beneficiary is entitled to recover the property in either its original or substituted form, except as against a *bona fide* transferee of the legal estate for value without notice ('equity's darling').

ACTIVITY

Compare Lord Browne-Wilkinson's essential characteristics of a trust laid down in *Westdeutsche Landesbank Girozentrale v Islington BC* (1996) with those laid down in the Recognition of Trusts Act 1987.

2.3 Characteristics of a trust

The distinctive features of a trust are outlined below. It is submitted that an understanding of these features is a more practical way of recognising and distinguishing a trust from other concepts.

2.3.1 Trust property

Any existing property which is capable of being assigned may form the subject-matter of a trust. Thus, the trust property may take the form of 'personalty', such as chattels or debts enforceable at law (choses in action), or an interest in land called 'realty' (freehold or leasehold interest in land). Moreover, the nature of the trust property may vary throughout the trust. The property may take the form of realty which is sold and the proceeds of sale reinvested in shares.

However, only subsisting property is capable of being the subject-matter of a trust. Accordingly, an expectancy or future property (such as a right under a will which has not vested because the testator is still alive) cannot be the subject-matter of a trust.

2.3.2 Separation of legal and equitable interests

The legal interest in property is the title which reflects the 'indicia' of ownership. The legal owner has the right to have his title to the property and the incidents of ownership respected by the rest of society. Thus he may enforce or protect his interest in the property through litigation. The equitable interest, on the other hand, is a right or an interest in property which, before the Judicature Acts of 1873 and 1875, was recognised solely by a Court of Chancery. The Judicature Acts effected a fusion of the administration of law and equity, so that in appropriate cases equitable principles may be applied in common law courts. The equitable title is the beneficial interest in property or the right to enjoy the property.

Generally, the trustee holds the legal title to property for the benefit of the beneficiary. The beneficiary enjoys the equitable interest. The rule is that whenever the two interests (legal and equitable) are separated, a trust is in existence. For example, T (a trustee) holds the legal title to shares in X Co (trust property) on trust for B, a beneficiary, absolutely. B acquires an equitable interest in the shares.

In addition, the same interests may be enjoyed jointly by the same persons under a trust. For example, T and B may hold the legal estate on trust for T and B equally. If, however, the legal and equitable interests are united in the hands of the same person without a separation of interest, no trust exists. Thus, no trust exists if T holds the legal estate for himself absolutely.

2.3.3 Sub-trusts

Sometimes the trustee may hold the equitable interest on behalf of a beneficiary. This would be the case where a beneficiary, who enjoys an equitable interest under a subsisting trust, creates a trust of his interest in favour of another, ie a beneficiary under a trust creates a sub-trust of his entire interest in favour of a sub-beneficiary. The effect of this arrangement is that the beneficiary under the original trust assigns his interest to the new beneficiary by way of a trust. In this situation the original beneficiary adopts the role of the settlor and trustee for the benefit of another:

T (legal owner) – B (original equitable owner) – C (sub-beneficiary or new equitable owner)

Indeed, it is possible for the original equitable owner to create a sub-trust and, at the same time, remain an equitable owner of trust property. This would be the position where the original equitable owner declares a trust of part of his equitable interest. For example, T (legal owner) holds on trust for B absolutely (equitable owner). B retains a life interest in the property and declares himself a trustee of the remainder for C absolutely.

The new arrangement may be illustrated as follows:

T (legal title) – <u>B (life interest) – C (remainder interest)</u>
(equitable owners)

It should be noted that in respect of the sub-trust, B will have active duties to perform on behalf of his new beneficiary, C.

2.3.4 Obligatory

A trust is mandatory in nature. The trustees have no choice as to whether they may fulfil the intention of the settlor. Instead, the trustees are required to fulfil the terms of the trust as stipulated in the trust instrument and implied by rules of law. The beneficiaries are given a *locus standi* to ensure that the trustees carry out their duties. (but note the anomalous nature of private purpose trusts – see Chapter 11).

2.3.5 *Inter vivos* or on death

Trusts may be created either *inter vivos* (during the lifetime of the settlor) or on death, by will or on an intestacy (under the Administration of Estates Act 1925, as amended).

2.3.6 The settlor's position

The settlor is the creator of an express trust. He decides the form that the trust property may take, the interests of the beneficiaries, the identity of the beneficiaries, the persons who will be appointed trustees and the terms of the trust. Indeed, he may appoint himself one of the trustees or the sole trustee. In short, the settlor is the author of the trust. But once the trust is created, the settlor *qua* settlor loses all control or interest in the trust property. Unless he has reserved an interest for himself, he is not entitled to derive a benefit from the trust property nor is he allowed to control the conduct of the trustees. In other words, following the creation of a trust the settlor, in his capacity as settlor, is treated as a stranger in respect of the trust.

ASE EXAMPLE

Re Bowden [1936] Ch 71

The settlor, before becoming a nun and in order to undertake the vows of poverty, chastity and obedience, transferred property to trustees on trust for specified beneficiaries. Later, she changed her mind when she left the convent and attempted to reclaim the property for her own benefit. The court held that, since the trust was created, the claimant as settlor lost all interest in the property and therefore could not recover the property.

> J '... the persons appointed trustees under the settlement received the settlor's interest ... and, immediately after it had been received by them, as a result of her own act and her own declaration ... it became impressed with the trusts contained in the settlement.'
>
> (Bennett J)

2.3.7 The trustees' position

The trustees bear the responsibility of controlling and managing the trust property solely for the benefit of the beneficiaries. This responsibility is treated as giving rise to a fiduciary relationship. Its characteristics are a relationship of confidence, trustworthiness to act for the benefit of the beneficiary and a duty not to act for his (the trustee's) own advantage.

They are the representatives of the trust. Owing to the opportunities to take advantage of their position the rules of equity were formulated to impose a collection of strict and rigorous duties on the trustees. Indeed, trustees' duties are so onerous that they are not even entitled to be paid for their services as trustees, in the absence of authority.

Trustees are liable in their personal capacity for mismanaging the trust funds and in extreme cases may be made bankrupt, should they neglect their duties.

2.3.8 The beneficiaries' position

The beneficiaries (as the owners of the equitable interest) are given the power to compel the due administration of the trust. They are entitled to sue the trustees and any third party for damages (joining the trustees in the action as co-defendants). In addition, the beneficiaries may trace the trust property in the hands of third parties with the exception of *bona fide* transferees of the legal estate for value without notice. The beneficiaries are given an interest in the trust property and are entitled to assign the whole or part of such interest to others. The beneficiaries are entitled to terminate the trust by directing the trustees to transfer the legal title to them, provided that they have attained the age of majority, and are *compos mentis* (mentally sound) and absolutely entitled to the trust property.

CASE EXAMPLE

Saunders v Vautier (1841) Cr & Ph 240, CA

Stock was bequeathed upon trust to accumulate the dividends until Vautier (V) attained the age of 25. At this age, the trustees were required to transfer the capital and accumulated income to V. V attained the age of majority (21) and claimed the fund at this age. The question in issue was whether the trustees were required to transfer the fund to V.

Held, since the income had vested in V, the sole beneficiary (by operation of law), subject to the enjoyment of the capital being postponed (ie the fund that produced the income), V acquired an indefeasible interest in the capital, subject to attaining the age of 25. As V was of full age, he was entitled to terminate the trust.

> J   'I think that principle has been repeatedly acted upon; and where a legacy is directed to be accumulated for a certain period, or where the payment is postponed the legatee, if he has an absolute indefeasible interest in the legacy, is not bound to wait until the expiration of that period, but may require payment the moment he is competent to give a valid discharge.'
>
> (Lord Langdale MR)

2.3.9 Equitable proprietary interests

The trustee's interest in the trust property is legal. This involves a right *in rem*. This refers to a right that attaches to the relevant property to such an extent that it is enforceable against the world. The legal owner cannot be deprived of his rights to the property by the fraud of some third person. A beneficiary's interest in the trust property is equitable which traditionally has been treated as a right *in personam*. This means that a claim against the wrongdoer trustee is against the trustee personally. In addition, the equitable interest is inviolable against everyone, except the *bona fide* transferee of the legal estate for value without notice of the equitable interest.

However, despite its origin, and the justification for the Chancellor's intervention to remedy injustice, on a practical level, the equitable title is treated as a proprietary interest. The beneficiary is entitled to protect his interest against everyone, except the *bona fide* transferee of the legal estate for value without notice. To this extent his interest is regarded as proprietary or exists *in rem*. His interest may be bought, sold or gifted away in the same way as the legal title.

2.3.10 *Bona fide* transferee of the legal estate for value without notice

The policy here was that in the fifteenth century, when the law of trusts was being moulded, the various Chancellors interceded only against those persons who, owing to the circumstances in which they had acquired the property, ought in conscience to be held responsible. Those persons were the heirs of the trustees, those who did not provide consideration and those who provided consideration, but bought the property in bad faith. Absent from this list was the *bona fide* transferee of the legal estate for value without notice of the equitable interest. Such a person acquired the legal title in priority over the beneficiary: see James LJ in *Pilcher v Rawlins* (1871) 7 Ch App 259.

J

'I propose simply to apply myself to the case of a purchaser for valuable consideration without notice, obtaining upon the occasion of his purchase, and by means of his purchase deed, some legal estate, some legal right, some legal advantage; and, according to my view of the established law of this court, such a purchaser's plea of a purchase for valuable consideration without notice is an absolute, unqualified, unanswerable defence, and an unanswerable plea to the jurisdiction of this court … but when the purchaser has satisfied the terms of the plea … this court has no jurisdiction whatever to do anything more than to let him depart in possession of that legal estate, that legal right, that legal advantage which he has obtained whatever it may be. In such a case the purchaser is entitled to hold that which, without breach of that duty, he has had conveyed to him.'

(James LJ)

In a more recent case, the court decided that the defendants were *bona fide* transferees of the legal title to the shares for value without notice and, thus, acquired good title to the shares. The claimants' cause of action in equity was therefore extinguished.

CASE EXAMPLE

MCC Proceeds Inc v Lehman Bros International (Europe), *The Times*, 14th January 1998, CA

Macmillan Incorporated, a Delaware company, was taken over in 1988 by Maxwell Communications Corporation plc (MCC) and became controlled by Robert Maxwell and members of his family. Macmillan Inc placed shares in a wholly owned subsidiary (Berlitz International Inc) together with the relevant share certificates, in the name of Bishopsgate Investment Trust plc (a nominee company controlled by Mr Maxwell). An agreement was entered into declaring that Bishopsgate held the legal title to the shares as nominees for Macmillan, who retained the beneficial interest in the shares. The agreement specified that, on Macmillan's written demand, Bishopsgate would immediately transfer the shares to

CONTINUED ▸

Macmillan. Without Macmillan's knowledge or consent, Bishopsgate pledged the certificates with the defendants as collateral under a stock lending scheme. The defendants, who were ignorant of Macmillan's interest in the shares and certificates, subsequently arranged for the cancellation of the certificates on transfer of the shares into a central depository paperless system in New York. The defendants subsequently sold the shares to an associated company, Shearson Lehman Bros Holdings plc. The claimants, who were Macmillan's successors and assignees, instituted proceedings against the defendants in conversion. The claim was based on the ground that Macmillan had a beneficial interest in the shares and certificates and was entitled to an immediate right to possession. Such interest, the claimants alleged, was sufficient to maintain an action in conversion and the defendants' lack of knowledge of Bishopsgate's wrongdoing or of Macmillan's interest was no defence to the conversion claim. The judge granted an application to the defendants to strike out the claim for conversion on the ground that no reasonable cause of action was disclosed on the facts. The claimants appealed to the Court of Appeal.

The Court of Appeal dismissed the appeal on the following grounds:

(a) the defendants, who were *bona fide* purchasers of the legal interest in the shares without notice of any breach of trust by Bishopsgate or of any claim by Macmillan, acquired good title to the shares and certificates, free from any adverse claims. Thus, the claimants' cause of action was extinguished. The claimants enjoyed an equitable interest in the shares and certificates and, in the circumstances, their interest was overreached

(b) a claim for conversion of goods was not maintainable by a person who had only an equitable interest in the property. Conversion was a common law cause of action and the common law did not recognise the equitable interests of beneficiaries under a trust. Accordingly, the common law recognised only the title of the trustee as a person normally entitled to immediate possession of the trust property. The claimants' action in conversion could not be maintained as its predecessor in title, Macmillan, had only an equitable interest in the shares and certificates. This rule of substantive law was not altered by the Judicature Acts 1873 and 1875, which merely fused the administration of law and equity.

2.4 Classification of trusts

The various forms of trusts may be classified into express and implied trusts. Express trusts are created in accordance with the express intention of the settlor. The term 'implied trusts' is a generic expression which includes resulting, constructive and statutory trusts.

The following is an indication of the various methods of classifying express trusts.

2.4.1 Private/public trusts

The broadest division is that between private and public (charitable) trusts.

Private trusts exist for the benefit of persons, or benefit a narrow section of the public, for instance a gift on trust for the education of the children of the settlor. There are a number of anomalous trusts in respect of which the beneficiaries are private purposes. These beneficiaries are obviously incapable of enforcing such trusts: for instance a trust for the benefit of the testator's pets or a trust for the execution and maintenance of a monument in memory of the testator. These are called 'hybrid' trusts, or trusts for imperfect obligations. Charitable trusts are public trusts which benefit the public as a whole in a number of specified ways such as the relief of poverty, the advancement of education, the propagation of religion, and other purposes which are beneficial to society within the spirit and intendment of the preamble to the Charitable Uses Act 1601.

Private trusts may be sub-divided into various categories, namely express, resulting, constructive and statutory trusts. An express trust is one that is created intentionally by a settlor or testator for the benefit of a person or group of persons (including purposes).

2.4.2 Fixed/discretionary trusts

Express trusts may be sub-divided into 'fixed' and 'discretionary' trusts. A fixed trust is one where the beneficiaries have settled and identifiable interests in the property which they are entitled to enjoy and protect. For instance:

APPLYING THE LAW

'On trust for A for life, remainder to B absolutely.' A enjoys the interest or income for as long as he lives, whereas B has a vested interest in the capital or the entire property subject to A's interest.

A discretionary trust is one whereby the trustees are given a duty to exercise their discretion in order to distribute the property in favour of a selected group of persons. The objects, individually considered, do not have an interest in the property but have only a hope ('*spes*') of acquiring an interest in the property, prior to the exercise of the discretion by the trustees. For instance:

APPLYING THE LAW

'For a period of 21 years from the date of the transfer to hold on trust to apply the income to such of the settlor's children as the trustees may decide in their absolute discretion.'

Discretionary trusts may be 'exhaustive' or 'non-exhaustive'.

An 'exhaustive' discretionary trust is one where the trustees are required to distribute the income and/or capital to the objects. The trustees are given a discretion to select which objects may benefit and the 'quantum' of the benefit.

A 'non-exhaustive' discretionary trust is one where the trustees are not required to distribute the entirety of the income and/or capital but may retain or accumulate the relevant property at their discretion (see later).

2.4.3 Resulting trusts

A 'resulting trust' is a trust created by the courts in accordance with the presumed intention of the settlor. The settlor or his estate is presumed to be the equitable owner. An occasion giving rise to this presumption is the purchase of property in the name of another. For instance, B purchases shares and directs the vendor to transfer the shares in the name of T. T is presumed to hold the shares on trust for B.

In addition, a resulting trust may be created when there is a surplus of trust funds left over after the trust purpose has been achieved. For instance, a surplus of trust funds is left over after the testator's pet, the sole beneficiary dies. This surplus is held on resulting trust for the testor's estate.

2.4.4 Constructive trusts

A 'constructive trust' is one created by the courts in the interests of justice and conscience. Thus, whenever a trustee abuses the confidence of the settlor by realising an unauthorised profit derived from trust property, that profit is held on constructive trust for the beneficiaries. The constructive trust extends beyond express trustees and may attach to strangers who intermeddle with trust property with notice that they are dealing with trust property. This is a subject that is in the process of development by the courts.

2.4.5 Statutory trusts

Statutory trusts are created by Parliament in special circumstances. For example, the Administration of Estates Act 1925 (as amended) created a statutory trust for the benefit of the deceased's heirs.

Section 33 of the Trustee Act 1925 created a protective trust, namely, a determinable life interest in favour of the principal beneficiary coupled with a discretionary trust in favour of a specified class of objects, including the principal beneficiary, on the occurrence of the determining event.

2.5 Reasons for the creation of express trusts

There are a variety of reasons why a settlor may wish to create an express trust. These may be loosely classified as 'family situations', to undertake commercial transactions or to promote charitable or non-charitable purposes. Some of the popular reasons are:

- to provide for secret beneficiaries after the death of the testator

- to create a marriage settlement for the benefit of the parties to a marriage and their issue, if any
- to obtain fiscal advantages by way of tax planning
- to protect property from spendthrift beneficiaries by means of discretionary or protective trusts
- to promote commercial arrangements and protect lenders and customers
- to provide an incentive to the workforce through employee trusts of various kinds
- to enable charitable objects to be carried out
- to make provision for a limited number of non-human objects such as pets and the maintenance of monuments.

■Key facts on constitution of trusts

KEY FACTS

Trust concept
- Underhill's definition
- Section 1 of the Recognition of Trusts Act 1987
- Lord Browne-Wilkinson's essential characteristics of a trust: *Westdeutsche Landesbank Girozentrale v Islington BC* (1996)

Characteristics of trusts
- Trust property
- Separation of legal and equitable interests
- Sub-trusts
- Mandatory duties imposed on the trustee
- *Inter vivos* or on death
- Settlor's position: *Re Bowden* (1936)
- Trustee's position (fiduciary; legal interest): *Westdeutsche Landesbank* (1996)
- Beneficiary's position (equitable interest): *Saunders v Vautier* (1841)
- Equitable proprietary interests
- *Bona fide* transferee of the legal estate for value without notice: *Pilcher v Rawlins* (1871); *MCC Proceeds Inc v Lehman Bros Int* (1998)

Classification of trusts
- Private/public trusts
- Fixed/discretionary trusts
- Resulting trusts

CONTINUED ▶

KEY FACTS

- Constructive trusts
- Statutory trusts: s 33 of the Trustee Act 1925

Reasons for the creation of express trusts
- To provide for secret beneficiaries
- To create marriage settlements
- To implement tax avoidance schemes
- To protect spendthrift beneficiaries
- To create commercial arrangements
- To create employee trusts
- To promote charitable activities
- To provide for a limited number of non-human objects

Express — Private/public, fixed/discretionary | Resulting — automatic, presumed | Constructive — fiduciary, strangers | Statutory — eg s 33 TA 1925

■ *Figure 2.1 Classification of trusts*

ACTIVITY

1. What difficulties are posed by any attempt to define a trust?

2. Identify the fundamental characteristics of trusts.

3. What essential features distinguish the various types of trusts that exist?

Further reading

Goodhart, W, 'Trust law for the 21st century' (1996) 10(2) Tru LI 38.

Hayton, D, 'Developing the law of trusts for the 21st century' (1990) 106 LQR 87.

Millett, P, 'Equity – the road ahead' (1995) 9(2) Tru LI 35.

chapter 3 THE 'THREE CERTAINTIES' TEST ■

3.1 Introduction

The creation of an express trust may be achieved by one of two modes. The first involves the transfer of the relevant property to the trustees subject to a declaration of trust in favour of the beneficiaries (a transfer and declaration). The second mode requires the settlor to declare himself a trustee of the relevant property for the beneficiaries (self-declaration). It is of crucial importance that the transferor/settlor and the transferee/trustee recognise their obligations. The transferor/settlor loses all interests, as settlor, on the creation of the trust. He is treated as a complete stranger in regard to the trust property and is incapable, as settlor, of bringing or defending a claim concerning property subject to an express trust. The transferees, in this context, involve the trustees and the beneficiaries. These are the parties who are entitled to bring proceedings in respect of the trust property.

The importance to the trustees of ascertaining whether a trust has been created is in respect of their duties. The trustees are the individuals who have control of the property and are required to comply with their fiduciary responsibilities to avoid litigation for breach of trust. The beneficiaries acquire equitable interests in the property on the creation of the trust and are given a bundle of rights in order to protect their interests.

It is imperative that the parties to a trust are familiar with their respective duties and rights. Equally, the courts are required to apply a rational set of rules in order to determine whether a trust has been validly created or not. The courts have formulated a test to determine this question, known as the 'three certainties' test laid down by Lord Langdale in *Knight v Knight* (1840) 3 Beav 148.

> **J** 'First, if the words were so used, that upon the whole, they ought to be construed as imperative; secondly, if the subject of the recommendation or wish be certain; and thirdly, if the objects or persons intended to have the benefit of the recommendation or wish be also certain.'
>
> (Lord Langdale MR)

Thus, the 'three certainties' are:

- certainty of intention (words)
- certainty of subject-matter
- certainty of objects.

3.2 Certainty of intention

The requirement here is whether the obligations of trusteeship are intended in respect of the property. This issue is determined by reference to all the circumstances of the case. Thus, oral and written statements as well as the conduct of the parties are construed by the courts to determine whether a trust relationship has been created.

3.2.1 Intention – a question of fact and degree

The test is purely subjective, in that the focus of attention involves the settlor's genuine intention as construed by the courts. The maxim 'Equity looks at the intent rather than the form' is applicable in this context. The word 'trust' need not be used but if used by the settlor is construed in its context. Alternative expressions will be construed by reference to the surrounding circumstances for the purpose of ascertaining whether the trust concept is intended. The doctrine of binding precedent is not applicable here and each case is determined on its own facts.

3.2.2 Intention to benefit distinct from intention to create a trust

An intention to create a trust is fundamentally different from the broader concept of an intention to benefit another *simpliciter*. There are many modes of providing a benefit to another, such as gifts, exchanges and sales of property. But the requirement here is whether the settlor intended to benefit another solely by creating a trust. Decided cases are used merely for illustrative purposes.

CASE EXAMPLE

Jones v Lock (1865) LR 1 Ch App 25

Robert Jones placed a cheque for £900 into the hand of his nine-month-old baby, saying 'I give this to baby and I am going to put it away for him'. He then took the cheque from the child and told his nanny: 'I am going to put this away for my son'. He put the cheque in his safe. A few days later, he told his solicitor: 'I shall come to your office on Monday to alter my will, that I may take care of my son'. He died the same day. The question in issue was whether the cheque funds belonged to the child or the residuary legatees under Robert Jones's will.

Held:

(a) No valid gift of the funds was made in favour of the child, for the funds were not paid over to him.

(b) No trust had been declared in favour of the child, for Robert Jones had not made himself a trustee for his child.

CONTINUED ▶

> J '... the case turns on the very short question whether Jones intended to make a declaration that he held the property in trust for the child; and I cannot come to any other conclusion than that he did not. I think it would be a very dangerous example if loose conversations of this sort, in important transactions of this kind, should have the effect of declarations of trust.'
>
> (Lord Cranworth LC)

Likewise, in the unusual case of *Duggan v Full Sutton Prison*, *The Times*, 13th February 2004, the court decided that no trust was created. In this case the claimant, a serving prisoner, contended that a trust was imposed on a prison governor to retain as a trustee and invest cash sums surrendered by prisoners. The Court of Appeal decided that only a debtor/creditor relationship had been created and it would have been impractical to impose a trust relationship on the prison authorities.

In *Paul v Constance* [1977] 1 WLR 527, CA the court considered the oral statements and conduct of the parties and concluded that there was sufficient evidence of an intention to create a trust. The court, however, acknowledged that this was a borderline case because it was not easy to pinpoint the specific time of the declaration of trust.

CASE EXAMPLE

Paul v Constance [1977] 1 WLR 527, CA

Ms Paul and Mr Constance lived together as man and wife. Mr C received £950 compensation for an industrial injury and both parties agreed to put the money in a deposit account in Mr C's name. On numerous occasions, both before and after the opening of the account, Mr C told Ms P that the money was as much hers as his. After Mr C's death, Ms P claimed the fund from Mrs C, the administrator.

Held: Mr C, by his words and deeds, declared himself a trustee for himself and Ms P of the damages. Accordingly, 50 per cent of the fund was held upon trust for Ms P.

> J 'In this court the issue becomes: was there sufficient evidence to justify the judge reaching that conclusion of fact? When one looks to the detailed evidence to see whether it goes as far as that – and I think that the evidence does have to go as far as that – one finds that from the time that Mr Constance received his damages right up to his death he was saying, on occasions, that the money was as much the

CONTINUED ▶

> plaintiff's as his. [The words] "This money is as much yours as mine," convey clearly a present declaration that the existing fund was as much the plaintiff's as his own. The 'judge accepted that conclusion. I think he was well justified in doing so and, indeed, I think he was right to do. It might, however, be thought that this was a borderline case, since it is not easy to pinpoint a specific moment of declaration … The question … is whether in all the circumstances the use of those words on numerous occasions as between Mr Constance and the plaintiff constituted an express declaration of trust. The judge found that they did. For myself, I think he was right so to find.'
>
> (Scarman LJ)

An express trust may be successfully created in a commercial context before a company becomes insolvent. Insolvency involves claims from creditors, both secured and unsecured, but with the prospect of some creditors receiving very little funds or nothing from a sale of the company's assets, the temptation to claim the existence of a trust of the company's funds may prove attractive. The trust concept was successfully created in *Re Kayford Ltd* [1975] 1 All ER 604, HC.

CASE EXAMPLE

Re Kayford Ltd [1975] 1 All ER 604, HC

A mail order company received advice from accountants as to the method of protecting advance payments of the purchase price or deposits for goods ordered by customers. The company was advised to open a separate bank account to be called 'Customer Trust Deposit Account' into which future sums of money received for goods not yet delivered to customers were to be paid. The company accepted the advice and its managing director gave oral instructions to the company's bank but, instead of opening a new account, a dormant deposit account in the company's name was used for this purpose. A few weeks later the company was put into liquidation. The question in issue was whether the sums paid into the bank account were held upon trust for customers who had paid wholly or partly for goods which were not delivered or whether they formed part of the general assets of the company.

Held   A valid trust had been created in favour of the relevant customers in accordance with the intention of the company and the arrangements effected. The position remained the same even though payment was not made into a separate banking account.

CONTINUED ▶

J '... it is well settled that a trust can be created without using the words "trust" or "confidence" or the like: t-he question is whether in substance a sufficient intention to create a trust has been manifested. The whole purpose of what was done was to ensure that the moneys remained in the beneficial ownership of those who sent them, and a trust is the obvious means of achieving this. No doubt the general rule is that if you send money to a company for goods which are not delivered, you are merely a creditor of the company unless a trust has been created. The sender may create a trust by using appropriate words when he sends the money (though I wonder how many do this, even if they are equity lawyers), or the company may do it by taking suitable steps on or before receiving the money. If either is done, the obligations in respect of the money are transformed from contract to property, from debt to trust.'

(Megarry VC)

Similarly, a trust may be created between two parties in order to promote a commercial venture in circumstances where the parties did not have the capacity to transfer property to each other by way of a contract. The trust property may take the form of a chose in action, ie an intangible personal property right. This was the approach of the court in *Don King Productions Inc v Warren* [1999] 2 All ER 218, CA.

CASE EXAMPLE

Don King Productions Inc v Warren [1999] 2 All ER 218, CA

The claimant, Don King Productions Inc (DKP), was owned by Don King, the leading boxing promoter in the USA. The first defendant, Frank Warren (W), was the leading boxing promoter in the UK. The other defendants were Mr Warren's business associates. In 1994, the parties entered into two partnership agreements intended to deal with the boxing, promotion and management interests of the two promoters. One of the agreements declared that the two parties would hold all promotion and management agreements relating to the business for the benefit of the partnership. Some of the promotion agreements contained non-assignment clauses. But none of the agreements contained a prohibition on the partners declaring themselves as trustees. The issue before the court was whether the benefit of the promotion and management agreements was capable of being the subject-matter of a trust, despite the express clause prohibiting the assignment of rights.

Held A valid trust of a chose in action was created in favour of the claimant. This was created in accordance with the intention of the parties. Accordingly, W's entry into the 'multi-fight agreement' intended for his benefit was in breach of the duties owed to the claimant.

CONTINUED ▶

> **J** 'In principle, I can see no objection to a party to contracts involving skill and confidence or containing non-assignment provisions from becoming trustee of the benefit of being the contracting party as well as the benefit of the rights conferred. I can see no reason why the law should limit the parties' freedom of contract to creating trusts of the fruits of such contracts received by the assignor or to creating an accounting relationship between the parties in respect of the fruits.'
>
> (Lightman J)

3.2.3 Precatory words

These are extremely ambiguous expressions used in wills, such as expressions of hope, desire, wish, recommendation or similar expressions which impose a moral obligation on the transferee. The issue here is whether such words impose a legal obligation on the recipient of property. For instance, a testator declares in his will: 'I leave all my property to my widow feeling confident that she will act fairly towards our children in dividing the same.' Did the testator create a trust?

The position today is that such words may or may not create a trust by reference to the will and surrounding circumstances. There was a time during the development of the law of trusts when such words did not impose a trust, with the effect that the executor of the will was entitled to retain the property beneficially. This was the approach of the ecclesiastical courts. When the Court of Chancery was formed it was believed that the solution allowing the executor to take the property beneficially was unacceptable. Thus, the Court of Chancery made strenuous efforts to avoid such a conclusion and decided that precatory words artificially created trusts (precatory trusts). The introduction of the Executors Act 1830 declared that the executor will be entitled to an interest under the testator's will, if this accords with the clear intention of the testator. This paved the way for the modern approach to precatory words, namely to construe them in their context.

In *Re Adams and Kensington Vestry* (1884) 27 Ch D 394 the court decided that on construction of the words used in the will, no trust was intended.

CASE EXAMPLE

Re Adams and Kensington Vestry (1884) 27 Ch D 394

A testator left his property by will 'unto and to the absolute use of my wife … in full confidence that she will do what is right as to the disposal thereof between my children'. The issue was whether a trust had been created.

Held   No trust had been created for the children, so the wife was entitled to the property absolutely.

A similar conclusion was reached in *Lambe v Eames* (1871) 6 Ch App 597.

In contrast, in *Comiskey v Bowring-Hanbury* [1905] AC 84 the court concluded that, on the facts
of the case, a trust was intended by the testator.

CASE EXAMPLE

Comiskey v Bowring-Hanbury [1905] AC 84

The testator transferred his property by his will to his widow, subject to the following terms:

> '… in full confidence that she will make such use of it as I should have made
> myself and that at her death she will devise it to such one or more of my nieces as
> she may think fit and in default of any disposition by her thereof by her will. I hereby
> direct that all my estate and property … shall at her death be equally divided
> among the surviving said nieces.'

The widow asked the court to determine whether she took the property absolutely or
subject to a trust in favour of the nieces.

Held   The intention of the testator was to transfer the property absolutely to his widow for
life and, after her death, one or more of his nieces was or were entitled to benefit, subject
to a selection by his widow. Failing such selection, the nieces were entitled equally.

3.2.4 Effect of uncertainty of intention

Where the intention of the transferor is uncertain as to the creation of a trust, no express trust is
created. The person who is in control of the property is entitled to retain it beneficially.
Accordingly, if the transferor disposes of the property to the transferee and no trust is intended, the
transferee takes it beneficially. Thus, in *Re Adams and Kensington Vestry* (1884) the testator's widow
was entitled to the property absolutely, and in *Jones v Lock* (1865), because of a failure to transfer
the property the deceased's estate was entitled to the £900.

■ Key facts on certainty of intention

	KEY FACTS	
Question of fact	Whether the settlor's words and conduct indicate an irrevocable intention to create a trust	*Re Kayford* (1975); *Paul v Constance* (1977); contrast *Jones v Lock* (1865); *Duggan v Gov of Full Sutton Prison* (2004)

CONTINUED ▸

31

3.3 Certainty of subject-matter

The term 'subject-matter', on its own, is ambiguous and inherently deals with two concepts: namely the trust property and the beneficial interest. Although the same test is applicable to both, it is important to distinguish each type of uncertainty. If the **trust property** is uncertain because the settlor did not specify it with sufficient clarity, the intended trust will fail. This has a reflex action on the transferor's intention, with the effect that the transferee retains the property beneficially. For instance, if A transfers 50,000 BT plc shares to X to hold 'some' of the shares upon trust for Y, the intended trust will fail and X will retain the property beneficially. This is because A has abandoned all interest in the property.

On the other hand, where the trust property is certain but the **beneficial interest** is uncertain, although the intended express trust will fail, a resulting trust for the transferor will arise. Thus, the legal owner will be required to hold the property on implied trust for the transferor. For instance, A transfers 50,000 BP plc shares to X on trust to provide some of the shares for Y and the remainder of the shares on trust for Z. The trust property is certain (50,000 shares), but the beneficial interest is uncertain, ie the number of shares to be held on trust for Y and the balance on trust for Z . The effect is that X cannot take the property beneficially and is required to hold on resulting trust for A.

The test for certainty of subject-matter is whether the trust property and the beneficial interest is ascertained or is ascertainable to such an extent that the court may attach an order on the relevant property. This is a question of law for the judge to decide and this issue is determined objectively.

3.3.1 Certainty of trust property

The issue here is whether the property that is subject to the trust is capable of satisfying the test for certainty. The determining factor is whether the formula specified by the settlor is sufficiently precise to identify the trust property.

CASE EXAMPLE

Sprange v Barnard (1789) 2 Bro CC 585

A testatrix transferred property by her will to Thomas Sprange for his sole use and added that at his death the remaining part of what was left that he did not want for his own use was to be divided equally between two named persons. The court decided that Thomas Sprange was not a trustee, and took the property beneficially.

CASE EXAMPLE

Palmer v Simmonds (1854) 2 Drew 221

A transfer by will to Thomas Harrison declared that, subject to a number of stipulations, he should leave the bulk of this property by will to four named persons equally. The court decided that no trust was intended and Thomas Harrison acquired the property beneficially.

In the context of insolvency law it may be advantageous for some creditors to promote the trust concept in an effort to gain priority over the other creditors. On an insolvency or liquidation the company's assets are available to pay its creditors. If a claimant is successful in establishing that some of the company's assets are subject to a trust these assets will not be available for distribution to its creditors. Such trust assets belong to the beneficiaries and not the company. The success of such a claim varies with the facts of each case.

CASE EXAMPLE

Re London Wine Co Ltd (1986) PCC 121

Customers bought wine from a wine company and contracted with the company to store the wine in its warehouse. On a liquidation of the company these customers claimed that a trust existed in their favour. The court decided that no property passed to the customers under the Sale of Goods Act 1979 because the customers' goods were not separated from the bulk and no valid trust was created because of uncertainty of trust property.

> J It seems to me any such trust must fail on the ground of uncertainty of subject-matter. It seems to me that in order to create a trust it must be possible to ascertain with certainty not only what the interest of the beneficiary is to be but to what property it is to attach.

CONTINUED ▸

> A farmer could, by appropriate words, declare himself to be a trustee of a specified proportion of his whole flock and thus create an equitable tenancy in common between himself and the named beneficiary, so that a proprietary interest would arise in the beneficiary in an undivided share of all the flock and its produce. But the mere declaration that a given number of animals would be held upon trust could not, I should have thought, without very clear words pointing to such an intention, result in the creation of an interest in common in the proportion which that number bears to the number of the whole at the time of the declaration. And where the mass from which the numerical interest is to take effect is not itself ascertainable at the date of the declaration, such a conclusion becomes impossible.
>
> In the instant case, even if I were satisfied on the evidence that the mass was itself identifiable at the date of the various letters of confirmation I should find the very greatest difficulty in construing the assertion that "you are the sole and beneficial owner of" 10 cases of such and such a wine as meaning or being intended to mean "you are the owner of such proportion of the total stock of such and such a wine now held by me as 10 bears to the total number of cases comprised in such stock."
>
> (Oliver J)

A similar result was reached by the courts in *Re Staplyton* [1994] 1 WLR 1181 and *Re Goldcorp Exchange Ltd* [1995] 1 AC 74. The Sale of Goods (Amendment) Act 1995 introduced a significant change in the law. The position today is that multiple purchasers of goods are deemed to acquire interests as tenants in common in the subject-matter.

Where the trust property consists of shares, or property other than goods which is indistinguishable, the quantification of the interest on its own may be sufficient to satisfy the test. Thus, one fully paid up BT plc share is the same as any other BT share of the same description. There may be no need to identify the relevant property by means of the share certificate numbers.

CASE EXAMPLE

Hunter v Moss [1994] 1 WLR 452

The defendant declared himself trustee for the claimant of 5 per cent of the issued share capital of a company (1,000 shares of one denomination were issued). The issue was whether the test for certainty of trust property was satisfied even though the defendant did not identify the share certificate numbers of the relevant shares. 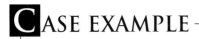The court held that a valid trust was created.

CONTINUED ▶

J
Dillon LJ referred to the case of *Re London Wine* (1986) and distinguished it thus: 'It seems to me that that case is a long way from the present. It is concerned with the appropriation of chattels and when the property in chattels passes. We are concerned with a declaration of trust, accepting that the legal title remained in the defendant and was not intended, at the time the trust was declared, to pass immediately to the plaintiff. The defendant was to retain the shares as trustee for the plaintiff.

… just as a person can give, by will, a specified number of his shares of a certain class in a certain company, so equally, in my judgment, he can declare himself trustee of 50 of his ordinary shares in MEL or whatever the company may be and that is effective to give a beneficial proprietary interest to the beneficiary under the trust. No question of a blended fund thereafter arises and we are not in the field of equitable charge.'

A similar result was reached in *Re Harvard Securities Ltd, The Times*, 18th July 1997.

3.3.2 Beneficial interests

Where the trust property is certain, but the interest to be acquired by the beneficiaries is uncertain, the express trust will fail and the property will be held on resulting trust for the transferor. This may be the case where the trustees acquire the trust property but some individual is required to divide the property between two or more beneficiaries. If that individual fails to allocate the relevant portions to the respective beneficiaries, and the issue cannot be resolved by the courts, the intended express trust will fail, thus giving rise to a resulting trust. This is the position where the settlor imposes a personal obligation on an individual to specify the relevant interests to be acquired by the beneficiaries.

CASE EXAMPLE

Boyce v Boyce (1849) 16 Sim 476

A testator devised two houses to trustees on trust to provide one for Maria, whichever she might choose, and the other to Charlotte. Maria died before the testator and had failed to make a selection. The question in issue was whether Charlotte might acquire one of the properties. The court decided that a personal obligation to select was imposed on Maria. No other person could have made the selection and the intended express trust failed but a resulting trust was set up for the testator's estate.

However, if no mode of distribution is provided in the trust instrument, the court may resolve the difficulty by adopting an arbitrary but fair means of distributing the property to the beneficiaries. This may take the form of equal division (if appropriate) or some other method of distribution.

CASE EXAMPLE

Re Knapton [1941] 2 All ER 573

The testatrix in her will provided for a number of houses to be distributed among several nephews and nieces. The will did not contain a method of distribution. The court decided that the beneficiaries had the right to choose a house in the order in which they were listed in the will.

3.3.3 Uncertainty of subject-matter

The consequences of uncertainty of subject-matter vary with the nature of the subject-matter. If the trust property is uncertain, then no express trust could have been intended by the settlor. The effect is that the transferee of the property retains the property beneficially. No resulting trust arises.

If the trust property is certain, however, but the beneficial interest is uncertain, the intended express trust will fail but a resulting trust will arise in favour of the transferor.

■Key facts on certainty of subject-matter

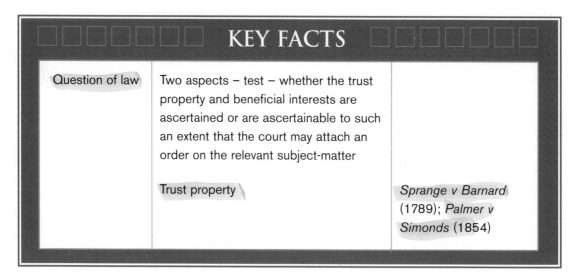

KEY FACTS

Question of law	Two aspects – test – whether the trust property and beneficial interests are ascertained or are ascertainable to such an extent that the court may attach an order on the relevant subject-matter	
Trust property		*Sprange v Barnard* (1789); *Palmer v Simonds* (1854)

CONTINUED ▸

		Re London Wine Co (1986); Re Staplyton (1994); Re Goldcorp (1995)
		Contrast Hunter v Moss (1994); Re Harvard Securities (1997)
	Beneficial interests	Boyce v Boyce (1849); contrast Re Knapton (1941)

3.4 Certainty of objects

The trustees owe their duties to, and are required to exercise the same for the benefit of, the beneficiaries under the trust. Accordingly, there is an obvious need for the trustees to be able to ascertain the beneficiaries under an express trust. The test for certainty of objects varies with the type of express trust created. There is a narrow test for certainty of objects for **fixed** trusts and a broader test for **discretionary** trusts. If the intended settlor fails to satisfy the relevant test for certainty of objects, the express trust will fail and a resulting trust will arise in his favour.

3.4.1 Fixed trusts

A fixed trust is one where the settlor has attempted to specify the number of beneficiaries and the extent of their interests in the trust instrument, for example a trust in favour of 'my children equally'. The trustees do not have a discretion to distribute the funds to the intended beneficiaries: on the contrary, in a fixed trust the intended beneficiaries acquire a vested interest in the trust property on the date of the creation of the trust. Thus, the beneficiaries may sell, exchange or give away their interest as they wish. The test for certainty of objects is whether the objects are ascertained or are ascertainable with clarity, so that the court may, if necessary, execute the trust. This is known as the 'list' test in the sense that the trustees are required to draw up a comprehensive list of all the beneficiaries. The test is sometimes also referred to as the 'class ascertainability' test. If the beneficiaries are not referred to by name, they are required to be identified as a class, such as the 'children' or 'relatives' of the settlor: see *IRC v Broadway Cottages Trust* [1955] Ch 20.

CASE EXAMPLE

IRC v Broadway Cottages Trust [1955] Ch 20

A settlement was created whereby trustees held property upon trust to apply the income for the benefit of all or any of a class of objects including, *inter alia*, the settlor's wife, specific relations of the settlor and the Broadway Cottages Trust, a charitable institution. The trustees paid income to the Broadway Cottages Trust and claimed exemption from income tax in respect of this. It was not possible to ascertain all the objects who might fall within the class of objects but it was possible to determine with certainty whether a particular person was a member of the class. The question in issue was whether the trust was valid or void. The court decided that the trust was void for uncertainty of objects, and the claim for a repayment of income tax failed.

In a more recent case, *OT Computers Ltd v First National Tricity Finance Ltd and Others* [2003] EWHC 1010, HL, the question arose as to whether the *Broadway Cottages* (1955) test was satisfied. One set of beneficiaries ('urgent suppliers') was defined in an inconclusive manner.

CASE EXAMPLE

OT Computers Ltd v First National Tricity Finance Ltd and Others [2003] EWHC 1010, HL

The claimant (company) traded as 'Tiny Computers' and was a retailer of computer products and accessories. In 2000 it started to make substantial losses. On 23rd January 2002 the company instructed its bank to open two separate trust accounts for the payment of customer deposits and of moneys due to 'urgent suppliers'. The company transferred sums from its current account into each of the trust accounts. The company created two schedules; one contained the names of customers and the other reflected some of the names of its suppliers, who were potential beneficiaries. The company was subsequently put into receivership. The bank later demanded repayment of a loan from the company. One of the defendants was an unpaid supplier whose name did not appear on the company's schedule.

The question in issue was whether valid trusts had been created for customers and 'urgent suppliers'.

Held

(1) It was clear that the directors of the company intended to create trusts in favour of its customers and 'urgent suppliers'.

(2) There was a valid declaration of trust in favour of the customers.

CONTINUED ▸

> (3)   However, it was not possible to identify each member of the class of 'urgent
> suppliers'. Accordingly, this trust failed and a resulting trust for the company's
> creditors was created.

Before 1971 this restricted test was applicable to all types of express private trusts – fixed and discretionary. Today, the 'list' test is applicable to fixed trusts only. Discretionary trusts, since 1971, have been subject to a much broader test.

3.4.2 Discretionary trusts

A discretionary trust is an express trust whereby the trustees are required to exercise their discretion to select the beneficiaries from among a class of objects and/or to determine the quantum of interest that the beneficiaries may enjoy. In other words, the trustees decide who, when and how much funds a beneficiary may enjoy. For example, £50,000 capital is transferred to trustees A, B and C to be held on trust to distribute the income for a period of 15 years to such of the relatives and dependants of the settlor as the trustees may decide in their absolute discretion. The effect is that the trustees are obliged to distribute the income only to members of the class or classes of objects. Prior to the exercise of the trustees' discretion the objects do not have an interest in the income, but merely a hope or '*spes*' of acquiring an interest.

The modern test for certainty of objects in respect of discretionary trusts is known as the 'individual ascertainability' test, or the 'is or is not' test, or the 'any given postulant' test. This test was laid down by the House of Lords in *McPhail v Doulton (sub nom Re Baden)* [1971] AC 424.

CASE EXAMPLE

McPhail v Doulton [1971] AC 424

The settlor, Bertram Baden, tranferred property to trustees to apply the net income, in their absolute discretion, to the officers, ex-officers, employees and ex-employees of a company or their relatives or dependants. The question in issue was whether the trust was valid as satisfying the test for certainty of objects. At this time the test for certainty of objects for all private trusts was the 'list' test as stated above. The trust objects were too broad to satisfy this narrow test. The House of Lords decided that the trust was valid and changed the test for certainty in respect of discretionary trusts. The new test for such trusts is whether the trustees may say with certainty that any given postulant is or is not a member of a class of objects, and there is no need to draw up a list of the objects.

The effect of the 'any given postulant' test is that the class or classes of objects are required to be defined by reference to a clear formula without necessarily drawing up a list of all the persons who are within the class or classes. Thus, the test is very much a 'definitional' exercise in order to determine the validity of the trust. The members of the class or classes of objects alone may benefit from the trust and the trustees who wish to distribute the property need to know whether the person selected for benefit falls within the class or classes of objects.

3.4.3 Powers of appointment

A mere power of appointment or power collateral is an authority to dispose of property in favour of members of a class of objects. Unlike a discretionary trust, a power of appointment does not impose an obligation on the donee of the power, or appointor, to distribute the property, but merely empowers him to distribute the property in his discretion. The only similarity with a discretionary trust lies in the fact that the discretion concerns a class of objects, rather than beneficiaries under a fixed trust. The individual members of the class of objects do not enjoy an interest prior to the exercise of the discretion but acquire a hope of enjoying an interest in the property.

The donee of the power may be granted either a personal or a fiduciary power of appointment in favour of the objects. A personal, or non-fiduciary, power is a power of appointment granted to a donee of the power in his capacity as an individual such as the testator's widow. There is no duty to consider exercising the authority, nor is there a duty to distribute the property in favour of the objects. In short, the donee of the power is given almost complete freedom in exercising his discretion. Indeed, the donee of the power may release the power even if this would mean that he will benefit from the release; for instance a testator may transfer property by will to his widow, W, for life with the remainder to such of his children A, B and C as W may appoint by will. In *Re Hay's Settlement Trust* [1982] 1 WLR 202, Megarry VC described the scope of the authority given to a non-fiduciary donee of the power thus: 'If he does exercise the power, he must, of course confine himself to what is authorised, and not go beyond it … A person who is not in a fiduciary position is free to exercise the power in any way he wishes unhampered by any fiduciary duties.'

A fiduciary power, unlike a personal power, is a power of appointment granted to an individual *virtute officio*, such as a trustee. The fiduciary power is similar to a personal power in only one respect in that there is no obligation to distribute the property. But unlike a personal power, the trustees are required to deal with the discretion in a responsible manner. Accordingly, a number of duties are imposed on the trustees, which were summarised by Megarry VC in *Re Hay's Settlement Trust* (1982):

> J 'The duties of a trustee which are specific to a mere power seem to be threefold. Apart from the obvious duty of obeying the trust instrument, and in particular of making no appointment that is not authorised by it, the trustee must, first, consider periodically whether or not he should exercise the power; second, consider the range of objects of the power; and third, consider the appropriateness of individual appointments. I do not assert that this list is exhaustive; but as the authorities stand it seems to me to include the essentials, so far as relevant to the case before me.'

Because of the lack of any obligation to distribute the property, the appointor is entitled to release the power and the beneficiaries entitled on an express gift over in default of appointment or a resulting trust may become entitled to the property. This rule is subject to one exception, namely a 'fiduciary power in the full sense'. A fiduciary power which is exercisable in respect of a pension fund is treated as a unique power which cannot be released. If the trustees fail to distribute the property the court is required to exercise the discretion. This type of fiduciary power was created by Warner J in *Mettoy Pension Trustees Ltd v Evans* [1990] 1 WLR 1587.

CASE EXAMPLE

Mettoy Pension Trustees Ltd v Evans [1990] 1 WLR 1587.

Mettoy Co plc launched an occupational pension scheme on 1st January 1968. The claimant, a wholly owned subsidiary of Mettoy, became the sole trustee of the scheme. In 1980, with the introduction of new legislation, new scheme rules were made. Rule 13(5) provided as follows:

> 'Any surplus of the trust fund remaining after securing all the aforesaid liabilities in full may, at the absolute discretion of the employer be applied to secure further benefits within the limits stated in the rules, and any further balance thereafter remaining *shall be properly apportioned amongst the principal employer and each participating employer.*'

Mettoy experienced financial difficulties and receivers were appointed in 1983. The company was wound up in 1984. As a consequence, the scheme was required to be liquidated. The claimant asked the court for directions in respect of a surplus of funds.

Warner J held that r 13(5) created a fiduciary power which could not be released or exercised by a receiver or liquidator. Accordingly, the court was required to decide what method of exercise would be appropriate.

■Key facts on certainty of objects (1)

KEY FACTS

• Fixed trusts	the 'list' test [whether the trustees are capable of drawing up a comprehensive list of all the objects]	*IRC v Broadway Cottages* (1955)
• Discretionary trusts [post-1971]	the 'any given postulant' test	*McPhail v Doulton* (1971)
• Powers of appointment [personal, fiduciary, fiduciary powers in the full sense]	the 'any given postulant' test	*Re Gestetner* (1953) (see below); *Re Gulbenkian* (1970) (see below); *Mettoy Pension Trustees v Evans* (1990)

3.4.4 Analysis of the 'any given postulant' test

The test for certainty of objects in respect of powers has always been whether the donee of the power may say with certainty that any given individual (postulant) is or is not a member of a class of objects. This test was laid down by Harman J in *Re Gestetner's Settlement* [1953] 1 Ch 672:

J
'The trustees as I see it, have a duty to consider whether or not they are to distribute any and, if so, what part of the fund and if so, to whom they should distribute it … if therefore, there be no duty to distribute, but only a duty to consider, there is no difficulty in ascertaining whether any given postulant is a member of the specified class. Of course, it can be easily postulated whether John Doe or Richard Roe is or is not eligible to receive the settlor's bounty. It is not necessary that the trustees worry their heads to survey the world from China to Peru when there are perfectly good objects of the class in England.'

In essence, the 'any given postulant test' will be satisfied if the boundaries concerning the identification of the classes of objects are clearly drawn and it is unnecessary to name each member of the class of objects, for example if a power of distribution is given in favour of the relatives of the settlor. The gift will be valid if the expression 'relatives' is capable of a legal definition so that the trustees may be able to distinguish the objects from the non-objects. It is unnecessary for the trustees to identify each object.

Prior to the House of Lords' decision in *Re Gulbenkian's Settlement* [1970] AC 508, the courts adopted a diluted approach to the 'any given postulant' test, namely whether at least **one person** fell within the class of objects, even though it may not be possible to say whether others come within the class or fall outside of it. The House of Lords in *Re Gulbenkian's Settlement* (1970) overruled this approach and reiterated the strict 'any given postulant' test.

CASE EXAMPLE

Re Gulbenkian's Settlement [1970] AC 508

A special power of appointment was granted to trustees to appoint in favour of Nubar Gulbenkian, 'any wife and his children or remoter issue … and any person … in whose house or apartment or in whose company or under whose care and control or by or with whom he may from time to time be employed or residing' subject to a gift over in default of appointment. The House of Lords overruled the diluted approach to the test adopted by the Court of Appeal and held that the gift created a valid power of appointment within the strict *Gestetner* (1953) test.

The point was made earlier that, prior to the decision in *McPhail v Doulton* (1971), the test for certainty of objects in respect of private trusts was the narrower *Broadway Cottages* (1955) 'list' test. The justification for this narrow test in respect of discretionary trusts concerned the notion of facilitating the court in the exercise of the discretion if the trustees failed to exercise their discretion. A discretionary trust is obligatory and any omission to exercise the discretion is required to be remedied by the court. It was believed that equal division of the funds in favour of the members of the class of objects would discharge the jurisdiction of the courts, hence the need, at this time, to equate the test for certainty of objects in respect of fixed and discretionary trusts. It was subsequently recognised by the courts that equal division of the funds in favour of the class of objects was merely one option. Other options included the appointment of new trustees or representative members of the classes of objects to prepare a scheme of distribuion. Accordingly, there was no longer a need to adopt the same test for certainty of objects in respect of both fixed and discretionary trusts. The modification in the test for certainty of objects for discretionary trusts was adopted in *McPhail v Doulton* (1971) (see above). Lord Wilberforce reasoned that it was striking how narrow and in a sense artificial is the distinction between discretionary trusts and powers. He recognised there were differences, but felt that such differences between discretionary trusts and powers of appointment did not justify the fundamentally different tests for certainty of objects. Accordingly, the test for certainty of objects in respect of powers was extended to discretionary trusts.

■Key facts on certainty of objects (2)

KEY FACTS

Question of law	Two separate tests: (a) Fixed trusts ('list' test)	IRC v Broadway Cottages Ltd (1955)
	(b) discretionary trusts ('any given postulant' test)	McPhail v Doulton (Re Baden) (1971)
		R v District Auditors, ex p W Yorkshire MCC (1986) (see below)

Three limitations

In *McPhail v Doulton* (1971) Lord Wilberforce laid down three limitations to the 'any given postulant' test – semantic uncertainty, evidential uncertainty and administrative unworkability.

- *Semantic uncertainty*   This is also referred to as linguistic or conceptual uncertainty. This involves uncertainty or vagueness in defining the class or classes of individuals in respect of whom the trustees are entitled or required to exercise their discretion, for example a distribution by the trustees, in their discretion in favour of anyone in respect of whom the trustees may consider to have a moral claim on the settlor. This proviso is applicable to both powers and trusts. If the gift suffers from such uncertainty, it is void.

- *Evidential uncertainty*   This principle applies to both powers and trusts but does not invalidate either if the class is not conceptually uncertain. This limitation concerns uncertainty in ascertaining the existence or whereabouts of objects. In this event, the trustees may apply to the courts for directions, referred to as a *Benjamin* order, and the courts may make such order as is appropriate in the circumstances.

- *Administrative unworkability*   This involves situations where the testator or settlor expressed the class of objects so broadly that it is difficult for the court to ascertain any sensible exercise of the discretion. In the event of the trustees failing to exercise their discretion, the court may find it difficult to exercise the discretion in a rational manner: for example, a duty to distribute a fund in favour of such of the residents of Greater London as the trustees may decide in their absolute discretion. This type of uncertainty does not affect the validity of powers of appointment but may invalidate discretionary trusts. In *R v District Auditors, ex p West Yorkshire*

Metropolitan County Council (1986) 26 RVR 24, the Divisional Court decided that a settlement of £400,000 on trust for the purposes of benefiting 'any or all or some of the inhabitants' of West Yorkshire (population approximately 2.5 million) was void as a discretionary trust, because of administrative unworkability. Accordingly, a resulting trust had arisen. In *Re Manisty's Settlement* [1974] Ch D 17, a settlement gave a power of appointment to the trustees to use a fund for the benefit of the settlor's relations, excluding those inserted in an excepted class. Templeman J held that the clause was valid, but in an *obiter* pronouncement stated that problems could arise if the class was 'capricious', such as 'residents of Greater London'.

3.4.5 Distinct approaches to the 'any given postulant' test

The House of Lords in *McPhail v Doulton* (1971), after reforming the test for certainty of objects in respect of discretionary trusts, remitted the case (*Re Baden (No 2)* [1972] 3 WLR 250) to the High Court to decide whether the new test was satisfied on the facts of the case. The High Court decided that the gift was valid and an appeal was made to the Court of Appeal which affirmed the decision of the High Court. However, each Lord Justice of Appeal adopted a different approach to the test.

The 'question of fact' approach

This approach is based on the assumption that the gift is conceptually certain (that is, linguistically certain). It then becomes a question of evidence or fact as to whether an individual proves to be within the class. Failure to discharge this burden of proof means that he is outside the class. In this respect it makes no difference whether the class is small or large. It is submitted that this approach concerns the practicalities of exercising the discretion as opposed to a test of validity of the gift. This mode of applying the test was laid down by Sachs LJ in *Re Baden (No 2)* (1972).

The 'substantial number' approach

This approach advocated by Megaw LJ in *Re Baden (No 2)* (1972) is to the effect that in terms of validity of the gift, the test for certainty of objects is whether a substantial number of objects is within the class of objects, and it is immaterial whether it is not possible to say with certainty that other objects are within or outside the class of objects. What is a substantial number of objects is for the courts to decide. Accordingly, the 'any given postulant' test is diluted to a 'substantial number of objects' test.

The advantage of this approach is that the gift remains valid despite the fact that the classes of objects are incapable of definition. To a limited extent, the broad objective of the settlor will be fulfilled. But this approach attracts a number of objections such as the striking similarity with the now-defunct 'one person' approach, which had been overruled by the House of Lords in *Re Gulbenkian* (1970). The 'substantial number' test seems to be a variant of the outdated approach. In addition, this diluted approach to the 'any given postulant' test creates a class within a class. The class as laid down by the settlor is varied to include only a substantial number of objects.

The 'strict' approach

In *Re Baden (No 2)* (1972) Stamp LJ subscribed to the view that the 'any given postulant test' requires the trustees to say of any individual that he either is clearly within or outside the class of objects. Accordingly, everyone is classified as being within or outside the class of objects. This requires clarity and precision in defining the qualifying class or classes of objects without listing the objects who fall within the class or classes. If such precise definitions are not forthcoming, the gift is void.

In addition, in *Re Tuck's Settlement Trust* [1978] Ch 49, the courts developed two further approaches that have a bearing on the 'any given postulant' test. The approaches involve conditional gifts and the 'dictionary' meaning of objects.

Gifts subject to conditions precedent and subsequent

Property law draws a distinction between two types of conditional gifts: conditions precedent and subsequent. In the case of gifts subject to conditions precedent, the requirement of certainty is less strict, as opposed to gifts subject to conditions subsequent. A gift subject to a condition precedent is one where the donee does not acquire an interest in the property until he satisfies the relevant condition, for example a gift of £500 to A provided that he passes his year one LLB examinations. A does not obtain the property until he passes the relevant examination. The approach of the courts is that the claimant donee needs to establish, if he can, that he satisfies the condition or qualification whatever be the appropriate test. If the formula is such as to involve questions of degree or description the uncertainty of the description or event contemplated will not necessarily invalidate the gift in the case of a condition precedent. What is required is that the claimant be able to convince the court by reference to any reasonable test that he satisfies the description or condition.

 CASE EXAMPLE

Re Allen [1953] Ch 810

A testator by his will left property to the eldest of his nephews 'who shall be member of the Church of England and an adherent to the doctrine of that Church'. The question in issue was whether the qualification was valid or void. The Court of Appeal held that the qualification created a condition precedent and, to satisfy it, it was not necessary that the condition be capable of exact definition. The claimant was required to prove that he, at least, satisfied the limitation.

Similarly, in *Re Tuck's Settlement Trust* [1978] Ch 49, the Court of Appeal decided that a gift subject to a condition precedent was valid.

CASE EXAMPLE

Re Tuck's Settlement Trust [1978] Ch 49

The settlor, Sir Adolf Tuck, the first baronet, executed a settlement in 1912 with the intention of ensuring that each baronet in succession would marry an 'approved wife'. The settlement provided for the payment of income to the baronet for the time being so long as he should be of the Jewish faith and married and living with an 'approved wife'. An 'approved wife' was identified in the settlement as 'a wife of Jewish blood by one or both of her parents and who has been brought up in and has never departed from and at the date of her marriage continues to worship according to the Jewish faith'. The settlor then added an arbitration clause to the effect that in the event of 'any dispute ... the decision of Chief Rabbi in London ... shall be conclusive'. Sir Adolf died in 1926. He was succeeded by his eldest son, Sir William Tuck, who married an approved wife. Sir William died in 1954 and was succeeded by his eldest son, Sir Bruce Tuck. Sir Bruce first married an approved wife but was divorced in 1964. In 1968, he married a lady who was not an approved wife. The question in issue was whether the limitation was valid or void.

The Court of Appeal held that the limitation was not void, on the grounds that the restriction created a condition precedent which was not wholly uncertain, and the Chief Rabbi clause constituted a valid delegation of decision-making power on the relevant questions of fact, in the event of a dispute. The clause was similar to an arbitration clause in contract law.

The same principle was applied in *Re Barlow's Will Trust* [1979] 1 All ER 296.

CASE EXAMPLE

Re Barlow's Will Trust [1979] 1 All ER 296

A testatrix, by her will, directed her executor to sell her collection of valuable paintings subject to the provision that 'any member of my family and any friends of mine' be allowed to purchase any of the paintings at a catalogue price compiled in 1970 (which was substantially below their market value on the date of death). The executors applied to the court to ascertain whether the direction was void for uncertainty and guidance as to the appropriate method for identifying members of the testatrix's family.

The court held that the direction as to 'friends' was valid, for the properties were to be distributed *in specie* and the quantum of the gifts did not vary with the class. Despite the expression 'friend' being conceptually uncertain, the transfer by will amounted to a series of individual gifts to persons who satisfied a specific description. The court also gave guidelines on the identification of friends namely:

CONTINUED ▸

(a) the relationship with the testatrix was required to be of long standing

(b) the relationship must have been social as opposed to business or professional

(c) when circumstances permitted they met frequently. The expression 'family' meant a blood relationship with the testatrix.

In *Re Barlow* (1979) the court drew a distinction between gifts where the quantum of the interest varies with the class of beneficiaries such as 'a gift of £1,000 to my friends to be divided equally'. In such a case if the class of beneficiaries is conceptually uncertain, the gift will fail. Whereas, as the facts of the case suggest, the quantum of the interest to be enjoyed by the beneficiaries did not vary with the class but involved a finite number of paintings. In such a case there was no need to identify the beneficiaries with precision, but instead the claimant was required to convince the trustees that he satisfied the description. The position would be the same if the testator had bequeathed £10 (from a pool of say £1,000) for 'each of my friends'.

A condition subsequent, on the other hand, operates to divest or determine a gift that had previously vested in the donee. If the condition is void, the gift or beneficial interest will remain in the donee. The courts are generally hesitant about divesting gifts or estates that have already vested and will hold a condition subsequent void only if its terms are such that it cannot clearly be known in advance or from the beginning what circumstances will cause the divesting or determination of the gift or estate: for instance an endowment to B until he is called to the Bar. Here, B obtains a vested interest which is determined when he is called to the Bar. Query whether the condition would be satisfied if B was called to the New York Bar. In *Clayton v Ramsden* [1943] AC 320, HL the court decided that a condition subsequent attached to a gift was so vague that the restriction was void.

CASE EXAMPLE

Clayton v Ramsden [1943] AC 320, HL

A testator bequeathed a legacy and a share of the residue of his estate upon trust for his daughter, Edna, for life with remainder on trust for her issue equally. The gift was subject to forfeiture (expressly inserted by the testator), if she should marry a person 'not of Jewish parentage and of the Jewish faith'. Edna married the appellant, Harold Clayton, who was an English Wesleyan who was admittedly not of Jewish parentage. The question in issue was whether the forfeiture clause was valid or void.

The House of Lords held that, on construction, the clause created a composite set of conditions subsequent which were void for uncertainty. The testator had given no indication of the degree of attachment or adherence to the faith which he required on the part of his daughter's husband. The forfeiture conditions were too vague to enable it to be said with certainty that a particular individual complied with the requirement.

The 'dictionary' approach

The 'dictionary' approach is based on the notion that the settlor may adopt a definition of the class or classes of objects specifically in a clause in the trust instrument. The effect is that there is likely to be little doubt as to the category of objects intended to benefit. For example, the settlor may give the trustees a discretion to distribute in favour of such of my 'old friends' as they may decide. He may then define the expression 'old friends' in any way he considers appropriate. In this way the class of objects which would otherwise have failed may be rescued by the settlor provided that the description offered by the settlor is clear enough for the courts to supervise. A variation on this theme entitles the settlor to appoint a third person as sole arbiter of the definition of the class of objects and perhaps all issues incidental to the exercise or non-exercise of the discretion. Difficulties have arisen if the arbitrator appointed by the settlor or testator happens to be the trustee. It must be observed that a settlor or testator cannot deprive a beneficiary of his right of access to the courts, at any rate on questions of law. Such clauses are void on the grounds of repugnancy to the beneficiary's rights and also public policy as an attempt to oust the jurisdiction of the courts, except in cases where the arbitrator has acted in bad faith.

CASE EXAMPLE

Re Raven [1915] 1 Ch 673

A provision in the testator's will giving the trustees the final say as to the identity of the beneficiary in the event of doubt was void on grounds of repugnancy and public policy because the province of the trustees' power involved a question of law.

On the other hand, in *Re Coxen* [1948] 2 All ER 492, the opinion of the trustees was treated as one of fact and the clause was treated as valid. However, in *Dundee General Hospital Board of Management v Walker* [1952] 1 All ER 896, the House of Lords appeared to suggest that a clause in a will making the trustees' decision final on questions of law was valid. Moreover, in *Re Tuck* (1978) (see above), Lord Denning MR decided that the arbitration clause requiring the Chief Rabbi to determine any dispute as to whether the beneficiary satisfied the descriptions 'of Jewish faith' and married to an 'approved wife' was valid on analogy with arbitration clauses in the law of contract.

J
'... I see no reason why a testator or settlor should not provide that any dispute or doubt should be resolved by his executors or trustees, or even a third person. To prove this, I will first state the law in regard to contracts. Here the general principle is that whenever persons agree together to refer a matter to a third person for decision, and further agree that his decision is to be final and binding upon them, then, so long as he arrives at his decision honestly and in good faith, the two parties are bound by it. They cannot reopen it for mistakes or errors on his part, either in fact or law, or for any reason other than fraud or collusion'.

(Lord Denning MR)

It ought to be observed that in *Re Tuck* (1978), the testator gave a partial definition of the description of the restrictive conditions, namely an 'approved wife'. It is unclear whether this was a significant feature of the case and what effect the absence of such definition or description may have had on the outcome of the case. In any event the court is entitled to admit extraneous evidence of the intention of the settlor.

It would appear that the application of the test for certainty of objects is far from clear although the modern approach attempts, to some extent, to give effect to the intention of the settlor or testator.

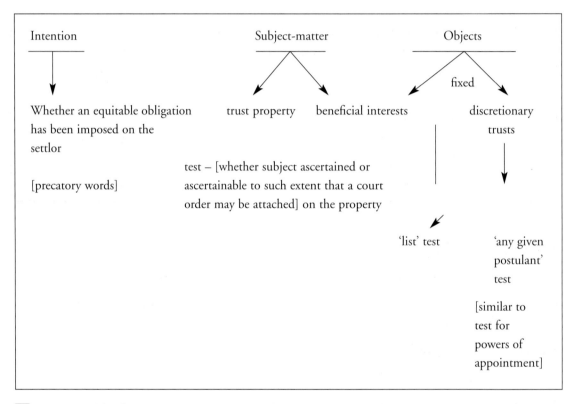

■ *Figure 3.1 The three certainties*

ACTIVITY

1. The Bargain Basement Co Ltd runs a mail order business. Finding itself in financial difficulties, it takes advice and as a result begins to pay all money as it is received from customers into a separate account (The Bargain Basement No 2 Deposit Account). Mrs Prudence orders £500 worth of goods and sends a deposit of £100 to the company which is paid into the No 2 account. Before the goods are delivered, Bargain Basement Co goes into liquidation.

   Is Mrs Prudence entitled to the return of her deposit and/or the interest it has earned in the account?

2. T, a testator, leaves a will containing the following gifts:

   (a) 'My three freehold houses to X and Y, my trustees, to hold two of the properties on trust for my daughter, to be selected by her, and the other on trust for my son.'

   The daughter survived the testator but died before making a selection.

   (b) '£5,000 to my wife, Hariett, knowing that she will employ a reasonable amount for the benefit of my aged housekeeper, Camilla.'

   Comment on the validity of these gifts.

Further reading

Battersby, G, 'A reconsideration of Property and Title in the Sale of Goods Act' [2001] JBL 1.

Goodhart, W, and Jones, G, 'The infiltration of equitable doctrine into English commercial law' (1980) 43 MLR 489.

Hayton, D, 'Certainty of objects – what is heresy?' [1984] Conv 307.

Hayton, D, 'Uncertainty of subject-matter of Trusts' (1994) 110 LQR 335.

Jones, A, 'Creating a trust over an unascertained part of a homogeneous whole' [1993] Conv 466.

Martin, J, 'Certainty of objects – what is heresy?' [1984] Conv 304.

Martin, J, 'Validity of trust of unidentified shares' [1996] Conv 223.

Worthington, S, 'Sorting out ownership interests in a bulk: Gifts, Sales and Trusts' [1999] JBL 1.

chapter 4 CONSTITUTION OF AN EXPRESS TRUST ■

4.1 Introduction

A settlor who wishes to create an express trust is required to adopt either of the following methods:

(a) a self-declaration of trust, or

(b) a transfer of property to the trustees, subject to a direction to hold upon trust for the beneficiaries.

This is known as the rule in *Milroy v Lord* [1862] 31 LJ Ch 798, HC. The effect of the perfect creation of a trust is that the beneficiary, who may be a volunteer, may enforce the trust. Alternatively, if the trust is incompletely constituted, the transaction involving an intended trust operates as an agreement to create a trust. Subject to the Contracts (Rights of Third Parties) Act 1999, this agreement may be enforced by a person who has provided consideration.

4.2 The rule in *Milroy v Lord* (1862)

The principle laid down by Turner LJ in *Milroy v Lord* (1862) identifies the various modes of creating an express trust. Generally, there are two modes of constituting an express trust and the onus is on the settlor to execute one (or in exceptional circumstances both) of these modes for carrying out his intention.

CASE EXAMPLE

Milroy v Lord [1862] 31 LJ Ch 798, HC

The settlor executed a deed purporting to transfer shares to Mr Lord on trust for Mr Milroy. The shares were only capable of being transferred by registration in the name of the transferee in the company's books. The settlor failed to complete the transfer, although Mr Lord held a power of attorney as agent for the settlor. On the settlor's death, Lord gave the share certificates to the settlor's executors and the question arose whether the shares were held upon trust for the claimant.

Held There was no gift of the shares to the objects nor was there a transfer of the shares to the intended trustee. The settlor having failed to transfer the shares to the trustee, the court will not infer that he is a trustee for the claimant.

CONTINUED ▶

> **J** '… in order to render a voluntary settlement valid and effectual, the settlor must have done everything which, according to the nature of the property comprised in the settlement, was necessary to be done in order to transfer the property and render the settlement binding upon him. He may, of course, do this … if he transfers the property to a trustee for the purposes of the settlement, or declares that he himself holds it in trust for those purposes … but, in order to render the settlement binding, one or other of these modes must … be resorted to, for there is no equity in this court to perfect an imperfect gift. The cases go further to this extent, that if the settlement is intended to be effectuated by one of the modes to which I have referred, the court will not give effect to it by applying another of those modes. If it is intended to take effect by transfer, the court will not hold the intended transfer to operate as a declaration of trust, for then every imperfect instrument would be made effectual by being converted into a perfect trust.'
>
> (Turner LJ)

On analysis, the court decided the following:

- there was no gift of the shares to Mr Milroy

- the settlor did not have an intention to create a trust

- in order to create a trust or to transfer the property (legal title), the settlor or transferor is required to do everything expected of him in order to vest the property in the name of the intended transferee

- the requirements necessary to be complied with in order to transfer the property vary with the type of property involved

- the settlor may transfer the property to the trustee subject to a valid declaration of trust or

- the settlor may declare himself a trustee

- if the trust is intended to be created by one of these modes the court will not automatically adopt another mode of creating the trust.

These are the primary rules concerning the constitution of a trust.

4.2.1 Transfer and declaration mode

A settlor may wish to create a trust by transferring the property to another person (or persons) as trustee(s), subject to a valid declaration of trust. In this context the settlor must comply with two requirements, namely a transfer of the relevant property or interest to the trustees complemented with a declaration of the terms of the trust (see the 'three certainties' test (above). If the settlor intends to create a trust by this method and declares the terms of the trust, but fails to transfer the property to the intended trustees, it is clear that no express trust is created. The ineffective transaction will amount to a conditional declaration of trust but without the condition (the transfer) being satisfied. For instance, S, a settlor, nominates T1 and T2 to hold 50,000 BT plc shares upon trust for A for life with remainder to B absolutely (the declaration of trust). In addition, S is required to transfer the property in the shares to T1 and T2. The declaration of trust on its own without the transfer is of no effect.

The formal requirements, if any, concerning the transfer of the legal title to property vary with the nature of the property involved. There are broadly two types of properties that exist – realty and personalty. In order to transfer the legal title to registered land the settlor is required to execute the prescribed transfer form and register the transfer in the names of the trustees at the appropriate Land Registry. The transfer of tangible moveable property requires the settlor to deliver the property to the trustees, accompanied by the appropriate intention to transfer; the transfer of the legal title to shares in a private company involves the execution of the appropriate transfer form and registration of the transfer in the company's share register. The various requirements for the transfer of the most common forms of properties can be summarised as follows:

- Legal estates and interests in land must be transferred by deed under s 52(1) of the Law of Property Act 1925.

- Equitable interests in either land or personalty must be disposed of in writing: see s 53(1)(c) of the Law of Property Act 1925.

- Choses in action (intangible personal property such as debts or intellectual property) may be assigned in law in writing in accordance with s 136 of the Law of Property Act 1925. As an alternative, an assignment may be executed in equity.

- Tangible moveable property (chattels) may be transferred by delivery accompanied by clear and unequivocal intention that the transferor intends to transfer property to the recipient, or by deed of gift. In *Re Cole* [1964] Ch 175, a husband showed his wife the furniture in a house and said that it was all hers. The question in issue was whether a transfer of the legal title had taken place. Held: no transfer had taken place as the words spoken were too loose to reflect an intention to donate.

- Shares in a private company will be transferred when the transfer procedure laid down in s 183 of the Companies Act 1985 has been complied with.

4.2.2 Transfer of shares in a private company

The owner of the legal title to shares in a private company is the person whose details are registered in the company's books. Thus, a new transferee acquires the legal title when he is registered with the company. Sections 182 and 183 of the Companies Act 1985 outline the procedure that is required to be followed in order to transfer shares in a private company. The transferor is required to execute a stock transfer form, issued under the Stock Transfer Act 1963, and send this, along with the share certificates, to the registered office of the company for registration. The company usually has an absolute discretion to decide whether to register the new applicant without giving reasons for its decision. In addition, the company deals only with the registered legal owner of the shares.

In accordance with the *Milroy v Lord* (1862) principle, if the transferor has done everything required of him and the only things remaining to be done are to be performed by a third party, the transfer will be effective in equity. The effect is that dividends declared at any time after the transferor has completed his duties in respect of the transfer, and before the new owner is registered, will be held on trust for the new transferee. Likewise, votes attaching to the shares are required to be cast as trustee for the new owner. Whether the transferor has done everything required of him to transfer the shares is essentially a question of fact.

The court applied this principle in *Re Rose* [1952] Ch 499, CA.

CASE EXAMPLE

Re Rose [1952] Ch 499, CA

Mr Rose executed two transfers of shares on 30th March 1943. He died more than five years after executing the transfers but less than five years (the claw-back period at this time) after the transfers were registered in the company's books, on 30th June 1943. For estate duty purposes it was necessary to know when the donee had received the shares.

Held The shares were transferred on 30th March 1943. At this time the transferor had done everything in his power to transfer the shares, and all that remained was for the directors of the company to consent to the transfer and register the new owner.

> J '... if a document is apt and proper to transfer the property – is, in truth, the appropriate way in which the property must be transferred – then it does not seem to me to follow from the statement of Turner LJ [in *Milroy v Lord* (1862)] that, as a result, either during some limited period or otherwise, a trust may not arise, for the purpose of giving effect to the transfer. Whatever might be the position during the period between the execution of this document and the registration of the shares, the transfers were, on 30th June 1943, registered. After registration, the title of Mrs Rose was beyond doubt complete in every respect, and if Mr Rose had received a dividend between execution and registration and Mrs Rose had claimed to have that dividend handed to her, what would Mr Rose's answer have been? It could no longer be that the purported gift was imperfect; it had been made perfect. I am not suggesting that the perfection was retroactive.'
>
> (Lord Evershed MR)

A similar conclusion was reached in *Mascall v Mascall* (1984) 49 P &CR 119, in respect of the execution of a transfer concerning registered land.

In contrast to the *Re Rose* (1952) principle, if the transferor has not done everything required of him, the transfer will not be effective in equity. This may be illustrated by *Re Fry* (1946).

CASE EXAMPLE

Re Fry [1946] Ch 312, HC

The donor of shares was domiciled in the USA, and needed the consent of the Treasury (under the Emergency Regulations (Defence (Finance) Regulations 1939)) to transfer shares in a British company. He sent the necessary forms to the company for registration of the new owner, save for Treasury approval. This he had applied for, but had not been granted at the time of his death. The question in issue was whether a transfer in equity had been made at the time of the donor's death.

Held   The shares had not passed to the donee at the time of the donor's death, for he had not done everything required of him: he had not obtained Treasury consent.

J

'Had they, however, arrived at the position which entitled them, as against that company, to be put on the register of members? Had everything been done which was necessary to put the transferees into the position of the transferor? If these questions could be answered affirmatively, the transferees would have had more than an inchoate title; they would have had it in their own hands to require registration of the transfers. Having regard, however, to the Defence (Finance) Regulations 1939, it is impossible, in my judgment, to answer the questions other than in the negative. The requisite consent of the Treasury to the transactions had not been obtained, and, in the absence of it, the company was prohibited from registering the transfers. In my opinion, accordingly, it is not possible to hold that, at the date of the testator's death, the transferees had either acquired a legal title to the shares in question, or the right, as against all other persons (including Liverpool Borax Ltd) to be clothed with such legal title.'

(Romer J)

The court decided that the donor had not everything required of him to secure registration of the shares, despite his death after his application for Treasury approval was made. The logic of the *Re Fry* (1946) decision may be understood on the ground that the donor might have been required to furnish more information to the Treasury before consent was obtained. In any event, the company was not entitled legitimately to consider registering the new owner until Treasury consent was obtained. The court came to a similar decision on the facts of *Milroy v Lord* (1862) (see above).

In the recent decision of *Pennington v Waine* [2002] All ER (D) 24; CA the Court of Appeal decided that where the donor had manifested an immediate and irrevocable intention to donate shares to another and had instructed her agent to execute the transfer, the donor will not be permitted to deny the interest acquired by the donee.

CASE EXAMPLE

Pennington v Waine [2002] All ER (D) 24, CA

The donor, Ada, was the owner of a number of shares in a company and was also one of its directors. Under instructions from Ada, one of the company's auditors, Mr Pennington, prepared a transfer form for 400 shares which was duly executed by Ada and sent to Mr Pennington. The transfer was in favour of Ada's nephew, Harold, to secure his appointment as a director as a 51 per cent holder of shares. The form was placed on the company's file. Mr Pennington assured Harold that he was appointed a director and nothing more was required to be done by him. No further action was taken in relation to the transfer. Ada died and by her will left her estate to others. The question in issue was whether a transfer in equity was made by Ada before her death in favour of Harold, or whether the shares passed to her heirs under her will.

Held   A transfer to Harold in equity was made during Ada's lifetime. Ada intended an immediate and irrevocable transfer in favour of Harold. The court considered that the test here was whether Ada had done everything required of her to secure the transfer, as distinct from whether she had done everything short of registration. The main ground for the decision was the fact that it would have been unconscionable for Ada and her heirs to deny the interest acquired by Harold. As an alternative ground the court decided that Ada and Mr Pennington were agents for Harold to submit the form to the company. The court also decided that the interim trust that arises, pending registration, is a constructive trust.

> J   'There was a clear finding that Ada intended to make an immediate gift. It follows that it would also have been unconscionable for Ada to recall the gift. It follows that it would also have been unconscionable for her personal representatives to refuse to hand over the share transfer to Harold after her death. In those circumstances, in my judgment, delivery of the share transfer before her death was unnecessary so far as perfection of the gift was concerned. I would also decide this appeal in favour of the respondent on this further basis ... the words used by Mr Pennington should be construed as meaning that Ada and, through her, Mr Pennington became agents for Harold for the purpose of submitting the share transfer to the Company.'
>
> (Lady Justice Arden)

It should be noted that the *Pennington v Waine* (2002) principle is distinct from the traditional *Re Rose* (1952) principle. In the former case, the court proceeded on the basis of 'unconscionability' on the part of the donor to deny that a transfer took place. This is a fairly broad concept and involves a question of law for the court to decide in its discretion, as opposed to the narrow *Re Rose*

(1952) question of fact as to whether the donor had done everything required of him to effect the transfer. Unconscionability may involve a promise made by the donor, relied on by the donee to his detriment. In these circumstances the court will prevent the donor from denying the promise and re-claiming the property as his own.

In addition to the transfer of the relevant property to the trustees, the settlor is required to declare the terms of a trust. In other words, the requirement here is that in order to constitute the trust the settlor must transfer the property to the trustees and, either before or after the transfer, he declares the terms of the trust. A transfer of the property to the trustees unaccompanied by a declaration of trust by definition will not create an express trust. Such a transfer may create a resulting trust for the settlor, eg S, an intended settlor, purports to create an express trust of 10,000 BTplc shares by transferring the legal title to the shares to T1 and T2 as trustees, but failed to declare the terms of the trust. The intended beneficiary of the shares was his son, B absolutely, but S failed to indicate the terms of the trust. Since T1 and T2 acquire the shares as trustees without a declaration of the terms of the trust, the intended express trust fails and a resulting trust for S will arise. Likewise, a declaration of trust of 10,000 BT plc shares in favour of B absolutely with the intention that T1 and T2 will acquire and hold the shares as trustees for B will fail if T1 and T2 did not acquire the relevant shares.

A declaration of trust involves a present, irrevocable intention to create a trust. This involves the 'three certainties' test: certainty of intention to create a trust, certainty of subject-matter and certainty of objects (see Chapter 3).

4.3 Self-declaration of trust

An alternative mode of creating an express trust is by way of a self-declaration. A settlor declares that he presently holds specific property on trust, indicating the interest, for a beneficiary. The settlor is the creator of the trust and the trustee. He simply retains the property as trustee for the relevant beneficiaries. Clear evidence is needed to convert the status of the original owner of the property to that of a trustee. This form of creating an express trust is as effective as the transfer and declaration mode. In the absence of specific statutory provisions to the contrary, no special form is required as long as the intention of the settlor is sufficiently clear to constitute himself a trustee, for 'Equity looks at the intent rather than the form'. Thus, the declaration of trust may be in writing or may be evidenced by conduct or may take the form of a verbal statement or a combination of each of these types of evidence: see *Paul v Constance* [1977] 1 WLR 527 (above); contrast *Jones v Lock* (1865) LR 1 Ch App 25 (above). What is required from the settlor is a firm commitment on his part to undertake the duties of trusteeship in respect of the relevant property for the benefit of the specified beneficiaries (see the 'three certainties' test, above). In this respect there is no obligation to inform the beneficiaries that a trust has been created in their favour. The effect of this mode of creation is to alter the status of the settlor from a beneficial owner to that of a trustee. For instance, S, the absolute owner of 50,000 shares in BP plc, declares that henceforth he holds the entire portfolio of shares upon trust for B, his son, absolutely. In these circumstances an express trust is created. S retains the *legal* title to the shares, but B acquires the entire *equitable* interest in the shares.

4.4 No self-declaration following imperfect transfer

The court will not automatically imply the self-declaration mode of creating a trust if there has been an imperfect transfer of the property to the intended recipient. This rule applies to imperfect gifts of property, see *Jones v Lock* (1865) (above) as well as imperfect transfers to trustees, for 'Equity will not perfect imperfect gifts'. The reason for the rule is that, despite the transferor's intention to benefit another by means of a transfer (whether on trust or not), the transferor ought not to be treated as a trustee if this does not accord with his intention: see *Richards v Delbridge* (1874) LR 18 Eq 11.

CASE EXAMPLE

Richards v Delbridge (1874) LR 18 Eq 11

A grandfather attempted to assign a lease of business premises to his grandson, R, by endorsing the lease and signing a memorandum: 'This deed and all thereto I give to R from this time henceforth with all stock in trade.' He gave the lease to R's mother to hold on his behalf. On the death of the grandfather it was ascertained that his will made no reference to the business premises. The question in issue was whether the lease was acquired by the grandson, R, during the grandfather's lifetime, or was transferred to the residuary beneficiaries under the grandfather's will.

Held   There was an imperfect gift *inter vivos*, as the assignment, not being under seal, was ineffectual to transfer the lease. Further, no trust had been created, as the grandfather did not declare himself a trustee of the lease for the grandson. The court will not construe an ineffectual transfer as a valid declaration of trust.

> J   … for a man to make himself a trustee there must be an expression of intention to become a trustee, whereas words of present gift show an intention to give over property to another, and not retain it in the donor's own hands for any purpose, fiduciary or otherwise.'
>
> (Sir George Jessel MR)

4.5 The settlor may expressly adopt both modes of creation

The settlor may expressly manifest an intention to transfer the relevant property to third party trustees (transfer and declaration mode) and, prior to completing the transfer, to declare himself a trustee for the beneficiaries (self-declaration mode). In this event, the trust will be perfect, provided that the third party trustee acquires the property during the settlor's lifetime. In other words, the self-declaration of trust is regarded as conditional on an effective transfer of the property to the third party trustee. This condition may only be satisfied during the lifetime of the settlor. The court has also decided that it is immaterial how the third party trustee acquires the property: see *Re Ralli's Will Trust* [1964] Ch 288, HC.

CASE EXAMPLE

Re Ralli's Will Trust [1964] Ch 288, HC

In 1899, a testator died, leaving the residue of his estate upon trust for his wife for life with remainder to his two children, Helen and Irene, absolutely. In 1924, Helen covenanted in her marriage settlement and under clause 7 to settle all her 'existing and after acquired property' upon trusts which failed, and ultimately on trust for the children of Irene. The settlement declared that all the property comprised within the terms of the covenant will, under clause 8, 'become subject in equity to the settlement hereby covenanted to be made'. Irene's husband was appointed one of the trustees of this marriage settlement. In 1946, Irene's husband was also appointed a trustee of the 1899 settlement. In 1956, Helen died and, in 1961, Helen and Irene's mother died. The question in issue was whether Helen's property from the 1899 settlement was held upon the trusts of Helen's marriage settlement, or subject to Helen's personal estate.

Held   By virtue of the declaration in Helen's settlement in 1924, Helen and, since her death, her personal representative (Irene's husband), held her share of the 1899 settlement subject to the trusts of Helen's settlement. This was the position even though the vesting of the property in Irene's husband came to him in his other capacity as trustee of the 1899 settlement. The same conclusion could be reached by applying the rule in *Strong v Bird* (1874) LR 18 Eq 315 (see below).

CONTINUED ▶

> **J** 'In my judgment the circumstance that the plaintiff holds the fund because he was appointed a trustee of the will is irrelevant. He is at law the owner of the fund and the means by which he became so have no effect on the quality of his legal ownership. The question is: for whom, if any one, does he hold the fund in equity? In other words, who can successfully assert an equity against him disentitling him to stand on his legal right? It seems to me to be indisputable that Helen, if she were alive, could not do so, for she has solemnly covenanted under seal to assign the fund to the plaintiff and the defendants can stand in no better position.'
>
> (Buckley J)

In this case it is worth noting the fortuitous event in 1946 when Irene's husband was appointed a trustee of the 1899 settlement. This meant that the third party trustee acquired the trust property, and since it was during Helen's lifetime the trust became perfect.

4.6 Multiple trustees including the settlor

In the case of *Choithram International v Pagarani* [2001] 1 WLR 1, PC, the Privy Council decided that where the settlor appoints multiple trustees, including himself, and declares a present, unconditional and irrevocable intention to create a trust for specific persons, a failure to transfer the property to the nominated trustees is not fatal, for his (settlor's) retention of the property will be treated as a trustee. Trusteeship for these purposes is treated as a joint office so that the acquisition of the property by one trustee is equivalent to its acquisition by all the trustees. For example, S nominates himself and T1 and T2 as trustees of property and specifies the terms. If S manifests an irrevocable and unconditional intention to create a trust, his failure to transfer the property to T1 and T2 is not fatal because S retains the property as a trustee. His retention of the property as one of the trustees is equivalent to all the trustees acquiring a right to acquire the property. Thus the trust is perfect.

CASE EXAMPLE

T Choithram International SA v Pagarani [2001] 1 WLR 1, PC

The settlor, Mr Choithram Pagarani (CP), intended to set up a foundation to serve as an umbrella organisation for four charitable bodies which he had already established. CP and the other trustees executed the foundation trust deed, despite CP's rapidly failing health. The trust deed was made between CP, as settlor and CP and seven other named individuals as trustees. CP transferred £1,000 to the trustees as the initial subject-matter of the trust, with further property to be placed under the control of the trustees. The deed also set out the terms of the trust. Immediately after signing the documents CP said words to the effect that 'I have

CONTINUED ▸

given all my wealth to the trust'. He then told his accountant, who was present at the time of signing, to transfer all his balances with the companies and his shares to the foundation trust. At a subsequent meeting of the trustees, CP reported that the foundation had been established and all his wealth had been given to the trust. The relevant documents were prepared, but CP refused to sign. Evidence was adduced that CP had an aversion to signing such documents and had been advised that it was not necessary to do so. However, CP repeatedly declared that he had done his 'bit': he had given all his wealth to the foundation and there was nothing more for him to do. In the end, CP had failed to execute the forms which were necessary to carry out the formal transfer of the further assets before his death.

The claimants, CP's first wife and her children, commenced proceedings in the British Virgin Islands for a part of CP's estate. The claim was made on the ground that the intended gifts to the foundation were ineffective because CP had failed to transfer the relevant properties, namely CP's shares and deposit balances in the companies, to the foundation. The trial judge found that CP intended to make immediate gifts of the relevant properties, but his intention was not irrevocable. In addition, the judge found that, despite CP's intention to make immediate gifts to the foundation, he had failed to vest the properties in the hands of all the trustees of the foundation. This decision was affirmed by the Caribbean Court of Appeal. The defendants (executors of CP) appealed to the Privy Council.

Held Effective transfers *inter vivos* had been made to the trustees subject to the trusts, on the following grounds:

(1) CP's intention was to make a present, immediate, unconditional and irrevocable gift to the foundation. This was manifested by the execution of the foundation deed, verbally declaring his intention upon signing the document and instructing his accountant to transfer all his balances with the companies and his shares to the foundation trust.

(2) Although the words used by CP were appropriate to an outright gift, 'I give to X', on construction, those words were intended to create a gift to the trustees of the foundation on trust for the foundation. This was partly attributed to the fact that the foundation had no legal existence apart from the trust declared by the foundation trust deed. Accordingly, the *Milroy v Lord* (1862) principle for the creation of an express trust had been satisfied.

(3) Since the property was vested in one of the trustees, namely CP himself, the express trust was constituted. Accordingly, there was a duty to transfer the property to all of the trustees of the foundation trust. In principle there was no distinction between a case where a settlor declared himself to be a sole trustee for a beneficiary and the case where he declared himself to be one of the trustees for that beneficiary. In both cases the trust was perfect and the beneficiary acquired an equitable proprietary interest in the property.

(4) The subject-matter of the trust comprised all of CP's wealth in the British Virgin Islands, namely CP's deposit balances and shares in the four companies. This was in accordance with CP's statements and conduct.

CONTINUED ▸

J The foundation has no legal existence apart from the trust declared by the foundation trust deed. Therefore the words "I give to the foundation" can only mean "I give to the trustees of the foundation trust deed to be held by them on the trusts of the foundation trust deed". Although the words are apparently words of outright gift they are essentially words of gift on trust …

What is the position here where the trust property is vested in one of the body of trustees, viz TCP? In their Lordships' view there should be no question. TCP has, in the most solemn circumstances, declared that he is giving (and later that he has given) property to a trust which he himself has established and of which he has appointed himself to be a trustee. All of this occurs at one composite transaction taking place on 17 February. There can in principle be no distinction between the case where the donor declares himself to be sole trustee for a donee or a purpose and the case where he declares himself to be one of the trustees for that donee or purpose. In both cases his conscience is affected and it would be unconscionable and contrary to the principles of equity to allow such a donor to resile from his gift.'

(Lord Browne-Wilkinson)

4.7 No trust of future property

It is not possible to create an express trust of property that does not exist or property that may or may not be acquired by the settlor simply because there is no property that is capable of being subject to an order of the court. Such property is referred to by a variety of names but the principle remains the same. Examples of terms used are 'future' or 'after-acquired' property or an 'expectancy' or a '*spes*' (or hope of acquiring property). Thus, it is not possible to create a trust of lottery winnings in the future.

CASE EXAMPLE

Re Ellenborough [1903] 1 Ch 697, HC

An intended beneficiary under a will voluntarily covenanted to transfer her inheritance to another upon trusts as declared. Before the testator had died the intended beneficiary (covenantor) changed her mind. The covenantee brought an action claiming that the covenantor was under a duty to transfer the relevant property.

Held No trust of the covenant had been created, because the property was not owned by the covenantor at the time of the covenant. In addition, the covenantee could not bring an action to enforce the agreement for he had not provided consideration.

It should be noted that although a trust cannot be created in respect of future property, a contract is capable of being created in respect of such property.

4.8 Trusts of choses in action

A chose in action is a right to intangible personal property such as a right to dividends attaching to shares, intellectual property and the creditor's right to have a loan repaid by the debtor. A trust is capable of being created in respect of any type of existing property, including a chose in action. The chose may be assigned to the trustees in accordance with the intention of the settlor.

ASE EXAMPLE

> *Don King Productions Inc v Warren* [1999] 2 All ER 218, CA
>
> K and W (two well-known boxing promoters) entered into partnership agreements in which W purported to assign the benefit of promotion and management agreements to the partnership. However, several of the contracts contained express prohibitions against assignment. The question in issue was whether a trust of the benefit of the agreements (choses in action) was created.
>
> **Held**   The benefit of promotion and management agreements was capable of being the subject-matter of a trust in accordance with the intention of the parties.

Similarly, the court may construe the subject-matter of a covenant as creating a chose in action, namely the benefit of the covenant. This intangible property right may be transferred to the trustees on trust for the relevant beneficiaries. What is needed to assign such a right or chose is a clear intention on the part of the assignor to dispose of the chose to the transferee. Accordingly, A may execute a covenant with B to transfer £10,000 to B upon trust for C. If the subject-matter of the trust is treated as the cash, namely £10,000 it becomes a question of fact as to whether the sum has been transferred to B. If we assume that A did not transfer the sum to B it is still possible that the trust may be treated as perfect. The court may construe the trust property as the 'benefit of the covenant' or the 'right to the cash', ie a chose in action. This chose may be transferred by operation of law in accordance with the intention of the parties. Therefore, in a sense the trust is perfect in that B has the trust property even though A did not transfer £10,000 in cash to B. B having acquired the right to the cash is entitled to claim the cash from A. This difficult principle is known as the rule in *Fletcher v Fletcher* (1844) 4 Hare 67.

CASE EXAMPLE

Fletcher v Fletcher (1844) 4 Hare 67

The settlor, Ellis Fletcher, covenanted (for himself, his heirs, executors and administrators) with trustees (their heirs, executors, administrators and assigns) to the effect that if either or both of his natural issue (illegitimate children), Jacob and John, survived him and attained the age of 21, Ellis's executors would pay to the covenantees (or heirs, etc) £60,000 within 12 months of his death, to be held on trust for the relevant natural issue. In the circumstances, Jacob alone survived the settlor and attained the age of 21. The surviving trustees (covenantees) declined to act in respect of the trust of the covenant, unless the court ordered otherwise. Jacob brought an action directly against the executors, claiming that he become solely entitled in equity to the property.

Held   A trust of the covenant was created in favour of Jacob, the claimant, who was entitled to enforce it as a beneficiary.

> J   '... where the relation of trustee and *cestui que trust* is constituted, as where property is transferred from the author of the trust into the name of a trustee, so that he has lost all power of disposition over it, and the transaction is complete as regards him, the trustee, having accepted the trust, cannot say he holds it, except for the purposes of the trust; if it is not already perfect. This covenant, however, is already perfect. The covenantor is liable at law, and the court is not called upon to do any act to perfect it.'
>
> (Wigram VC)

On analysis, in *Fletcher v Fletcher* (1844), the court decided that:

(a) on construction of the terms of the covenant, the intended trust property was the 'benefit of the covenant' or a right to the cash sum, ie a chose in action, and not the cash sum of £60,000

(b) since the sum had existed in Ellis Fletcher's estate at the time of the covenant, this chose in action was transferred to the covenantees, trustees, on the date of the creation of the covenant

(c) the covenantees therefore became trustees, subject to the achievement of the stipulated conditions, surviving the settlor and attaining the age of 21

(d) since Jacob satisfied these conditions he became a beneficiary unconditionally and was therefore entitled to protect his interest.

It is questionable who had the 'benefit of the covenant'. Was it Ellis Fletcher or the covenantees, trustees? Did Ellis Fletcher have the benefit of the covenant? He was the covenantor. He (or his estate) was under a duty to transfer the sum to the covenantees, trustees. He (or his estate) therefore had the **burden** of transferring the sum to the coveantees, trustees. It is true that Ellis Fletcher had the cash in his estate at the time of the covenant, but this did not derive from the covenant. This sum existed independently of the covenant.

Alternatively, it could be argued that the covenantees, trustees had the 'benefit of the covenant' as covenantees. They were nominated as the recipients of the sum of £60,000, albeit in a representative capacity. In other words, between the two parties to a voluntary covenant – the covenantor and the covenantees – only the covenantees may be treated as acquiring the 'benefit of the covenant'. If this is the true position, then only the covenantees may create a trust of this chose or benefit, ie only the covenantees may become the settlors of the chose in action. On the facts of *Fletcher v Fletcher* (1844), this was clearly not the intention of the covenantees, trustees.

A separate analysis of the *Fletcher v Fletcher* (1844) rule which is consistent with the *Milroy v Lord* (1862) principle, is to identify the trust property as the cash sum of £60,000, and not the 'benefit of the covenant' or the chose in action. The issue then is whether the covenantees, trustees, acquired, or were entitled to acquire, the cash sum and, if so, when. It could be argued that the terms of the covenant were unique and imposed a positive duty, not on Ellis Fletcher, but his personal representatives to transfer £60,000 to the covenantees as trustees for Jacob. Under the covenant Ellis Fletcher merely had a duty to retain the cash sum in his estate at the time of his death. If he had done this at the time of his death then Ellis Fletcher would have done everything in his power, barring his death, to perfect the trust under the *Re Rose* (1952) principle. He was merely required to die (an issue outside his control), leaving the cash sum in his estate. This he had done. At this point a positive duty would be imposed on Ellis Fletcher's personal representatives to transfer the property to the covenantees, trustees.

4.8.1 *Fletcher* restricted to debts enforceable at law

Owing to the difficulties posed by the *Fletcher v Fletcher* (1844) principle and the opportunities for intended beneficiaries under an imperfect trust, it is not surprising that the principle has been restricted by the courts to one type of chose in action, namely debts enforceable at law. A debt enforceable at law involves a legal obligation to pay a quantified amount of money. It does not concern an obligation to transfer shares or paintings. In addition the obligation involves existing, and not future, property. This restriction was imposed in an *obiter* pronouncement in *Re Cook's Settlement Trust* [1965] Ch 902, HC.

CASE EXAMPLE

Re Cook's Settlement Trust [1965] Ch 902, HC

A number of valuable paintings were gifted by his father to Sir Francis Cook, who covenanted with trustees to the effect that if any of the paintings was sold during his lifetime, the net proceeds of sale were required to be settled on trust for stated beneficiaries. Sir Francis gave one of the paintings to his wife who wanted to sell it. The question in issue was whether the covenant may be enforced as an agreement to create a trust or as a trust.

Held (a) the parties to the agreement were volunteers who could not enforce the covenant

(b) the intended trust was imperfect for the subject matter concerned future property i.e. the proceeds of sale in the future. For this reason the *Fletcher* (1844) principle was not applicable. In any event the *Fletcher* principle was applicable to debts enforceable at law.

> J 'The covenant with which I am concerned did not, in my opinion, create a debt enforceable at law, that is to say, a property right, which, although to bear fruit only in the future and on a contingency, was capable of being made the subject of an immediate trust, as was held to be the case in *Fletcher v Fletcher*... this covenant on its true construction is, in my opinion, an executory contract to settle a particular fund or particular funds of money which at the date of the covenant did not exist and which might never come into existence. It is analogous to a covenant to settle an expectation or to settle after acquired property.'
>
> (Buckley J)

■ Key facts on constitution of express trusts

KEY FACTS

Rule in *Milroy v Lord* (1862) (a) self declaration of trusts	Settlor is the trustee ('three certainties' test) Re Kayford (1975); *Paul v Constance* (1977)

CONTINUED ▶

(b) Transfer to trustees and declaration of trusts	Vesting of property in the hands of the trustees accompanied by a valid declaration of trust
Transfer of the legal title – nature of the property	Land – registration under the LRA 1925 chattels – deed of gift or delivery – *Re Cole* (1964) Shares in a private company – execution of a stock transfer form and registration in the company's share register choses in action – assignment at law under s 136 LPA 1925
Transfer of the equitable interest Whether the transferor has done everything required of him to effect the transfer?	Writing under s 53(1)(c) of the LPA 1925 *Re Rose* (1952); *Mascall v Mascall* (1984); *Pennington v Waine* (2002)
Where there are multiple trustees nominated by the settlor (including the settlor) and the latter has manifested an irrevocable intention to create a trust, the trust is valid even though the other named trustees have not acquired the property	*Choithram v Pagarani* (2001)
An imperfect transfer to the trustees will not automatically be treated as a valid declaration of trust	*Richards v Delbridge* (1874); *Jones v Lock* (1865)
A settlor may expressly declare himself a trustee pendinga transfer to the third party trustees. If the transfer takes place during the lifetime of the settlor the trust will be perfect	*Re Ralli* (1964)
The benefit of a covenant (chose in action of a debt) may be the subject-matter of a trust	*Fletcher v Fletcher* (1844)

4.9 Consequences of a perfect trust

If a trust is perfect or completely constituted, the beneficiary acquires an equitable interest and before 1873/75 was entitled to enlist the assistance of the Court of Chancery to protect this interest.

- If the beneficiary is *sui juris* and absolutely entitled to the property he may terminate the trust by directing the trustees to transfer the legal title to him (see Chapter 2).

- The beneficiary is given a right *in rem* (in the thing), ie a right that is inherent in the trust property and is entitled to trace his property against anyone except the *bona fide* transferee of the legal estate for value without notice (see Chapter 2). This right to trace is exempt from the limitation period.

- The result is that it is immaterial whether the beneficiary is a volunteer or not (see below). He is given a right or a *locus standi* to enforce the trust, simply by proving that he is an authorised equitable owner of the property. He may bring the claim in his own name and is entitled to join the trustee as a co-defendant. In the normal course of events the trustees bring the claim on behalf of the trust. If, however, the intended trust is imperfect the transaction operates as an agreement to create a trust and, subject to the Contracts (Rights of Third Parties) Act 1999, may only be enforced by parties who have provided consideration: see *Jeffreys v Jeffreys* (1841) Cr & Ph 138.

CASE EXAMPLE

Jeffreys v Jeffreys (1841) Cr & Ph 138

A father voluntarily conveyed a freehold property to trustees upon trust for the benefit, *inter alia*, of his daughters. He also covenanted with the trustees to surrender copyhold property to the trustees upon the same trusts. He died without surrendering the copyhold property and by his will devised both the freehold and copyhold properties to his widow. After the father's death, the daughters sought to have the trusts of the deed carried into effect and to compel the widow to surrender her interest under the will to the freehold and copyhold properties.

Held As far as the freehold property was concerned, the trust was completely constituted and the daughters, as beneficiaries, succeeded in the claim. In respect of the copyhold property the trust was imperfect and because the daughters were volunteers, they were not entitled to compel the widow to part with the legal interest, which she acquired under her deceased husband's will.

4.10 Incompletely constituted trusts

If the intended trust is imperfect by reference to the *Milroy v Lord* (1862) rule the transaction operates as an agreement to create a trust. This involves the law of contract, as opposed to the law of trust. An agreement to create a trust may only be enforced in equity by non-volunteers. The rule is that 'Equity will not assist a volunteer' and 'Equity will not perfect an imperfect gift'. To obtain an equitable remedy, the claimant is required to establish that he has furnished consideration. For instance, if A agrees to transfer specific property to B upon trust for C, a volunteer, and A has failed to transfer the relevant property to B, the trust is imperfect. The question in issue is whether C may enforce the agreement to create a trust. The general rule is that if C is a volunteer he cannot enforce the agreement in equity. It is of great importance to classify C's status (volunteer or non-volunteer) if the trust is imperfect.

A 'volunteer' is one who has not provided valuable consideration. Valuable consideration refers either to common law consideration in money or money's worth or marriage consideration. Common law consideration is the price by each party to an agreement. 'Marriage consideration' takes the form of an ante-nuptial settlement made in consideration of marriage, or a post-nuptial settlement made in pursuance of an ante-nuptial agreement. A post-nuptial settlement *simpliciter* is not within the marriage consideration. An ante-nuptial agreement is one made before or at the time of a marriage, on condition that the marriage takes place, on the occasion of the marriage and for the purpose of facilitating the marriage. The persons who are treated as providing marriage consideration are the parties to the marriage and the issue of the marriage, including remoter issue. Any other children affiliated to the parties to the marriage are volunteers. Thus, illegitimate, legitimated and adopted children as well as children of a subsequent marriage are volunteers. Such volunteer children may derive an incidental benefit if their interests are intertwined with the interests of the non-volunteers, ie in special circumstances, the non-volunteers in bringing a claim may be required to acknowledge the interests of the volunteers. This was stated in an *obiter* pronouncement in *Attorney-General v Jacob-Smith* [1895] 2 QB 341. Good consideration such as natural love and affection is insufficient for these purposes.

4.10.1 Agreements enforceable by non-volunteers

It follows that if the trust is imperfect and the claimant wishes to obtain equitable assistance, he is required to demonstrate that he has furnished valuable consideration. If this is the case, the imperfect trust will be treated to all intents and purposes as though it was perfect. In other words, the claimant who has furnished valuable consideration will derive from the agreement to create a trust all the benefits accorded to a beneficiary under a perfect trust. Thus, the non-volunteer will be entitled to bring a claim directly against the reluctant settlor for an equitable remedy in order to have the agreement enforced and the limitation period will not operate.

CASE EXAMPLE

Pullan v Koe [1913] 1 Ch 9

By a marriage settlement made in 1859, a wife covenanted to settle after-acquired property of £100 and over. In 1879, she received a gift of £285 but did not transfer the relevant sum to the trustees. Instead, the money was paid into her husband's bank account and he later invested it in bonds, which remained in his estate at the time of his death in 1909. The trustees of the marriage settlement claimed the securities from the husband's executors on behalf of the children of the marriage. The executors pleaded the Statute of Limitations as a defence.

Held The trustees, as representatives of non-volunteers, were entitled to trace the intended trust assets on behalf of the non-volunteers. The claim was treated as equivalent to an action brought in respect of a perfectly created trust.

> **J** 'In my opinion as soon as the £285 was paid to the wife it became in equity bound by and subject to the trusts of the settlement … the property being thus bound, these bonds became trust property, and can be followed by the trustees and claimed from a volunteer … the trustees are entitled to come into a court of equity to enforce a contract to create a trust, contained in a marriage settlement, for the benefit of the wife and the issue of the marriage, all of whom are within the marriage consideration.'
>
> (Swinfen Eady J)

4.10.2 Covenants to create trusts before the Contracts (Rights of Third Parties) Act 1999

Assume that A voluntarily promises (ie without consideration) to transfer 10,000 BP plc shares to B to hold on trust for C, a volunteer and non-party, absolutely. A fails to transfer the shares to B. The trust is therefore imperfect. Since B and C are volunteers, neither may bring an action in equity against A to enforce the promise. The rule that only persons who have provided consideration may claim rights under a promise to create a trust, is subject to one limitation, namely that a party to a voluntary covenant (ie a deed) may claim the common law remedy of damages for breach of covenant. The rule at common law is that in a 'specialty' contract (ie a deed) the absence of consideration does not prevent a party from enforcing the contract at law by claiming damages. In this respect 'Equity follows the law' and does not prevent the party from enforcing his legal rights. At the same time, the volunteer is not entitled to claim equitable assistance, for 'Equity will not assist a volunteer'. In the above example if the voluntary promise between A (an intended settlor) and B (an intended trustee) is incorporated in a deed for the benefit of C (an intended beneficiary). Although B and C are volunteers, B, in theory, is entitled to claim damages at common law for breach of contract. This was decided in *Re Cavendish-Browne's Settlement Trust* [1916] WN 341 (substantial damages were awarded). However, the court came to a different conclusion in *Re Kay's Settlement* [1939] 1 All ER 245 (B was prevented from bringing an action for damages on behalf of C), applying the principle laid down in *Re Pryce* [1917] 1 Ch 234 (C was not entitled to apply to the court for directions to force B to bring a claim for damages on behalf of C, because the volunteer ought not to obtain by indirect means, relief that he cannot obtain by direct procedure). The quantum of damages may or may not pose a problem depending on the circumstances. The approach in *Re Pryce* (1917) and *Re Kay* (1939) appears to be based on the premise that if B were to succeed in the claim for damages and obtain substantial damages he may be required to hold the damages on trust for the volunteer, non-covenantee, C. Thus, C may obtain a remedy indirectly.

A different solution is adopted if C, a volunteer, is also a party to the covenant. He will be entitled to claim damages in his own right, but of course will not be entitled to a equitable remedy because of his status as a volunteer.

CASE EXAMPLE

Cannon v Hartley [1949] Ch 213

A deed of separation made between the defendant, his wife (non-volunteer) and his daughter (volunteer) contained a clause requiring the defendant to settle future property. The daughter brought a claim for damages against her father for breach of covenant.

Held   The daughter was entitled to substantial damages because she was a party to the deed.

'In the present case the plaintiff, although a volunteer, is not only a party to the deed of separation but is also a direct covenantee under the very covenant upon which she is suing. She does not require the assistance of the court to enforce the covenant for she has a legal right herself to enforce it. She is not asking for equitable relief for damages at common law for breach of covenant.'

(Romer J)

It would appear that if the claimant has provided consideration, he may bring a claim in equity (perhaps specific performance) on behalf of a volunteer who was entitled to benefit from the agreement: see *Beswick v Beswick* [1968] AC 58, HL.

CASE EXAMPLE

Beswick v Beswick [1968] AC 58, HL

Peter Beswick executed a deed with his nephew to transfer his business in return for a salary payable to Peter during his life and after his death an annuity payable to his (Peter's) widow. After Peter's death the nephew refused to pay his aunt the annuity. She brought a claim for specific performance against her nephew in the capacity of her deceased's husband's personal representative.

Held   The aunt was entitled to succeed in her claim

4.10.3 Effect of the Contracts (Rights of Third Parties) Act 1999

Under the Contracts (Rights of Third Parties) Act 1999, the decisions in *Re Pryce* (1917) and *Re Kay* (1939) are reversed. Under s 1 of the Act, a third party to a contract is entitled 'in his own right' to enforce a term of the contract if, *inter alia*, a 'term of the contract purports to confer a benefit on him'. This is clearly covered by a contract to create a trust for the benefit of C. Section 1(5) enacts the policy of treating the volunteer third party C as 'if he had been a party to the contract'. The effect is that even though C is not a party to the contract, he will be treated as if he is a party. Today, C would be entitled to claim substantial damages from A, even though he is not a party to the contract. The statutory changes endorse the principle in *Re Cavendish-Browne* (1916) and equate the process with the method in *Cannon v Hartley* (1949) (see above). At the same time, the Act has reversed the decisions in *Re Pryce* (1917) and *Re Kay* (1939). However, notwithstanding the reforms enacted in the 1999 Act, C, a volunteer, would not be entitled to an equitable remedy of specific performance. Such a remedy would not have been available to him even if he had been a party to the contract, for 'Equity will not assist a volunteer'.

Figure 4.1 Perfect trusts

ACTIVITY

1. Explain and illustrate the maxim 'Equity will not perfect an imperfect gift'.

2. What is meant by marriage consideration?

3. What changes have the Contracts (Rights of Third Parties) Act 1999 introduced by way of assistance to a volunteer in enforcing an agreement to create a trust?

Further reading

Rickett, C, 'Completely Constituting an inter vivos trust: Property Rules' (2001) Conv 515.

Roe, T, 'Contractual Intention under s 1(1)(b) and s1(2) of the Contracts (Rights of Third Parties) Act 1999' [2000] 63 MLR 887.

chapter 5 — EXCEPTIONS TO THE RULE THAT EQUITY WILL NOT ASSIST A VOLUNTEER ■

5.1 Introduction

There are a number of occasions when, although a gift or trust is imperfect, equity would give assistance to volunteers and force the defendant to complete the intended gift or trust.

5.2 The rule in *Strong v Bird*

The rule in *Strong v Bird* (1874) LR 18 Eq 315 is that if an *inter vivos* gift is imperfect by reason only of the fact that the transfer to the intended donee is incomplete, the incomplete gift will become perfect when the donee acquires the property in the capacity of executor of the donor's estate. This rule is applicable to both personal and real property.

In probate law, a deceased's estate devolves on his executor as appointed in his will; the executor's function is to administer the estate of the deceased. The executor is treated in law as the *alter ego* of the deceased. All that is needed to transfer the estate to the executor are:

- the valid execution of a will in which an executor is appointed and
- the acquisition of probate by the nominated executor. The probate document has the effect in law of vesting the estate of the deceased in the executor. Third parties wishing to deal with the estate of the deceased are required to act through the executor.

The donee/executor will take the property beneficially in accordance with the *inter vivos* intention of the donor, even though he acquires the asset in a different capacity. In short, the defective gift, because of the failure to transfer the property *inter vivos*, will be cured by operation of law when the donee/executor obtains probate.

CASE EXAMPLE

Strong v Bird (1874) LR 18 Eq 315

The defendant's stepmother became a lodger and agreed to pay for her board and lodging. The defendant borrowed £1,000 from her and it was agreed that the sum would be repaid by reductions from each quarter's rent. After £200 had been repaid the stepmother generously refused to hold the defendant to the loan and paid the full rent. This new arrangement was not binding at law, for lack of consideration, but the intention to release the debt continued until her death. The defendant was appointed her executor until her will. The next of kin claimed that the defendant was required to repay the balance of the loan.

Held The intended gift of the balance of the loan became perfect on the death of the testatrix.

J

'... when a testator makes his debtor executor, and thereby releases the debt at law, he is no longer liable at law. It is said that he would be liable in this court: and so he would, unless he could shew some reason for not being made liable. Then what does he shew here? Where he proves to the satisfaction of the court a continuing intention to give; and it appears to me that there being the continuing intention to give, and there being a legal act which transferred the ownership or released the obligation – for it is the same thing – the transaction is perfected ...'

(Sir George Jessel MR)

5.2.1 The nature of the donor's intention

The donor's intention is of paramount importance. The claimant is required to establish that the donor manifested a present, continuous intention to make an *inter vivos* gift to him. The *Strong v Bird* (1874) rule concerns only intended *inter vivos* gifts or transfers. The rule was never intended for purely testamentary transfers. Such transfers are required to be made by wills. Accordingly, there is no contradiction of the requirements under the Wills Act 1837.

Present intention of the donor

In order to activate the rule, the intended transferee is required to prove that the donor had the intention to transfer the property immediately and not in the future. Thus, if the donor promised to transfer the property after he had modified the property and he fails to modify the property, the test will not be satisfied. Moreover, if the modification of the property has been completed, the donor is required to make a further promise to transfer the property to the donee.

CASE EXAMPLE

Re Freeland [1952] 1 Ch 110

The claimant alleged that the testatrix promised to transfer her car to the claimant after it was repaired. The car was repaired but was not delivered to the claimant; instead the defendant, who had borrowed the car from the testatrix, kept possession of the car until the testatrix's death. The claimant was appointed executor of the deceased's estate. The issue was whether the imperfect gift was completed.

Held The *Strong v Bird* (1874) rule was not applicable to these facts, for the intention of the testatrix was to transfer the car in the future.

> J
>
> There was no room for the application of the principle [in *Strong v Bird* (1874)] where there was an intention to give which was not completed because the intended donor desired first to apply the subject matter of the gift to some other purpose. In such a case the intended donee when appointed executor could not say that nothing remained to complete his gift …'
>
> (Evershed MR)

Continuous intention

The claimant is required to prove that the donor manifested an intention to transfer the relevant property to him and that this intention remained unaltered up to the time of the donor's death. Any break in the continuity of the intention would disentitle the transferee of the property. The date of the execution of the will may offer some evidence of the inconsistency of the intention of the testator. If a will is executed after a declaration of intent by the testator and the will transfers the relevant property to another donee, this may be sufficient to break the continuity of the testator's intention. This is a question of fact. It follows that if the donor had forgotten his intention to donate the property to the donee and treated the property as his own, the requisite intention would not be satisfied.

> Re Wale [1956] 1 WLR 1346
>
> The testatrix, Elizabeth Wale, declared her intention in 1939 to make a transfer of shares
> to trustees subject to a trust in favour of her daughter. The testatrix had taken no steps to
> transfer the shares to the trustees and for the remainder of her life showed no indication
> of remembering the 1939 settlement. By her will she left her estate to her two sons. Her
> daughter was appointed one of the executors. The issue was whether the imperfect gift of
> the shares was perfected on Elizabeth Wale's death.
>
> **Held**   The rule in *Strong v Bird* (1874) was not applicable, for the donor's intention was
> not continuous until her death.

The rule was originally intended to perfect an imperfect gift in favour of the transferee, beneficially. But the principle has been extended to transfers to trustees to hold on trust for beneficiaries. There ought to be no reason in principle to prevent such an extension. It is not an essential part of the rule that the transferee is required to be a beneficial owner of the property. Instead, the purpose of the rule is merely to complete an imperfect transfer when probate of the will is obtained by the intended transferee/executor. The donee's status is immaterial. Accordingly, the rule is applicable where the donor intends to transfer property to X (executor) as trustee for Y: see *Re Ralli* [1964] Ch 288, HC (Chapter 4).

Extension to intestacies

The *Strong v Bird* (1874) principle has been extended to transfers to the administrator of a deceased's estate on his death intestate. A person dies intestate when he dies without making a will. The deceased's next of kin is entitled to administer his estate. His function is to distribute the deceased's estate in accordance with the intestacy rules. He is treated as the equivalent to the executor in the case of a person dying testate. In *Re James* [1935] Ch 449, the court extended the *Strong v Bird* (1874) rule to transfers on an intestacy.

CASE EXAMPLE

> Re James [1935] Ch 449
>
> A inherited his father's house on the latter's death intestate. A 'gave' the house to his father's
> housekeeper, handing her the title deeds, but he did not convey the house to her. She occupied
> the house as donee and A had a continuing intention to give her the house until his own death
> intestate, nine years later. The housekeeper was appointed one of two administratrixes of A's
> estate. The legal interest in the house therefore vested in the housekeeper jointly with the other
> administratrix. The issue was whether the claimant was entitled to enlist the assistance of equity
> to complete the transfer beneficially to the housekeeper.
>
> **Held**   The imperfect transfer was required to be perfected under the *Strong v Bird*
> (1874) rule.

However, in *Re Gonin* [1979] Ch 16, the High Court in an *obiter* pronouncement, severely criticised the *Re James* (1935) solution. The tenor of this criticism was that although the donor promised to transfer the relevant property to the donee, his appointment as the deceased's next of kin did not constitute a conscious effort of the deceased, but a fortuitous event. Accordingly, the court ought not to intervene to assist such a volunteer.

CASE EXAMPLE

Re Gonin [1979] Ch 16

A mother who wanted to make a gift of her house to her daughter erroneously believed that she could not do so because the daughter was illegitimate. As an alternative, she wrote a cheque for £33,000 in the daughter's favour. This cheque was found after the mother's death. At this time it was too late to cash the cheque as the funds in the account of the deceased became frozen. The daughter became the administratrix of her mother's estate and claimed the house in accordance with the *Strong v Bird* (1874) rule.

Held: that the rule in *Strong v Bird* (1874) was not applicable as there was no continuing intention to give the house to the daughter.

> J   'The appointment of an administrator is not the act of the deceased but of law. It is often a matter of pure chance which of many persons equally entitled to a grant of letters of administration finally takes them out. Why, then, should any special tenderness be shown to a person so selected by law and not the will of the testator. It would seem an astonishing doctrine of equity that if the person who wishes to take the benefit of the rule in *Strong v Bird* manages to be the person to obtain a grant then he will be able to do so ...'
>
> (Walton J)

Gilbert Kodilinye, in an article entitled 'A fresh look at the rule in *Strong v Bird*' [1982] Conv 14, analyses the attack by Walton J on *Re James* (1935) and suggests that his criticisms were unfounded. The policy of the *Strong v Bird* (1874) rule is simply to vest the property in the hands of the legal representative of the deceased. In this respect, it makes no difference whether during the intended donor's lifetime the transferee was, or was not, consciously appointed to act as his representative on death. The material issue is the defective transfer *inter vivos* is cured by the transfer to the intended donee by operation of law on the death of the donor.

5.3 *Donatio mortis causa*

A *donatio mortis causa* (DMC) involves an *inter vivos* transfer of control over property by the donor while contemplating death but on condition that the gift will become perfect on death. The principle here is that immediately on the death of the donor the transfer becomes perfect or the donee is entitled to have the imperfect transfer perfected on death. The transferor may make a 'complete' delivery or transfer of the property but conditional on death, as would suffice in the case of an *inter vivos* gift, for example the delivery of a watch or a bracelet to the donee before undergoing surgery. In these circumstances the donee's title becomes unconditional on the death of the donor and no action on the part of the donor's personal representatives is needed to perfect the donee's title. The donee will simply retain the property beneficially. Alternatively, there could be a valid DMC even though the delivery or transfer does not vest the donor's title in the donee. For example, the transfer of a chose in action, such as a passbook to funds in the donor's building society account in contemplation of and conditional on death, does not vest the funds in the account to the donee on the death of the donor. In this event, the donor's personal representatives are required to hold the legal title to the property on trust for the donee. This is a true case of 'equity perfecting an imperfect gift', or 'equity assisting a volunteer'.

A DMC has been described by Buckley J in *Re Beaumont* [1902] 1 Ch 889 as a 'singular form of gift', something between an unconditional *inter vivos* gift and a gift on death. It is a transfer of property *inter vivos,* but conditional on death.

> J
>
> 'A *donatio mortis causa* is a singular form of gift. It may be said to be of an amphibious nature, being a gift which is neither entirely *inter vivos* nor testamentary. It is an act *inter vivos* by which the donee is to have absolute title to the gift not at once but if the donor dies. If the donor dies the title becomes absolute not under the will but as against the executor. In order to make the gift valid it must be made so as to take complete effect on the donor's death.'
>
> (Buckley J)

There are a number of condtions that are required to be satisfied in order to establish a valid DMC. These are:

- the donor is required to contemplate death
- the donor is required to transfer the property *inter vivos* and conditional on death
- the donor is required to transfer dominion over the property during his lifetime
- certain types of property are incapable of forming the subject-matter of a DMC.

5.3.1 Contemplation of death

The requirement here is that the donor contemplates impending death or death in the near future. It is not sufficient for the donor to contemplate the mere possibility of death. The requirement is much more specific than that we will all have to die some day. However, the donor need not contemplate immediate death or be on his death-bed in order to satisfy this principle. The test here is essentially subjective and involves a question of fact.

The donor need not express his personal sentiments: very often, in the appropriate environment, the courts will infer this condition from the surrounding circumstances. The donor may contemplate death as a result of undertaking a dangerous mission or undergoing surgery. Contemplation of death by suicide may also suffice, since suicide is no longer a crime.

5.3.2 Conditional on death

The donor must intend the gift to become absolute only on his death. In the meantime the gift is revocable. There can be no DMC if the donor intends to make an immediate gift *inter vivos*. In that case the gift stands or falls as an ordinary gift *inter vivos*. Likewise, there can be no DMC if the donor intends to make a gift by will, ie he intends his wishes to take effect on his death but he does not wish to part with dominion over the asset *inter vivos*. To satisfy this condition the donor is required to part with dominion over the asset *inter vivos* but with the intention that the gift will become complete on death.

During the donor's lifetime the transfer of the asset is required to be revocable. This is a question of fact. Revocation is automatic if the donor recovers from the illness which he contemplated leading to death. Alternatively, the donor may expressly revoke the transfer by resuming dominion over the property. There is no revocation of the transfer by will, for the will speaks from the date of death and the time of death makes the transfer perfect.

In exceptional circumstances, the donor may specify that death alone from a specific ailment will make the gift complete. If that be the case then only death from that source will suffice. In the ordinary course of events, if the donor contemplates death from a specific condition then death from any condition will be sufficient to satisfy this requirement.

CASE EXAMPLE

Wilkes v Allington [1931] 2 Ch 104

The donor knew that he was suffering from cancer and had no hope of recovery. He did not know how long he had to live when he transferred property to the donee. One month later he caught a cold on a bus journey and died from pneumonia.

Held   A valid DMC of the property had been made.

5.3.3 Parting with dominion

The donor is required to part with dominion or control over the property during his lifetime. It is required to be established that the donor has lost control over the asset during his lifetime and, at the same time, the donee has acquired control over the subject-matter of the gift. With regard to tangible moveable property (chattels) this condition will be satisfied if the donor has delivered the chattel to the donee with the intention that property in the chattel will be transferred on death. This test will not be satisfied where the donor has merely transferred custody over the property to the donee.

ASE EXAMPLE

> *Reddel v Dobree* (1834) 10 Sim 244
>
> The donor, in declining health, delivered a locked ash box to X, telling her that the box contained money for her. He insisted that the box be returned to him for inspection every three months during his lifetime and that, on his death, X would be entitled to obtain the key from his son. The question was whether a valid DMC had been created.
>
> **Held**   No valid DMC was created, for the donor had retained dominion over the property.

It is immaterial whether the delivery of the chattel is made before or after the donor expresses his intention to make the transfer.

ASE EXAMPLE

> *Cain v Moon* [1896] 2 QB 283
>
> A daughter delivered a deposit note to her mother for safe custody. Two years later, when the daughter was seriously ill she told her mother 'The bank note is for you if I die'. The issue was whether a valid DMC was created. The court held that the antecedent delivery sufficed and it was not necessary for the mother to hand back the note and for the daughter to re-deliver it when she expressed her intention. Thus, a valid DMC was created.

However, in *Re Craven's Estate* [1937] 1 Ch 423, Farwell J in an *obiter* pronouncement declared broadly that the retention of a spare set of keys by the donor is inconsistent with the test of parting with dominion over the property. However, in *Woodard v Woodard* [1995] 3 All ER 980, CA the Court of Appeal refused to follow this statement and, instead, considered the circumstances responsible for the donor retaining a spare set of keys. If the donor consciously and deliberately retained the spare set of keys in order to maintain control over the property, this is inconsistent with his parting with dominion. However, if the spare set of keys was retained by the donor through absentmindedness, or without a deliberate effort to retain control over the property, dominion may be transferred. The retention of the spare set of keys would be irrelevant in these circumstances.

ASE EXAMPLE

Woodard v Woodard [1995] 3 All ER 980, CA

A father who was dying fom cancer was admitted to hospital. He was driven to the hospital by his son (the defendant) in the father's car. The father told the defendant, in the presence of the claimant, the defendant's mother, that he might keep the keys as he (the father) would not be driving his car any more. The father died three days later. The defendant sold the car and the claimant, as administrator and sole beneficiary of her deceased husband's estate, brought an action against the defendant for the recovery of the proceeds of sale. The defendant argued that his father had made either an outright *inter vivos* gift or a DMC. The trial judge decided that the father had made an outright gift to his son. The claimant appealed to the Court of Appeal.

Held   A valid DMC had been created in favour of the son.

• It was clear from the evidence that the defendant would have had to give the car back if his father had recovered. There was therefore no outright gift of the car, but a transfer conditional on the death of the father.

• It was also clear that the transfer was made in contemplation of death owing to the surrounding circumstances.

• It was irrelevant that the defendant already had possession of the car and set of keys. There was no need for the defendant to return the car and keys to the father and for the latter to re-transfer the car and keys to the defendant; reliance was placed on *Cain v Moon* [1896] 2 QB 283 and *Re Stoneham* [1953] Ch 59.

Likewise, in *Re Lillingston* [1952] 2 All ER 184 the test was satisfied where the subject-matter of the gift is transferred, or the means of acquiring the asset is transferred to the donee.

ASE EXAMPLE

Re Lillingston [1952] 2 All ER 184

D, a donor in contemplation of death, handed X a collection of jewellery and the keys to her trunk, telling her that the trunk contained the key to her Harrods safe deposit, which in turn contained the key to her city safe deposit. D said that she wished X to have all her jewellery and that after her death, X could go and get the jewellery in these safe deposits. D and X agreed that the jewellery should be kept in the trunk, which was in D's room and X placed the collection of jewellery in the trunk, whereupon D said: 'Keep the key, it's now yours.' On D's death the issue arose as to whether valid DMCs were created in favour of X.

CONTINUED ▸

> **Held**   There were valid DMCs of the collection of jewellery and of the jewellery in the two safe deposits.

> **J**   '[It did not matter] in how many boxes the subject of a gift may be contained or that each, except the last, contains a key which opens the next, so long as the scope of the gift is made clear.'
>
> (Wynn-Parry J)

Transfer of dominion over choses in action

In the case of a chose in action which cannot be transferred by delivery, the donor is required to transfer the legal title to the donee by complying with the relevant formalities. Alternatively, the donor is required to deliver a document of title or essential evidence of title concerning the chose in action in order to secure a transfer of the property. The latter test was laid down in *Birch v Treasury Solicitor* [1951] 1 Ch 298, CA.

CASE EXAMPLE

Birch v Treasury Solicitor [1951] 1 Ch 298, CA

A, a donor, in contemplation of death, delivered to the donee, B, her Post Office Savings Bank book, London Trustee Savings Bank book, Barclays Bank deposit passbook and Westminster Bank deposit account book, intending that the money in these accounts should belong to B on A's death. The issue was whether valid DMCs were created. Expert evidence was tendered on behalf of the Trustee Savings Bank that the passbook was essential evidence of title to the funds in the account.

Held   There was sufficient delivery of documents to establish valid DMCs of the funds in each of the bank accounts.

> **J**   '… we think that the real test is whether the instrument "amounts to a transfer" as being the essential *indicia* or evidence of title, possession or production of which entitles the possessor to the money or property purported to be given … We think, accordingly, that in the case of both banks the condition stated on the face of the deposit books must be taken to have remained operative, ie, that the book was, and is, the essential *indicia* of title and that delivery of the book "amounted to transfer" of the chose in action.'
>
> (Evershed MR)

5.3.4 The types of property

In general, most properties are capable of being the subject-matter of a DMC. However, there are a number of properties that may not be suitable to be transferred by a DMC.

- **Cheques**   The cheque of the donor, drawn on his own bank, is a revocable mandate which is revoked on his death. During the donor's lifetime the cheque may be cashed by the donee. In this event, the issue is whether the donee is entitled to retain the funds or not. This is not related to a DMC. Alternatively, the payee of the cheque may present the cheque for payment after the death of the payer. In this event the gift is imperfect and cannot be perfected by a DMC. The donor's cheque is incapable of being the subject-matter of a DMC: see *Re Beaumont* [1902] 1 Ch 889, HC.

- **Land**   Lord Eldon in *Duffield v Elwes* (1827) 1 Bli NS 497, in an *obiter* pronouncement, took the view that land cannot be the subject-matter of a DMC. It was widely believed that this view was too broad and was finally tested in *Sen v Headley* [1991] 2 WLR 1308, CA. The Court of Appeal decided that Lord Eldon's view could not be supported in respect of unregistered land.

CASE EXAMPLE

Sen v Headley [1991] 2 WLR 1308, CA

The deceased, while suffering from inoperable cancer, was looked after by the claimant, with whom he lived. The claimant visited him in hospital every day. Three days before he died, he told the claimant that 'The house [was hers] … You have the keys … The deeds are in the steel box'. The sole key to the box was given to her. In addition, the claimant had her own house keys. The issue was whether there was a valid DMC of the house (unregistered land).

Held   The transfer of the title deeds to the house was a sufficient parting with dominion over the house, but the retention of the house keys, on its own, was insufficient to transfer the house. Further, a DMC operates by way of a constructive trust.

> **J**   'It cannot be doubted that title deeds are the essential *indicia* of title to unregistered land. Moreover, on the facts found by the judge, there was here a constructive delivery of the title deeds of 56 Gordon Road equivalent to an actual handing of them by Mr Hewett to Mrs Sen. And it could not be suggested that Mr Hewett did not part with dominion over the deeds … We hold that land is capable of passing by way of a *donatio mortis causa* and that the three general requirements for such a gift were satisfied in this case.'
>
> (Nourse LJ)

- **Stocks and shares**   The question of whether shares are capable of being the subject-matter of a DMC is the subject of a number of contradictory judicial rulings.

ASE EXAMPLE

Ward v Turner (1752) 2 Ves Sen 431

The court decided that the delivery of receipts for the purchase price of South Sea annuities was not a sufficient delivery of the annuities to the donee by way of a DMC.

> **J**   '[A DMC of company stock could not be made] without a transfer, or something amounting to that. The receipts were nothing but waste paper.'
>
> (Lord Hardwicke)

CASE EXAMPLE

Staniland v Willott (1850) 3 Mac & G 664

The donor, in contemplation of death, made a valid legal transfer of shares in a public company to the donee, but the transfer was revoked by the recovery of the intended donor from his illness. Accordingly, there was no DMC, but the court decided that, had the facts been different, shares were capable of being the subject-matter of a DMC.

In *Moore v Moore* (1874) LR 18 Eq 474, the court decided that railway stock could not be the subject-matter of a DMC. This decision was followed in *Re Weston* [1902] 1 Ch 680, where the court decided that building society shares were an inappropriate subject of a DMC.

The effect of these cases is that an unattractive distinction between shares in a public company and shares in a private company has been drawn. The decision in *Staniland v Willott* (1850) seems difficult to justify, for share certificates are not documents of title. With regard to shares in a private company, if the donor has executed a share transfer form in favour of the transferee (so that he has done everything required of him), the transfer may be effective in accordance with the *Re Rose* [1952] Ch 499, CA principle, see Chapter 4). There will be no need to seek equitable assistance in order to perfect the gift, for the gift will already be perfect in equity.

5.4 Proprietary estoppel

Proprietary estoppel is a right given to a volunteer whenever a landowner stands by and allows the volunteer to improve his property by incurring expenditure on the property on the assumption that there will be a transfer to him. The landowners and successors in title are estopped from denying the interest acquired by the volunteer. Unlike promissory estoppel which may be used only 'defensively', proprietary estoppel may be used 'offensively' (as a cause of action) in order to perfect the imperfect gift made. This principle is sometimes referred to as the rule in *Dillwyn v Llewellyn* (1862) 4 De GF&J 517.

CASE EXAMPLE

Dillwyn v Llewellyn (1862) 4 De GF&J 517

A father, wishing his son to live nearby, offered him a farm so that he could build a house on the land. The son accepted the offer, expended a sum of money and built a house on the land, to the knowledge and approval of the father. The father died before a conveyance of the legal estate was ever made to the son. The son claimed to have the land conveyed to him.

Held   The father's actions gave the son the impression that the land would be conveyed to him. Thus, it would have been unconscionable to deny the son an interest in the property. Likewise, the father's personal representatives were estopped from denying the interest acquired in the property. They were obliged to convey the fee simple to the claimant, son.

> **J**   'If A puts B in possession of a piece of land and tells him "I give it to you that you may build a house on it", and B, on the strength of that promise, with the knowledge of A expends a large sum of money in building a house, I cannot doubt that the donee acquires a right from the subsequent transaction to call on the donor to perform that contract and complete the imperfect donation which was made.'
>
> (Lord Westbury)

The principle was explained in the dissenting speech of Lord Kingsdown in *Ramsden v Dyson* (1866) LR 1 HL 129, thus:

> **J**   '… if a man, under a verbal agreement with a landlord for a certain interest in the land, or, what amounts to the same thing, under an expectation, created or encouraged by the landlord, that he shall have a certain interest, takes possession of such land, with the consent of the landlord, and upon the faith of such promise or expectation, with the knowledge of the landlord, and without objection by him, lays out money upon the land, a court of equity will compel the landlord to give effect to such promise or expectation.'
>
> (Lord Kingsdown)

5.4.1 Five *probanda*

In *Willmot v Barber* (1880) 15 Ch D 96, Fry J set out the requirements in more detail:

> **J** 'It has been said that the acquiesence which will deprive a man of his legal rights must amount to fraud, and in my view that is an abbreviated statement of a very true proposition. A man is not to be deprived of his legal rights unless he has acted in such a way as would make it fraudulent for him to set up those rights. What then are the elements necessary to constitute fraud? In the first place, the plaintiff must have made a mistake as to his legal rights. Secondly, the plaintiff must have expended some money or must have done some act (not necessarily upon the defendant's land) on the faith of his mistaken belief. Thirdly, the defendant, the possessor of the legal right must know of the existence of his own right which is inconsistent with the right claimed by the plaintiff. Fourthly, the defendant must know of the plaintiff's mistaken belief of his rights … Lastly, the defendant must have encouraged the plaintiff in his expenditure of money or in the other acts which he has done, either directly or by abstaining from asserting his legal right. Where all these elements exists, there is fraud of such a nature as will entitle the court to restrain the possessor of the legal right from exercising it, but nothing short of this will do.'
>
> (Fry J)

These five *probanda*, as they are called, have not been applied consistently by the courts. Some courts refer to the propositions as factors as opposed to essential requirements in in order to establish the principle. The test laid down by Fry J was endorsed by Scarman LJ in *Crabb v Arun District Council* [1975] 3 All ER 865:

> **J** 'If the plaintiff has any right, it is an equity arising out of the conduct and relationship of the parties. In such a case I think it is now well settled law that the court, having analysed and assessed the conduct and relationship of the parties, has to answer three questions. First, is there an equity established? Secondly, what is the extent of the equity, if one is established? And thirdly, what is the relief appropriate to satisfy the equity?'
>
> (Scarman LJ)

In *Greasley v Cooke* [1980] 3 All ER 710, CA, the Court of Appeal decided that the claimant is not obliged to incur expenditure in order to succeed in the claim; instead the claimant is required to suffer a detriment in reliance on the promise made by the defendant, to such an extent that it would be unjust and inequitable for the promissor to go back on his promise. The notion of reliance is presumed in favour of the claimant.

CASE EXAMPLE

Greasley v Cooke [1980] 3 All ER 710, CA

The claimant had given assurances to the defendant, a maid, to the effect that she was entitled to remain in the house for as long as she wished. The defendant remained in the house, caring for the family (including a mentally retarded child), without payment. Possession proceedings were brought against the maid.

Held that an equity in the defendant's favour was raised and an order was made entitling her to occupy the house rent free for as long as she wished to stay there. Further there is a presumption of reliance once the claimant has established a promise.

> 'There is a presumption that [she remained in the house] relying on assurances given to her … The burden is not on her but on them to prove that she did not rely on their assurances. They did not prove it, nor did their representatives. So she is presumed to have relied on them … It so happens that in many of these cases of proprietary estoppel there has been expenditure of money. But that is not a necessary element.'
>
> (Lord Denning MR)

5.4.2 Unconscionability

The modern approach to proprietary estoppel is to broaden its scope and to focus on the defendant's unconscionability, rather than strict, rigid rules. This test was laid down by Oliver J in *Taylors Fasions Ltd v Liverpool Victoria Friendly Society* [1982] 1 All ER 897:

> The more recent cases indicate that the application of the *Ramsden v Dyson* principle … requires a very much broader approach which is directed rather at ascertaining whether it would be unconscionable for a party to be permitted to deny that which, knowingly or unknowingly, he has allowed or encouraged another to assume to his detriment than to inquiring whether the circumstances can be fitted within the confines of some preconceived formula serving as a universal yardstick for every form of unconscionable behaviour. So regarded, knowledge of the true position by the party alleged to be estopped becomes merely one of the relevant factors (it may even be a determining factor in certain cases) in the overall inquiry. This approach, so it seems to me, appears very clearly from the authorities.'
>
> (Oliver J)

5.4.3 Nature of the interest acquired

Once it is established that a right by way of a proprietary estoppel exists in favour of the claimant, the court will strive to find the most appropriate way of giving effect to the claimant's interest. This will depend on all the circumstances of the case. Solutions adopted by the courts include a transfer of the freehold estate, a decree of specific performance of the renewal option in a lease, a lien for the amount expended by the claimant and the creation of a licence for the claimant.

ACTIVITY

J

'A *donatio mortis causa* is a singular form of gift. It may be said to be of an amphibious nature, being a gift which is neither entirely *inter vivos* nor testamentary. It is an act *inter vivos* by which the donee is to have absolute title to the gift not at once but if the donor dies. If the donor dies the title becomes absolute not under the will but as against the executor.'

(per Buckley LJ in *Re Beaumont* (1902))

Explain and analyse this statement by reference to decided cases.

chapter 6 FORMALITIES FOR THE CREATION OF EXPRESS TRUSTS

6.1 Introduction

As a general rule, equity does not insist on special formal requirements in order to create an express trust: 'Equity looks at the intent rather than the form'. However, occasionally Parliament has intervened and has imposed a number of formal requirements. These formalities vary with the subject-matter of the trust, such as land, the nature of the interest involved, such as an equitable interest, and the mode of creation, such as *inter vivos* or by will. These formalities are distinct from the necessary formalities (see above) needed to transfer the property to the trustees and so constitute the trust. Many of these formalities were originally enacted in the Statute of Frauds 1677. This was a statute passed in order to prevent fraud and require writing in appropriate circumstances.

6.2 Declaration of a trust of land

Section 53(1)(b) of the Law of Property Act 1925 (originally s 7 of the Statute of Frauds 1677) enacts that:

 'A declaration of trust respecting any land or any interest therein must be manifested and proved by some writing signed by some person who is able to declare such trust or by his will.'

The subsection is only applicable to *inter vivos* trusts concerning land and not personal property, thus, a trust concerning one square inch of land is subject to the subsection, but a trust of £1m of personalty may be declared orally.

6.2.1 'Land or an interest in land'

'Land', under Sch 1 to the Interpretation Act 1978, 'includes buildings and other structures, land covered with water, and any estate, interest, easement, servitude or right in or over land'.

Section 205 (1)(ix)–(x) of the Law of Property Act 1925 enacts:

 '(ix) "land" includes land of any tenure, and mines and minerals, whether or not held apart from the surface, buildings or parts of buildings (whether the division is horizontal, vertical or made in any other way) and other corporeal hereditaments; also a manor, an advowson, and a rent and other incorporeal hereditaments, and an easement, right, privilege, or benefit in, over, or derived from land; and 'mines and minerals' include any strata or seam of minerals or substances in or under the land, and powers of working and getting the same; and "manor" includes a lordship, and reputed manor or lordship; and "hereditament" means any real property which on an intestacy occurring before the commencement of this Act might have devolved upon an heir;

(x) "legal estates" mean the estates, interests and charges, in or over land (subsisting or created in law) which are by this Act authorised to subsist or to be created as legal estates; "equitable interests" mean all the other interests and charges in or over land; and equitable interest "capable of subsisting as a legal estate" means such as could validly subsist or be created as a legal estate under this Act.'

Thus, included in the definition of 'land' are all rights to the land. In addition, s 2(6) of the Law of Property (Miscellaneous Provisions) Act 1989 defines an 'interest in land' as 'any estate, interest or charge in or over the land'. Thus, a mortgagee's right over the land is treated as an interest in land.

6.2.2 'Declarations of trusts'

Section 53(1)(b) of the Law of Property Act 1925 is only applicable in respect of declarations of trusts as the means of benefiting another. A declaration of trust was examined in Chapters 3 and 4. The test is whether a present, irrevocable intention to create a trust was manifested by the settlor. This requires the settlor to comply with the 'three certainties' test: certainty of intention, subject-matter and objects.

6.2.3 'Manifested and proved by some writing'

The requirement here is that the declaration of trust is only required to be **proved** by writing. It is not required to be **made** in writing. The trust is merely required to be evidenced in writing for the purposes of enforcement. The trust may validly be declared orally, but it simply would not be enforceable in a court. Thus, the writing need not be contemporaneous with the declaration but may be adduced some time after the declaration of trust and may enforce the trust retrospectively.

For instance, on Day 1, S, a settlor orally declares a trust in respect of land in favour of B, absolutely. This declaration is within s 53(1)(b) of the LPA 1925 and, because it is not supported by writing, it is unenforceable. However on Day 2, S executes a document endorsing the terms of the trust declared on Day 1. The trust is now enforceable, not from Day 2, but retrospectively, from Day 1.

The effect of non-compliance with s 53(1)(b) is to render unenforceable the valid declaration of trust.

6.2.4 'Writing'

'Writing' for these purposes does not assume any special mode and has taken the most diverse set of forms, ranging from recitals in an instrument to affidavits, answers to interrogatories, telegrams and even letters to third parties. The test is whether the material terms of the trust are included in a document (or series of documents) signed by the settlor. The material terms, of course, involve the 'three certainties' test.

A 'document' has been defined in s 13 of the Civil Evidence Act 1995 as 'anything in which information of any description is recorded'. Thus, a document for these purposes may include an audio or video casette, and even information stored in electronic form.

The material terms of the trust need not be contained in one document but may be contained in a variety of documents. There is a need for each document to refer to the other to such an extent that the documents, taken as a whole, form a complete memorandum of the terms of the trust.

For instance, Document 1 may manifest the settlor's intention to create a trust and signed by him, Document 2 may contain the subject-matter of the trust and Document 3 may contain the objects of the trust. Provided that all three documents are joined, a complete memorandum of the terms of the trust may exist. In this event, the documents may refer to each other with sufficient certainty to identify them. Each document or at least one of the documents is required to be signed by the settlor.

This requirement is fundamentally different from the test enacted in s 2(1) of the Law of Property (Miscellaneous Provisions) Act 1989 concerning contracts for the sale or other dispositions of land. Under this Act the terms of the contract are required to be included in one document.

6.2.5 Signature

Section 53(1)(b) of the Law of Property Act 1925 requires the person able to declare the trust to sign the document(s). The requirement here is that the settlor must endorse the document containing the terms of the trust. The signature need not be the full, formal signature of the settlor but may take the form of some mark attributed to the settlor and intended by him to authenticate the document(s). Thus, initials or the thumb print of the settlor will be sufficient. Section 1(4) of the Law of Property (Miscellaneous Provisions) Act 1989 enacts that '"sign" in relation to an instrument includes making one's mark on the instrument and "signature" is to be construed accordingly'. Likewise, the settlor's voice or image on a recording may amount to a signature.

However, the signature of the settlor's agent is not effective for these purposes.

6.3 Exclusion

Section 53(2) of the Law of Property Act 1925 (replacing s 8 of the Statute of Frauds 1677) provides that 'This section shall not affect the creation or operation of implied, resulting and constructive trusts'. Resulting and constructive trusts are types of implied trusts that are created by the courts. These trusts are exempt from the above formal requirement. Accordingly, an *inter vivos* resulting trust of land may arise without the terms being reduced into writing.

CASE EXAMPLE

Hodgson v Marks [1971] Ch 892

Mrs Hodgson (Mrs H), a widow aged 83, owned a house in Edgware, London. She took a lodger, Mr Evans, whom she trusted, but who was disliked by her nephew who also lived in the house. In order to prevent her nephew turning Mr Evans out of the house, Mrs H voluntarily transferred the house to Mr Evans, who was duly registered as the legal owner of the property. Mrs H had orally declared that the house was to remain hers. Mr Evans later attempted to transfer the house to Mr Marks. When Mrs H discovered this, she claimed that she was entitled in equity to the house. Mr Marks argued that no trust was created in favour of Mrs H because the oral statement by Mrs H was not reduced into writing signed by her.

Held   Mrs H had retained the absolute equitable interest in the house by way of a resulting trust. This trust was enforceable by virtue of s 53(2) of the LPA 1925.

> J   '... the evidence is clear that the transfer [to Mr Evans] was not intended to operate as a gift, and, in those circumstances, I do not see why there was not a resulting trust of the beneficial interest to the plaintiff, which would not, of course, be affected by s 53(1).'
>
> (Russell LJ)

In *Hodgson v Marks* (1971) it would have been ironic that the precursor to s 53(1)(b) of the LPA 1925, namely s 7 of the Statute of Frauds 1677, a statute passed to prevent fraud, could have been used to perpetrate a fraud, but for s 53(2) of the LPA 1925. In any event, a similar conclusion could have been reached by adopting the constructive trust institution, namely to prevent a fraud being committed on Mrs Hodgson.

6.4 Dispositions under section 53(1)(c) of the Law of Property Act 1925

Section 53(1)(c) of the LPA 1925 (substantially, but not completely, reflecting the terms of s 9 of the Statute of Frauds 1677) provides as follows:

 'A disposition of an equitable interest or trust subsisting at the time of disposition, must be in writing signed by the person disposing of the same, or by his agent thereunto lawfully authorised in writing or by will.'

(Section 9 of the Statute of Frauds 1677, before its repeal, provided:

' ... all grants and assignments of any trust or confidence shall be in writing signed by the party granting or assigning the same or by such last will or devise or else shall be utterly void and of no effect'.)

Rationale of the provision

The policy underlying the enactment is to:

(i) prevent fraud by prohibiting oral hidden transfers of equitable interests under trusts and

(ii) assist trustees by enabling them to identify the whereabouts of the equitable interest subsisting under a trust: see Lord Upjohn in *Vandervell v IRC* [1967] 2 AC 291.

' ... the object of the section [53(1)(c)], as was the object of the old Statute of Frauds, is to prevent hidden oral transactions in equitable interests in fraud of those truly entitled, and making it difficult, if not impossible, for the trustees to ascertain who are in truth his beneficiaries.'

Lord Upjohn in *Vandervell v IRC* [1967] 2 AC 291

Effect of non-compliance

The effect of non-compliance with this provision is that the purported disposition is void. This is distinct from s 53(1)(b): see above. The wording of the statutory provision (s 53(1)(c)) is mandatory in nature. The operative words are 'must be in writing'.

Subsisting equitable interest

An essential restriction on the operation of s 53(1)(c) is that it is applicable only to subsisting equitable interests. In other words, the provision is applicable to the interest of a beneficiary under a subsisting trust. The subsection is not applicable to *the original creation of a trust*, but is activated only when a beneficiary under a trust seeks to dispose of his interest. For instance, S, a settlor, tranfers property to the trustees, A and B, to hold property upon trust for for C absolutely. Thus, A and B hold the legal title to property and C enjoys the equitable interest. The formalities that S will need to comply with, if any, will depend on the type of property concerned. But this arrangement does not involve s 53(1)(c). If C wishes to dispose of his equitable interest (subsisting) he is required to comply with the statutory provision. A subsisting equitable interest may exist under any type of trust, express, resulting, constructive or statutory.

Land and personalty

The subsection is applicable to subsisting equitable interests in realty or personalty and contains no restriction as to the type of property. Indeed, the provision focuses on the type of *interest*, and not the type of property in which that interest is enjoyed. This is the position despite the definition of 'equitable interests' under s 205(1)(x) of the Law of Property Act 1925, which states that 'equitable interests mean all the other interests and charges in or over **land**'.

Writing

Writing may take a variety of forms, including video recordings, photographs and audio tapes. The test is whether a permanent form of representation exists of the transfer of the relevant interest: see above. (See earlier regarding s 53(1)(b).)

Signature

The signature of the disponer or his agent may take any form which endorses the document, including thumb prints, initials and perhaps the disponer's voice on a tape recording: see above.

Agent's signature

The section authorises the signature of an agent, provided the agent was lawfully authorised in writing. The position here is different from s 53(1)(b): see above.

Disposition

The key feature of s 53(1)(c) is the meaning of the term 'disposition'. This has not been defined in the statute. But the term 'conveyance' has been defined in s 205(1)(ii) of the Law of Property Act 1925 as including a disposition. The subsection provides as follows:

> **S** ' "Conveyance" includes a mortgage, charge, lease, assent, vesting declaration, vesting instrument, disclaimer, release and every other assurance of property or of an interest therein by any instrument, except a will; "convey" has a corresponding meaning; and "disposition" includes a conveyance and also a devise, bequest, or an appointment of property contained in a will; and "dispose of" has a corresponding meaning.'

In *Timpson's Executors v Yerbury* [1936] 1 KB 645, Romer LJ described a disposition thus:

> **J** 'The equitable interest in property in the hands of the trustee can be disposed of by the person entitled to it in favour of a third party in any one of four different ways. The person entitled to it:
>
> (1) can assign it to the third party directly;
>
> (2) can direct the trustees to hold the property in trust for the third party;
>
> (3) can contract for valuable consideration to assign the equitable interest to him; or
>
> (4) can declare himself to be a trustee for him of such interest.'
>
> (Romer LJ)

6.4.1 Direction to trustees

Romer LJ, in his second classification of a disposition in *Yerbury* (1936), declared that a direction by a beneficiary under a subsisting trust to the trustees (holding the legal title) to hold upon trust for another beneficiary is within s 53(1)(c). For instance, S creates a trust of 50,000 shares in BT plc to T1 and T2, as trustees, by transferring the legal title to the shares for B absolutely. If B directs T1 and T2 to hold the property on trust for C, this intended disposition would be within s 53(1)(c). Thus, B is required to issue the direction in writing otherwise it is void.

In *Grey v IRC* [1960] AC 1, HL, the House of Lords decided that an oral direction by an equitable owner to the trustees of a trust fund to hold the property upon trust for another was a purported disposition and void for non-compliance with s 53(1)(c).

 CASE EXAMPLE

Grey v IRC [1960] AC 1, HL

In 1949, Mr Hunter (the settlor) transferred shares of a nominal sum to trustees upon trust for his six grandchildren. In 1955, the settlor transferred 18,000 £1 shares to the same trustees upon trust for himself. In an attempt to avoid *ad valorem* stamp duty (payable on instruments which transfer any property or interest in property), the settlor verbally instructed the trustees to hold the shares upon trust for the grandchildren. The trustees subsequently executed confirmatory documents affirming the oral instructions. The Revenue assessed the documents to *ad valorem* stamp duty.

Held The oral instructions by Mr Hunter were ineffective and void for non-compliance with s 53(1)(c), but the confirmatory documents had the effect of transferring the equitable interests to the grandchildren. Accordingly, the documents were stampable.

CONTINUED ▶

J   'If the word "disposition" is given its natural meaning it cannot, I think, be denied that a direction given by the beneficiary whereby the beneficial interest in the shares theretofore vested in another or others is a disposition.'

(Lord Simonds)

J   '... the short question [is] whether the oral direction that Mr Hunter gave to his trustees on 18 February 1955, amounted in any ordinary sense of the words to a "disposition of an equitable interest or trust subsisting at the time of the disposition", I do not feel any doubt as to my answer. I think that it did. Whether we describe what happened in technical or in more general terms, the full equitable interest in the eighteen thousand shares concerned, which at that time was his, was (subject to any statutory invalidity) diverted by his direction from this ownership into the beneficial ownership of the various equitable owners, present and future, entitled under his six existing settlements.'

(Lord Radcliffe)

Mr Hunter, the settlor, would have been better advised, from the point of view of avoiding stamp duty, to have omitted the transaction involving the transfer of the legal title to the 18,000 shares to the trustees and, as the absolute legal and equitable owner of the shares, orally declare himself a trustee in favour of his six grandchildren. This would have amounted to a self-declaration of trust of 18,000 shares with Mr Hunter holding the legal title as trustee for the beneficiaries. The effect of such a declaration would have been to create an original trust and would have been outside s 53(1)(c). No writing would have been required. Further, if Mr Hunter wanted the original trustees to hold on trust, he could have transferred the legal title to the shares to them in a subsequent transaction. This would have attracted only nominal stamp duty.

Section 53(1)(c) did not consolidate s 9 of the Statute of Frauds 1677

In *Grey v IRC* (1960), counsel for the taxpayer argued that the Law of Property Act 1925 is a consolidating Act and, in effect, consolidated s 9 of the Statute of Frauds 1677. It was submitted that a consolidating Act does not change the law and as this transaction would have been effective under the 1677 Statute, it ought to be equally effective under the 1925 legislation. This argument was rejected by the House of Lords. Lord Radcliffe pointed out that s 9 of the Statute of Frauds was repealed and replaced (or consolidated) by the Law of Property Act 1922. The 1922 Act was amended by the Law of Property (Amendment) Act 1924 by the introduction of the broad concept of 'disposition', as opposed to the old narrower expressions 'grants or assignments'. The 1925 Law of Property Act then consolidated the law that existed after 1924. Thus, the link between the 1677 Statute and the 1925 Act was broken by the 1924 Act.

J 'The Law of Property Act 1925 itself was, no doubt, strictly a consolidating statute. But what it consolidated was not merely the Law of Property Act 1922, a statute which had itself effected massive changes in the law relating to real property and conveyancing, but also the later Law of Property (Amendment) Act 1924. The Statute of Frauds sections had not been touched by the Act of 1922, but they were, in effect, repealed and re-enacted in altered form by the operation of s 3 of the Act of 1924. This new wording is what is carried into s 53 of the Act of 1925. For these reasons I think that there is no direct link between s 53(1)(c) of the Act of 1925 and s 9 of the Statute of Frauds.'

(Lord Radcliffe (*in Grey v IRC*))

6.4.2 Transfer of both the legal and equitable titles to a third party

In *Vandervell v IRC* [1967] 2 AC 291, HL, the House of Lords decided that s 53(1)(c) has no application where the equitable owner, under a subsisting trust, directs the legal owner to transfer his title to a third party, and in the same transaction, the equitable owner, without writing, transfers his interest to the same third party. In other words, the effect of the transaction is to terminate the trust by uniting both the legal and equitable interests in the hands of the third party. Clearly, such a transaction is outside the mischief of s 53(1)(c): see above. There can be no fraudulent dealing with the equitable interest simply because it is now incorporated with the legal title. The trustees do not need to identify the movement of the equitable interest because this is united with the legal title and, in any event, the position of the trustee is redundant because the trust no longer subsists.

CASE EXAMPLE

Vandervell v IRC [1967] 2 AC 291, HL

In 1958, Mr Vandervell decided to donate £150,000 to the Royal College of Surgeons to found a chair of pharmacology. He decided to achieve this purpose by transferring 100,000 ordinary shares in Vandervell Products Ltd (a private company controlled by Mr Vandervell) to the College subject to an option (vested in a separate company, Vandervell Trustee Company) to re-purchase the shares for £5,000. In pursuance of this scheme, Mr Vandervell orally directed the National Provincial Bank (which held the legal title to the shares on behalf of Mr Vandervell) to transfer the shares to the College, subject to the option exercisable by the Trustee Company. The bank complied with the directions. During the tax years 1958–59 and 1959–60, dividends on the shares amounting to £162,500 and £87,500 respectively were paid to the College. The Inland Revenue assessed Mr Vandervell to surtax in respect of the dividends, on two grounds:

CONTINUED ▶

(a) that Mr Vandervell had not absolutely divested himself from the shares, so that the dividends fell to be treated as his income within s 415 of the Income Tax Act 1952 (now s 683 Income and Corporation Taxes Act 1988)

(b) in the alternative, that Mr Vandervell had not transferred his equitable interest in the shares to the College because of his failure to comply with s 53(1)(c) of the Law of Property Act 1925.

Held: (i) The Revenue succeeded on the first ground because Mr Vandervell had transferred only the legal title to the option to the Trustee Company. The equitable title to the option had not been consciously transferred to the Trustee Company or anyone. Accordingly, Mr Vandervell retained an interest in the option, namely an equitable interest by way of a resulting trust. Since Mr Vandervell retained an interest in the option to acquire the 100,000 shares he, therefore, retained an interest in the shares by way of a resulting trust.

(ii) Mr Vandervell won the argument on the second ground of the assessment. The court decided that in a composite transaction the transfer of both the legal and equitable interests in property to a third party is outside the mischief of s 53(1)(c).

> J '... when the beneficial owner owns the whole beneficial estate and is in a position to give directions to his bare trustee with regard to the legal as well as the equitable estate there can be no possible ground for invoking the section [s 53(1)(c)] where the beneficial owner wants to deal with the legal estate as well as the equitable estate.'
>
> (Lord Upjohn)

> J '... when the taxpayer instructed the bank to transfer the shares to the college, and made it abundantly clear that he wanted to pass, by means of that transfer, his own beneficial or equitable interest, plus the bank's legal interest, he achieved the same result as if there had been no separation of the interests. The transfer thus made, pursuant to his intentions and instructions, was a disposition, not of the equitable interest alone, but of the entire estate in the shares. In such a case, I see no room for the operation of s 53(1)(c) ...'
>
> (Lord Donovan)

As an additional point, in *Vandervell v IRC* (1967), instead of transferring his subsisting equitable interest in the shares to the College without writing, Mr Vandervell could have achieved the same result by first terminating the trust under the *Saunders v Vautier* (1841) 4 Beav 115 principle (termination of trust on the direction of the beneficiaries, provided that they are *sui juris* and absolutely entitled to the equitable interest, see above). The effect would have been that Mr Vandervell would then acquire the legal title. Second, armed with both the legal and equitable interests in the shares, Mr

Vandervell could have created a trust for the College by orally declaring himself a trustee for the same beneficiary. This transaction would have been effective outside s 53(1)(c), for there would no longer be a subsisting equitable interest and the arrangement would have involved the creation of a new trust.

6.4.3 Section 53(2) of the Law of Property Act 1925

Section 53(2) (re-enacting s 8 of the Statute of Frauds 1677) provides as follows:

 'This section shall not affect the creation or operation of resulting, implied or constructive trusts.'

The issue which is considered in this section is: how far does s 53(2) restrict the operation of s 53(1)(c)? The groundswell of opinion is to the effect that the resulting and constructive trusts referred to in s 53(2) are created by the courts. Accordingly, a court will not contradict itself by requiring a disposition under such trust (constructive) to be in writing. Either the court feels that the circumstances of the case warrant the imposition of a trust or it does not. If the court favours the creation of a trust, it ought not to be a defence that the transfer of the equitable interest has not been reduced into writing.

The relationship between s 53(1)(c) and s 53(2) was examined in *Oughtred v IRC* [1960] AC 206. In this case the House of Lords decided that a specifically enforceable contract between a mother and son to exchange their interests in shares created a constructive trust when the mother disposed of her interest to her son before he reciprocated. The purpose of the transaction was to reduce the level of estate duty payable on the mother's estate on her death and to avoid stamp duty. Despite the trust, a majority of the Law Lords decided that the document was liable to stamp duty. But only three Law Lords considered the relationship between s 53(1)(c) and s 53(2). It is believed that the opinion of Lord Denning on this issue is no longer tenable.

> **J** 'I do not think the oral agreement was effective to transfer Peter's reversionary interest to his mother. I should have thought that the wording of section 53(1)(c) of the Law of Property Act, 1925, clearly made a writing necessary to effect a transfer: and section 53(2) does not do away with that necessity.'
>
> (Lord Denning)

> **J** 'The appellant as a result of what was done on June 26 was, as the release recognised, absolutely entitled to the settled shares, but that was not because the equitable interest was transferred to or vested in her by the transfer but because Peter, having become a constructive trustee for her of his equitable interest, could not, after his nominees had received the consideration shares, as they did on June 26, 1956, dispute the appellant's title to the settled shares.'
>
> (Lord Cohen (dissenting))

This appears to be the language of an estoppel.

> **J** 'On June 18, 1956, the son owned an equitable reversionary interest in the settled shares: by his oral agreement of that date he created in his mother an equitable interest in her reversion, since the subject-matter of the agreement was property of which specific performance would normally be decreed by the court. He thus became a trustee for her of that interest *sub modo*: having regard to subsection (2) of section 53 of the Law of Property Act, 1925, subsection (1) of that section did not operate to prevent that trusteeship arising by operation of law. On June 26 Mrs Oughtred transferred to her son the shares which were the consideration for her acquisition of his equitable interest: upon this transfer he became in a full sense and without more a trustee of his interest for her. She was the effective owner of all outstanding equitable interests. It was thus correct to recite in the deed of release to the trustees of the settlement, which was to wind up their trust, that the trust fund was by then held upon trust for her absolutely. There was, in fact, no equity to the shares that could be asserted against her, and it was open to her, if she so wished, to let the matter rest without calling for a written assignment from her son.'
>
> (Lord Radcliffe (dissenting))

In respect of the relationship between ss 53(1)(c) and 53(2), in *Oughtred v IRC* (1960) only Lord Radcliffe's opinion reflected a degree of rationality and realism. A constructive trust is created by the court in order to prevent unjust enrichment. It is the conduct of the defendant that justifies the imposition of the trust. It would be unrealistic for the court to shackle its jurisdiction on the sole ground of the lack of writing, particularly if it feels that the circumstances justify the imposition of a constructive trust. Accordingly, the subsequent authorities refused to follow Lord Denning's and Lord Cohen's opinions.

In *Re Holt's Settlement* [1968] 1 All ER 470, Megarry J adopted Lord Radcliffe's judgment in *Oughtred v IRC* (1960) in the context of schemes under the Variation of Trusts Act 1958.

> **J** 'Mr Millett for the tenant for life, provided … [a] means of escape from s 53(1)(c) in his helpful reply. Where, as here, the arrangement consists of an agreement made for valuable consideration, and that agreement is specifically enforceable, then the beneficial interests pass to the respective purchasers on the making of the agreement. Those interests pass by virtue of the species of constructive trust made familiar by contracts for the sale of land, whereunder the vendor becomes a constructive trustee for the purchaser as soon as the contract is made … S 53(2), he continued, provides that "This section does not affect the creation or operation of resulting, implied or constructive trusts." Accordingly, because the trust was constructive, s 53(1)(c) was excluded … It seems to me that there is considerable force in this argument in cases where the agreement is specifically enforceable, and in its essentials I accept it … '.
>
> (Megarry J)

In *Chinn v Collins* [1981] AC 533, the House of Lords decided that a specifically enforceable contract was immaterial in order to effect a transfer of an equitable interest. This was declared in the context of a tax avoidance scheme:

> 'The legal title to the shares was at all times vested in a nominee and dealings related to the equitable interest in these required no formality. As soon as there was an agreement for their sale accompanied or followed by payment of the price, the equitable title passed at once to the purchaser and all that was needed to perfect his title was notice to the trustees or the nominee, which notice both had at all material times.'
>
> (Lord Wilberforce)

More recently, the Court of Appeal, in *Neville v Wilson* [1996] 3 WLR 460, reviewed the diverse opinions delivered in *Oughtred v IRC* (1960) and endorsed Lord Radcliffe's view that s 53(2) restricted the operation of s 53(1)(c).

Nourse LJ in *Neville v Wilson* (1996), after referring to *Oughtred v IRC* (1960), said:

> 'Why then should sub-section (2) not apply? No convincing reason was suggested in argument and none has occurred to us since. Moreover, to deny its application in this case would be to restrict the effect of general words when no restriction is called for, and to lay the ground for fine distinctions in the future. With all the respect that is due to those who have thought to the contrary, we hold that sub-section (2) applies to an agreement such that we have in this case.'

In *Neville v Wilson* (1996), shares in U Ltd were held in trust for J Ltd, a family company. The shareholders in J Ltd agreed informally to liquidate J Ltd and divide the equitable interest in U Ltd shares among themselves in proportion to their existing shareholdings. The question in issue was whether s 53(1)(c) invalidated this agreement. The Court of Appeal held that each shareholder's agreement gave rise to a constructive trust so that s 53(2) exempted them from the requirements of s 53(1)(c).

In addition, s 2(5) of the Law of Property (Miscellaneous Provisions) Act 1989 exempts 'implied resulting and constructive trusts' from the requirement that a contract for the sale of land or an interest in land must be in writing.

6.4.4 Overlap between subsections 53(1)(b) and (c) of the Law of Property Act 1925

Section 53(1)(b) of the Law of Property Act 1925 concerns a declaration of trust respecting land and s 53(1)(c) deals with the disposition of a subsisting equitable interest in land or personalty. It follows that a beneficiary under a trust of land, who declares a trust of such property, will attract the requirements of both subsections. Since s 53(1)(c) is expressed in a mandatory form, no disposition of the equitable interest will take place until the transfer (or declaration) is in writing.

6.4.5 Estoppel

In the controversial case, *Re Vandervell Trusts (No 2)* [1974] Ch 269, the Court of Appeal decided *inter alia* that the doctrine of equitable estoppel creates an exception to the s 53(1)(c) requirements.

> **J** 'If he (Mr Vandervell) had lived, and not died, he could not have claimed it back. He could not be heard to say that he did not intend the children's trust to have it. Even a court of equity would not allow him to do anything so inequitable and unjust.'
>
> (Lord Denning MR)

In *Re Vandervell Trusts (No 2)* Mr V orally directed the trustee company, VT Ltd, to exercise the option to re-purchase the shares. This was done by VT Ltd and the legal title to the shares was vested in VT Ltd. The issue here was whether the equitable interest in the shares was acquired for the benefit of the children's settlement or was retained for Mr V (and his estate following his death). The Court of Appeal decided that the equitable interest in the shares was held by VT Ltd for the children's settlement. Section 53(1)(c) was not applicable to a transaction which extinguished a resulting trust.

6.4.6 Self-declaration of trust of part of an equitable interest

A disposition may be effected by means of a self-declaration. This method was referred to by Romer LJ in the *Yerbury* decision (1936): see above. Thus, B, a beneficiary, may declare himself a trustee of his entire interest in favour of C. This arrangement is valid only if it is reduced into writing.

However, it is debatable whether a self-declaration of trust of part of a subsisting equitable interest amounts to a disposition within s 53(1)(c). For example, B, a beneficiary who enjoys an absolute interest under a trust, retains a life interest and orally declares himself a trustee of the remainder interest in favour of C. It is arguable that since B has active duties to perform, the sub-trust created by B amounts to the creation of a new trust. Accordingly, the policy of enacting s 53(1)(c) is not relevant and such a disposition is outside of the provision: see *Grainge v Wilberforce* (1889) 5 TLR 436, *Re Lashmar* [1891] 1 Ch 258 and A Underhill and D Hayton, *Law of Trusts and Trustees* (16th edn, Butterworths, 2002). On the other hand, Lewin, in *Trusts and Trustees* (17th edn, Sweet

& Maxwell, 2003), and Brian Green in an article entitled '*Grey, Oughtred* and *Vandervell*: a contextual reappraisal' (1984) 47 MLR 385, assert that a self-declaration of trust, whether as to part of the equitable interest or the entirety, is a disposition within s 53(1)(c) and requires writing.

6.4.7 Disclaimers

Disclaimers are exempt from s 53(1)(c), despite being included in the definition of a 'conveyance' within s 205(1)(ii). A disclaimer involves a conscious decision on the part of the individual to abandon his interest in the property. There is no positive intention on his part to transfer the interest to any specific person. The effect of the disclaimer is that the property is transferred or acquired by another, but this is distinct from a conscious decision to dispose of the property or interest to another.

> J
>
> 'A disclaimer operates by way of avoidance and not by way of disposition. For the general aspects of disclaimer we refer briefly to the discussion in *Re Stratton's Disclaimer* [1958] Ch 42.'
>
> (Danckwerts LJ: *Re Paradise Motor Co* [1968] 1 WLR 1125)

A surrender of an equitable interest, on the other hand, would appear to be a disposition within s 53(1)(c), despite academic commentary to the contrary. The argument, which is not very convincing, is that a surrender involves an extinguishment of an interest which is distinct from a disposition. If this is true it would amount a relatively simple exercise in avoiding the rigour of s 53(1)(c).

6.4.8 Pension scheme nominations

Nominations by staff pension fund holders of the persons who will become entitled to benefits under a pension fund after the deaths of the pension holders are not dispositions within s 53(1)(c).

> J
>
> 'The question is thus whether an instrument with this elective, contingent and defeasible quality, which takes effect only on the death of the person signing it, can fairly be said to be a "a disposition of an equitable interest or trust subsisting at the time of the disposition". Mr Ferris put much emphasis on the word "subsisting": however wide the word "disposition" might be in its meaning, there was no disposition of a subsisting equity, he said, I should hesitate to describe an instrunent which has a mere possibility of becoming a "disposition" as being in itself a disposition *ab initio*; and I agree that the word, "subsisting" also seems to point

CONTINUED ▸

> **J** against the nomination falling within section 53(1)(c) … I very much doubt whether the nomination falls within section 53(1)(c).'
>
> (Megarry J: *Re Danish Bacon Co Ltd. Staff Pension Fund* [1971] 1 WLR 248)

■Key facts on formalities

KEY FACTS

Declarations of trusts of land (s 53(1)(b) LPA 1925)

• Land or an interest in land	s 205(1)(ix) LPA 1925; s 2(6) LP (Miscellaneous Provisions) Act 1989
• Declarations of trusts	'Three certainties' test
• Manifested and proved	Unenforceable if not complied with
• Writing	s 13 Civil Evidence Act 1995
• Signature	Endorsement: s 1(4) LP (Miscellaneous Provisions) Act 1989
• Exemption	s 53(2) LPA 1925; *Hodgson v Marks* (1971)

KEY FACTS

Dispositions of subsisting equitable interests (s 53(1)(c) LPA 1925)

• Disposition	*Timpson's Executors v Yerbury* (1936); *Grey v IRC* (1960); *Vandervell v IRC* (1967); *Re Vandervell Trusts (No 2)* (1974); *Oughtred v IRC* (1960); *Re Holt* (1968); *Neville v Wilson* (1996); *Re Paradise Motor Co* (1968); *Re Danish Bacon Staff Pension Fund* (1971)
• Subsisting equitable interest	
• Land or personalty	
• 'Must be in writing'	Intended transfer is void for non-compliance with the provision
• Signature (inclusive of agent's signature)	

ACTIVITY

> Peter transfers his freehold property, Blackacre, to Jason and Joseph to hold upon trust for the benefit of Anthony absolutely.
>
> Consider the effect of the following alternative directions:
>
> (i) Anthony orally declares himself a trustee of his interest on behalf of Hamish absolutely.
>
> (ii) Anthony orally declares himself a trustee of his interest for himself for life with remainder to Hamish absolutely.
>
> (iii) Anthony orally contracts with Hamish to transfer his interest to him in return for a payment of £30,000.
>
> (iv) Anthony orally directs Jason and Joseph to transfer their legal interest to Hamish and Anthony orally promises Hamish to transfer his equitable interest to him.
>
> (v) Anthony orally disclaims his interest which, if effective, will enable Peter to obtain his interest absolutely.

Further reading

Clarke, P, 'Mr Vandervell again' (1974) 38 Conv 405.

Green, B, '*Grey, Oughtred* and *Vandervell*: a contextual reappraisal' (1984) 47 MLR 385.

Hill, G, 'Section 2 of the Law of Property (Miscellaneous Provisions) Act 1989' (1990) 106 LQR 396.

Howell, J, 'Informal conveyances and s 2 of the Law of Property (Miscellaneous Provisions) Act 1989' [1990] Conv 441.

Thompson, M, 'Disposition of equitable interests' [1996] Conv 368.

Youdan, T, 'Formalities for trusts of land and the doctrine in *Rochefoucauld v Boustead*' [1984] CLJ 306.

chapter 7 DISCRETIONARY TRUSTS

7.1 Introduction

A discretionary trust exists where the trustees are given a discretion to pay or apply property (the income or capital or both) to or for the benefit of all or anyone selected from a group or class of objects on such terms and conditions as the trustees may see fit. In tax law this type of trust is known as a trust without an interest in possession. The trust is created in accordance with the express intention of the settlor. The relevant property is transferred to the trustees and the scope of the trustees' discretion expressed in the trust instrument.

For example, S, a settlor, transfers a cash fund of £100,000 to trustees on trust to pay or apply the income and capital (including accumulations of income) to or for the benefit of any or all of the settlor's children, A, B and C, as the trustees may decide in their absolute discretion.

In this example, a discretionary trust is created in respect of both income and capital. The trustees are required to decide in whose favour the property (income and capital) may be distributed. In Year 1, the trustees may distribute the entire income to A. In Year 2, the trustees may distribute the income and a portion of the capital to B and in Year 3 the income may be distributed equally to A, B and C and the entire capital distributed to C.

Fixed trusts

The alternative type of express trust that may be created is a 'fixed' trust or a trust with an interest in possession. This is the case if, on the date of the creation of the trust, the settlor has not only identified the beneficiaries under the trust but also quantified the interest vested in each beneficiary. Thus, each beneficiary is entitled to sell, exchange or gift away his interest, subject to provisions to the contrary as detailed in the trust instrument. In a fixed trust the trustees do not have a discretion to decide the extent of the beneficial interest which the objects may enjoy, eg trustees hold specified property on trust for the children of the settlor, D, E and F, in equal shares absolutely. On the date of the creation of the trust, each beneficiary has a fixed one-third share of the fund that he may retain or dispose of as he likes.

Discretionary trusts

Under a discretionary trust, the individual members of the class of objects have only a hope or '*spes*' of acquiring a benefit under the trust. In other words, under a discretionary trust, the members of the class of objects, prior to the exercise of the trustees' discretion, do not enjoy an interest in the trust property but are treated as potential beneficiaries and are incapable of disposing of their potential interests by way of a trust.

7.2 Exhaustive/non-exhaustive discretionary trusts

A discretionary trust may be either 'exhaustive' or 'non-exhaustive'. This is determined by reference to the intention of the settlor.

An exhaustive discretionary trust is one where, during the trust period, the trustees are required to distribute the income or capital, or both, but retain a discretion as to the mode of distribution and the persons to whom the distribution may be made. The trustees are required to distribute the income each year as it arises, but have a discretion in favour of the persons who may actually benefit.

A non-exhaustive discretionary trust is one where the trustees are given a discretion as to whether or not to distribute the property (either income or capital). A non-exhaustive discretionary trust of income exists where the trustees may legitimately decide not to distribute the income and the settlor has specified the effect of non-distribution; for instance, the undistributed income may be accumulated or paid to another. In short, a non-exhaustive discretionary trust of the income is a trust for distribution of the income coupled with a power to accumulate or otherwise dispose of the undistributed income.

For example, a settlor transfers £50,000 to trustees, T1 and T2, upon trust to distribute the income in their discretion in favour of the settlor's children, A, B and C, as the trustees may decide in their absolute discretion. At this stage this is an exhaustive discretionary trust of the income in favour of the children of the settlor. But if the settlor had inserted in the trust instrument a power to accumulate the income in the trustees' discretion, the trust would become non-exhaustive with regard to the income.

It follows that the distinction between an exhaustive and non-exhaustive discretionary trust is based on the power of the trustees to refrain from distributing the property that is within the discretion of the trustees. In the ordinary course of events the trustees will be required to accumulate the income that has not been distributed. The accumulated income is treated as capitalised income or capital in both trust law and tax law. In *IRC v Blackwell Minor's Trustees* (1925) 10 TC 235, the accumulation of undistributed surplus income at the discretion of the trustees was treated as capital of the beneficiary, and not liable to income tax.

7.3 Period of accumulation

The combined effect of s 164 of the Law of Property Act 1925 and s 13 of the Perpetuities and Accumulations Act 1964 is that the settlor is entitled to select any one (but only one) of the following periods as the maximum period during which the trustees may accumulate the income. These periods are as follows:

Section 164 LPA 1925

1. The life of the settlor.

2. A term of 21 years from the death of the settlor or testator.

3. The minority or respective minorities of any person or persons living or '*en ventre sa mère*' at the death of the settlor or testator.

4. The minority or respective minorities only of any person or persons who, under the limitations of the instrument directing the accumulations, would for the time being, if of full age, be entitled to the income directed to be accumulated.

Section 13 Perpetuities and Accumulations Act 1964

1. A term of 21 years from the date of the making of the disposition.

2. The minority or respective minorities of any person or persons in being at that date.

A direction to accumulate which exceeds the periods mentioned above, but which is otherwise valid, will be void only in so far as it exceeds the appropriate statutory period.

7.4 Reasons for creating discretionary trusts

7.4.1 Flexibility

Where a settlor wishes to make a present disposition on trust but is uncertain as to future events and would like the trustees to react to changed circumstances and the needs of the potential beneficiaries, he may create a discretionary trust. This would require the trustees to take into consideration the circumstances, including fiscal factors surrounding individual members of the class of objects. The trustees may well take into account that the distribution of income will be more tax efficient if paid to objects with lower income and transfers of capital may be more beneficial to those with larger incomes. The effect is that the discretionary trust has the advantage of flexibility. The settlor may nominate himself as one of the trustees and, even if he does not, he may still be entitled to exercise some influence over the trustees.

7.4.2 Protection of objects from creditors

Since an object under a discretionary trust is not entitled to an interest in the trust property, prior to the exercise of the discretion in his favour, but is merely entitled to a hope of acquiring a benefit, the bankruptcy of such an object does not entitle the trustee in bankruptcy to a share of the trust fund. The trustee in bankruptcy is only entitled to funds paid to the object in the exercise of the discretion of the trustees. Moreover the trustee in bankruptcy is not entitled to claim funds paid to third parties (such as tradesmen and hoteliers) in discharge of obligations *bona fide* undertaken by the potential beneficiaries.

7.5 Administrative discretion

Discretionary trusts are distinct from the administrative discretions that accompany all trusts. Thus, the trustees may have a power or discretion over the type of investments that may be made by the trust, whether to appoint agents on behalf of the trust, whether to apply income for the maintenance of infant beneficiaries, whether to make an advancement on behalf of a beneficiary, whether to appoint additional trustees, etc. But these powers and discretions are of an administrative nature and do not affect the beneficial entitlement of the objects. Accordingly, the existence of such administrative powers does not create discretionary trusts but is consistent with both fixed and discretionary trusts.

7.6 Mere powers and trust powers

The settlor may authorise another or others to distribute property to a class of objects but without imposing an obligation to distribute the same. This is called a mere power of appointment (or bare power, or power collateral).

For example, S may transfer property by will to his widow, W, for life with remainder to such of his children A, B and C, as W may appoint by will. W is referred to as a donee of the power and A, B and C as the objects of the power. They are not beneficiaries but, like the objects of a discretionary trust, are potential beneficiaries or have a '*spes*' of enjoying a benefit prior to the exercise of the power in their favour. If W makes a valid appointment in favour of the objects they become beneficiaries in respect of the amount of property distributed in their favour. On the other hand, if the donee of the power fails to make an appointment, the property is held on resulting trust for the settlor or his estate.

In order to dispense with the resulting trust, it is customary for the settlor to insert an 'express gift over in default of appointment' in the trust instrument. If this clause is inserted, the objects under the 'gift over' take the property unless the donee of the power validly exercises the power. Indeed, *prima facie*, the individuals entitled on a gift over in default of appointment are entitled to the property subject to such interest being defeated on a valid exercise of the power.

It was pointed out in Chapter 3 that a mere power of appointment may be 'personal' or 'fiduciary'. A 'personal' power is one granted to a donee of the power in his personal capacity, such as the testator's widow in the above example. Such powers impose no duties on the donee of the power, save for a distribution in favour of the objects if the appointor wishes to exercise his discretion. Conversely, a fiduciary power is created where the appointor acquires the property in his capacity as a fiduciary or trustee. A number of fiduciary duties are imposed on the appointor. These were listed by Megarry VC in *Re Hay's Settlement Trust* [1982] 1 WLR 202, as a duty to consider periodically whether or not the power ought to be exercised, a duty to consider the range of objects of the power and a duty to consider the appropriateness of individual appointments.

Both personal and fiduciary powers may be released by the appointor, but Warner J in *Mettoy Pension Fund Trustees Ltd v Evans* [1990] 1 WLR 1587, created a further category of powers, called 'fiduciary powers in the full sense'. The distinctive feature of this last type of power is that it cannot be released by the appointor. If the donee of the power fails to exercise his discretion the court will ensure that the discretion is exercised in favour of the objects.

7.7 Trust powers

A trust power is in substance a discretionary trust but, in form, the gift resembles a power. The court construes the instrument and decides that in accordance with the intention of the settlor a trust was intended. Accordingly, the trustees may not release their discretion and if they refuse to exercise their discretion the court will intervene.

> J
> 'There are not only a mere trust and a mere power, but there is also known to this court a power, which the party to whom it is given, is entrusted and required to execute; and with regard to that species of power the court considers it as partaking so much of the nature and qualities of a trust, that if the person who has that duty imposed on him does not discharge it, the court will, to a certain extent, discharge the duty in his room and place ...'
>
> (Lord Eldon: *Brown v Higgs* (1803) 8 Ves 561)

CASE EXAMPLE

Burrough v Philcox (1840) 5 My & Cr 72

The testator transferred property on trust for his two children for life, with remainder to his issue, and declared that if they should die without issue, the survivor should have the power to dispose by will 'among my nieces and nephews, or their children, either all to one or to as many of them as my surviving child shall think fit'. The testator's children died without issue and without any appointment having been made by the survivor. It was held that a trust was created in favour of the testator's nieces and nephews and their children. The trust was subject to a power of selection in the surviving child.

> J
> 'Where there appears a general intention in favour of a class, and a particular intention in favour of individuals of a class to be selected by another person, and the particular intention fails from that selection not having been made, the court will carry into effect the general intention in favour of the class.'
>
> (Lord Cottenham)

On the other hand, in *Re Weekes's Settlement* [1897] 1 Ch 289, the court, on construction of the instrument, concluded that a mere power was created.

CASE EXAMPLE

Re Weekes's Settlement [1897] 1 Ch 289

The testatrix transferred property to her husband for life with 'power to dispose of all such property by will amongst our children'. There was no gift over in default of appointment. There were children but the husband died intestate without having exercised the power. It was held that a mere power of appointment was given to the husband and not a trust power. The court was not entitled to intervene in favour of the children. Thus the property was not divided among the children equally but went to the testatrix's heir.

> J '... now, apart from the authorities, I should gather from the terms of the will that it was a mere power that was conferred on the husband, and not one coupled with a trust that he was bound to exercise. I see no words in the will to justify me in holding that the testatrix intended that the children should take if her husband did not execute the power.'
>
> (Romer LJ)

Ultimately, the question whether a 'mere power of appointment' or a 'trust power' was created varies with the intention of the settlor. This is a question of fact. Decided cases illustrate how unpredictable this question is likely to be. There are two types of gifts that are consistent with the conclusion that a mere power of appointment was intended by the settlor. These are:

- The creation of an express gift over in default of appointment. This is an express alternative gift in the event of the donee of the power failing to exercise the power. The settlor has made provision by declaring alternative beneficiaries in the event of the failure to exercise the power, for example '£50,000 is transferred to trustees to distribute the income for a period not exceeding 15 years in favour of such of the relatives of the settlor as the trustees may decide in their absolute discretion. In the event of the trustees failing to distribute any part of the income to the relatives, Mr X will be entitled to the same'. In this case the clause entitling Mr X to a beneficial interest is an express gift over in default of appointment. The material feature is that the clause is only activated if the trustees fail to distribute the property in favour of the relatives of the settlor. *Re Mills* [1930] 1 Ch 654 illustrates this principle.

- A general power of appointment is incapable of being a trust power, for the courts are incapable of exercising such power. A general power of appointment is one which entitles the donee of the power to appoint in favour of anyone, including himself. Thus, there are no limits to the objects of such a power of appointment. Similarly, a hybrid power of appointment is incapable of being a trust power. A hybrid power is similar in appearance to a general power save for the disqualification of an excluded class of objects, for example 'on trust for X to appoint in favour of anyone except the settlor and his spouse'.

In *Blausten v IRC* [1972] Ch 256, the settlement gave the trustees the power to introduce any person other than the settlor as a member of a class of objects, but subject to the written consent of the settlor. It was held that a hybrid power of appointment was created.

Likewise, in *Re Manisty's Settlement* [1973] 3 WLR 341, the court decided that a hybrid power was created. In this case the trustees were given a power to add objects to a class of potential beneficiaries which excluded the settlor, his wife and certain named persons.

However, a special power of appointment may or may not create a trust power. A special power of appointment confers on the trustee an authority or a duty to distribute the fund in favour of a specific class of objects, such as the children of the settlor. If there is no express gift over in default of appointment, it is extremely difficult to know whether a special power of appointment creates a trust power or a mere power. The issue is one of construction of the terms of the gift. The absence of an express gift over in default of appointment is nothing more than an argument that the settlor did not intend to create a trust. The weight of such an argument will vary with the facts of each case.

> J
>
> 'The authorities do not show, in my opinion, that there is a hard-and-fast rule that a gift to A for life with a power to A to appoint among a class and nothing more must, if there is no gift over in the will, be held a gift by implication to the class in default of the power being exercised. In my opinion the cases show… that you must find in the will an indication that the testatrix did intend the class or some of the class to take – intended in fact that the power should be regarded in the nature of a trust…'
>
> (Romer LJ: *Re Weekes's Settlement* (1897))

ACTIVITY

How would you distinguish a mere power of appointment from a trust power?

7.8 Duties imposed on fiduciaries

A discretionary trust is mandatory and a power is merely permissive, but similar duties are imposed on both discretionary trustees and those exercising fiduciary powers. Thus, under a fiduciary power, the trustees are required to act responsibly and *bona fide* to consider, from time to time, whether to exercise their discretion but they may legitimately fail to exercise their discretion. In this event the gift over in default of appointment will take effect. Under a discretionary trust, however, if the discretionary trustees fail to exercise their discretion the courts will intervene and repair the omission by the trustees.

It may be recalled that there are two kinds of discretionary trusts: exhaustive and non-exhaustive discretionary trusts (see earlier). In an exhaustive discretionary trust the trustees are required to distribute the relevant property (income or capital) within a reasonable period of time. On the other hand, a non-exhaustive discretionary trust is one where the trustees may legitimately fail to distribute the property. In this event the property is retained by the trustees. For instance, in the case of a non-exhaustive discretionary trust of income, on a failure to distribute the income within a reasonable time the income will be accumulated and becomes capitalised (or capital). Thus, in such a case the discretion may be exercised by a decision to accumulate the income.

Whether the trust is exhaustive or not, the trustees are under a duty to refrain from acting capriciously, but are under a duty to act in a responsible manner, surveying the range of objects both in terms of the categories of objects and the qualifications of individual objects with a view to distribution.

> **J** 'a trustee with a duty to distribute, particularly among a potentially very large class, would surely never require the preparation of a complete list of names, which any how would tell him little that he needs to know. He would examine the field, by class and category; might indeed make diligent and careful enquiries, depending on how much money he had to give away and the means at his disposal, as to the composition and needs of particular categories and of individuals within them; decide on certain priorities or proportions and then select individuals according to their needs and qualifications.'
>
> (Lord Wilberforce: *McPhail v Doulton* [1971] AC 424)

If the trustees act in good faith and with due care and attention, confirming the exercise of their discretion within the terms authorised by the settlor, the courts will not interfere with the trustees' discretion.

The distinction between an exhaustive and a non-exhaustive discretionary trust becomes significant when the trustees fail to exercise their discretion. This will be evident if the trustees fail to distribute the relevant property (exhaustive) or fails to take relevant factors into consideration (non-exhaustive). In these circumstances the court will intervene and execute the unfulfilled duty of the trustees. The court has a variety of options available to it in order to execute the trust but whichever course is adopted its objective would be to give effect to the intentions of the settlor or testator. The court is entitled to appoint new trustees able and willing to exercise the discretion or by directing the trustees to distribute the fund. Alternatively, the court may direct representatives of the classes of objects to prepare a scheme of distribution or in appropriate cases the court may order an equal division of the funds in favour of the objects. This last course of action would be appropriate in cases of family trusts of a limited class.

CASE EXAMPLE

Re Locker's Settlement [1977] 1 WLR 1323

An exhaustive discretionary trust of income was created but the trustees failed to distribute the income. They subsequently declared an intention to repair their omission by distributing accumulated income and asked the court for directions. The court granted directions to the effect that the trustees were entitled to make the distribution.

7.9 Status of objects under discretionary trusts

Under a fixed trust the beneficiaries are given quantifiable interests in the trust property which each may enjoy, sell, exchange or gift away. Each beneficiary is entitled to the protection of a court of equity and is empowered to pursue actions in order to enforce such rights.

For example, in a gift to the trustees on trust for A for life, remainder to B absolutely, A has a vested interest in possession and is entitled to the income as of right from the trust fund for life. B has a vested interest in the capital of the fund as of right and would acquire an absolute interest on A's death.

7.9.1 Individual interest

Under a discretionary trust the trustees are given a discretion to decide what interest, if any, may be distributed to the objects. The objects are dependent on the trustees exercising their discretion in their favour. In *Gartside v IRC* [1968] 1 All ER 121, a case involving a non-exhaustive discretionary trust, the House of Lords reiterated the principles that the objects have rights in competition with each other. No object is entitled to a quantifiable interest in the property. Prior to the exercise of the discretion, the objects, individually considered, have an expectation or hope of acquiring a benefit. Each object does not have a right to the income of the fund, but merely a right to require the trustees to consider whether they will distribute any property to the object. If the trustees decide to distribute property to an object, he gets it not by reason of having the right to have his case considered, but only because the trustees have decided to distribute the property to him. This is the position whether the discretionary trust is exhaustive or non-exhaustive. The same principles apply to objects under a power of appointment.

It follows that if an object assigns his rights under a discretionary trust to a third party or becomes bankrupt, the assignee or trustee-in-bankruptcy can be in no better position than the object. Accordingly, the assignee or trustee-in-bankruptcy obtains property at the discretion of the trustees and have no right to demand the income as it arises.

CASE EXAMPLE

Re Coleman (1888) 39 Ch 443

An object under a discretionary trust assigned his interest for consideration to a third party. The trustees declined to pay the income to the third party. The question in issue was whether the trustees had retained their discretion concerning the income. It was held that the third party was entitled to no interest in the income as it arose.

However, following an assignment of rights to third parties any income actually paid to the assignor may be claimed by the assignee or trustee-in-bankruptcy in the capacity as a representative of the assignor *vis-à-vis* the trust. But a payment in a non-traceable form by the trustees to another, on behalf of the object of the trust, may not be claimed by the assignee or trustee-in-bankruptcy.

'If the trustees were to pay an hotel-keeper to give him a dinner he would get nothing but the right to eat a dinner, and that is not property which could pass by assignment or bankruptcy.'

(Cotton LJ: *Re Coleman* (1888))

Of course, income legitimately paid to an object in the exercise of the discretion of the trustees becomes the property of the beneficiary as and when the trustees exercise their discretion in his favour. Moreover, it is not accurate to say that individual objects under a discretionary trust do not have rights under the trust. Each object has the right to be considered to be entitled to the property in the exercise of the discretion of the trustees. In addition, each object has the right to require the trustees to exercise their discretion *bona fide* in a responsible manner and within the limits as laid down by the settlor.

'No doubt in a certain sense a beneficiary under a discretionary trust has an "interest": the nature of it may, sufficiently for the purpose, be spelt out by saying that he has a right to be considered as a potential recipient of benefit by the trustees and a right to have his interest protected by a court of equity.'

(Lord Wilberforce: *Gartside v IRC* [1968] 1 All ER 121)

7.9.2 Group interest

In trusts law, if all the objects entitled to both income and capital act in unison and if they are of full age and sound mind, they are entitled to terminate the discretionary trust and acquire the property for their own benefit. This principle is applicable to both exhaustive and non-exhaustive trusts; for instance, if trustees hold property on discretionary trust to distribute the income in favour of all or any of a closed group of persons, A, B and C, for 21 years and subject thereto the capital is held on trust for D. Provided that A, B, C and D are of full age and sound mind and are in agreement, they may terminate the trust.

Similarly, the sole objects collectively are entitled to assign their interests to a third party. In these circumstances, the third party is entitled to demand the fund from the trustee.

CASE EXAMPLE

Re Smith, Public Trustee v Aspinall [1928] Ch 915

A testator gave one-quarter of the residue of his estate to trustees on trust to pay, at their absolute discretion, the income for the maintenance of Mrs Aspinall for life and/or all or any of her children. On the death of Mrs Aspinall the trustees were required to pay both income and capital, including capitalised income, to the children in equal shares. Mrs Aspinall joined with her two surviving children and the personal representative of her deceased child in executing an assignment of their interest in favour of Legal and General Assurance Company in order to secure a mortgage. The question in issue was whether the trustees were required to pay the income, as it arose, to the company until the discharge of the mortgage, or whether they were at liberty to pay the income at their discretion to Mrs Aspinall. It was held that the income was payable to the company because the sole objects of the trust were entitled to dispose of the entire income.

J 'What is to happen where the trustees have a discretion whether they will apply the whole or only a portion of the fund for the benefit of one person, but are obliged to apply the rest of the fund, so far as not applied for the benefit of the first-named person, to or for the benefit of a second-named person? There, two people together are the sole objects of the discretionary trust and, between them, are entitled to have the whole fund applied to them or for their benefit … you treat all the people put together just as though they formed one person, for whose benefit the trustees were directed to apply the whole of a particular fund.'

(Romer J)

ACTIVITY

What rights do objects enjoy under a discretionary trust?

7.10 Protective trusts under s 33 of the Trustee Act 1925

A protective trust under s 33(1) of the Trustee Act 1925 involves a determinable life interest in favour of the principal beneficiary and, in the event of a termination or forfeiture of the interest taking place, the establishment of a discretionary trust of the income in favour of a class of objects, including the principal beneficiary, his spouse and issue. But, if the principal beneficiary has no spouse or issue, the capital and income will be held on discretionary trust in favour of the principal beneficiary and his next of kin.

This 'ready-made' protective trust exists as a device to obviate the risk to the settlor of inadvertently creating a conditional interest instead of a determinable interest.

Trustee Act 1925, s 33(1)

'Where any income … is directed to be held on protective trusts for the benefit of any person (in this section called "the principal beneficiary") for the period of his life or for any less period, then, during that period (in this section called the "trust period") the said income shall … be held [on the trusts laid down in s 33(1)(i) and (ii)].'

In *Re Wittke* [1944] Ch 166, it was decided that it is unnecessary for the settlor to set out the details of the trust. All that is required is that the settlor manifest an intention to create a protective trust. The model trust under s 33 will be adopted.

In any event, the settlor is entitled to set up his special express protective trust incorporating as much detail as he considers appropriate. Furthermore, s 33(2) entitles the settlor to adopt any variation of the structure of the protective trust as laid down in s 33(1). For example, the settlor may incorporate the s 33 trust, but exclude the discretionary trust that arises when the forfeiture event takes place and substitute a remainder interest of both capital and income in favour of the principal beneficiary's issue or, failing issue, his next of kin.

Trustee Act 1925, s 33(2)

'This section … has effect subject to any variation of the implied trusts aforesaid contained in the instrument creating the trust.'

Section 33(3) enacts what would have been implied in any event, namely, that s 33 does not validate any provision which would be liable to be set aside. Accordingly a determinable life interest in favour of the settlor is void as against his trustee in bankruptcy.

Trustee Act 1925, s 33(3)

'Nothing in this section operates to validate any trust which would, if contained in the instrument creating the trust, be liable to be set aside.'

7.10.1 Determining events (forfeiture)

Section 33(1)(i) adopts a broad formula for ascertaining the occasions when the life interest will be determined.

Trustee Act 1925, s 33(1)(i)

' ... when the principal beneficiary does or attempts to do or suffers any act or thing, or until any event happens, other than an advance under any statutory or express power, whereby, if the said income were payable during the trust period to the principal beneficiary ... he would be deprived of the right to receive the same on any part thereof ... '

It is to be noted that an advancement under an express or statutory power (such as s 32 of the Trustee Act 1925) is excluded from the forfeiting events. An advancement involves the provision of an enduring benefit on behalf of a beneficiary such as the provision of a house or the setting up of a business.

The burden of proving a forfeiture lies on any party who claims that a determining event has taken place. In this respect, the principal beneficiary may rely on a presumption that the forfeiting event has not taken place, until the contrary is proved to the satisfaction of the court.

The determining event formula under s 33 of the Trustee Act 1925 not only includes the acts or omissions of the principal beneficiary, but also circumstances outside his control which deprive him of the right to receive the income under the trust.

CASE EXAMPLE

Re Gourju [1943] Ch 24.

The principal beneficiary, an English national, became marooned in German-occupied Nice. The effect was that the income from the trust became payable to the Custodian of Enemy Property under the Trading With The Enemy Act 1939. It was decided that this event triggered a forfeiture of the beneficiary's interest.

In *Re Hall* [1944] Ch 46, however, in similar circumstances, there was no forfeiture in respect of a French national who lived in France, and was regarded as an 'enemy' under the 1939 Act. It appears that, subject to an express provision to the contrary, a positive act on the part of the beneficiary which is outside the ordinary course of events is required to be done in order to trigger a forfeiture.

Accordingly, the purported sale, gift or other disposition by the principal beneficiary of his interest, as well as his bankruptcy have the effect of activating the determining event.

7.10.2 Other examples of forfeiting events

- *Re Balfour's Settlement* [1938] Ch 928: the impounding by trustees of part of the income of the principal beneficiary in order to repair a breach of trust instigated by the beneficiary prior to the date of bankruptcy of the beneficiary.

- *Re Baring's Settlement Trust* [1940] Ch 737: a sequestration order against the beneficiary following her failure to obey a court order to return her infant children to the jurisdiction of the court.

- *Re Dennis's Settlement Trusts* [1942] Ch 283: the execution of a deed of variation releasing the principal beneficiary's right to part of the income. It seems that there is forfeiture if a representative of the principal beneficiary is appointed in order to look after the beneficiary's interests, as opposed to a transfer of property to a representative for the benefit of another.

- *Re Oppenheim's Will Trusts* [1950] Ch 633: the appointment of a receiver to handle the affairs of the beneficiary, who was certified as a person of unsound mind, did not cause a forfeiture.

- Likewise, in *Re Westby's Settlement* [1950] Ch 296: fees paid to the receiver, who was appointed in order to represent the interests of a person of unsound mind, did not cause a forfeiture.

■Key facts on dispositive discretions

KEY FACTS

Mere powers	– authoritative – may be released by appointor	
↓		
Personal powers	– authoritative – may be released by appointor	– *Re Weekes* (1897)
OR		
Fiduciary powers	– authoritative – may be released by appointor	– *Blausten v IRC* (1972); *Re Manisty* (1974)
OR		
Fiduciary powers in the full sense	– authoritative – may not be released by appointor	– *Mettoy Pension v Evans*(1990)
Discretionary trusts/	– mandatory – may not be released by trustees	– *McPhail v Doulton* (1971)
Trust powers		
↓		
Exhaustive/ non-exhaustive		

Further reading

Gardner, S, 'Fiduciary powers in Toytown' (1991) 107 LQR 214.

Grubb, A, 'Powers, trusts and classes of objects – *Re Hay's Settlement*' [1982] Conv 432.

Harris, J, 'Trust, power and duty' (1971) 87 LQR 31.

Sheridan, L, 'Discretionary trusts' (1957) 21 Conv 55.

chapter 8

RESULTING TRUSTS ■

8.1 Introduction

So far, we have been considering various aspects of express trusts. These trusts, it may be recalled, are created in accordance with the express intention of the settlor. This intention is required to be clearly expressed to the satisfaction of the court. All the circumstances are considered by the courts including verbal and written statements as well as the conduct of the settlor. The effect is that the material terms of an express trust are complete. There are no shortcomings by the draftsperson. A resulting trust, on the other hand, is implied by the court in favour of the settlor/transferor or his estate, if he is dead. Such trusts arise by virtue of the unexpressed or implied intention of the settlor or testator. The settlor or his estate becomes the beneficial owner under the resulting trust when no other suitable claimants can be found. It is as though the settlor has retained a residual interest in the property, albeit one that is implied or created by the courts. The trust is created as a result of defective drafting. The draftsperson omitted to deal with an event that has taken place, and the court is asked to deal with the beneficial ownership of the property. The expression 'resulting trust' derives from the Latin verb *resultare*, meaning to spring back (in effect, to the original owner). Examples are the transfer of property subject to a condition precedent which cannot be achieved, the intended creation of an express trust which becomes void, or the incomplete disposal of the equitable interest in property. In *Vandervell v IRC* [1967] 2 AC 291 (see Chapter 6) the House of Lords decided that the equitable interest in the option to purchase shares was vested in Mr Vandervell by way of a resulting trust.

> J
>
> 'If A intends to give away all his beneficial interest in a piece of property and thinks he has done so but, by some mistake or accident or failure to comply with the requirements of the law, he has failed to do so, either wholly or partially, there will, by operation of law, be a resulting trust for him of the beneficial interest of which he had failed effectually to dispose. If the beneficial interest was in A and he fails to give it away effectively to another or others or on charitable trusts it must remain in him. Early references to equity, like nature, abhorring a vacuum, are delightful but unnecessary …'
>
> (Lord Upjohn)

8.2 Automatic and presumed resulting trusts

In *Re Vandervell's Trusts (No 2)* [1974] 1 All ER 47, Megarry J classified resulting trusts into two categories, namely 'automatic' and 'presumed'. 'Automatic' resulting trusts arise where the beneficial interest in respect of the transfer of property remains undisposed of. Such trusts are created in order to fill a gap in ownership. The equitable or beneficial interest cannot exist in the air and ought to remain with the settlor/transferor. The resulting trust here does not depend on any intentions or presumptions, but is the automatic consequence of the transferor's failure to dispose of property that was vested in him. In other words, if the transfer is made subject to an intended express trust that fails, the resulting trust that arises does not establish the trust but merely carries back the beneficial interest to the transferor. The 'presumed' resulting trust arises, in the absence of evidence to the contrary, when property is purchased in the name of another, or property is voluntarily transferred to another. For instance, A purchases property and the legal title is conveyed in the name of B, or A transfers the legal title to property in the name of B. In these circumstances B *prima facie* holds the property on resulting trust for A. This is a rebuttable presumption of law that arises in favour of A. The question is not one of the automatic consequences of a dispositive failure by A in respect of the equitable interest, but one of presumption: the legal title to the property has been transferred to B, and because of the absence of consideration and any presumption of advancement, B is presumed not only to hold the entire interest on trust, but also to hold the beneficial interest for A absolutely. The presumption thus establishes both that B is to take on trust and also the nature of that trust.

In *Westdeutsche Landesbank Girozentrale v Islington BC* [1996] AC 669, Lord Browne-Wilkinson declared that a resulting trust gives effect to the common intention of the parties. In his Lordship's opinion this trust arises in two sets of circumstances, namely the purchase of property in the name of another and the existence of surplus trust funds after the trust purpose has been fulfilled.

The classification by Megarry J in *Vandervell v IRC* (1967), despite criticism, serves the useful purpose of simplifying the categories of resulting trusts and for the purpose of exposition we will rely on it.

8.3 Automatic resulting trusts

The rationale behind this type of resulting trust, as indicated above, is that the transfer of property was subject to a condition precedent that has not been achieved or that the destination of the beneficial interest has not been dealt with. This type of resulting trust arises in a variety of situations.

CASE EXAMPLE

Re Ames [1946] Ch 217

A transfer to trustees was made subject to a marriage settlement that turned out to be void. The court decided that the fund was held on resulting trust for the settlor's estate on the ground that the money was paid on a consideration that had failed.

A similar result was reached in *Essery v Cowlard* (1884) 26 Ch D 191, where the court decided that the contract to marry had definitely and absolutely been put to an end.

In *Vandervell v IRC* [1967] 2 AC 291, the transfer of the legal title to property was made but the transferor omitted to deal with the destination of the equitable interest in a share option scheme.

In *Barclays Bank v Quistclose* [1970] AC 56, a resulting trust was created with regard to a loan made for a specific purpose which was not carried out. It must be emphasised that in order to implement the law of trust the specific loan to the borrower must be such that the sum does not become the general property of the borrower. The specific purpose of the loan identified by the lender must be sufficient to impress an obligation on the borrower to use the amount solely for the purposes as stated by the lender.

CASE EXAMPLE

Barclays Bank v Quistclose [1970] AC 56

Quistclose Ltd loaned £209,719 to Rolls Razors Ltd, subject to an express condition that the latter would use the money to pay a dividend to its shareholders. Q Ltd's cheque for the relevant sum was paid into a separate account opened specifically for this purpose with Barclays Bank Ltd, which knew of the purpose of the loan. Before the dividend was paid, Rolls Ltd went into voluntary liquidation and Barclays Ltd claimed to use the amount to set off against the overdrafts of Rolls Ltd's other account at the bank.

The House of Lords held that the terms of the loan were such as to impress on the money a trust in favour of Quistclose Ltd in the event of the dividend not being paid, and since Barclays had notice of the nature of the loan, it was not entitled to set off the amount against Rolls Ltd's overdraft. Lord Wilberforce broadened the basis on which the resulting trust arose by deciding that there were two trusts posed by these facts – a primary trust to pay a dividend and a secondary trust that arises if the purpose of the primary trust has not been carried out.

CONTINUED ▸

'... when the money is advanced, the lender acquires an equitable right to see that it is applied for the primary designated purpose ... when the purpose has been carried out (ie, the debt paid) the lender has his remedy against the borrower in debt: if the primary purpose cannot be carried out, the question arises if a secondary purpose (ie, repayment to the lender) has been agreed, expressly or by implication: if it has, the remedies of equity may be invoked to give effect to it, if it has not (and the money is intended to fall within the general fund of the debtor's assets) then there is the appropriate remedy for recovery of the loan. I can appreciate no reason why the flexible interplay of law and equity cannot let these practical arrangements, and other variations if desired: it would be to the discredit of both systems if they could not. In the present case the intention to create a secondary trust for the benefit of the lender, to arise if the primary trust, to pay the dividend, could not be carried out, is clear and I can find no reason why the law should not give effect to it ... '

(Lord Wilberforce)

8.3.1 *Quistclose* analysis

Lord Wilberforce's reasoning in *Quistclose* (1970) has attracted a great deal of judicial and academic comment. Millett P writing extra-judicially ('The *Quistclose* trust: who can enforce it?' (1985) 101 LQR 269), questioned whether a valid 'primary trust' had existed in *Quistclose* (1970). An express trust, subject to limited exceptions, assumes the existence of a person with a *locus standi* to enforce the trust. Without such a person the intended express trust is void (see later). The intended 'primary trust' was to pay a dividend. This lacks a beneficiary to enforce the trust. Thus, it is doubtful whether there could be a valid express trust in order to pay a dividend as Lord Wilberforce decided. In addition such a primary trust may lack precision or certainty which the law requires.

In *Twinsectra v Yardley* [2002] All ER 377 Lord Millett restated his views:

'In several of the cases the primary trust was for an abstract purpose with no one but the lender to enforce performance or restrain misapplication of the money ... It is simply not possible to hold money on trust to acquire unspecified property from an unspecified vendor at an unspecified time.'

(Lord Millett: *Twinsectra v Yardley* (2002))

In addition there have been a variety of approaches to the 'secondary trust' in favour of the lender as laid down by Lord Wilberforce in *Quistclose* (1970). In *Carreras Rothmans Ltd v Freeman*

Matthews Treasure Ltd [1984] 3 WLR 1016, Peter Gibson J decided that this trust affects the conscience of the borrower if the terms of the agreement have not been carried out. This is consistent with a constructive trust as distinct from a resulting trust.

CASE EXAMPLE

Carreras Rothmans Ltd v Freeman Matthews Treasure Ltd [1984] 3 WLR 1016

The claimant company (a cigarette manufacturer) engaged the services of the defendant, an advertising agency. The defendant fell into financial difficulty and needed funds to pay its production agencies and advertising media. The claimant made a special agreement with the defendant to pay such of its debts which were directly attributable to the claimant's involvement with the defendant. A large fund was paid into a special bank account established in the name of the defendant. A few months later the defendant went into liquidation. The creditors called on the claimant to meet the defendant's debts. The claimant complied with their demands and took assignments from the creditors of their rights against the defendant. The liquidator of the defendant company refused to pay the claimant any sums from the special account. The claimant sought a declaration that the moneys in the special account ought to be repaid to the claimant. The court held that the funds in the account were held on resulting trust for the claimant because the sum had been paid for a specific purpose that had not been achieved. Accordingly, the sum was not part of the defendant's assets to be distributed among its creditors. The court applied the *Quistclose* principle despite differences in the facts of this case and *Quistclose*. The differences were that in *Quistclose* the transaction was one of loan with no contractual obligation on the part of the lender to make payment prior to the agreement for the loan. In the present case there was no loan but there was an antecedent debt owed by the claimant. These were considered insignificant.

J

'In my judgment the principle … is that equity fastens on the conscience of the person who receives from another property transferred for a specific purpose only and not therefore for the recipient's own purposes, so that such person will not be permitted to treat the property as his own or to use it for other than the stated purpose. If the common intention is that property is transferred for a specific purpose and not so as to become the property of the transferee, the transferee cannot keep the property if for any reason that purpose cannot be fulfilled. In my judgment therefore the [claimant] can be equated with the lender in *Quistclose* as having an enforceable right to compel the carrying out of the primary trust.'

(Peter Gibson J)

A similar conclusion was reached by the Court of Appeal in *Re EVTR* [1987] BCLC 646:

CASE EXAMPLE

Re EVTR [1987] BCLC 646

The claimant acquired a windfall sum of money and decided to assist the company that employed him by purchasing new equipment. He paid a sum of money to the company's solicitors to be released to the company 'for the sole purpose of buying new equipment'. The new equipment was ordered but before it was delivered the company went into receivership. The claimant alleged that the sum of money was repayable to him in accordance with trusts law. The court held in the claimant's favour. The court applied the *Quistclose* principle and decided the sum was held on resulting trust for the claimant. However, in confusing the terminology as to the type of trust involved, the court also reasoned that a constructive trust was created when the sum was originally received by the defendant.

> **J** 'On *Quistclose* principles, a resulting trust in favour of the provider of the money arises when money is provided for a particular purpose only, and that purpose fails ... It is a long established principle of Equity that, if a person who is a trustee receives money or property because of, or in respect of, trust property, he will hold what he receives as a constructive trustee on the trusts of the original trust property. It follows, in my judgment, that the repayments made to the receivers are subject to the same trusts as the original [sum] in the hands of the company. There is now, of course, no question of the [amount] being applied in the purchase of new equipment for the company, and accordingly, in my judgment, it is now held on a resulting trust for the [claimant].'
>
> (Dillon LJ)

The objection to the imposition of a constructive trust in the context of a *Quistclose* trust is that such a trust is not dependent on the intention of the lender or transferor. The trust is created by the courts in order to promote good conscience or to prevent unjust enrichment. The date on which the trust is created is also significant, for if the constructive trust is imposed at the time when the defendant receives the funds, then the equitable interest of the lender would appear to be created before the defendant performs an unconscionable act. The same argument may be raised with regard to the resulting trust. The point here is that the claimant's (lender's) equitable interest does not leave him until the sum is applied for the purpose stipulated by the lender. Accordingly, on receipt of the relevant amount the borrower merely acquires the legal title to the funds to be used for the stipulated purpose. If the sum is not used for such purpose the proprietary interest of the claimant may be asserted by him. In *Twinsectra v Yardley* [2002] 2 All ER 377, Lord Millett expressed his opinion that a *Quistclose* trust is a resulting trust for the lender:

> '... the *Quistclose* trust is a simple commercial arrangement akin (as Professor Bridge observes) to a retention of title clause (though with a different object) which enables the borrower to have recourse to the lender's money for a particular purpose without entrenching on the lender's property rights more than necessary to enable the purpose to be achieved. The money remains the property of the lender unless and until it is applied in accordance with his directions, and insofar as it is not so applied it must be returned to him. I am disposed, perhaps pre-disposed, to think that this is the only analysis which is consistent both with orthodox trust law and with commercial reality.'
>
> (Lord Millett)

An alternative analysis is to consider that the resulting trust is created only when the fund is not used for the stipulated purpose. Here it could be argued that the defendant receives both the legal and equitable interests in the fund subject to perhaps a contractual obligation to use the fund for the stipulated purpose. If the fund is used in accordance with the common intention of the parties the defendant acquires both the legal and equitable interests. But if the defendant fails to carry out the stipulated purpose a resulting trust automatically springs up in favour of the claimant.

ACTIVITY

To what extent is it possible to formulate a comprehensive theory regarding resulting trusts?

8.3.2 Surplus of trust funds

Where the trust exhausts only some of the trust property leaving a surplus of funds after the trust purpose has been satisfied, a resulting trust for the transferor or settlor may arise in respect of the surplus. This principle is based on two assumptions: (a) the trust purpose has been satisfied and (b) a surplus of funds has been left over.

CASE EXAMPLE

Re Abbott [1900] 2 Ch 326

An appeal was launched to raise funds for two sisters who were destitute. The purpose of the appeal was to enable the beneficiaries to live in lodgings in Cambridge and to provide for their 'very moderate wants'. Considerable sums were raised and a surplus was left over after the ladies died. The question in issue involved the destination of this surplus. The

CONTINUED ▶

court decided that the surplus was held on resulting trust for the subscribers. The court dismissed the assertion that the fund was intended to become the absolute property of the ladies entitling them to demand a transfer to themselves or if they became bankrupt transferring the funds to their trustee in bankruptcy. On construction of the terms of the appeal and the surrounding circumstances, the intention of the subscribers was to give a wide discretion to the trustees as to whether any, and if so what, part of the fund ought to be applied for the benefit of the ladies. This approach was only consistent with a resulting trust.

It is to be noted that a material factor in these types of cases is the intention of the transferor. If the intention is expressed an express trust will be created for the transferor. In the absence of an express intention the court is required to consider whether there is any evidence of an implied intention that the transferor retained an interest in the property. Such evidence will vary with the facts of each case. In *Re Abbott* (1900) some of the factors that appealed to the court were that virtually all the contributors were identifiable and acquainted with the ladies, the terms of the appeal indicated that the basic needs of the ladies were to be taken care of and the trustees were given a wide discretion as to the means of caring for the ladies. These factors were sufficient to impress on the court that an implied resulting trust ought to be created in favour of the contributors.

In *Re Gillingham Bus Disaster Fund* [1958] Ch 300, the court concluded that a resulting trust is created even though the contributors were anonymous.

CASE EXAMPLE

Re Gillingham Bus Disaster Fund [1958] Ch 300

A disaster took place on the streets of Gillingham. A bus had careered into a group of marching cadets, killing several persons and maiming several more. An appeal was launched to raise funds by means of collecting boxes to be used for funeral expenses, caring for the disabled and 'for worthy causes' in memory of the dead boys (non-charitable purposes). A surplus of funds remained after the bus company admitted liability and paid substantial sums for similar purposes. The court was asked to determine the destination of the surplus. Harman J decided, on construction of the circumstances, that a resulting trust for contributors was created. The donors did not part 'out and out' with their contributions, but only for the specific purposes as stated in the appeal. In this respect, it was immaterial that the donors contributed anonymously. Accordingly, the surplus amount was held on resulting trust for the donors. The sum was paid into court to await claimants. Failing claimants, the fund was taken by the Crown on the basis of *bona*

CONTINUED ▶

vacantia. The court took the view that the ordinary resulting trust rule ought to be followed despite the fact that the vast majority of the contributors were anonymous. The ruling of the court was to the effect that all the contributors (small and large, anonymous and identifiable) were to be treated as having the same intention. The position was analogous to trustees who could not find their beneficiaries. But the court could easily have come to the opposite conclusion, namely the donors being anonymous, manifested an intention not to have the property returned to them. They would then have parted with their funds 'out and out', leaving no room for a resulting trust. The Crown would then have been entitled to the property on the basis of *bona vacantia*. This case was heavily criticised in *Re West Sussex Constabulary Trusts* [1971] Ch 1 (see later).

No resulting trust – beneficial interest taken by the transferee

An alternative construction that may be adopted by the court is to the effect that the transferee may take the property beneficially in accordance with the implied intention of the transferor/settlor. In this event there is no room for a resulting trust. This approach may be adopted where the beneficiary is still capable of enjoying the benefit from the settlement. The issues concerning the implied intention of the transferor and whether the purpose of the transfer is still capable of being achieved remain questions of construction of the circumstances of each case.

CASE EXAMPLE

Re Andrew's Trust [1905] 2 Ch 48

The first Bishop of Jerusalem died, leaving several infant children. An appeal was launched to raise funds 'for or towards' their education. The children had subsequently completed their formal education with use of some of the funds. The question in issue concerned the destination of the remainder of the funds. The court held that the surplus was taken by the children in equal shares in accordance with the implied intention of the contributors. There was no resulting trust for the contributors. The court was influenced by the fact that the children were still capable of deriving benefits from the fund, unlike *Re Abbott* (1900) (where the ladies had died: see above). In addition, the court was willing to construe 'education' in a broad sense and did not restrict it to formal education. In any event, the court decided that education in the narrow sense as referring to formal education was merely the motive for the gift, as distinct from the intention underlying the gift.

A similar result was reached in *Re Osoba* [1979] 1 WLR 24.

CASE EXAMPLE

Re Osoba [1979] 1 WLR 24

A testator bequeathed the residue of his estate which comprised rents from certain leasehold properties to his widow 'for her maintenance and for the training of my daughter up to University grade'. The widow died and the daughter completed her formal education. The testator's son claimed remainder of the residue which had not been used for the daughter's education. The court held that the widow and daughter took as joint tenants. This joint tenancy was not severed. Thus, on the death of the widow the daughter succeeded to the entire fund. The references to maintenance and education in the will were merely declarations of the testator's motive for the gift.

> J
> '... the testator has given the whole fund; he has not given so much of the fund as the trustee or anyone else should determine, but the whole fund. This must be reconciled with the testator having specified the purpose for which the gift is made. This reconciliation is achieved by treating the reference to the purpose as merely a statement of the testator's motive in making the gift. Any other interpretation of the gift would frustrate the testator's expressed intention that the whole subject matter should be applied for the benefit of the beneficiary.'
>
> (Buckley LJ)

An additional factor that had influenced the court was that the transfer was made in a residuary clause in the testator's will. The significance of this was the fact that any failure of the gift would have resulted in an intestacy which would have frustrated the testator's intention.

■Key facts on automatic resulting trusts

KEY FACTS

Transfer of the legal title to trustees subject to an intended trust which is void	*Re Ames* (1946)
Transfer of the bare legal title to trustees without disposing of the equitable interest	*Vandervell v IRC* (1967); *Hodgson v Marks* (1971)
Disposal of property to another subject to a specific limitation which has not been achieved	*Barclays Bank v Quistclose* (1971); *Carreras Rothmans v Freeman Matthews* (1984); *Re EVTR* (1987)
Surplus of trust funds left over after the trust purpose had been achieved	*Re Abbott* (1900); *Re Gillingham Bus Disaster Fund* (1958); contrast *Re Andrew's Trust* (1905); *Re Osoba* (1979)

ACTIVITY

Consider the ownership of the equitable interests in the relevant properties, in respect of each of the dispositions made by Alfred of properties which he originally owned absolutely:

(a) A transfer of 10,000 shares in British Telecom plc to his wife, Beryl, subject to an option, exercisable by their son, Charles, at any time within the next five years, to repurchase 5,000 of the shares. The shares have been duly registered in Beryl's name and she pays 50 per cent of the dividends received to Alfred.

(b) A transfer of £50,000 to trustees 'upon trust to distribute all or such part of the income (as they in their absolute discretion shall think fit) for the maintenance and training of my housekeeper's daughter, Mary, until she graduates from University or reaches the age of 25, whichever happens earlier', subject to gifts over. Mary, aged 24, has recently graduated from the Utopia University.

8.3.3 Dissolution of unincorporated associations

An unincorporated association comprises a group of individuals joined together to promote a common purpose or purposes, not being commercial activities and creating mutual rights and duties among its members. Many sports clubs are run as unincorporated associations. Such associations vary in size and objectives; some may be long standing or exist with a view to making profits and have open or restricted membership. They differ from incorporated associations in that they lack a legal personality – separate and distinct from those of its members. The title of the association is treated as a label to identify its members. The association may sue or be sued through its officers who act on behalf of the members collectively. The association is regulated by its rules which have the effect of imposing an implied contract between all the members *inter se*. Thus, all the members are collectively joined together by the rules of the association. Its affairs are normally handled by a committee and its assets may be held on trust for the members of the association in order to ensure that the association's property is kept separate from that of its members.

In the leading case of *Conservative and Unionist Central Office v Burrell* [1982] 1 WLR 522, Lawton LJ defined an 'unincorporated association'.

> J
>
> '... two or more persons bound together for one or more common purposes, not being business purposes, by mutual undertakings, each having mutual duties and obligations, in an organisation which has rules which identify in whom control of it and its funds rests and upon what terms and which can be joined or left at will. The bond of union between the members of an unincorporated association has to be contractual.'
>
> (Lawton LJ)

The issue in this case involved the legal status of the Conservative Party and whether it was liable to corporation tax on its profits. The court decided that the party was not an unincorporated association but an amorphous combination of various elements. The party lacked a central organisation which controlled local organisations.

In *Re Bucks Constabulary Fund (No 2)* [1979] 1 WLR 936, Walton J graphically described the structure of an unincorporated association.

> J
>
> 'If a number of persons associate together, for whatever purpose, if that purpose is one which involves the acquisition of cash or property of any magnitude, then, for practical purposes, some one or more persons have to act in the capacity of treasurers or holders of the property. In any sophisticated association there will accordingly be one or more trustees in whom the property which is acquired by the association will be vested. These trustees will of course not hold such property on their own behalf. Usually there will be a committee of some description which will run the affairs of the association; though, of course, in a small association the committee may well comprise all the members; and the normal course of events will be that the trustee, if there is a formal trustee, will declare that he holds the property of the

CONTINUED ▶

> **J** association in his hands on trust to deal with it as directed by the committee. If the trust deed is a shade more sophisticated it may add that the trustee holds the assets on trust for the members in accordance with the rules of the association. Now in all such cases it appears to me quite clear that, unless under the rules governing the association the property thereof has been wholly devoted to charity, or unless and to the extent to which the other trusts have validly been declared of such property, the persons, and the only persons, interested therein are the members. Save by way of a valid declaration of trust in their favour, there is no scope for any other person acquiring any rights in the property of the association, although of course it may well be that third parties may obtain contractual or proprietary rights, such as a mortgage, over those assets as the result of a valid contract with the trustees or members of the committee as representing the association.'
>
> (Walton J)

The rules of the association usually provide the procedure for enforcing rights and ownership of interests in respect of a distribution of the assets of the society on a dissolution. If the rules make provision for the distribution of assets on a liquidation those rules will be decisive and the court will merely give effect to such rules. But in the event that the rules are silent as to the destination of the surplus funds on dissolution, the courts are required to resolve the mode of distribution of the assets. The analysis here is twofold:

(a) What is meant by a 'dissolution'?

(b) What rules will be applied by the courts in order to ascertain ownership of the funds on the date of dissolution?

Dissolution

In the vast majority of cases the date of the dissolution of the association will not be in dispute. This will be the date when a formal resolution is passed to wind up the association. But, occasionally, an association may be dormant for a considerable period of time and the traditional formal resolution to wind up the body may not accurately identify the date of termination. If the inactivity is so prolonged, or the circumstances are exceptional, the court may infer that the association has become dissolved. In such cases there may be some difficulty in determining the precise date of dissolution. The less activity there is, the greater the difficulty of determining the specific date of dissolution. In such cases the court will choose a date somewhere between the time when the club could still be said to exist, and the time when its existence had clearly come to an end. The subsisting members of the association will then be entitled to participate in the distribution of the assets.

In *Re William Denby & Sons Ltd Sick and Benevolent Fund* [1971] 1 WLR 973, Brightman J classified four categories of cases in which an unregistered friendly society or benevolent fund should be regarded as having been dissolved or terminated so that its assets became distributable:

(1) in accordance with the rules

(2) by agreement of all persons interested

(3) by order of the court in the exercise of its inherent jurisdiction

(4) when the substratum on which the society or fund was founded had gone, so that the society or fund no longer had any effective purpose.

On the facts of the case, it was held that the substratum had not gone, so that the fund was not distributable.

In *Re GKN Bolts & Nuts* [1982] 1 WLR 774 the court decided that mere inactivity, by itself, is insufficient to constitute spontaneous dissolution. The association may be treated as merely going through a dormant period.

CASE EXAMPLE

Re GKN Bolts & Nuts [1982] 1 WLR 774

In 1946 the trustees of a social club bought a sports ground for use for the benefit of employees of a company. By 1969 the club was in financial difficulties and the sports ground was no longer in use. In February 1975 the last general meeting was held. In September 1975 the stock of the club was sold. On 18th December 1975 a special meeting of the club was convened to consider an offer to buy the sports ground and the members voted unanimously to sell the property. On 18th August 1978 the sale was completed. One of the issues involved the date of dissolution. The court held that the club ceased to exist on 18th December 1975.

J 'The question is whether on the facts of the present case the society ceased to exist on 18th December 1975. On that date, the position was that the club had ceased to operate as a club for several months. The picture was not one of mere inactivity alone; there were positive acts towards the winding up of the club. The sale of the club's stock of drinks was one instance, and others were the ending of the registration for VAT, and the dismissal of the steward. The cessation of any club activities, the ending of the use of the sports ground and the abandonment of preparing accounts or issuing membership cards were all in one sense examples of inactivity; but I think that there was in all probability some element of deliberation in these matters, and not a mere inertia.

However that may be, the resolution to sell the sports ground seems to me to conclude the matter. Having taken all steps, active or passive, required to terminate the activities of the club, short of passing a formal resolution to wind it up or dissolve it, the general meeting of the club resolved to sell the club's last asset.'

(Megarry VC)

Basis of distribution

The court initially adopted the resulting trust solution on the ground that the funds provided by the members were for the benefit of themselves. Not all the members may realistically enjoy the same benefits; some of them may get nothing whilst others may qualify and receive a good deal of benefits under the rules. But if they were all equally entitled to a contingent benefit on the happening of certain events, a resulting trust in their favour was considered to be the fairest way of distributing the fund. The division will be in favour of the subsisting members of the association on the date of dissolution.

CASE EXAMPLE

Re Printers and Transferrers Society [1899] 2 Ch 84

A trade union society was founded by weekly subscriptions to raise funds for strikes and other benefits for its members. The scale of benefits varied with the duration of membership and different conditions applied to printers as opposed to transferrers. The rules of the society were silent as to the mode of distribution of assets on a dissolution. There were assets of £1,000 and the society consisted of 201 subsisting members. On the question of the distribution of the fund, the court held that a resulting trust had existed in favour of the subsisting members on the date of distribution in proportion to the amount contributed over the years. It is to be noted in this case that the court did not discount the benefits received by those sharing in the distribution.

On the other hand, in *Re Houbourn Aero Components Ltd's Air Raid Distress Fund; Ryan v Forrest* [1946] Ch 144, the court decided that all members, both past and present, were entitled to a share in the distribution of the fund.

CASE EXAMPLE

Re Houbourn Aero Components Ltd's Air Raid Distress Fund; Ryan v Forrest [1946] Ch 144

Employees of a company voluntarily contributed to a fund for the purpose of relieving air raid losses during the Second World War. After the war a surplus of funds had existed. On the destination of the surplus, the court decided that all the subscribers were entitled to share in the distribution, because each retained an interest in the amount of his contributions, but subject to reductions in respect of benefits received from the fund.

An alternative basis for distribution concerns the law of contract rather than the trust. Megarry J in *Re Sick and Funeral Society of St John's Sunday School v Golcar* [1973] Ch 51 (see below) explained the significance of the law of contract in this context.

> **J** '... membership of a club or association is primarily a matter of contract. The members make their payments, and in return they become entitled to the benefits of membership in accordance with the rules. The sums they pay cease to be their individual property, and so cease to be subject to any concept of resulting trust. Instead, they become the property, through the trustees of the club or association, of all the members for the time being, including themselves. A member who, by death or otherwise, ceases to be a member thereby ceases to be the part owner of any of the club's property: those who remain continue owners. If, then, dissolution ensues, there must be a division of the property of the club or association among those alone who are owners of that property, to the exclusion of former members.'
>
> (Megarry LJ)

It follows that if members of a society subscribe to a fund, not for their own personal benefit but to provide for a third party, perhaps their widows, the members would have parted 'out and out' with the funds subject to the hope that a surviving widow will take the property. If the members die without leaving a widow they are not entitled to recover their contributions. Likewise, when all the widows die the estates of the members are not entitled to claim the property.

CASE EXAMPLE

Cunnack v Edwards [1896] 2 Ch 679

A society was formed to provide annuities for the widows of deceased members. By 1879, all the members had died and by 1892 the last widow had died. There was a surplus of funds of £1,250. The personal representatives of the last widow claimed the fund. The court held that the Crown took the fund as *bona vacantia*. There was no room for a resulting trust in favour of past members.

A similar result was reached in *Re West Sussex Constabulary's Widows, Children and Benevolent Fund Trusts* [1971] Ch 1.

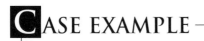

CASE EXAMPLE

Re West Sussex Constabulary's Widows, Children and Benevolent Fund Trusts [1971] Ch 1

A fund was established for providing payments to widows of deceased members of the West Sussex Constabulary. The rules provided that, with exceptions, a member who resigned would forfeit all claims to the fund. Receipts were derived from four classes of contributors, namely:

CONTINUED ▶

(a) identifiable donations and legacies

(b) members' subscriptions

(c) collecting boxes and

(d) proceeds of entertainment, sweepstakes and raffles.

On 1st January 1968, the Constabulary was amalgamated with other police forces and the fund came to an end. The question in issue concerned the distribution of the fund. The court held that a resulting trust was created for the first category of contributors but the remainder of the fund was taken by the Crown as *bona vacantia* subject to an indemnity given by the Crown to honour continuing payments to surviving widows. The court decided that the first category contributors paid sums for a specific purpose which was no longer feasible. The second category of contributors provided funds not for their benefit but for third party widows and had therefore deprived themselves of any interest in the property. The third category of contributors, by virtue of their anonymity , had never expected the return of their funds (distinguishing *Re Gillingham Bus Disaster Fund* (1958)) and the fourth category of contributors received consideration for their payments.

In *Re Bucks Constabulary Widows' and Orphans Fund Friendly Society (No 2)* [1979] 1 WLR 936, on similar facts the court decided that on a dissolution of a friendly society the subsisting members were entitled to the funds.

CASE EXAMPLE

Re Bucks Constabulary Widows' and Orphans Fund Friendly Society (No 2) [1979] 1 WLR 936

The objects of the society included the relief of widows and orphans of deceased members of Bucks Constabulary. On an amalgamation with other societies a surplus of funds was available for distribution. Walton J held that the subsisting members were entitled to the property equally. The court was able to distinguish *Re West Sussex Constabulary Fund* (1971) on the ground that that case did not involve a friendly society. Further, the court ruled that the rights of entitlement on a dissolution of an unincorporated association are based on the law of contract as opposed to the law of trusts.

J

'... so far as the members are concerned it is a matter of pure contract, and, being a matter of pure contract, it is, in my judgment, as far as distribution is concerned, completely divorced from all questions of equitable doctrines.'

(Walton J)

If the rules of the association distinguish between the members in terms of entitlement, such as creating two or more forms of membership with correlative entitlement, then on a liquidation this discrimination is required to be reflected in the distribution. Thus, members who were required to pay double subscriptions while the society continued will be entitled to double the funds available for distribution.

CASE EXAMPLE

Re Sick and Funeral Society of St John's Sunday School v Golcar [1973] Ch 51

A Sunday school society was formed to provide sickness and death benefits for its members. Subscriptions were based on a sliding scale according to age; those under 13 paid half of one old penny per week and those over 12 paid one old penny. The benefits for those paying the full subscription were twice those of the younger subscribers. It was resolved to wind up the society. No further subscriptions were paid. There was some £4,000 of surplus assets. The court held that the distribution took the form of full shares for full members and half shares for the other members.

> **J** 'On the footing that the rules of a club or association form the basis of the contract between all the members, I must look at the rules of the society to see whether they indicate any basis other than that of equality. It seems to me that they do. Those aged from five to 12 years old pay contributions at half the rate, and correspondingly their allowances and death benefit (rule 14) are also paid at half the rate. Where the rules have written into them the basis of inequality this ought also to be applied to the surplus property of the society.'
>
> (Megarry LJ)

Similar principles are applicable to surplus funds within pension schemes. However, since the pension trustee hold the funds upon trust for the investors it would be logical if the resulting trusts principles were applicable in this context. In *Davis v Richards and Wallington Industries* [1990] 1 WLR 1511, the court decided that in respect of a pension fund surplus, the employers' contributions were held on resulting trust but the employees' contributions and other transferred funds were taken by the Crown as *bona vacantia*. The reason stated by Scott J for the *bona vacantia* solution concerned the difficulties in calculating the shares that would have been subject to such trusts, in view of the different benefits received by employees. In *Air Jamaica Ltd v Charlton* [1999] 1 WLR 1399, the Privy Council decided that a resulting trust of the surplus fund was created in favour of the employer and employees equally. In distinguishing *Davis v Richards* (1990), the court decided that the fact that the transferors did not intend to retain a benefit was not sufficient to militate against the imposition of a resulting trust.

> **J** ' ... like a constructive trust, a resulting trust arises by operation of law, though unlike a constructive trust it gives effect to intention. But it arises whether or not the transferor intended to retain a beneficial interest – he almost always does not – since it responds to the absence of any intention on his part to pass a beneficial interest to the recipient. It may arise even where the transferor positively wished to part with the beneficial interest, as in *Vandervell v Inland Revenue Commissioners* [1967] 2 AC 291.'
>
> (Lord Millett: *Air Jamaica Ltd v Charlton* (1999))

■Key facts on dissolution of unincorporated associations

KEY FACTS

'Unincorporated associations' – meaning		*Conservative & Unionist Central Office v Burrell* (1982) – *per* Lawton LJ
		Re Bucks Constabulary Fund (No 2) (1979) – *per* Walton J
Date of dissolution		*Re GKN Bolts & Nuts* (1982)
Basis of distribution	Resulting trust	*Re Printers and Transferrers Society* (1899) (subsisting members)
	Resulting trust	*Re Houbourn Air Raid Distress Fund* (1946) (past and current members)
	Contract	*Cunnack v Edwards* (*bona vacantia*) (1896)
	Contract	*Re West Sussex Constabulary Fund* (1971) (*bona vacantia*)
	Contract	*Re Bucks Constabulary Fund* (No 2) (1979) (subsisting members)
		Re Sick and Funeral Society of St John's Sunday School v Golcar (1973) (subsisting members)

ACTIVITY

The Dealing Tennis Club, an unincorporated association, has just been offered a substantial sum of money for its site by a property developer. The club was founded 40 years ago and derives its funds from subscriptions, fetes, bazaars and other entertainment activities, collection boxes in respect of special tournaments and legacies. The committee of the club is minded to accept the offer to liquidate the association but wishes to know (i) on what basis the site is held and (ii) how any surplus assets following the winding-up of the association will be distributed.

Advise the committee.

8.4 Presumed resulting trusts

A presumption of law is a conclusion which the court is obliged to draw on proof of specific facts. A presumed resulting trust is a *prima facie* rule of evidence that creates a rebuttable presumption of law. It is a default mechanism that comes into play when there is a purchase of property in the name of another or the voluntary transfer of property to another, and there is no definitive evidence in the first place concerning the transferor's real intention. If there is clear evidence as to the destination of the equitable interest, either a gift or an express trust would be created and there would be no room for a presumed resulting trust. For instance, if A transfers the legal title to 500 BT plc shares to B and expresses his intention that B will retain the equitable interest in the shares, a gift is created by A in favour of B. In other words, the transaction is clear as to the location of the legal and equitable titles. B has both titles. Equally, the equitable interest is clearly identifiable when an express trust is created. For instance, C transfers the legal title to 2,000 BAA plc shares to D, subject to an express trust in favour of E absolutely. D acquires the legal title and E enjoys the equitable interest absolutely. But if the location of the equitable interest is uncertain, equity *prima facie* imposes a trust on the transferee for the benefit of the transferor. The transferor is presumed to have retained the equitable title and the transferee is presumed to obtain a nominal interest in the property. The rule is arbitrary in the sense that the two transactions mentioned below trigger the presumption. In this respect the presumption has the advantage of clarifying the ownership of the beneficial interest, subject to evidence to the contrary.

There are two types of transactions that give rise to the presumption, namely:

- a purchase of property in the name of another and
- a voluntary conveyance of property in the name of another.

8.4.1 Purchase in the name of another

The rule is that where property (real or personalty) is vested in the name of another or in the purchaser jointly with others, a resulting trust will be presumed in favour of those who provide the purchase monies and in proportion to the contribution made by each person. Parol evidence is admissible in order to identify the purchaser. If A and B jointly purchase a house and have it conveyed in the name of B so that B becomes the legal owner of the house, B is presumed to hold the house on trust for both A and B in proportion to the contribution made by each of them. If A provides four-fifths and B one-fifth of the purchase monies, B is presumed to hold the house for himself beneficially as to one-fifth and the remainder on trust for A.

> 'The clear result of all the cases, without a single exception is that the trust of a legal estate, whether taken in the names of the purchasers and others jointly, or in the names of others without that of the purchaser, whether in one name or several; whether jointly or successive – results to the man who advances the purchase money. It is the established doctrine of a court of equity that this resulting trust may be rebutted by circumstances in evidence.'
>
> (Eyre CB: *Dyer v Dyer* (1788) 2 Cox Eq 92)

In order to trigger the presumption it is essential that the provision of the money is by way of a purchase and not as a loan. If a loan is provided the relationship of the parties is that of creditor and debtor and no presumed resulting trust will arise. Likewise, it is essential that the parties contribute to the purchase of property and not merely the payment of rent. In *Savage v Dunningham* [1973] 3 All ER 429 an attempt was made to extend the presumed resulting trust to a flat-sharing arrangement. The court rejected this application and decided that rent, unlike purchase money, is not paid for the acquisition of a capital asset but merely for the right to use the property.

Members of a lottery syndicate who pay their subscriptions to nominees on behalf of the syndicate may become beneficiaries of any winnings. The members of the lottery on making a contribution acquire a chose in action or a right to the lottery winnings by way of a resulting trust: see *Abrahams v Abrahams, The Times*, 26th July 1999.

CASE EXAMPLE

Abrahams v Abrahams, The Times, 26th July 1999

Mr and Mrs Abrahams paid a weekly subscription of £1 each as members of a lottery syndicate. Mrs A left her husband but continued to make contributions on his behalf. There was no secrecy about the circumstances and extent of her contributions and no syndicate member objected. Mr A subsequently became bankrupt and later the syndicate won the jackpot. Mr A's trustee in bankruptcy claimed Mr A's share of the winnings. This was opposed by Mrs A. The court held that Mrs A had purchased a property right in the name of her husband. The right was to have winnings duly administered in accordance with the rules of the syndicate. Accordingly, Mr A's share of the winnings was held in trust for Mrs A.

8.4.2 Voluntary transfer in the name of another

Where the legal title to property is voluntarily (without consideration) transferred to another and there is no indication as to the destination of the equitable interest, the transaction may give rise to a presumed resulting trust. It is necessary to distinguish personalty from realty.

In relation to personalty, the voluntary nature of the transfer of the legal title and the uncertainty in the location of the equitable interest are sufficient to trigger the presumed resulting trust in favour of the transferor.

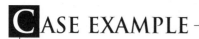CASE EXAMPLE

Re Vinogradoff [1935] WN 68

A grandmother voluntarily transferred £800 worth of war loan stock into the joint names of herself and her granddaughter, then aged four. The grandmother continued to receive the dividends until her death. By her will, the grandmother transferred her interest in the stock to another. On her death, leaving her will unchanged, the question arose as to the beneficial ownership of the stock. The court held that a presumed resulting trust for the grandmother's estate was created and there was no evidence to rebut the presumption.

In respect of realty, prior to the enactment of the Law of Property Act 1925 a voluntary conveyance had the effect of creating a presumed resulting trust in favour of the grantor. To prevent the resulting trust from arising the grantor was required to insert a trust in favour of the grantee. This principle was reversed by s 60(3) of the Law of Property Act 1925.

Section 60(3) of the Law of Property Act 1925 declares:

'In a voluntary conveyance a resulting trust for the grantor shall not be implied merely by reason that the property is not expressed to be conveyed for the use or benefit of the grantee.'

The effect of s 60(3) is to prevent the implication of a resulting trust in favour of transferor by reason only of a voluntary conveyance. However, a presumed resulting trust may still arise in accordance with the intention of the transferor: see *Hodgson v Marks* (1971) (above).

8.4.3 Presumption of advancement

In *Murless v Franklin* (1818) 1 Swanst 13, Lord Eldon enunciated the principle with regard to the presumption of advancement:

> 'The general rule that on a purchase by one man in the name of another, the nominee is a trustee for the purchaser is subject to an exception where the purchaser is under a species of natural obligation to provide for the nominee.'
>
> (Lord Eldon)

In *Bennet v Bennet* (1879) 10 Ch D 474, Jessel MR laid down the modern version of the presumption:

> 'The doctrine of equity as regards presumption of gifts is this, that where one person stands in such a relation to another that there is an obligation on that person to make a provision for the other, and we find either a purchase or investment in the name of the other, or in the joint names of the person and the other, of an amount which could constitute a provision for the other, the presumption arises of an intention on the part of the person to discharge the obligation to the other; and therefore, in the absence of evidence to the contrary, that purchase or investment is held to be in itself evidence of a gift. In other words, the presumption of gift arises from the moral obligation to give.'
>
> (Jessel MR)

A presumption of advancement, as distinct from a presumption of a resulting trust, is a presumption of a gift in favour of the transferee. Where a 'special relationship' exists between the transferor and transferee, a purchase of property in the name of another or the voluntary transfer of real or personal property in another's name gives rise to a presumption of a gift. Thus, the transferor is presumed to lose his beneficial interest in the property.

This presumption, like the presumption of a resulting trust, may be rebutted by evidence of the intention of the transferor.

The special relationship with the transferee produces occasions which, in the past, the courts had recognised as giving rise to an obligation on the part of the transferor to provide or support the transferee.

These are occasions where:

- the transferee is the wife of the transferor
- a transfer is made by a father to his legitimate child
- the transferor stands *in loco parentis patris* to the child: see *Re Paradise Motor Co* [1968] 1 WLR 1125.

Transfers by husband to his wife

A presumption of advancement arises when a husband transfers real or personal property to his wife. In other words, a husband may be construed as making a gift to his wife by purchasing property in her name or voluntarily conveying property to her.

> J
> 'The law of this court is perfectly settled that where a husband transfers money or other property into the name of his wife only, then the presumption is that it is intended as a gift or advancement to the wife absolutely.'
>
> (Malins VC: Re Eykyn's Trusts (1877) 6 Ch D 115)

The presumption does not arise if the parties are not married or where the wife transfers property in the name of her husband. In these circumstances the general rule concerning the presumption of a resulting trust will arise. The presumption of advancement has been severely weakened since the 1940s as a result of the socio–economic and cultural changes concerning married couples: see later.

Transfers by fathers to their legitimate children

A voluntary transfer of property or a purchase of property by a father in the name of his legitimate child is presumed to create a gift in favour of the child. The reason for this is that the father is under a moral obligation to care for his child.

> J
> 'the father is under [an] obligation from the mere fact of his being the father, and therefore no evidence is necessary to show the obligation to provide for his child, because that is part of his duty. In the case of a father, you have only to prove the fact that he is the father, and when you have done that the obligation at once arises.'
>
> (Jessel MR: Bennet v Bennet (1879) 10 Ch D 474)

This presumption is treated as extremely weighty and is not rebutted by slight evidence.

CASE EXAMPLE

Shephard v Cartwright [1955] AC 431.

The claimants' father transferred a number of shares in the names of his legitimate children. The children, under instructions from their father, signed documents without understanding their effect. These documents permitted the father to sell the shares and ultimately withdraw and dissipate the funds from their bank accounts. Following the death of the father the children claimed an account from the estate. The court held in favour of the children. A presumption of advancement had arisen and was not rebutted.

However, the presumption of advancement does not arise where the child transfers property in the name of their father. The general rule of resulting trust operates here. The child therefore is presumed to retain the beneficial interest.

Transfers by persons who stand *in loco parentis*

In accordance with the general rule, a presumption of resulting trust operates when a mother transfers property in the name of her child. In *Bennet v Bennet* (1879) 10 Ch D 474, a transfer of £3,000 from a mother to her son was treated as giving rise to a loan.

> **J** 'as regards a child, a person, not the father of the child, may put himself in the position of one *in loco parentis* to the child, and so incur the obligation to make provision for the child … in the case of a person *in loco parentis* you must prove that he took upon himself the obligation.'
>
> (Jessel MR)

But where a person stands in the shoes of a male parent (*in loco parentis patris*) and transfers property to his surrogate child, a presumption of advancement arises.

The question as to whether a person stands *in loco parentis* is a question of degree. The person is required to undertake the duties of parenthood and in particular a male parent. To this extent only a person of the male gender who undertakes the responsibility to care for the child will satisfy the test.

> **J** 'A person *in loco parentis* means a person taking upon himself the duty of a father of a child to make provision for that child. It is clear that the presumption can only arise from that obligation, and therefore the doctrine can only have reference to the obligation of a father to provide for his child, and nothing else.'
>
> (Jessel MR)

In *Re Paradise Motor Co* (1968), the transferor, a stepfather, treated his stepson as his own. He transferred shares to the stepson and this was treated as giving rise to a presumption of advancement.

8.4.4 Rebuttal of the presumptions

The presumptions of resulting trusts and advancement are capable of being rebutted by evidence that establish the true intention of the transferor. The weight of the presumptions will vary with the facts of each case and the court will consider all the circumstances of the case.

CASE EXAMPLE

Fowkes v Pascoe (1875) LR 10 Ch App 343

A testatrix bought stock which she put into the joint names of herself and Pascoe. In her will she left her residuary estate to her daughter-in-law and then to Pascoe and his sister. The question in issue was whether the stock formed part of the residuary estate. The court decided the presumption of resulting trust had arisen initially but on the facts the presumption was rebutted. The testatrix intended to make a gift to Pascoe. There was sufficient evidence that the testatrix was a wealthy woman, she was clearly fond of Pascoe and considered herself as having no near relations.

- In *Lord Grey v Lady Grey* (1677) 2 Swan 594, the court decided that the presumption of advancement was not rebutted when a son allowed a father to receive income from land, the subject-matter of the transfer. Such conduct amounted to reverence and good manners.

- In *Shephard v Cartwright* (1955) (see above) the court decided that the children's conduct in signing documents under the instructions and control of their father was not admissible in order to rebut the presumption of advancement.

- In *Re Paradise Motor Co* (1968) (see above) the verbal disclaimer by a stepchild of rights to shares amounted to a rebuttal of the presumption of advancement.

ACTIVITY

Evaluate the status of the presumptions of resulting trusts and advancement in contemporary society.

8.4.5 Intended unlawful activity and rebuttal evidence

A transferor may voluntarily convey property to a nominee in an attempt to implement some unlawful activity, such as to avoid his creditors. Later the transferor repents, withdraws from the illegal purpose and wishes to claim the property back from the nominee. The issue is whether the claimant ought to be allowed to recover the property in the light of his impropriety concerning the original transfer. In effect, should the claimant be allowed to rely on the presumption of resulting trust?

In *Tinker v Tinker* [1970] 1 All ER 540, the court applied the maxim 'He who comes to equity must come with clean hands', and prohibited the adduction of evidence of the true intention of the transferor.

CASE EXAMPLE

Tinker v Tinker [1970] 1 All ER 540

A husband transferred the matrimonial home to his wife in order to defeat his creditors, should his business fail. His business flourished but his wife claimed the house as hers. The court decided that the presumption of advancement arose in favour of the wife and the husband was not entitled to rebut the presumption by adducing evidence of his own impropriety.

The law was reviewed by the House of Lords in *Tinsley v Milligan* [1994] 1 AC 340. It was decided that if a party does not rely on the illegality in order to establish a claim to an equitable interest, the illegality is no bar to a successful action. In other words, if the claimant enjoys an equitable interest by way of a resulting trust, his subsequent illegality is not decisive.

CASE EXAMPLE

Tinsley v Milligan [1994] 1 AC 340

The defendant transferred property into the name of her friend, the claimant in order to facilitate a fraud on the Department of Social Security. Both litigants were parties to the fraud which was carried on for a few years. The parties fell out and the claimant sought to evict the defendant from the property. The defendant claimed that the property was held on trust for both parties in equal shares. The House of Lords decided in favour of the defendant. The court ruled that where a party based her claim on title to property (whether legal or equitable) that was acquired in the course of an illegal transaction, that party may recover the property so long as she was not forced to plead, or rely on, the illegality. In this case the presumption of a resulting trust applied. Consequently, the defendant did not have to rely on the illegality since she only had to establish a contribution to the purchase price.

> 'The presumption of a resulting trust is, in my view, crucial in considering the authorities. On that presumption (and on the contrary presumption of advancement) hinges the answer to the crucial question "does a plaintiff claiming under a resulting trust have to rely on the underlying illegality?". Where the presumption of resulting trust applies, the plaintiff does not have to rely on the illegality. If he proves that the property is vested in the defendant alone but that the plaintiff provided part of the purchase money, or voluntarily transferred the property to the defendant, the plaintiff establishes his claim under a resulting trust unless either the contrary presumption of advancement displaces the presumption of resulting trust or the defendant leads evidence to rebut the presumption of resulting trust.'
>
> (Lord Browne-Wilkinson)

In *Tinsley v Milligan* (1994) it would appear that a party may be entitled to assert his equitable interest in the property by relying on the presumption of a resulting trust, if he withdraws from the intended unlawful activity. On the other hand, if the presumption of advancement operates against the claimant so that he is required to rebut the presumption in order to establish an equitable interest in the property the claimant may be prohibited from adducing evidence of his illegality:

> **J**
>
> 'In cases where the presumption of advancement applies, the plaintiff is faced with the presumption of gift and therefore cannot claim under a resulting trust unless and until he has rebutted that presumption of gift: for those purposes the plaintiff does have to rely on the underlying illegality and therefore fails.'
>
> (Lord Browne-Wilkinson)

However, in *Tribe v Tribe* [1995] 4 All ER 236, the Court of Appeal seemed to have extended *Tinsley v Milligan* (1994) by allowing the illegal purpose to be used to rebut the presumption of advancement.

CASE EXAMPLE

Tribe v Tribe [1995] 4 All ER 236

The claimant owned 459 out of 500 shares in a company. He was the tenant of a number of clothing shops which were occupied by the company as a licensee. The landlords of two of the shops served dilapidation notices on the claimant, requiring him to carry out substantial repairs to the property. He was advised that if these claims were valid, he might be forced to sell the company or dispose of his shares. In order to avoid this, he transferred the shares to one of his sons for an alleged consideration of £79,995. It was never intended that this amount would be paid. The dispute with the landlords was subsequently resolved and the claimant requested a re-transfer of the shares from his son. The son refused. The court decided in favour of the father.

> **J**
>
> '... a person who seeks to recover property transferred by him for an illegal purpose can lead evidence of his dishonest intention whenever it is necessary for him to do so provided that he has withdrawn from the transaction before the illegal purpose has been carried out.'
>
> (Millett LJ)

■Key facts on resulting trusts

KEY FACTS

Automatic resulting trusts	
• Failure of an intended express trust	*Re Ames* (1946); *Vandervell v IRC* (1967)
• Transfers subject to conditions precedent which fail to materialise	*Barclays Bank v Quistclose* (1970); *Carreras Rothmans v Freeman Matthews Ltd* (1984); *Re EVTR* (1987); *Twinsectra v Yardley* (2002)
• Surplus of trust funds	*Re Abbott* (1900); *Re Gillingham Bus Disaster Fund* (1958)
• Surplus beneficial interest acquired by beneficiary	*Re Andrew's Trust* (1905); *Re Osoba* (1979)
• Dissolution of unincorporated associations: 'dissolution'	*Re William Denby Benevolent Fund* (1971); *Re GKN Bolts & Nuts* (1982)
'unincorporated associations'	*Conservative and Unionist Central Office v Burrell* (1982)
	Re Bucks Constabulary Fund (No 2) (1979)
• Resulting trust	*Re Printers and Transferrers Society* (1899); *Re Houbourn Air Raid Distress Fund* (1946)
• Contract	*Cunnack v Edwards* (1896); *Re West Sussex Constabulary Fund* (1971); *Re Bucks Constabulary Fund* (1979); *Re Sick and Funeral Society v Golcar* (1973)

CONTINUED ▸

KEY FACTS

Presumed resulting trusts	
• Purchase of property in the name of another	*Dyer v Dyer* (1788); *Abrahams v Abrahams* (1999)
• Voluntary transfer of personal property to another	*Re Vinogradoff* (1935)
• Section 60(3) LPA 1925	*Hodgson v Marks* (1971)
• Exception – presumptions of advancement	
• transfers by a husband to his wife	*Tinker v Tinker* (1970)
• transfers by fathers to their legitimate children	*Shephard v Cartwright* (1955)
• transfers by persons who stand *in loco parentis patris*	*Re Paradise Motor Co Ltd* (1968)
• Rebuttal of presumptions	*Fowkes v Pascoe* (1875)
• Intended unlawful activity and rebuttal evidence	*Tinker v Tinker* (1970); *Tinsley v Milligan* (1994); *Tribe v Tribe* (1995)

ACTIVITY

How far are the presumptions of resulting trusts and advancement significant in the context of property transferred to another subject to the unfulfilled intention of defeating creditors?

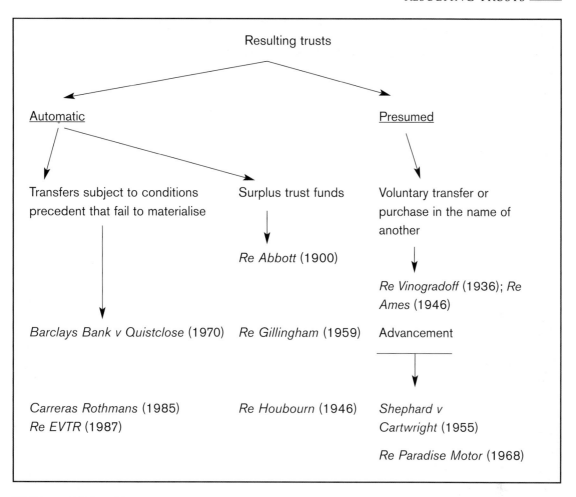

■ *Figure 8.1 Resulting trusts*

Further reading

Cotterill, I, 'Property and Impropriety – The *Tinsley v Milligan* Problem Again' (1999) LMCLQ 465.

Creighton, P, 'The recovery of property transferred for illegal purposes' (1997) 60 MLR 102.

Ho L, and Smart, P S J, 'Reinterpreting the *Quistclose* Trust: A critique of Chambers' Analysis' (2001) 210 JLS 267.

Millett, P, 'The *Quistclose* trust: who can enforce it?' (1985) 101 LQR 269.

Pettit, P, 'Illegality and repentance' (1996) 10 Tru LI 51.

Rickett, C, 'Unincorporated associations and their dissolution' [1980] CLJ 88.

Rose, F, 'Gratuitous transfers and illegal purposes' (1996) 112 LQR 386.

Swadling, W, 'A new role for resulting trusts' (1996) 16 LS 110.

chapter 9 CONSTRUCTIVE TRUSTS ■

9.1 Introduction

A constructive trust is an implied trust created by the courts in the interests of fairness and justice. This type of trust attaches to specific property, held by a person in circumstances where it would be inequitable to allow him to assert full beneficial ownership of the property. The trust is categorised as a residual type of trust which is called into play whenever the court desires to create a trust that does not correspond to any other category. The trust may be imposed on express trustees and other fiduciaries in respect of the receipt of any unauthorised benefit. In addition, the trust may be imposed on strangers or third parties who intermeddle with the affairs of the trust. Thus, a stranger or third party who receives property subject to a fiduciary relationship, and who has actual or constructive knowledge that it is trust property that has been transferred to him in breach of trust or fiduciary duties, will be a constructive trustee of that property. If the constructive trustee becomes bankrupt the property is not available for his general creditors but for the beneficiaries in whose favour the constructive trust operates. In addition, the limitation periods for bringing a claim do not operate.

9.2 Constructive trusts/duty to account

The expression 'constructive trust' is sometimes used in a different sense, in that no specific property is subject to the trust. But the defendant is treated constructively as if he is a trustee so that he is personally liable to account to the claimants for any losses or gains resulting from his misconduct. The effect is that a claim *in personam* arises in favour of the beneficiary. This type of 'constructive trust' concerns, in reality, a personal liability to account. The limitation periods for bringing claims apply to such actions and if the fiduciary becomes bankrupt the beneficiaries do not acquire priority over his ordinary creditors.

Lord Millett in *Paragon Finance plc v Thakerar* [1999] 1 All ER 410 referred to the two interpretations of constructive trusts:

J

'The expressions "constructive trust" and "constructive trustee" have been used by equity lawyers to describe two entirely different situations. The first covers those cases where the defendant, though not expressly appointed as trustee, has assumed the duties of a trustee by a lawful transaction which was independent of and preceded the breach of trust and is not impeached by the plaintiff. The second covers those cases where the trust obligation arises as a direct consequence of the unlawful transaction which is impeached by the plaintiff.

A constructive trust arises by operation of law whenever the circumstances are such that it would be unconscionable for the owner of property (usually but not necessarily the legal estate) to assert his own beneficial interest in the property and deny the beneficial interest of another. In the first class of case, however, the constructive trustee really is a trustee. He does not receive the trust property in his own right but by a transaction by which both parties intend to create a trust from the outset and which is not impugned by the plaintiff. His possession of the property is coloured from the first by the trust and confidence by means of which he obtained it, and his subsequent appropriation of the property to his own use is a breach of that trust. Well known examples of such a constructive trust are *McCormick v Grogan* (1869) LR 4 HL 82 [a case of secret trust] and *Rochefoucald v Boustead* [1897] 1 Ch 196 [where the defendant agreed to buy property for the plaintiff but the trust was imperfectly recorded]. *Pallant v Morgan* [1952] 2 All ER 951 [where the defendant sought to keep for himself property which the plaintiff trusted him to buy for both parties] is another. In these cases the plaintiff does not impugn the transaction by which the defendant obtained control of the property. He alleges that the circumstances in which the defendant obtained control make it unconscionable for him thereafter to assert a beneficial interest in the property.

The second class of case is different. [See *A-G for Hong Kong v Reid* [1994] 1 AC 324.] It arises when the defendant is implicated in a fraud. Equity has always given relief against fraud by making any person sufficiently implicated in the fraud accountable in equity. In such a case he is traditionally, though I think unfortunately described, as a constructive trustee and said to be "liable to account as a constructive trustee". Such a person is not in fact a trustee at all, even though he may be liable to account as if he were. He never assumes the position of a trustee, and if he receives the trust property at all it is adversely to the plaintiff by an unlawful transaction which is impugned by the plaintiff. In such a case the expressions, "constructive trust" and "constructive trustee" are misleading, for there is no trust and usually no possibility of a proprietary remedy; they are nothing more than a formula of equitable relief.

CONTINUED ▸

> J
>
> The importance of the distinction between the two categories of constructive trust lies in the application of the statutes of limitation. Constructive trusts of the first kind are treated in the same way as express trusts and were often confusingly described as such; claims against the trustees were not barred by the passage of time. Constructive trusts of the second kind however were treated differently. They were not in reality trusts at all, but merely a remedial mechanism by which equity gave relief for fraud. The Court of Chancery, which applied the statutes of limitation by analogy, was not misled by its own terminology, it gave effect to the reality of the situation by applying the statute to the fraud which gave rise to the defendant's liability.'
>
> (Lord Millett)

9.3 Institutional and remedial constructive trusts

Constructive trusts are sometimes described as institutional or remedial. An institutional constructive trust is the traditional constructive trust that is declared by the courts retrospectively from the date of the misconduct by the constructive trustees. The courts merely declare the existence of such trust.

A remedial constructive trust is imposed in order to prevent unjust enrichment. This type of trust is essentially a remedy that may be called into play whenever the claimant seeks to recover his property from a fiduciary (or his successors in title) who acts in breach of his duties. In short it is a judicial remedy that gives rise to an enforceable obligation. The court order creates the right with a correlative remedy as opposed to being simply confirmatory.

In *Westdeutsche Landesbank Girozentrale v Islington BC* [1996] AC 669 Lord Browne-Wilkinson described the distinction between institutional and remedial constructive trusts:

> J
>
> Under the institutional constructive trust, the trust arises by operation of law as *from the date when the circumstances give rise to it*. The function of the court is merely to declare that such trust has arisen in the past. The consequences which flow from such trust having arisen (including the possibly unfair consequences to third parties who in the interim receive trust property) are also determined by rules of law, not under discretion. A remedial constructive trust is different. It is a judicial remedy giving rise to an enforceable equitable obligation; the extent to which it operates retrospectively to the prejudice of third parties lies in the discretion of the courts.'
>
> (Lord Browne-Wilkinson)

Moreover, it is equally unwarranted to equate a constructive trust with a resulting trust. In *Hussey v Palmer* [1972] 1 WLR 1286, Denning MR declared that a constructive trust exists as a remedy. In the United States of America, the constructive trust is treated as a remedy which is defined in terms of preventing unjust enrichment. In English law, quasi-contractual remedies based on the prevention of unjust enrichment are available and traditionally, the constructive trust has been treated as a substantive right. However, Denning MR attempted to equate English law with the law in the United States of America.

> J
>
> '[The constructive trust] is an equitable remedy by which the court can enable an aggrieved party to obtain restitution.'
>
> (Denning MR)

In the UK, remedies exist in quasi-contract which are based on unjust enrichment. It is arguable that the use of the constructive trust to provide a remedy is not justifiable. This is the predominant view of the English courts. This is reflected in the judgment of Peter Gibson LJ in *Halifax Building Society v Thomas* [1996] 2 WLR 63.

CASE EXAMPLE

Halifax Building Society v Thomas [1996] 2 WLR 63

The defendant obtained a mortgage by a fraudulent misrepresentation of a building society. He fell into arrears and after the property was sold, a surplus remained. The society claimed the surplus by way of a constructive trust, in order to prevent the defendant from profiting from his fraud. The court rejected this claim, on the ground that a remedial constructive trust does not exist in English law.

> J
>
> 'English law has not followed other jurisdictions where the constructive trust has become a remedy for unjust enrichment. As is said in *Snell's Equity*, 29th edn, 1990, p 197: In England the constructive trust has in general remained essentially a substantive institution; ownership must not be confused with obligation, nor must the relationship of debtor and creditor be converted into one of trustee and *cestui que* trust.'
>
> (Peter Gibson LJ)

9.4 Recognised categories of constructive trusts

9.4.1 Trustee or fiduciary making unauthorised profit

A trustee or fiduciary is not allowed to put himself in a position where his duty and interest may conflict. Moreover if there is such a conflict, any profit or benefit obtained by the trustee or fiduciary is required to be transferred to the beneficiary.

CASE EXAMPLE

Keech v Sandford [1726] Sel Cas Ch 61

The defendant, an express trustee, held the profits of a lease of Romford market on trust for a minor. Before the expiration of the lease, the defendant requested a renewal of the lease in favour of the beneficiary personally, but this was refused. The trustee than attempted to renew the lease in his capacity as trustee for the infant but this was also refused. The lessor agreed to renew the lease in favour of the trustee personally and this was done. A claim was brought on behalf of the beneficiaries. The court held that the profits of the renewed lease were held on constructive trust in favour of the beneficiaries. The court declared that the trustee was the only person of all mankind who was not entitled to have the benefit of the lease. But it was crucial that the rule be strictly adhered to for it was obvious what would be the consequences of letting trustees have the lease, on refusal to renew in favour of the beneficiary. The trustees were in control of the property and could, in theory, have obtained sensitive information about the property which is concealed from the public.

In effect, the claimant is required to establish each of the following three elements:

(a) the defendant holds a fiduciary position *vis-à-vis* the claimant

(b) the defendant obtained a benefit derived from the property and

(c) there is a causal connection between the relationship and the benefit.

9.4.2 Fiduciary relationship

A fiduciary is an individual who is aware that his judgment and confidence is relied on, and has been relied on, by the claimant in some particular matter. This concept is extremely wide and is interpreted fairly flexibly by the courts. Material factors are whether the parties stand on an equal footing, whether there has been an abuse of one's position and whether there has been full disclosure between the parties. Obvious fiduciary relationships include trustee/beneficiary, principal/agent, director/company, partner/co-partners. Ultimately, the question is one of fact and degree.

- In *Reading v A-G* [1951] AC 507 the court decided that a uniformed officer in the Armed Forces was a fiduciary in respect of unauthorised benefits received.

- Likewise, in *English v Dedham Vale Properties* [1978] 1 WLR 93 a fiduciary relationship was created in respect of a purchaser of land who abused his position by pretending to have the vendor's permission to apply for and obtain planning permission in respect of the property. But in *Swain v Law Society* [1982] 3 WLR 261, it was decided that the Law Society was not in a fiduciary relationship with respect to members of the solicitors' profession.

A fiduciary is expected to act in the interests of the other, to act selflessly and with undivided loyalty.

A definition of a fiduciary was offered by Millett LJ in *Bristol and West BS v Mothew* [1996] 4 All ER 698 as follows:

> **J** 'A fiduciary is someone who has undertaken to act for or on behalf of another in a particular matter in circumstances which give rise to a relationship of trust and confidence. The distinguishing obligation of a fiduciary is the obligation of loyalty. The principal is entitled to the single minded loyalty of his fiduciary. This core liability has several facets. A fiduciary must act in good faith; he must not make a profit of his trust; he must not place himself in a position where his duty and interest may conflict; he may not act for his own benefit or the benefit of a third person without the informed consent of his principal. This is not intended to be an exhaustive list but it is sufficient to indicate the nature of fiduciary obligations. They are defining characteristics of the fiduciary.'

9.4.3 Unauthorised remuneration or financial benefit received by trustee or fiduciary

In *Boardman v Phipps* [1967] 2 AC 46, a solicitor to a trust was treated as a fiduciary and accountable to the trust in respect of profits received.

CASE EXAMPLE

Boardman v Phipps [1967] 2 AC 46

Mr Boardman, a solicitor to a trust, was a fiduciary when he received confidential information concerning the company that assisted in him obtaining control of the company and re-organising it. Although he acted in good faith he was liable to account as a constructive trustee for the profits made. The opportunity to make the profit arose by virtue of his fiduciary relationship with the trust. On behalf of Mr Boardman it was argued that information concerning the trust was incapable of being treated as trust property. The court rejected this argument and decided that the confidential information acquired in this case which was capable of being and was turned to account can be properly regarded as the property of the trust. However, the court awarded him generous remuneration in recognition of his outstanding contribution to the trust.

ASE EXAMPLE

Banner Homes v Luff [2000] 2 WLR 772

Two rival bidders made an arrangement concerning the purchase of property. The defendant conducted itself in a way inconsistent with the agreement, and in an inequitable manner. The court decided that a constructive trust (or a duty to account) arose in the circumstances. It was essential that the circumstances made it inequitable for the acquiring party to retain the property for himself in a manner inconsistent with the arrangement or understanding on which the non-acquiring party had acted.

ASE EXAMPLE

Williams v Barton [1927] 2 Ch 9

Mr Barton, one of two trustees, received commission as a stockbroker's clerk when he introduced the trust to his firm of stockbrokers. Mr Barton took no part in the work of valuation. The co-trustee now claimed to recover the commission on behalf of the trust. The court held that despite the valuation was quite proper in the circumstances, Mr Barton was required to account for the commission because the opportunity to earn the reward derived from his position as trustee.

9.4.4 Bribes or secret profits received by fiduciaries

When a bribe is received in money or in kind, the money or property constituting the bribe belongs in law to the recipient, ie the property in the bribe passes to the recipient of the bribe in accordance with the intention of the parties. Equity, however, acts *in personam* and insists that it is unconscionable for a fiduciary to obtain and retain a benefit in breach of duty. Thus, he is under a duty to pay and account for the bribe to the person to whom that duty was owed. If, however, the bribe consists of property which increases in value, or if a cash bribe is invested advantageously, the fiduciary is accountable not only for the original amount or value of the bribe but also for the increased value of the property representing the bribe. As soon as the bribe was received it should have been paid or transferred instantly to the person who suffered from the breach of duty. Equity considers as done that which ought to have been done. As soon as the bribe was received, whether in cash or in kind, the fiduciary holds it on a constructive trust for the person injured. If the property representing the bribe decreases in value, the fiduciary must pay the difference between that value and the initial amount of the bribe, because he should not have accepted the bribe or incurred the risk of loss. In addition, if the fiduciary becomes insolvent his unsecured creditors will be deprived of their right to share in the proceeds of that property, for the unsecured creditors cannot be in a better position than their debtor. This result was achieved in *A-G for Hong Kong v Reid* [1994] 1 All ER 1.

CASE EXAMPLE

A-G for Hong Kong v Reid [1994] 1 All ER 1

The DPP of Hong Kong received bribes which were invested in properties in New Zealand. The Attorney-General for Hong Kong brought an action for an account in respect of bribes received by Mr Reid and a declaration that the properties in New Zealand were held on trust for the Government of Hong Kong. In the meantime the value of the properties had decreased in value. The question in issue concerned the status of a fiduciary who received a bribe, in particular, whether such a fiduciary became a mere debtor for the innocent party or alternatively a trustee for the aggrieved party. The defendants mounted an argument claiming that the fiduciary became a debtor for the innocent party and had no equitable interest in the properties, relying on the Court of Appeal decision in *Lister v Stubbs* (1890) 45 Ch D 1. The claimants asserted that the decision in *Lister v Stubbs* (1890) should not be followed, as it was inconsistent with basic equitable principles. The Privy Council decided in favour of the claimant on the ground that the bribe and representative property acquired by the fiduciary were subject to the claims of the injured party. Since the representative property had decreased in value, the fiduciary was liable to account for the difference between the bribe and the undervalue.

9.4.5 Trustee-director's remuneration

The requirement of a share qualification of a director may be provided for in the articles of association. If the trustee uses the shareholding of the trust to secure his appointment as a director, he is accountable to the trust for the remuneration received, in the absence of authority. This is the position, despite the payment being made for services as director of the company. If the opportunity to receive the remuneration was gained as a result of the conduct of the trustee, then he would have put himself in a position where his interest and duty conflicted.

CASE EXAMPLE

Re Macadam [1946] Ch 73

The articles of a company provided that the trustees of a will had a power to appoint two persons to directorships. The trustees appointed themselves directors and received remuneration. The court held that they were liable to account to the trust for the directors' fees received from the company.

But if the defendant is appointed a director before he acquires the trust shares or secures his appointment as director by the use of shares held in his personal capacity, he is not accountable to the trust.

CASE EXAMPLE

Re Gee [1948] Ch 284

The issued capital of a private company, Gee & Co Ltd, was 5,000 £1 shares. Immediately before his death, Alfred Gee (the testator) was the registered holder of 4,996 shares in Gee & Co. The remaining four shareholders, who held one share each, were: Miss Gee (the testator's sister); the testator's wife; his daughter, Mrs Hunter; and his son-in-law, Mr Staples. By his will, the testator appointed his wife, Mrs Hunter and Mr Staples to be his executors and trustees after his death. After the death of the testator and before his will was probated, Mr Staples was appointed managing director of the company by the unanimous agreement of the three executors and Miss Gee, who together constituted all the registered beneficial shareholders at that time. Mr Staples agreed to act as director of the company, and received £15,721 as remuneration for the 10 years that he managed the company. The beneficiaries under the will now claimed that Mr Staples was liable to account for the profit. The court rejected the claim and decided that Mr Staples was not accountable because he was appointed a director unanimously by the shareholders for qualities independent of the trust votes. The trust votes were not brought into play to secure his appointment.

J   'After the death of the testator, only four persons remained on the register of this company, and they alone could attend meetings of it. As I have said before, the meeting of 6th January 1938, was attended by all the corporators. Each of them held one share, and as the resolutions were passed unanimously, they must be supposed to have voted in favour by the use of that share. If the corporators, as I think, held their shares beneficially, they were entitled to vote as they chose. If, on the other hand, they were nominees of the testator, there were still three of them whose votes outweighed the vote of Mr Staples if it was his duty to vote against his own interest. In neither event did the trust shares come into the picture at all.'

(Harman J)

9.4.6 Occasions when a trustee may receive remuneration
Authority in the trust instrument

Trustees may negotiate with the settlor to be paid for their services. Such clauses are frequently included where a professional trustee is appointed. Charging clauses are construed strictly against the trustee. However, s 28 of the Trustee Act 2000 introduced a degree of flexibility with charging clauses for professionals. The section enacts that in the case of a express charging clause if the trustee is a trust corporation or acts in a professional capacity, the trustee is entitled to be paid even if the services are capable of being provided by a lay person. On the occasions when trustees are entitled to be paid under charging clauses they are entitled to charge only a reasonable amount.

Statutory authority

Section 29 of the Trustee Act 2000 creates an implied power of payment on the part of professional trustees. A trust corporation is entitled to receive reasonable remuneration for services provided. A professional trustee who is neither a trust corporation nor a sole trustee is entitled to receive reasonable remuneration if the other trustees agree in writing. The reason for the exclusion of the sole trustee is to promote objectivity concerning this decision. The implied authority to remuneration does not apply to trustees of a charitable trust.

In addition, by virtue of s 42 of the Trustee Act 1925, where the court appoints a corporation to be a trustee it (the court) may authorise the corporation to charge such remuneration for its services as the court may think fit.

Reimbursements

Section 31 of the Trustee Act 2000 (which repeals and replaces s 30(2) of the Trustee Act 1925) entitles trustees to be reimbursed for expenses properly incurred when acting on behalf of the trust. Whether an expense was properly incurred would depend on general principles and the circumstances surrounding the expense.

Authority of the court

The court will only authorise reasonable remuneration for services performed by trustees which are of exceptional benefit to the trust. In *Boardman v Phipps* (1967), generous remuneration was awarded by the court for the efforts of the appellants.

Moreover, the court is entitled to increase the amount of the remuneration as laid down in the charging clause: see *Re Duke of Norfolk's Settlement Trusts* [1981] 3 All ER 220.

ASE EXAMPLE

Foster v Spencer, *The Times*, 14th June, 1995

The court decided that, in the exercise of its inherent jurisdiction, trustees of a cricket club were entitled to remuneration for past services, but not to future remuneration. The trustees were extremely active in bringing about a sale of the site for a reasonable price. The decisive factors were:

(i) there were no funds out of which to pay remuneration at the time of the appointment of the trustees

(ii) the refusal of the claim to remuneration would have resulted in the beneficiaries being unjustly enriched at the expense of the trustees

(iii) there was no true appreciation of the extent of the task at the time of appointment. Had the trustees realised what they were in for, they would have declined to act unless remunerated in some way.

Agreement with all the beneficiaries

If all the beneficiaries are *sui juris* and absolutely entitled to the trust property, they may agree to remunerate the trustees. It is essential that the beneficiaries act independently and without any undue influence from the trustees.

The rule in *Cradock v Piper* (1850) 1 Mac & G 664

A trustee/solicitor may act as a solicitor for himself and co-trustee in litigation involving the trust and may recover the costs for acting on behalf of his co-trustee. This anomalous rule is restricted to litigious work and may not be extended beyond the relationship of trustee/solicitor.

The rule in *Re Northcote* [1949] 1 All ER 442

The principle is that English executors and trustees, who are entitled to earn a commission under a foreign jurisdiction in which the trust assets are situated, are empowered to retain such remuneration for their own benefit.

ASE EXAMPLE

Re Northcote [1949] 1 All ER 442

A testator, domiciled in England, died leaving assets in England and the United States. His executors obtained a grant of probate in England. They also obtained a grant in New York in respect of the American assets. They collected the American assets and were entitled to agency commission under the law of that state. The question in issue was whether they were accountable for the commission. The court held that the executors were not accountable.

9.4.7 Purchases of trust property (rule against self-dealing)

The courts have developed a rule prohibiting trustees and other fiduciaries, without authority, from purchasing the trust property. If the purchase takes place the transaction is treated as voidable at the instance of the beneficiaries.

> '... the purchase is not permitted in any case, however honest the circumstances; the general interests of justice requiring it to be destroyed in every instance ...'
>
> (Lord Eldon: *Ex p James* (1803) 8 Ves 337)

Reasons commonly associated with this harsh rule are that the trustees would otherwise be both vendors and purchasers and it would be difficult to ascertain whether an unfair advantage had been obtained by the trustees. In addition, the property may become virtually unmarketable since the title may indicate that the property was at one time trust property. Third parties may have notice of this fact and any disputes concerning the trust property may affect their interest. The aggrieved beneficiary is required to act within a reasonable time in order to avoid the sale. The rule cannot be avoided by conveying the property to a nominee of the trustees for the court will consider all the circumstances to ascertain whether an unfair advantage has been acquired by the trustees.

CASE EXAMPLE

Wright v Morgan [1926] AC 788

A testator by his will gave his son, Harry Herbert, the option to purchase a plot of land provided that the price was fixed by an independent valuer. Harry was also a trustee under the will. Harry assigned the option to Douglas Wright, his co-trustee and brother, but who was not authorised to purchase the property. Douglas retired from the trust and purported to exercise the option at a price fixed by the valuers. The beneficiaries under the will brought an action to set aside the sale. The court held that the sale ought to be set aside on the ground of a conflict of duty and interest.

CASE EXAMPLE

Regal (Hastings) Ltd v Gulliver [1942] 1 All ER 378

Regal Ltd received an offer from one of Its subsidiaries to sell to Regal a quantity of shares. Regal did not have the specified amount of funds but four of Its directors subscribed for the shares personally and later sold them for a profit. It was found as a fact that all the transactions were *bona fide*. Regal now claimed that the directors were accountable for their profit. The House of Lords held that the directors were accountable to the company.

> **J** 'I am of opinion that the directors standing in a fiduciary relationship to Regal in regard to the exercise of their powers as directors, and having obtained these shares by reason and only by reason of the fact that they were directors of Regal and in the course of the execution of that office, are accountable for the profits which they have made out of them. The equitable rule laid down in *Keech v Sandford* and *Ex p James*, and similar authorities applies to them in full force.'
>
> (Lord Russell)

CASE EXAMPLE

Industrial Development Consultants v Cooley [1972] 1 WLR 443

The defendant was the managing director of the claimant company. He was approached by the Chairman of the Eastern Gas Board to work for them, although at the time the claimant company was interested in a project for the Gas Board. In his capacity as managing director, he had obtained special knowledge which should have been passed on to the claimant company. Concealing this knowledge, he obtained his release from the service of the claimant, basing his request on alleged ill health. The claimant would not have released him had it known the full facts. The claimant sued the director alleging that he was a trustee of profits of his new contract on behalf of the claimant. The court held in favour of the claimant in view of the conflict of duty and interest in failing to pass on the information to the claimant.

Although the general principle of avoiding a conflict of duty and interest is applied strictly by the courts, there are exceptional circumstances when a fiduciary may retain an unauthorised benefit. Each case is determined on its own facts. In *Holder v Holder* [1968] Ch 353, the Court of Appeal found a number of exceptional circumstances that entitled an executor to retain a benefit.

CASE EXAMPLE

Holder v Holder [1968] Ch 353

The testator appointed his widow, daughter and one of his sons, Victor, to be his executors and trustees. Victor at first took a few minor steps in connection with the administration of the estate (signing cheques, etc) but then abstained from taking any further part in the administration. One of the assets of the estate included a farm. Victor had acquired no special knowledge of the farm in his capacity as executor and all his knowledge about the farm was acquired as a tenant of that farm. The farm was then offered for sale at an auction, subject to Victor's tenancy. At the auction, Victor made a successful bid for the farm. Another son applied to the court for the sale to be set aside. The court held that the sale ought not be set aside for the following reasons:

- Victor had not instructed the valuer nor had he arranged the auction. Thus, Victor could not be construed as both a vendor and purchaser.

- Victor had never assumed the duties of executor, for he had done virtually nothing in the administration of the estate, nor had Victor any influence on the two other executors in respect of the sale.

- In any case, Victor had made no secret of his intention to buy the farm and had paid a good price for the property.

- Victor was not relied upon by other beneficiaries to protect their interests.

> **J** 'In this case Victor's ... interference with the administration of the estate was of a minimal character and the last cheque he signed was in August before he executed the deed of renunciation. He took no part in the instructions for probate, nor in the valuations or fixing of the reserves. Everyone concerned knew of the renunciation and of the reason for it, namely, that he wished to be a purchaser.'
>
> (Harman LJ)

A similar principle applies in respect of the purchase by the trustee of the beneficiary's interest. This is known as the 'fair dealing' rule. The test here is whether the beneficiary was capable of exercising an independent judgement after full disclosure by the trustee. The presumption is that the trustee exercised undue influence on the beneficiary. The burden of proof is therefore on the trustee to rebut this presumption. In disputed cases the trustee is required to establish that the contract with the beneficiary is distinct and clear, after a jealous and scrupulous examination of all the circumstances, proving that the beneficiary intended the trustee to purchase his interest; and that there was no fraud, no concealment, no advantage taken, by the trustee of information, acquired by him in the character of trustee. This is a question of degree.

9.5 Contracts for the sale of land

It is a fundamental principle of property law that when a contract for the sale of land is made but the sale had not been completed, the vendor becomes a constructive trustee for the purchaser from the date of the exchange of the contract until the date of completion for 'Equity regards as done that which ought to be done'. On the date of the completion of the contract the legal title to the property is acquired by the purchaser, but in the interim period the beneficiary acquires a proprietary interest commencing on the date of the creation of the contract.

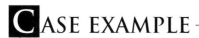 **CASE EXAMPLE**

> *Lysaght v Edwards* (1876) 2 Ch D 499
>
> Edwards agreed in writing to sell real property to the claimant but, before completion, Edwards died. By his will, he devised his real property to trustees on trust to sell and invest the proceeds of sale. On a claim by the purchaser for an order requiring the executors to complete the sale the court decided in favour of the purchaser, on the ground that on the date of the creation of the contract, the equitable title to the property was acquired by the purchaser by operation of law.

9.6 Equity will not allow a statute to be used as an engine for fraud

The court is entitled to suspend the operation of a statutory provision if insistence on its strict compliance will have the tendency to perpetuate a fraud. The court will not sit back and acquiesce in a defendant abusing his position by committing a fraud on the claimant in reliance on a statutory formal provision.

CASE EXAMPLE

> *Rochefoucauld v Boustead* [1897] 1 Ch 196
>
> The claimant was the mortgagor of several estates but found himself in financial difficulty. The defendant purchased the properties from the mortgagee and orally agreed to hold them on trust for the claimant, subject to the repayment to the defendant of the purchase price and expenses. The defendant sold the estates and later became bankrupt. The

CONTINUED ▸

claimant sued the trustee in bankruptcy for an account. The trustee in bankruptcy alleged that the oral agreement was not enforceable as the predecessor to s 53(1)(b) of the Law of Property Act 1925 (namely s 7 of the Statute of Frauds 1677) was not complied with and the claimant had no interest in the proceeds of sale. The court decided in favour of the claimant on the ground that it will not allow s 7 of the Statute of Frauds 1677 to be used as an engine for fraud. It would be a fraud for a person to whom land is conveyed on trust, to deny the trust and claim the land as his own. Even if there was insufficient evidence to constitute a memorandum in order to satisfy s 7 of the 1677 Act, parol evidence was admissible to establish that the defendant bought the properties as trustee.

■Key facts on constructive trusts – duty to account

KEY FACTS

Trustee (fiduciary) making unauthorised profits [to prevent unjust enrichment]	*Keech v Sandford* (1726); *Boardman v Phipps* (1967); *Banner Homes v Luff* (2000)
Secret profits received by fiduciary	*A-G for Hong Kong v Reid* (1994) (contrast *Lister v Stubbs* (1890))
Unauthorised receipt of remuneration by trustee or fiduciary	*Re Macadam* (1946); *Williams v Barton* (1927)
Unauthorised purchases of trust property	*Wright v Morgan* (1926); *Regal (Hastings) Ltd v Gulliver* (1942)
Contracts for the sale of land	*Lysaght v Edwards* (1876)
Equity will not allow a statute to be used as an engine for fraud	*Rochefoucauld v Boustead* (1897); *Hodgson v Marks* (1971)

9.7 Proprietary rights in the family home

The presumptions of resulting trusts and advancements in the context of the family home and other family assets were regarded as outmoded and best suited for a different society. In their place the courts have substituted settled principles of property law – the resulting and constructive trusts.

9.7.1 Legal title in the joint names of the parties

The legal title to property may be conveyed in the joint names of the partners, subject to an express trust of the land for themselves as equitable joint tenants or tenants in common. Such an express declaration of trust will be conclusive of the equitable interests of the parties, in the absence of fraud or mistake or evidence varying the declaration of trust.

CASE EXAMPLE

Goodman v Gallant [1986] 2 WLR 236

The claimant and defendant purchased a house which was conveyed in their joint names 'upon trust to sell … and until sale upon trust for themselves as joint tenants'. The defendant left the house following a dispute between the parties. The claimant gave written notice of severance of the joint tenancy and claimed a declaration to the effect that she was entitled to a three-quarters share in the house. The court decided that in the absence of any claim for rectification or rescission, the express declaration in the conveyance was conclusive as to the intentions of the parties. The notice of severance had the effect of terminating the joint tenancy and substituting a tenancy in common in respect of the beneficial interest.

But the mere fact that that the legal title to property is vested in the joint names of the parties does not, on its own, entitle the surviving legal owner to an equitable interest in the property, if this does not accord with the intention of the parties.

CASE EXAMPLE

Goodman v Carlton [2002] All ER (D) 284

The claimant was the son and next of kin of Mr Goodman (G), who died intestate. The defendant, Anita (A), was the surviving legal owner of real property. The legal title to the house was acquired by G and A in 1994. G accepted an offer to purchase the house at a discount. His original intention was to purchase the house alone and register it in his sole name. As G did not have sufficient income to finance a mortgage he arranged to purchase the property with A as co-mortgagee. In 1997 G tentatively instructed his solicitors to transfer the house into his sole name but this was not followed up. Shortly afterwards G died. As surviving joint tenant, A acquired the legal title to the house and G's son commenced proceedings, claiming that A held the house on trust for G's estate absolutely. The trial judge decided in favour of the claimant. A appealed to the Court of

CONTINUED ▸

Appeal. The court dismissed the appeal and decided that the property was held on resulting trust for the claimant, as administrator of G's estate. A failed to contribute to the purchase of the property and there was no evidence of any agreement, understanding or common intention to share the beneficial ownership with A, who therefore acquired no interest.

J

'Mr Goodman was the person at whose expense the House was provided. He paid all the deposit. The discount in the price was solely referable to him as sitting tenant. He was to pay (and did in fact pay) all the mortgage payments and all the premiums on the endowment policy. There was no intention that the transfer of the House into joint names should confer a beneficial interest on Anita. It was part of the arrangements undertaken to acquire the House for his sole use, occupation and benefit. Anita's participation was intended only to be a temporary involvement on the basis of the limited understanding between them. A resulting trust arose by operation of law for the sole benefit of Mr Goodman.'

(Mummery LJ)

Alternatively, the parties may declare the terms of the trust outside the conveyance. Provided that s 53(1)(b) of the Law of Property Act 1925 has been complied with (evidence in writing), the declaration of trust will be conclusive as to the beneficial interests of the parties, in the absence of fraud or mistake.

9.7.2 Legal title in the name of one party only

Where the legal title to property is conveyed in the name of one party only, and his or her partner wishes to claim a beneficial interest, the claimant is required to establish the existence of a trust – resulting or constructive. The presumptions of resulting trust and advancement will not be readily adopted in order to quantify the interests of the parties because such presumptions have outlived their usefulness in this context. It was not until after the Second World War that the courts were required to consider the proprietary rights in family assets of a different social class. It was considered to be an abuse of legal principles for ascertaining or imputing intention, to apply to transactions between the post-war generation of married couples artificial 'presumptions' as to the most likely intentions of a culturally different generation of spouses in the nineteenth century. These sentiments were expressed by the House of Lords in two definitive decisions: *Pettitt v Pettitt* [1970] AC 777 and *Gissing v Gissing* [1971] AC 886.

Pettitt v Pettitt [1970] AC 777

Mrs Pettitt purchased a cottage with her own money and had the legal title conveyed in her name. Mr Pettitt from time to time redecorated the property, expending a total of £725. On a breakdown of the marriage he claimed a proportionate interest in the house (£1,000 *pro rata* value). The court decided that Mr Pettitt's expenditure was not related to the acquisition of the house. In the absence of an agreement or understanding, his expenditure was to be treated as a gift. The court decided that settled principles of property law were applicable in this context.

Gissing v Gissing [1971] AC 886

Mr Gissing purchased the matrimonial home in his name out of his own resources. Mrs Gissing paid £220 for furnishings and laying a lawn. There was no common understanding as to the beneficial interest in the house. On a breakdown of the marriage, the question arose as to the beneficial ownership of the house. The court decided that Mrs Gissing was not entitled to an interest in the house, for she had made no contributions to the purchase price.

9.7.3 Resulting trust

A resulting, implied or constructive trust will be created whenever the trustee has so conducted himself that it would be inequitable to allow him to deny to the beneficiary an equitable interest in the land acquired. He will be treated as having conducted himself inequitably if, by his words or conduct, he had induced the beneficiary to act to his own detriment in the reasonable belief that by so acting he will acquire a beneficial interest in the land. In other words, the court gives effect to the implied trust that reflects the common intention of the parties that if each acts in the manner provided for in the agreement the beneficial interests in the matrimonial home will be held as they have agreed; for example, if both the husband and wife contributed to the purchase of the house but the legal title to the property was placed in the name of the husband the wife will need to establish that it would be inequitable for the husband to deny her a share in the property. This would be the case if the court is satisfied that it was the common intention of both spouses that the contributing wife should have a share in the beneficial interest and that her contributions were made upon this understanding. The court, in the exercise of its equitable jurisdiction, would not permit the husband in whom the legal estate was vested and who had accepted the benefit of the contributions to take the whole beneficial interest merely because, at the time the wife made her contributions, there had been no express agreement as to how her share in it was to be quantified.

The intention of the parties is determined objectively, by reference to their statements and conduct. The court is required to draw inferences from such evidence and make value judgements as to the intentions of the parties. This is the position even though a party did not consciously formulate that intention in his own mind or may have acted with some different intention which he did not communicate to the other party. The subjective intentions of the parties are not decisive; more so, if such intention has not been communicated to the other party.

The time for drawing an inference as to what the parties said and did which led up to the acquisition of a matrimonial home is on a different footing from what they said and did after the acquisition was completed. The material time for the court to draw inferences from the conduct of the parties is up to and including the time of the acquisition of the property. In exceptional circumstances, subsequent evidence may be relevant only if it is alleged that there was some subsequent fresh agreement, acted upon by the parties, to vary the original beneficial interests created when the matrimonial home was acquired. In other words, what the parties said and did after the acquisition was completed will be relevant if it is explicable only upon the basis of their having manifested to one another at the time of the acquisition some particular common intention as to how the beneficial interests should be held.

9.7.4 Common intention

The common intention of the parties, based on inferences drawn by the courts, will reflect the quantum of the interest acquired by the parties. It is only if no such inference can be drawn that the court is driven to apply as a rule of law, and not as an inference of fact, the maxim 'Equality is equity,' and to hold that the beneficial interest belongs to the spouses in equal shares.

Domestic duties

It follows that domestic duties undertaken by a party (such as caring for and bringing up the children), unconnected with a common intention to share the property in reliance on such duties, are insufficient to create an interest in the property.

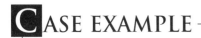**ASE EXAMPLE** ─────────────────────────

Burns v Burns [1984] 1 All ER 244

The defendant bought a house in his sole name with the assistance of a mortgage. The claimant made no financial contributions to the purchase of the house but gave up paid employment in order to perform the duties of bringing up their children. The defendant gave her a generous housekeeping allowance and did not ask her to contribute to household expenses. Subsequently, the claimant became employed and used her earnings for household expenses and to purchase fixtures and fittings. Ultimately, the claimant left the defendant and claimed a beneficial interest in the house. The court rejected the claim and held that the claimant had failed to prove that she had made a contribution, directly or indirectly, to the acquisition of the property, and therefore did not have an interest in the property. A common intention that the claimant had acquired an interest in the property cannot be imputed to the parties on the basis that the claimant lived with the defendant for 19 years, brought up the children and did a fair share of domestic duties.

9.7.5 Indirect contributions

Indirect contributions to the purchase price of the house (like direct contributions) would equally give the party contributing to the purchase an interest in the property. The claimant may acquire an interest in the property by making a substantial indirect contribution to the acquisition of the property (including mortgage repayments). This arrangement may be achieved by an undertaking between the parties to the effect that the claimant agrees to pay the household expenses on condition that the legal owner pays the mortgage instalments. In short, a link between the mortgage payments and the expenses undertaken by the claimant is required to be established and the claimant's expenses are required to be of a substantial nature (*per* Lord Pearson in *Gissing v Gissing* (1971)).

> J 'Contributions are not limited to those made directly in part payment of the price of the property or to those made at the time when the property is conveyed into the name of one of the spouses. For instance there can be a contribution if by arrangement between the spouses one of them by payment of the household expenses enables the other to pay the mortgage instalments.'
>
> (Lord Pearson)

The concept of indirect contributions may be illustrated by the Court of Appeal decision in *Grant v Edwards* [1986] Ch 638:

CASE EXAMPLE

Grant v Edwards [1986] Ch 638

The claimant, a woman who lived with the defendant, was given a false reason for not having the house put in their joint names. The woman made substantial contributions to the family expenses in the hope of acquiring an interest in the house. The expenses undertaken by the woman enabled the man to keep up the mortgage instalments. The claimant applied to the court for a declaration concerning an interest in the house. The court decided that the claimant was entitled to a half-share in the property. She would not have made the substantial contributions to the housekeeping expenses, which indirectly related to the mortgage instalments, unless she had an interest in the house. This was the inevitable inference of the claimant's conduct which established a common intention and reliance to her detriment. The court reviewed the earlier case of *Eves v Eves* [1975] 1 WLR 1338 and declared that that case involved indirect contributions in kind made in reliance on a promise by the legal owner to grant her an equitable interest in the property.

In *Grant v Edwards* (1986) two Lords Justices of Appeal disagreed as to the type of conduct that may constitute indirect contributions. Nourse LJ adopted a narrow interpretation of such conduct. In his view it is conduct in respect of which the actor could not have been reasonably expected to embark unless he or she had an interest in the house. On the other hand, Browne-Wilkinson LJ was prepared to adopt a wider interpretation of conduct that may give rise to indirect contributions. In his view, once a common intention is established, 'any act done by her to her detriment relating to the joint lives of the parties is … sufficient to qualify. The acts do not have to be referable to the house.'

In *Burns v Burns* [1984] 1 All ER 244, Fox LJ identified payments which may be referable to the acquisition of the house. This is the case if '… the payer (a) pays part of the purchase price or (b) contributes regularly to the mortgage instalments or (c) pays off part of the mortgage or (d) makes substantial financial contributions to the family expenses so as to enable the mortgage to be paid'.

9.7.6 The principles in *Pettitt* and *Gissing*

The House of Lords in *Lloyds Bank v Rosset* [1990] 1 All ER 1111, reviewed the principles laid down in *Pettitt* (1970) and *Gissing* (1971) and issued guidelines concerning the relevant principles. In *Lloyds Bank v Rosset* (1990), Lord Bridge laid down two guidelines which are capable of establishing a beneficial interest:

J

Evidence of agreement

'Any agreement, arrangement or understanding reached between the parties that the property is to be shared beneficially... this can only be based on *evidence of express discussion between the partners.* The [claimant is then required to show] that he or she acted to his or her detriment or significantly altered his or her position.'

Illustrations of this principle include *Eves v Eves* (1975) and *Grant v Edwards* (1986).

Evidence of conduct

'Where the court must rely entirely on the conduct of the parties... to infer a common intention to share the property beneficially and ... to give rise to a constructive trust. In this situation *direct contributions to the purchase price* by the [claimant], whether initially or by payment of mortgage instalments, will readily justify the inference necessary to the creation of a constructive trust. But ... it is extremely *doubtful whether anything less will do.*'

This principle may be illustrated by *Pettitt v Pettitt* (1970) and *Gissing v Gissing* (1971).

(Lord Bridge)

9.7.7 Scope of the *Rosset* principles
Constructive or resulting trust?

The second category of evidence seems consistent with a resulting trust, but Lord Bridge categorises this as evidence of a constructive trust. The boundaries surrounding the resulting trust are clearly drawn. It is confusing and unnecessary to merge resulting trusts with the constructive trust.

Indirect financial contributions?

Has this been abolished by implication? Such contributions were acknowledged in *Gissing v Gissing* (1971) and *Burns v Burns* (1984) and *Grant v Edwards* (1986). It is unlikely that Lord Bridge intended to abolish the concept of indirect contributions. His objective was to clarify the law as laid down in *Pettitt* (1970) and *Gissing* (1971) rather than to change the law. On this basis indirect contributions are still capable of creating an interest in the property. In the recent case of *Le Foe v Le Foe* [2001] All ER (D) 325, the High Court analysed Lord Bridge's judgment and decided that he did not intend to exclude indirect contributions.

CASE EXAMPLE

Le Foe v Le Foe [2001] All ER (D) 325

The parties were married and the family home was put in the husband's sole name with the assistance of a mortgage. The wife was in paid employment and assisted the husband in the repayment of the mortgage. On a breakdown of the marriage the issue arose as to the extent of the wife's interest in the house. The court decided that by virtue of the wife's indirect contributions to the mortgage repayments the court was entitled to infer that the parties had a common intention that the wife would acquire an interest in the property. This was quantified at 50 per cent.

The unwarranted requirement for express discussions between the parties

This appears to be over-simplistic, for an agreement or understanding may be inferred from conduct.

In *Hammond v Mitchell* [1991] 1 WLR 1127 the High Court adopted the narrow approach of express discussion as evidence of the intention of the parties as laid down by Lord Bridge in *Rosset* (1990).

CASE EXAMPLE

Hammond v Mitchell [1991] 1 WLR 1127

The parties, Mr Hammond (H) and Miss Mitchell (M), lived together from 1977 to 1988. In 1979, the couple moved into a bungalow in Essex, which was bought in H's name with the assistance of a mortgage. H assured M that as he was going through a divorce it would be in their best interests if the house was put in his name. He then told her: 'Don't worry about the future because when we are married it will be half yours anyway …'. In 1980, surrounding land was bought and the bungalow was extended. M assisted H in his business ventures. H purchased a house in Spain and for a short while they lived there, but never gave up possession of the Essex house. In 1988, the relationship was terminated and M brought an action claiming a beneficial interest in the properties and other assets. The court held that in relation to the bungalow, there was evidence of an express understanding that M should have a beneficial interest, quantified as one-half. But in relation to the Spanish house there was no evidence to justify an intention to share the beneficial interest.

> **J** 'In relation to the bungalow there was express discussion which, although not directed with any precision as to proprietary interests, was sufficient to amount to an understanding at least that the bungalow was to be shared beneficially.'
>
> (Waite J)

Similarly, in *Springette v Defoe* [1992] 2 FLR 388, the court adhered rigidly to the *Rosset* (1990) principles.

ASE EXAMPLE

> *Springette v Defoe* [1992] 2 FLR 388
>
> The parties lived as man and wife in a council house. In 1982, they made a formal offer to purchase the house for £14,445, which represented a discount of 41 per cent because the claimant, Miss Springette (S), had been a council tenant for 11 years or more. They bought the house jointly with the aid of a mortgage of £12,000. By agreement, they each contributed 50 per cent of the mortgage instalments. The balance of the purchase price was provided by S. The legal title was registered in their joint names but no quantification of their interests was registered in the Land Registry. During 1985, the relationship between the parties became strained and the defendant (D) left the home. S claimed that she was entitled to a 75 per cent share of the proceeds of sale of the house, as represented by her contribution to the purchase. The learned Recorder decided that the beneficial interests were shared equally, despite the lack of evidence of any discussion concerning this issue. S appealed to the Court of Appeal. The interests of the parties were determined by reference to the contributions made. There was no evidence which had the effect of varying the interest acquired by way of a resulting trust because there was no discussion between the parties to that effect. Accordingly, the interests were shared in a 75:25 ratio.

> **J** 'It is not enough to establish a common intention which is sufficient to found an implied or constructive trust of land that each of them happened at the same time to have been thinking on the same lines in his or her uncommunicated thoughts, while neither had any knowledge of the thinking of the other.'
>
> (Dillon LJ)

9.7.8 The *Cooke* approach

In *Midland Bank v Cooke* [1995] 4 All ER 562, the court adopted a modified approach to the *Rosset* (1990) principle. The approach is to the effect that where a party acquires an equitable interest in property by way of direct contributions to the purchase price of the property the court may take into consideration the conduct of the parties in order to quantify their shares. The court is not bound to deal with the matter on the strict basis of the trust resulting from the cash contribution to the purchase price, and is free to attribute to the parties an intention to share the beneficial interest in some different proportions.

ASE EXAMPLE

Midland Bank v Cooke [1995] 4 All ER 562

H and W married and moved into a house which was purchased with the assistance of a mortgage in H's sole name. The deposit was raised through H's savings and a wedding gift. This mortgage was replaced by a general mortgage in favour of the Midland Bank in order to secure H's business overdraft. The property was subsequently transferred into the joint names of H and W. There was no discussion between the parties as to their beneficial interests. In proceedings brought by the bank against H and W for arrears of payments and possession of the property, W claimed a declaration that she was entitled to a 50 per cent share in the house. The judge held that W was entitled to a beneficial interest of 6.74 per cent in the property, equivalent to a half-share of the wedding gift. W appealed to the Court of Appeal. The court allowed the appeal and awarded W a 50 per cent share in the value of the house, in accordance with the principles in *Pettitt v Pettitt* (1970), *Gissing v Gissing* (1971) and *Grant v Edwards* (1986). Since W had established an interest in the house through direct contributions, the court was entitled to look at all the circumstances in order to give effect to the true intentions of the parties. Accordingly, the court might attribute to the parties an interest in the property which was different from the resulting trust contributions to the purchase price.

Similarly, in *Drake v Whipp* [1996] 1 FLR 826, the court gave a broad interpretation of the intention of the parties. This intention is not measured solely by the direct contributions of the parties, in the absence of evidence to the contrary. The court is entitled to look at all the circumstances of the case to identify the scope of the common intention of the parties. Direct contributions being only one factor to be taken into account. The court also classified the types of trusts involved into constructive and resulting trusts.

CASE EXAMPLE

Drake v Whipp [1996] 1 FLR 826

The claimant and the defendant purchased a barn with the intention of converting it into a residence. The property was conveyed into the sole name of the defendant. Both parties contributed to the purchase price and the cost of the conversion work. The claimant made a direct contribution of one-fifth. It was found that the parties had a common intention that the claimant would acquire a beneficial interest. The court decided that it was entitled to adopt a 'broad brush' approach in determining the parties' respective shares under the constructive trust. It was entitled to look at the parties' entire course of conduct in evaluating their respective shares. This might involve direct and indirect contributions in money or money's worth and *any other evidence of intention* of the parties. Accordingly the claimant acquired a one-third interest in the property.

9.7.9 Section 37 of the Matrimonial Proceedings and Property Act 1970

Section 37 of the Matrimonial Proceedings and Property Act 1970 provides as follows:

'It is hereby declared that where a husband and wife contributes in money or money's worth to the improvement of real or personal property in which or in the proceeds of sale of which either or both of them has or have a beneficial interest, the husband or wife so contributing shall, if the contribution is of a substantial nature and subject to any agreement between them to the contrary express or implied, be treated as having then acquired … a share or an enlarged share… in that beneficial interest of such an extent as may have been agreed or, in default of such agreement, as may seem in all the circumstances just to any court …'

Section 37 is only applicable to married couples. Unmarried spouses who make contributions in similar circumstances may only rely on the common law rules. The court decides in its discretion whether a contribution is substantial or not.

9.7.10 Date and method of valuation

If the claimant has an interest in the house, the value of that interest is ascertained at the time the property is sold. Accordingly, any increases or decreases in the value of the property are taken into consideration. If a party remains in occupation paying the mortgage, rates and other outgoings, he is credited with these expenses. Conversely, the party in occupation is debited with occupation rent for using the premises partly owned by the other. In *Oxley v Hiscock* [2004] EWCA 546, the Court of Appeal declared that decided cases had created three methods of valuation. These are:

- The approach adopted by Lord Diplock in *Gissing v Gissing* (1971) and by Nourse LJ in *Stokes v Anderson* [1991] 1 FLR 391: the respective shares of the parties are not to be determined at the time of the acquisition of the property but are left to be determined when their relationship comes to an end or the property sold. Thus, a complete picture of the whole course of dealing is available to the court in order to determine what is fair.

- The approach suggested by Waite LJ in *Midland Bank v Cooke* (1995): the court undertakes a survey of the whole course of dealing between the parties in order to determine what proportions the parties must be assumed to have intended from the outset for their beneficial ownership. Thus evidence of what the parties intended at the time of the acquisition may be inferred from the conduct of the parties while they were living together.

- The suggestion put forward by Browne-Wilkinson VC in *Grant v Edwards* (1986) and approved by Walker LJ in *Yaxley v Gotts* [2000] Ch 162: the court in its discretion makes such an order as the circumstances require in order to give effect to the beneficial interest in the property of the one party, the existence of which the party with the legal title is estopped from denying.

In *Oxley* (2004) the Court of Appeal expressed a preference for the third approach. The second approach was capable of leading to an artificial or fictional intention of the parties. Likewise, the same point could be made of the first approach, ie at the time of the acquisition the parties' intention was that their shares should be left for late determination.

9.7.11 Order of sale

Section 14 of the Trusts of Land and Appointment of Trustees Act 1996 Act repeals and replaces s 30 of the Law of Property Act 1925. The section declares that any person interested in the trust property (including the trustees of land), may apply to the court for an order relating to the exercise of the trustees' functions or declaring the extent of the beneficial interests.

The court is directed in s 15 of the 1996 Act to have regard to a number of factors when deciding an application under s 14. These are:

(a) the intentions of the settlor

(b) the purposes for which the property subject to the trust is held

(c) the welfare of any minor who occupies or might reasonably be expected to occupy any land subject to the trust as his home

(d) the interests of the mortgagee of any beneficiary

(e) in the case of an application relating to the beneficiary's right to occupy under s 13, the circumstances and wishes of each of the beneficiaries entitled to occupy

(f) in all other cases, except conveying the land to beneficiaries absolutely entitled, the circumstances and wishes of the adult beneficiaries entitled to possession.

The underlying purpose of the trust, including the rights of children, are required to be taken into account before any decision is reached by the court. The approach of the courts was declared in *Mortgage Corporation v Silkin* [2000] 2 FCR 222, concerning an application by a mortgagee for an order of sale:

> **J** '… it does not seem to me unlikely that the legislature intended to relax the fetters on the way in which the court exercised its jurisdiction … so as to tip the balance somewhat more in favour of families and against banks and other chargees … As a result of s 15, the court has greater flexibility than heretofore, as to how it exercises its jurisdiction on an application for an order of sale … Once the relevant factors to be taken into account have been identified, it is a matter for the court as to what weight to give to each factor in a particular case.'
>
> (Neuberger J)

■Key facts on proprietary rights in the family home

KEY FACTS

• The legal title to property may be conveyed in the joint names of the partners, subject to an express trust for land for themselves as equitable joint tenants or tenants in common. Alternatively, the parties may declare the terms of the trust outside the conveyance. Provided that s 53(1)(b) of the Law of Property Act 1925 has been complied with, the declaration of trust will be conclusive as to the beneficial interests of the parties, in the absence of fraud or mistake.	*Goodman v Gallant* (1986); *Goodman v Carlton* (2002)
• Where the legal title to property is conveyed in the name of one party only, and his or her partner wishes to claim a beneficial interest,the claimant is required to establish the existence of a trust – resulting or constructive.	s 53(2) of the LPA 1925
• The presumptions of resulting trust or advancement will not be readily adopted in order to quantify the interests of the parties.	*Pettitt v Pettitt* (1970); *Gissing v Gissing* (1971)
• Domestic duties undertaken by a party are insufficient to create an interst in the property.	*Burns v Burns* (1984)
• The principles laid down in *Lloyd's Bank v Rossett* Lord Bridge laid down two guidelines which are capable of establishing a beneficial interest: **(i) Evidence of agreement:** 'Any agreement, arrangement or understanding reached between the parties that the property is to be shared beneficially … this can only be based on *evidence of express discussion between the partners.* The [claimant is then required to show] that he or she acted acted to his or her detriment or significantly altered his or her position.'	*Eves v Eves* (1975); *Grant v Edwards* (1986)

CONTINUED ▸

KEY FACTS

(ii) **Evidence of conduct:** 'Where the court must rely entirely on the conduct of the parties … to infer a common intention to share the property beneficially and … to give rise to a constructive trust. In this situation *direct contributions to the purchase price* by the [claimant], whether initially or by payment of mortgage instalments, will readily justify the inference necessary to the creation of a constructive trust. But … it is extremely *doubtful whether anything less will do*.'	*Pettitt v Pettitt* (1970); *Gissing v Gissing* (1971); *Re Rogers' Question*
Difficulties created by this dichotomy of evidence	
• Constructive or resulting trust? The second category of evidence seems consistent with a resulting trust, but Lord Bridge categorises this as evidence of a constructive trust.	
• Indirect financial contribution? Has this been abolished by implication?	*Gissing v Gissing* (1971); *Burns v Burns* (1984); *Le Foe v Le Foe* (2001)
• The unwarranted requirement for express discussions between the parties. This appears to be over-simplistic for an agreement or understanding may be inferred from conduct.	*Hammond v Mitchell* (1991); *Springette v Defoe* (1992); *Midland Bank v Cooke* (1995); *Drake v Whipp* (1996)
• Equation of constructive trust (first category) with proprietary estoppel.	
• Date and method of valuation.	*Midland Bank v Cooke* (1995); *Drake v Whipp* (1996); *Oxley v Hiscock* (2004)
• s 37 of the Matrimonial Proceedings and Property Act 1970.	
• ss 14 and 15 of the Trusts of Land and Appointment of Trustees Act 1996.	

ACTIVITY

Harold and Winifred have been living together as man and wife for several years
(although not married). Consider the extent of their beneficial interests in the family
home (bought for £200,000), which is now worth £600,000, in each of the following
alternative sets of circumstances:

(i)   The purchase price was entirely provided by Harold and the title to the property
      vested in his sole name. Harold repeatedly told Winifred that the beneficial interest
      belonged to both of them in equal shares.

(ii) The entire purchase price was provided by Winifred but the house was conveyed into
      the sole name of Harold in the hope of preventing the house falling into the hands
      of her creditors should her business fail. As things turned out, her fears regarding
      her business proved unfounded and her business flourished.

(iii) Winifred provided £50,000 of the purchase price of £200,000 and the remainder of
      the purchase price was obtained by way of a mortgage of the house. The mortgage
      was taken in Harold's name as the legal title was vested in the sole name of Harold.
      Winifred provided housekeeping money and extensively redecorated the house.

(iv) Assume the facts as in (iii) above, but Harold and Winifred were legally married.

9.8 Strangers as constructive trustees

9.8.1 Introduction

Generally, third parties, strangers to a trust or agents of the trustees, do not become constructive
trustees simply because of a breach of trust committed by the trustees or even a neglect of duties by
the agent. The third party may be liable to the trust to pay damages for breach of contract or in the
law of tort in accordance with general principles of law.

CASE EXAMPLE

Mara v Browne [1896] 1 Ch 199

A solicitor acting on behalf of the trustees unlawfully invested trust funds on certain
mortgages and the trust suffered loss. The court held that the solicitor was not liable as a
constructive trustee, though he would have been liable in contract for his negligence had
the action not become time-barred.

An agent or stranger to a trust becomes a constructive trustee if he intermeddles with trust
property. A person intermeddles in the affairs of a trust if he undertakes the mantel of a trustee. He

may do so by assuming the duties of trusteeship or abusing the trust relationship reposed in him in his dealings with the trust property. Lord Selborne in *Barnes v Addy* (1874) LR 9 Ch App 244 identified the categories of constructive trusteeship as follows:

> J 'Those who create a trust clothe the trustee with a legal power and control over the trust property, imposing on him a corresponding responsibility. That responsibility may no doubt be extended in equity to others who are not properly trustees, if they are found either making themselves trustees *de son tort*, or actually participating in any fraudulent conduct of the trustee to the injury of the *cestui que* trust ... Strangers are not to be made constructive trustees merely because they act as agents of trustees in transactions within their legal powers, transactions, perhaps, of which a court of equity may disapprove, unless those agents:
>
> (a) receive and become chargeable with some part of the trust property; or
>
> (b) they assist with knowledge in a dishonest or fraudulent design on the part of the trustees.'
>
> (Lord Selbourne)

CASE EXAMPLE

Barnes v Addy (1874) LR 9 Ch App 244

A solicitor advised the settlement trustees against the appointment of a beneficiary as the sole trustee of a part of the trust funds, but nevertheless prepared the necessary documents. The sole trustee misapplied the property and became bankrupt. An action was brought against a solicitor and the trustees of a trust settlement. The court held that the solicitor was not liable for the loss for he did not receive the trust property but acted honestly and within the course of his authority. The settlement trustees were liable.

Thus, an intermeddler in the affairs of a trust becomes a constructive trustee within one of the following categories:

- a trustee *de son tort* (of his own wrongdoing)
- knowingly receiving or dealing with trust property for his own use
- dishonest assistance or accessory liability (formerly 'knowingly assisting in a fraudulent or dishonest transaction on the part of the trustee/fiduciary').

9.8.2 Trustees *de son tort*

A trustee *de son tort* is a person who has not been appointed a trustee but such a person assumes that he has been validly appointed a trustee. The phrase was coined on analogy with an executor *de son tort*, ie a person who assumes the function of an executor and intermeddles in the estate of a deceased. A trustee *de son tort* undertakes the duties of a trustee and deals with the trust property, not for his own benefit, but on behalf of the beneficiaries.

In *Boardman v Phipps* (1967), a solicitor inaccurately believed that he had the permission of all of the beneficiaries to take over a company in which trust shares were held. He was accountable for the profits that he had made, although generous remuneration was awarded to him by the court for his exceptional effort.

9.8.3 Knowingly receiving or dealing with trust property for his own use

The rationale behind the trustee's liability under this head is based on the premise that the stranger or agent has received the trust property with knowledge of the same, before he acts, or fails to act, for his own benefit in a manner inconsistent with the trust. In effect, the stranger to the trust claims a proprietary interest in the subject-matter of the trust and thus attempts to compete with the interests of the beneficiaries. The claimant is required to prove, firstly, a disposal of his assets in breach of fiduciary duty; secondly, the beneficial receipt by the defendant of assets which are traceable as representing the assets of the claimant; and thirdly, knowledge on the part of the defendant that the assets he received are traceable to a breach of fiduciary duty. Thus, liability may arise where the stranger:

- receives trust property knowing that his possession is in breach of trust or
- receives trust property initially without knowledge that his acquisition is in breach of trust, but subsequently becomes aware of the existence of the trust and acts in a manner inconsistent with the trust.

CASE EXAMPLE

Belmont Finance Corporation v Williams Furniture & Others (No 2) [1980] 1 All ER 393

Belmont Co, a wholly owned subsidiary of Williams Co, entered into a scheme for the unlawful purchase of its own shares and was subsequently put into receivership. The receiver claimed damages for conspiracy and also sought to recover from the directors as constructive trustees the proceeds of sale which were still traceable. The Court of Appeal held in favour of the receiver on the ground that the participating companies and their directors were liable as constructive trustees. Liability arose by the receipt of trust monies and the fact that the directors knew of all the circumstances, in particular, the unlawfulness of the transaction, and had knowledge or ought to have known that the sum received from the sale of Belmont's shares was trust money. There was no need to prove fraud.

Test for 'knowledge'

In *Re Baden Delvaux and Lecuit v Societé Générale pour Favoriser le Developpement du Commerce et de l'Industrie en France SA* [1983] BCLC 325, Peter Gibson J, in a lengthy judgment, postulated five categories of 'knowledge':

> **J** 'What types of knowledge are relevant for the purposes of constructive trusteeship? … knowledge can comprise anyone of the five different mental states as follows:
>
> (i) actual knowledge;
>
> (ii) wilfully shutting one's eyes to the obvious;
>
> (iii) wilfully and recklessly failing to make such inquiries as an honest and reasonable man would make;
>
> (iv) knowledge of circumstances which would indicate the facts to an honest and reasonable man;
>
> (v) knowledge of circumstances which would put an honest and reasonable man on inquiry.
>
> More accurately, apart from actual knowledge, they are formulations of circumstances which may lead the court to impute knowledge of the facts to the alleged constructive trustee, even though he lacked actual knowledge of those facts.'
>
> (Peter Gibson J)

The first three categories of knowledge involve a subjective or partly subjective enquiry, whereas categories (iv) and (v) require a purely objective assessment of the circumstances. Actual knowledge within category (i) concerns such facts of which the stranger is aware, positively and consciously. Wilfully shutting one's eyes to the obvious within category (ii) is a common law notion involving abstinence from making enquiries because the defendant knows what the result would entail. Similarly, knowledge within category (iii) embraces circumstances when the defendant foresees or suspects the likelihood of a serious risk of loss of the trust property if reasonable enquiries are not made, but is indifferent as to the consequences of failing to make such enquiries. Knowledge within categories (iv) and (v) involve a wholly objective enquiry in that the reasonable man would have made reasonable enquiries or would have been put on enquiry. The court adopts its own standard in fixing an individual with knowledge within categories (iv) and (v). The effect is that the degree of culpability that is required to make a stranger a constructive trustee within the latter two categories borders between fraud and negligence. It is arguable that this test is divorced from dishonesty or want of probity, which ought to be the basis of the liability to account. In other words, an innocent failure to make reasonable enquiries is distinct from acting dishonestly, or consciously acting with impropriety.

It ought to be noted that in accordance with the traditional rationale for liability here, all five types of *Re Baden Delvaux* (1983) knowledge were applicable in order to impose liability on the intermeddler. Such a view was laid down in the majority of cases, for liability under this head is restitution based.

CASE EXAMPLE

International Sales and Agencies Ltd v Marcus [1982] 3 All ER 551

The defendant made a personal loan of £30,000 to a major shareholder of the claimant company. After the death of the debtor, a friend and director of the claimant company repaid the loan with the company's funds, to the knowledge of the defendant. The claimant sought to make the defendant a constructive trustee of the funds. The court held in favour of the claimant.

> J
>
> 'The knowing recipient of trust property for his own purposes will become a constructive trustee of what he receives if either he was in fact aware at the time that his receipt was affected by a breach of trust, or if he deliberately shut his eyes to the real nature of the transfer to him (this could be called imputed notice), or if an ordinary reasonable man in his position and with his attributes ought to have known of the relevant breach. This I equate with constructive notice. Such a position would arise where such a person would have been put on enquiry as to the probability of a breach of trust ...'
>
> (Lawson J)

In *Polly Peck International plc v Nadir and Others (No 2)* [1992] 4 All ER 769, the Court of Appeal applied the restitution based test of liability and decided that any category of *Re Baden Delvaux* (1983) knowledge would be sufficient to impose liability on the defendant.

CASE EXAMPLE

Polly Peck International plc v Nadir and Others (No 2) [1992] 4 All ER 769

The administrators of the claimant's company (PPI) alleged that N and IBK (a bank controlled by him) had misapplied £142m of PPI's funds. Part of that money had been transferred by the bank to the London account of the fourth defendant, the Central Bank of the Turkish Republic of Northern Cyprus. The Central Bank exercised the supervisory and regulatory role of a central bank in a sovereign State. The administrators claimed that a scheme whereby PPI's funds were transferred via IBK to Northern Cyprus was, at best, in breach of fiduciary duties owed by N to PPI and, at worst, a dishonest means of diverting PPI's funds for improper purposes. The

CONTINUED ▶

claimants also contended that either the Central Bank had actual knowledge of the fraudulent scheme or, at best, was put on enquiry as to the impropriety of the scheme. Accordingly, the claimants alleged that the Central Bank was a constructive trustee, requesting a tracing order in respect of some £8.9m standing to the Central Bank's account at the London clearing bank, and a Mareva injunction (a 'freezing' order) against the Central Bank to protect the £8.9m. The judge granted the injunction subject to a proviso to enable the Central Bank to carry on its banking business in the normal way. The bank appealed against the order. The Court of Appeal, allowing the appeal and discharging the order, held that there was insufficient evidence for finding that the Central Bank had knowledge of the alleged impropriety perpetrated by N and IBK. The tracing claim failed for the same reason.

J

'Liability as constructive trustee in a "knowing receipt" case does not require that the misapplication of the trust funds should be fraudulent. It does require that the defendant should have knowledge that the funds were trust funds and that they were being misapplied. Actual knowledge obviously will suffice. Mr Potts has submitted that it will suffice if the defendant can be shown to have had knowledge of facts which would have put an honest and reasonable man on inquiry, or at least, if the defendant can be shown to have wilfully and recklessly failed to make such inquiries as an honest and reasonable man would have made (see categories (iii) and (v) of the categories of mental state identified by Peter Gibson in *Baden*'s case). I do not think there is any doubt that, if the latter of the two criteria can be established against the Central Bank, that will suffice. I have some doubts about the sufficiency of the former criterion but do not think that the present appeal is the right occasion for settling the issue. The various categories of mental state identified in *Re Baden*'s case are not rigid categories with clear and precise boundaries. One category may merge imperceptibly into another.

The real question, however, is whether the circumstances in which the transfers were made should have made the Central Bank suspicious of the propriety of what was being done. Millett J thought so. He thought so because of "the sheer scale of the payments".

I find myself unimpressed by the "sheer scale" argument in so far as it is put forward as a ground for contending that the Central Bank ought to have suspected impropriety. Millett J commented that "these payments were on a scale which was completely unjustified by any legitimate business requirement which Polly Peck or its trading subsidiaries in Northern Cyprus could possibly have had". With the greatest respect to the judge, I do not think this conclusion is a fair one so far as the Central Bank is concerned ... the constructive trust test, the "honest and reasonable banker" being put on enquiry (if that is indeed the test), postulates inquiry as to whether or not impropriety is being committed. The test is not satisfied by the inference of no more than curiosity.

CONTINUED ▸

> **J** It should be noted that in *Polly Peck International plc v Nadir* the Court of Appeal identified the test of liability under the "knowingly receiving" head as restitution based. The rationale for imposing liability on the defendant is based on the premise that he has acquired the claimant's property. Dishonesty or want of probity ought not to be the touchstones of liability. The issues in this context are: whether the defendant had acquired the claimant's property, and whether he knows that his acquisition was in breach of trust. The reverse situation, which will entitle the defendant to take free of the claimant's allegation, depends on whether he is a *bona fide* purchaser for value without notice of the breach of trust. Accordingly, "knowledge" within any of the five categories laid down in *Re Baden* will be sufficient to impose liability on the defendant.'
>
> (Scott LJ)

In *Carl Zeiss Stiftung v Herbert Smith & Co (No 2)* [1969] 2 Ch 276, the court decided that the claimant failed to establish an equitable interest in the property in the first place and consequently failed in its attempt to make the defendant a constructive trustee. A 'doubtful equity' is insufficient to support a claim under this head.

ASE EXAMPLE

Carl Zeiss Stiftung v Herbert Smith & Co (No 2) [1969] 2 Ch 276

An East German firm, Carl Zeiss, brought a passing off action against a West German firm of the same name. It was alleged that following the partition of Germany members of the claimant firm fled to the West and set up a competing business. Solicitors of the West German firm were paid a sum of money for work done for their clients. The East German firm claimed this money from the solicitors, contending that they had received the sum knowing that the same belonged to the claimant. The court held in favour of the defendants, for the ownership of the assets of the claimant firm was seriously in dispute on reasonable grounds. The solicitors could have no knowledge that the funds belonged to the claimants.

9.8.4 Alternative rationale of liability

Megarry VC, in *Re Montagu's Settlement* [1987] Ch 264, reviewed the basis of liability under this head and concluded that 'the constructive trust should not be imposed unless the conscience of the recipient is affected; this depends on knowledge, not "notice"; want of probity includes actual knowledge, shutting one's eyes to the obvious, or wilfully and recklessly failing to make such inquiries as a reasonable and honest man would make; it does not include knowledge of circumstances which would indicate the facts to an honest and reasonable man or would put the latter on enquiry'. In short, the test for knowledge is based only on the first three categories of *Re Baden Delvaux* (1983) knowledge because the basis of liability is dependent on want of probity.

CASE EXAMPLE

Re Montagu's Settlement [1987] Ch 264

Under a subsisting trust, the trustees, on advice from a firm of solicitors, settled chattels in favour of the beneficiary, the tenth Duke of Manchester, absolutely. The transfer was in breach of trust but as a result of an honest mistake on the part of the solicitors and the Duke. The Duke disposed of a number of chattels during his lifetime. After his death, the eleventh Duke claimed that his predecessor had become a constructive trustee of the chattels and was liable to re-transfer the remaining assets (and traceable proceeds of sale of the disposed chattels) and was also personally liable in respect of the value of any assets disposed of and in respect of which the proceeds were not traceable. The court held that the Duke (or his estate) was not personally liable as a constructive trustee because he did not have subjective knowledge of the breach but was liable to re-transfer to the settlement trustees undisposed trust assets and traceable proceeds as an innocent volunteer.

J **Megarry VC** summarised the following propositions:

'(1) The equitable doctrine of tracing and the imposition of a constructive trust by reason of the knowing receipt of trust property are governed by different rules and must be kept distinct. Tracing is primarily a means of determining the rights of property, whereas the imposition of a constructive trust creates personal obligations that go beyond mere property rights.

(2) In considering whether a constructive trust has arisen in a case of the knowing receipt of trust property, the basic question is whether the conscience of the recipient is sufficiently affected to justify the imposition of such a trust.

(3) Whether a constructive trust arises in such a case primarily depends on the knowledge of the recipient, and not on notice to him; and for clarity it is desirable to use the word "knowledge" and avoid the word "notice" in such cases.

(4) For this purpose, knowledge is not confined to actual knowledge, but includes at least knowledge of types (ii) and (iii) in the *Baden* case [1983] BCLC 325, p 407, ie, actual knowledge that would have been acquired but for shutting one's eyes to the obvious, or wilfully and recklessly failing to make such inquiries as a reasonable and honest man would make; for in such cases there is a want of probity which justifies imposing a constructive trust.

CONTINUED ▶

J

(5) Whether knowledge of the *Baden* types (iv) and (v) suffices for this purpose is at best doubtful; in my view, it does not, for I cannot see that the carelessness involved will normally amount to a want of probity.

(6) For these purposes, a person is not to be taken to have knowledge of a fact that he once knew but has genuinely forgotten: the test (or a test) is whether the knowledge continues to operate on that person's mind at the time in question.

(7) (a) It is at least doubtful whether there is a general doctrine of "imputed knowledge" that corresponds to "imputed notice".

(b) Even if there is such a doctrine, for the purposes of creating a constructive trust of the "knowing receipt" type the doctrine will not apply so as to fix a donee or beneficiary with all the knowledge that his solicitor has, at all events if the donee or beneficiary has not employed the solicitor to investigate his right to the bounty, and has done nothing else that can be treated as accepting that the solicitor's knowledge should be treated as his own.

(c) Any such doctrine should be distinguished from the process whereby, under the name "imputed knowledge", a company is treated as having the knowledge that its directors and secretary have.

(8) Where an alleged constructive trust is based not on "knowing receipt" but on "knowing assistance", some at least of these considerations probably apply; but I need not decide anything on that, and I do not do so.'

Judicial support for Megarry VC's view followed in a spate of subsequent High Court authorities, including *Cowan de Groot Properties Ltd v Eagle Trust plc* [1992] 4 All ER 700, *Barclays Bank v Quincecare Ltd* [1992] 4 All ER 363 and *Lipkin Gorman v Karpnale* [1992] 4 All ER 363. In the Court of Appeal decision of *BCCI v Akindele* [2000] 3 WLR 1423, Nourse LJ reviewed the law with regard to liability under the head of knowingly receiving trust property. He endorsed the approach adopted by Megarry VC in *Re Montagu* [1987], which he considered a seminal judgment. The effect is that in his view liability under this head is based on actual or subjective knowledge on the part of the defendant that the assets received were linked to a breach of trust. He equated liability under this head with accessory liability and doubted the utility of the five categories of knowledge laid down by Peter Gibson J in *Re Baden Delvaux* [1983]. Nourse LJ identified the basis of liability under this head as involving the conscience of the defendant, ie 'whether the defendant's state of knowledge is such as to make it unconscionable for him to retain the property'.

CASE EXAMPLE

BCCI v Akindele [2000] 3 WLR 1423

The defendant received US$6.68m in 1988 as profit on a payment of US$10m he had paid to the bank in 1985 under an artificial loan agreement. The transaction involved a fraudulent breach of fiduciary duties owed to the bank. It was found that the defendant had no subjective knowledge of the frauds at the time of the transaction. The claimants contended that the defendant was liable to account to them for US$6.79m as a constructive trustee. The Court of Appeal dismissed the claim on the ground that the test for liability for knowing receipt cases is whether a recipient could conscientiously retain the funds as against the company. Just as there is now a single test of dishonesty for knowing assistance, so ought there to be a single test of knowledge for knowing receipt cases. Further, it was debatable whether the fivefold categorisation of knowledge laid down by Peter Gibson J in *Re Baden Delvaux* (1983), was of any use in knowing receipt cases. The material date for determining the defendant's state of knowledge was 1985, the date of the agreement. Additional knowledge that he acquired between 1985 and 1987, press rumours of irregularities involving BCCI, warnings to him from business figures in Nigeria and his becoming aware of the arrest of BCCI officials in connection with money laundering, did not make it unconscionable for him to retain the receipt. The additional knowledge went to the general reputation of BCCI. It was not sufficient to question the propriety of the 1985 transaction.

J

'... I have come to the view that, just as there is now a single test of dishonesty for knowing assistance, so ought there to be a single test of knowledge for knowing receipt. *The recipient's state of knowledge must be such as to make it unconscionable for him to retain the benefit of the receipt.* A test in that form, though it cannot, any more than any other, avoid difficulties of application, ought to avoid those of definition and allocation to which the previous categorisations [in *Baden Delvaux*] have led. Moreover, it should better enable the courts to give commonsense decisions in the commercial context in which claims in knowing receipt are now frequently made.'

(Nourse LJ)

9.8.5 Dishonest assistance or accessory liability

Under the head of accessory liability, the defendant (alleged constructive trustee) does not acquire control of the property, but merely assists in a dishonest breach of trust. He is under a duty to account and strictly, he ought not to be labelled a constructive trustee, for liability is personal and not *in rem*. Provided that the defendant is solvent, there are no difficulties. But if the defendant is insolvent, the classification of his status will have important consequences. A proprietary remedy (tracing process) may subsist even though the defendant is insolvent. The same applies to the limitation period. The assertion of a right *in rem* is not subject to limitation periods. Millett LJ in *Paragon Finance v Thakerar* (1999) made reference to the importance of adopting the correct classification of this principle and declared that since the fiduciary defendant does not obtain control of the relevant property he is only liable to account:

J 'The expressions "constructive trust" and "constructive trustee" have been used by equity lawyers to describe two entirely different situations. The first covers those cases where the defendant, though not expressly appointed as trustee, has assumed the duties of a trustee by a lawful transaction which was independent of and preceded the breach of trust and is not impeached by the plaintiff. The second covers those cases where the trust obligation arises as a direct consequence of the unlawful transaction which is impeached by the plaintiff.

A constructive trust arises by operation of law whenever the circumstances are such that it would be unconscionable for the owner of property (usually but not necessarily the legal estate) to assert his own beneficial interest in the property and deny the beneficial interest of another. In the first class of case, however, the constructive trustee really is a trustee. He does not receive the trust property in his own right but by a transaction by which both parties intend to create a trust from the outset and which is not impugned by the plaintiff. His possession of the property is coloured from the first by the trust and confidence by means of which he obtained it, and his subsequent appropriation of the property to his own use is a breach of that trust. Well known examples of such a constructive trust are *McCormick v Grogan* (1869) LR 4 HL 82, [a case of secret trust] and *Rochefoucald v Boustead* [1897] 1 Ch 196, [where the defendant agreed to buy property for the plaintiff but the trust was imperfectly recorded]. *Pallant v Morgan* [1952] 2 All ER 951, [where the defendant sought to keep for himself property which the plaintiff trusted him to buy for both parties] is another. In these cases the plaintiff does not impugn the transaction by which the defendant obtained control of the property. He alleges that the circumstances in which the defendant obtained control make it unconscionable for him thereafter to assert a beneficial interest in the property.

The second class of case is different [see *A-G for Hong Kong v Reid* [1993] 3 WLR 1143]. It arises when the defendant is implicated in a fraud. Equity has always given relief against fraud by making any person sufficiently implicated in the fraud accountable in equity. In such a case he is traditionally, though I think unfortunately described, as a constructive trustee and said to be "liable to account as a

CONTINUED ▸

J constructive trustee". Such a person is not in fact a trustee at all, even though he may
be liable to account as if he were. He never assumes the position of a trustee, and if he
receives the trust property at all it is adversely to the plaintiff by an unlawful transaction
which is impugned by the plaintiff. In such a case the expressions, "constructive trust"
and "constructive trustee" are misleading, for there is no trust and usually no possibility
of a proprietary remedy; they are nothing more than a formula of equitable relief.'

(Millett LJ)

This head of liability was formerly known as 'knowingly assisting in a fraudulent or dishonest
transaction on the part of the trustee/fiduciary'. This was the original basis on which the test of
liability was presented by Lord Selborne in *Barnes v Addy* (1874) (see above) but in the leading case
of *Royal Brunei Airlines v Tan* [1995] 2 AC 378, Lord Nicholls reviewed the law concerning
'accessory liability'. He opined that the liability of a third party who assisted a trustee to commit a
breach of trust is dependent on the state of mind of the third party and is fault based. Dishonesty
on the part of the third party is an essential ingredient of liability, irrespective of the state of mind
of the trustee who committed the breach of trust. The trustee will be liable in any event for breach
of trust, even if he acted innocently, unless he is relieved by the court or is protected by an
exclusion clause in the trust instrument. Dishonesty on the part of the trustee is, however, not a
prerequisite in order to attach liability to the dishonest third party.

9.8.6 *Royal Brunei v Tan* analysis

The leading authority under this head is now *Royal Brunei v Tan* (1995). In this case the Privy
Council reviewed the authorities and concluded that the test of liability is dishonesty. In addition,
there is no pre-condition for the liability of the defendant to establish that the trustee was fraudulent.

CASE EXAMPLE

Royal Brunei Airlines v Tan [1995] 2 AC 378

The claimant appointed a travel agent, Borneo Leisure Travel (BLT), to act as its general
travel agent for the sale of passenger and cargo transportation. BLT was required to
account to the claimant for all amounts received from such sales. In breach of trust, sums
received were not paid into a separate account, but were paid into BLT's current account
and used for its own purposes. The defendant was BLT's managing director and principal
shareholder. BLT's payments fell into arrears and the claimant terminated the agreement.
The company later became insolvent. The claimant commenced an action against the
defendant claiming an account in respect of the unpaid money. This claim was based on

CONTINUED ▶

the second limb of Lord Selborne's *dictum* in *Barnes v Addy* (1874): 'strangers are not to be made constructive trustees merely because they act as the agents of trustees in transactions ... unless they assist with knowledge in a dishonest and fraudulent design on the part of the trustees'. The question in issue was whether the breach of trust, which was a prerequisite to liability, had to be a dishonest and fraudulent breach of trust by the trustee. The Privy Council allowed the claim on the ground that a stranger to a trust is liable to make good resulting loss if he dishonestly procured or assisted in a breach of trust or fiduciary obligation. It was not a prerequisite of that liability that, in addition, the trustee or fiduciary acted dishonestly.

J 'What matters is the state of mind of the third party sought to be made liable, not the state of mind of the trustee ... If the liability of the third party is fault-based, what matters is the nature of his fault, not that of the trustee. In this regard dishonesty on the part of the third party would seem to be a sufficient basis for his liability, irrespective of the state of mind of the trustee who is in breach of trust ... Given, then, that in some circumstances a third party may be liable directly to a beneficiary, but given also that the liability is not so strict that there would be liability even when the third party was wholly unaware of the existence of the trust, *the next step is to seek to identify the touchstone of liability. By common accord, dishonesty fulfils this role* ... their Lordships' overall conclusion is that dishonesty is a necessary ingredient of accessory liability. It is also a sufficient ingredient. A liability in equity to make good resulting loss attaches to a person who dishonestly procures or assists in a breach of trust or fiduciary obligation. It is not necessary that, in addition, the trustee or fiduciary was acting dishonestly, although this will usually be so where the third party who is assisting him is acting dishonestly. "Knowingly" is better avoided as a defining ingredient of the principle, and in the context of this principle the *Baden* ... scale of knowledge is best forgotten.'

(Lord Nicholls of Birkenhead)

In *Heinl v Jayske Bank (Gibraltar)*, *The Times*, 28th September 1999, the Court of Appeal decided that the standard of proof for dishonestly assisting in breaches of fiduciary duties exceeds a balance of probabilities, but is not as high as beyond a reasonable doubt.

9.8.7 Dishonesty

In 2002, the House of Lords in *Twinsectra Ltd v Yardley*, considered the standards that are required to be adopted in order to determine whether the defendant has acted dishonestly. The Law Lords treated the opinion of Lord Nicholls in *Royal Brunei Airlines v Tan* (1995) as definitive and subjected his speech to detailed analysis. The Law Lords cosidered that there were three possible standards by which a person's dishonesty may be judged – purely subjectively, purely objectively and a combination of objectivity and subjectivity. The majority of the Law Lords (Lord Millett dissenting) rejected the first two standards and decided in favour of the combined standard. The purely subjective standard was rejected for it would have been impractical for the defendant to set his own standards of honesty. The purely objective standard (which appealed to Lord Millett) was rejected by the majority of the Law Lords on the basis that dishonesty involves an element of subjectivity. The personal attributes of the defendant ought to be taken into account. The majority of the Law Lords adopted the criminal law test for dishonesty (as laid down by Lord Lane CJ in *R v Ghosh* [1982] QB 1053), namely the defendant's conduct is dishonest by reference to the ordinary standards of reasonable and honest people **and** that he himself realised that his conduct was dishonest by those standards.

CASE EXAMPLE

Twinsectra Ltd v Yardley [2002] UKHL 12, HL

Mr Leach (L), the second defendant, was a solicitor. He acted for an entrepreneur, Mr Yardley (Y), in a transaction involving a loan of £1m from Twinsectra Ltd. L did not deal directly with Twinsectra. Another firm of solicitors, Sims (S), acted on behalf of Y. S received the money in return for an undertaking to the effect that the fund would be applied solely in the acquisition of a specified property. Contrary to the undertaking, S did not retain the money, but paid it over to L. The latter in turn took no steps to ensure that it was utilised for the stated purpose but simply paid it out upon Y's instructions. The result was that £357,700 was used by Y for purposes other than the acquisition of property. The loan was not repaid. Twinsectra sued all the parties involved, including L. The claim against him was based on dishonestly assisting S in a breach of trust. The trial judge made a significant finding to the effect that L did not act dishonestly (but was misguided) in receiving the money and paying it to Y without concerning himself about its application. The issue before the House of Lords was whether L was liable for dishonestly assisting S in a fraudulent breach of trust. The court decided that the claim did not succeed, on the following grounds:

(a) (Lord Millet dissenting.) In determining whether a defendant acted dishonestly under accessorial liability a combined objective/subjective test was applicable. The test requires the claimant to prove that the defendant was (i) dishonest by the ordinary standards of reasonable and honest people (objective) and (ii) that he himself realised that his conduct was dishonest by those standards (subjective).

(b) A reversal of the decision of the trial judge on a question of fact may only be done in exceptional circumstances. On the facts there was sufficient evidence to indicate that the trial judge had not misdirected himself as to the appropriate test for dishonesty.

CONTINUED ▶

J

'There is a passage in the earlier part of the judgment in *Royal Brunei* [1995] 2 AC 378 which suggests that Lord Nicholls considered that dishonesty has a subjective element. Thus in discussing the honest trustee and the dishonest third party, he stated: "These examples suggest that what matters is the state of mind of the third party ... But [the trustee's] state of mind is essentially irrelevant to the question whether the third party should be made liable to the beneficiaries for breach of trust." However, after stating that the touchstone of liability is dishonesty, Lord Nicholls went on to discuss the meaning of dishonesty: "Before considering this issue further it will be helpful to define the terms being used by looking more closely at what dishonesty means in this context. Whatever may be the position in some criminal or other contexts (see, for instance, *R v Ghosh* [1982] QB 1053), in the context of the accessory liability principle acting dishonestly, or with a lack of probity, which is synonymous, means simply not acting as an honest person would in the circumstances. This is an objective standard." Further, Lord Nicholls said: "Ultimately, in most cases, an honest person should have little difficulty in knowing whether a proposed transaction, or his participation in it, would offend the normally accepted standards of honest conduct. Likewise, when called upon to decide whether a person was acting honestly, a court will look at all the circumstances known to the third party at the time. The court will also have regard to personal attributes of the third party, such as his experience and intelligence, and the reason why he acted as he did."

The use of the word "knowing" in the first sentence would be superfluous if the defendant did not have to be aware that what he was doing would offend the normally accepted standards of honest conduct, and the need to look at the experience and intelligence of the defendant would also appear superfluous if all that was required was a purely objective standard of dishonesty. Therefore I do not think that Lord Nicholls was stating that in this sphere of equity a man can be dishonest even if he does not know that what he is doing would be regarded as dishonest by honest people.'

(Lord Hutton)

In *Satnam v Heywood* [1999] 3 All ER 652, the Court of Appeal decided that in order to make a third party liable as a constructive trustee, a link has to be established between a profit made by the third party and confidential information obtained from a fiduciary.

CASE EXAMPLE

Satnam v Heywood [1999] 3 All ER 652

Satnam Investments (S Ltd), a property development company, acquired an option to purchase a site with development potential. The site owners were entitled to terminate the option if S Ltd went into receivership. S Ltd was placed into receivership by its banks. Shortly afterwards Dunlop Heywood Ltd (H Ltd), a company of surveyors which had acted for S Ltd in respect of the site, disclosed to Morbaine Ltd (M Ltd), a rival development company, that S Ltd had an interest in the site, administrative receivers had been appointed and that the local planning authority was well disposed towards development. This information was disclosed without S Ltd's authority. After receiving the information M Ltd sought to acquire an interest in the site. The owners of the site terminated S Ltd's option and sold the site to M Ltd. After the discharge of the receivers, S Ltd brought proceedings against H Ltd and M Ltd contending that H Ltd had breached its fiduciary obligations by disclosing the information to M Ltd and that M Ltd had been aware of the breach and became a constructive trustee of the site for S Ltd. The trial judge upheld the claim even though he made no finding that M Ltd had acted dishonestly or participated in H Ltd's breach of fiduciary duty. M Ltd appealed.

The Court of Appeal allowed the appeal on the following grounds:

(1) H Ltd was a fiduciary and acted in breach of its duties to S Ltd in disclosing confidential information to M Ltd without S Ltd's authority.

(2) Some of the information disclosed to M Ltd was either available to M Ltd or would have been available on reasonable enquiry, once the news of S Ltd's receivership had become known.

(3) If the information could be treated as trust property, there was insufficient *nexus* between the information and the acquisition of the site in order to make M Ltd liable as a constructive trustee for knowingly receiving trust property.

(4) Since the judge made no finding that M Ltd acted dishonestly, M Ltd could not be liable as an accessory to a dishonest breach of trust by H Ltd.

■Key facts on strangers as constructive trustees

KEY FACTS

General rule

- Third parties, strangers to a trust or agents of the trustees do not become constructive trustees simply because of a breach of trust committed by the trustees or even a neglect of duties by the agent.

Mara v Browne (1896); *Barnes v Addy* (1874)

Intermeddlers/constructive trustees

- **A trustee *de son tort*** (of his own wrongdoing)

Boardman v Phipps (1967)

- **Categories of knowledge**

Re Baden Delvaux (1983)

- **Knowingly receiving or dealing with trust property for his own use**

Belmont Finance Corporation v Williams Furniture & Others (No 2) (1980); *International Sales and Agencies Ltd v Marcus* (1982); *Carl Zeiss Stiftung v Herbert Smith & Co (No 2)* (1969); *Re Montagu's Settlement* (1987); *Cowan de Groot Properties Ltd v Eagle Trust plc* (1992); *Barclays Bank v Quincecare Ltd* (1992); *Lipkin Gorman v Karpnale* (1992); *Satnam v Heywood* (1999)

CONTINUED ▶

KEY FACTS

• Alternative rationale – unconscionability, dishonesty	*BCCI v Akindele* (2000)
• Dishonest assistance or accessory liability	*Polly Peck International plc v Nadir and Others (No 2)* (1992); *Re Baden Delvaux* (1983); *Royal Brunei Airlines v Tan* (1995)
• Is dishonest assistance a genuine category of constructive trust?	*Paragon Finance Ltd v Thakerar* (1999)
• The standard of proof	*Heinl v Jayske Bank (Gibraltar)* (1999)
• Test for dishonesty	*Twinsectra Ltd v Yardley* (2002)

ACTIVITY

1. In what circumstances will an agent or stranger to a trust be liable to account for 'knowingly receiving and dealing' with trust property and 'knowingly assisting in a fraudulent design'?

2. During negotiations for the purchase of Blackacre, Paul, the purchaser, purporting to act on behalf of the vendors, sought and obtained planning permission for the land, thereby greatly increasing its value. Victor, the vendor, was unaware of this, but had he known, would have demanded a higher price for Blackacre. Paul has recently sold the property to Thomas for a handsome profit

   Victor seeks your advice as to whether he may force Paul to account for the profit resulting from the grant of planning permission.

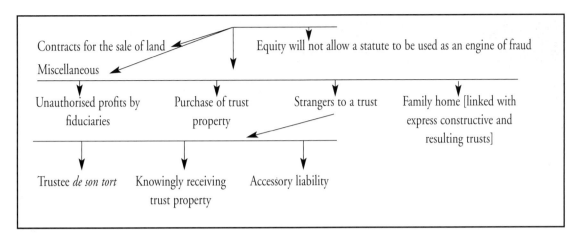

■ *Figure 9.1 Constructive trusts*

Further reading

Baughen, S, '*Quistclose* Trusts and Knowing Receipt' (2000) Conv 351.

Clark, P, 'The Family Home: Intention and Agreement' [1992] Fam Law 73.

Ferris, G, 'The advice of the Privy Council in *Royal Brunei Airlines v Tan*' (1996) 30 *Law Teacher* 111.

Gardner, S, 'Two maxims of equity: casenote on *A-G for Hong Kong v Reid*' (1995) 54 CLJ 60.

Gardner, S, 'Knowing assistance and knowing receipt: taking stock' (1996) 112 LQR 56.

Hayton, D, 'Constructive trusts of homes – a bold approach' (1993) 109 LQR 485.

Hibbert, T, 'Dishonesty and Knowledge of Accesories and Recipients' (2000) JIBL 138.

Millett, P, 'Restitution and Constructive Trusts' (1998) 114 LQR 399.

Millett, Lord, 'The Husband the Wife and the Bank' (2001) PCB 238.

Panesar, S, 'A loan subject to a Trust and Dishonest Assistance by a Third Party' (2003) 18 JIBL 9.

SECRET TRUSTS AND MUTUAL WILLS ■

10.1 Introduction

A secret trust is an equitable obligation communicated to an intended trustee during the testator's lifetime, but which is intended to attach to a gift arising under the testator's will.

A testator who wishes to create a trust over his property upon his death is required to express this intention as well as the terms of the trust in his will. The formalities necessary to create a valid will are required to be complied with. These formalities are enacted in s 9 of the Wills Act 1837 (as amended). The basic requirement is the need for writing signed by the testator and witnessed by two or more witnesses. The secret trust is an exception to this rule because in limited circumstances where a testator has not fully complied with the necessary formalities, equity will nevertheless impose a duty upon the party acquiring the property under the will (legatee or devisee) to carry out the wishes of the testator. This will require the legatee or devisee to hold the property upon trust for the secret beneficiaries.

On a testator's death his will becomes a public document and wills are consequently open to public scrutiny. But the testator may wish to make provision, after his death, for what he considers to be some embarrassing object, such as a mistress or an illegitimate child. To avoid adverse publicity, he may make an apparent gift by will to an intended trustee, subject to an understanding to hold the property for the benefit of the secret beneficiary.

10.2 Two types of secret trusts

There are two types of secret trust:

- fully secret trusts
- half-secret trusts.

A fully secret trust is an obligation which is fully concealed on the face of the will. The obligation is communicated to the legatee during the lifetime of the testator and the will transfers the property to the legatee without mention of the existence of a trust; ie the existence and *a fortiori* the terms of the trust are fully concealed on the face of the instrument creating the trust, namely the will. For example, a disposition by will 'to A absolutely'.

A half-secret trust is intended when the will indicates or acknowledges the existence of the trust but the terms are concealed on the face of the will. The trustee will then take the property on trust subject to a valid communication of the terms effected *inter vivos*, for example a disposition by will 'to A on trust for purposes communicated to him'.

Thus, assuming there has been a valid communication of the terms of the trust, the category of secret trust involved depends on whether the trust has been acknowledged on the face of the will or not. This is important, for the two types of secret trust are subject to different rules.

In enforcing secret trusts, equity does not contradict s 9 of the Wills Act 1837, as amended, because the trust operates outside (*dehors*) the Wills Act. Indeed, the secret trust complements the will in that a valid will is assumed, but it is recognised that the will on its own does not reflect the true intention of the testator. The bare minimum requirements are a validly executed will which transfers property to the trustees, whether named as such under the will or not; and the acceptance by the trustees *inter vivos* of an equitable obligation. Section 15 of the Wills Act 1837 is not applicable in this context. Section 15 of the 1837 Act enacts that an attesting witness (including his spouse) loses his interest under the will. It will be recalled that one of the formalities under the Wills Act 1837 involves two or more attesting witnesses. The Wills Act 1968 amended this requirement to allow additional attesting witnesses (and their spouses) exceeding two to acquire property under the testator's will. Accordingly, if there are three attesting witnesses under a will and one of these has been bequeathed property under the will, that witness's interest will not lapse. In *Re Young* [1951] Ch 344, the court decided that the secret trust operated outside the will in the sense that it was immaterial that one of the intended beneficiaries under *the trust*, as distinct from the *will*, witnessed the will.

CASE EXAMPLE

Re Young [1951] Ch 344

A testator made a bequest to his wife subject to a direction made outside the will to the effect that on her death she would leave the property for the purpose which he had communicated to her. One of the purposes was that she would leave a legacy of £2,000 to the testator's chauffeur, who witnessed the will. The question in issue was whether the chauffeur had forfeited his interest. The court held that the trust in favour of the chauffeur was not contained in the will but was created separately outside the will. Section 15 of the Wills Act 1837 was not applicable.

> J   'The whole theory of the formation of a secret trust is that the Wills Act 1837 has nothing to do with the matter because the forms required by the Wills Act are entirely disregarded, since the persons do not take by virtue of the gift in the will, but by virtue of the secret trusts imposed upon the beneficiary who does in fact take under the will.'
>
> (Danckwerts J)

A variation of the *dehors* theory is to the effect that the trust is created *inter vivos* and outside or independently of the will. The notion here is that is that the trust is created by reason of the personal obligation accepted by the legatee. Thus, the argument proceeds on the assumption that the date of the creation of the trust is during the lifetime of the settlor: see *Re Gardner (No 2)* [1923] 2 Ch 230. This theory is fundamentally flawed in both trusts and probate law. On the date of the communication of the terms of the trust to the legatee (trustee) the trustee has not acquired the intended property. Thus, there cannot be a valid trust. In probate law a will speaks from the date of the death of the testator. Before this date the legatee has merely a hope of acquiring a benefit under the will.

Traditionally, the trust property is transferred by will on condition that the trustee (who takes under the will as legatee or devisee) holds the property subject to an agreement entered into between the testator and himself. Likewise, the secret trust principles will extend to intestacies. These are occasions (as illustrated by *Sellack v Harris* (1708)) where the settlor decides not to make a will on the faith of a promise by his next of kin to dispose of the property in accordance with the settlor's wishes as disclosed to him during the lifetime of the settlor.

ASE EXAMPLE

Sellack v Harris (1708) 5 Vin Ab 521

A father was induced by his heir presumptive (entitled to realty on an intestacy before 1925) not to make a will on the ground that the heir himself would make provision for his mother. After the death of his father, the heir refused to make provision as promised. The court held that the heir was obliged to make the relevant provision for he had induced his father to refrain from making a will.

10.3 Basis for enforcing secret trusts

The theoretical justification for enforcing secret trusts is said to be the need to prevent fraud. The court originally applied the maxim 'Equity will not allow a statute to be used as an engine for fraud'. The statute in this respect is the Wills Act 1837. The jurisdiction adopted by the courts in order to enforce secret trusts was to prevent the legatee or devisee fraudulently denying the binding nature of his promise and attempting to set up s 9 of the Wills Act 1837 as a defence, eg if, during his lifetime, a testator (T) made an agreement with A (a legatee) to the effect that on T's death, £50,000 would be transferred to him to hold on trust for B and T made a will to that effect. Following T's death, it would be a fraud on the estate of T and B for A to deny the agreement or non-compliance with s 9 of the 1837 Act and claim the property beneficially. Consequently the court will step in and compel A to honour his agreement. This theory was enunciated by Lord

Westbury in *McCormick v Grogan* (1869) LR 4 HL 82. However, in the same case, Lord Hatherley put forward a different interpretation of the notion of fraud. His view of the fraud focused on an inducement by the intended legatee (trustee) to assure the testator that the transfer of property to the legatee will be held upon trust in accordance with his wishes, and the legatee subsequently attempts to deny the promise. In the above example the court proceeded on the basis of frustrating A's course of action if he induced T to transfer property to him in order to carry out T's wishes, and after T's death A attempts to claim the property beneficially by relying on the statute. Half-secret trusts cannot be justified on this basis, for the will transfers the property to persons named as trustees and such persons are not allowed to take property beneficially. Thus, the trustee may not profit from his fraud. If the intended half-secret trust fails, a resulting trust will be set up.

An alternative basis for enforcing secret trusts is the transfer and declaration theory. The approach here is that the will transfers the property to the trustee, subject to an express, conditional declaration of trust executed by the testator outside the will. The conditional declaration of trust will be activated when the trustee acquires the relevant property under the testator's will. The secret trust becomes effective when the trustee acquires the property under the testator's will, subject to the valid declaration. The court steps in and compels the trustee to carry out the wishes of the testator as indicated in the declaration. The conditional *inter vivos* declaration becomes effective on the death of the testator and specifically when the legatee acquires the property. The trust is not created *inter vivos*, but on death, and subject to an *inter vivos* declaration or communication of the testator's wishes. This approach was advocated by Lord Sumner in *Blackwell v Blackwell* [1929] AC 318:

> **J** 'The court of equity finds a man in the position of an absolute legal owner of a sum of money, which has been bequeathed to him under a valid will and it declares that, on proof of certain facts relating to the motives of the testator, it will not allow the legal owner to exercise his legal right to do what he wishes with the property. In other words it lets him take what the will gives him and then makes him apply it as the Court of Conscience directs, and it does so in order to give effect to the wishes of the testator, which would not otherwise be effectual.'
>
> (Lord Sumner)

A variation on this theory is the *dehors* analysis, as outlined above.

10.4 Requirements for the creation of fully secret trusts

- The claimant is required to prove that the testator, during his lifetime, communicated the terms of the trust to the legatee. It is immaterial whether the communication was made before or after the execution of the will provided that it was made before the death of the testator.

207

Communication may take place directly by means of an oral statement or in writing outside the will. In addition, communication may take place constructively, ie by delivery of a sealed envelope containing the terms of the trust to the trustee during the lifetime of the testator, but headed 'Not to be opened before my death'. Provided that the trustee is aware that the contents of the envelope is connected with the testator's will, communication is deemed to be effective on the date of the delivery of the envelope. This is illustrated by *Re Keen* [1937] Ch 236 (below).

- The trustee is required to accept the trust obligation during the testator's lifetime. This may be manifested by means of an acknowledgement by the legatee (trustee) to be bound by the terms of the trust. Alternatively, acceptance may exist through acquiescence or silence on the part of the legatee. Once the legatee is aware of the intention of the testator and this intention is complete in the sense that all the terms have been communicated to the legatee, he is bound to hold on trust for those purposes. The legatee is not required to do anything positive to demonstrate acceptance, he is deemed to accept the terms of the trust once he is aware of the testator's wishes during his lifetime.

Brightman J, in *Ottaway v Norman* [1972] Ch 698, identified the basic requirements for a fully secret trust thus:

> **J** 'It will be convenient to call the person upon whom such a trust is imposed the "primary donee" and the beneficiary under the trust the "secondary donee". The essential elements which must be proved to exist are:
>
> (i) the intention of the testator to subject the primary donee to an obligation in favour of the secondary donee;
>
> (ii) communication of that intention to the primary donee; and
>
> (iii) the acceptance of that obligation by the primary donee either expressly or by acquiescence. It is immaterial whether these elements precede or succeed the will of the donor.'

As a corollary to the communication principle where the legatee does not wish to be bound by the terms of the trust communicated to him he is under an obligation to notify the testator of his refusal during the testator's lifetime. Failure to accomplish this means that the legatee is bound by the terms communicated to him. In *Moss v Cooper* (1861) 1 J & H 352, it was decided that a legatee's failure to communicate his intention to the testator during the latter's lifetime did not absolve him from the liability to hold on trust for purposes known to him.

10.4.1 No agreement for transferee to hold as trustee

If there is no agreement between the testator and the legatee whereby the transferee is intended to hold as trustee, the transferee takes beneficially and may set up s 9 of the Wills Act 1837 as a defence. The distinction here is between a legacy *simpliciter* and a legacy upon trust.

CASE EXAMPLE

Wallgrave v Tebbs (1855) 2 K & J 313

A testator, by will, transferred personal and real property to two individuals absolutely. The testator was contemplating the identities of the ultimate beneficiaries under the trust but failed, during his lifetime, to notify the two individuals of his selection. The court decided that the two individuals were entitled to the properties beneficially. They had not acted unconscionably by claiming the properties beneficially because they did not make an agreement to hold on trust.

> 'I am satisfied that I ought not overstep the clear line which separates "mere trusts" from 'devises and bequests" ... Where a person, knowing that a testator in making a disposition in his favour intends it to be applied for purposes other than for his own benefit either expressly promises, or by silence implies, that he will carry out the testator's intention into effect, and the property is left to him upon the faith of an undertaking, it is in effect a case of trust and the court will not allow the devisee to set up the Statute of Frauds – or rather the Statute of Wills as a defence. But the question here is totally different. Here there has been no promise or undertaking on the part of the legatee. The latter knew nothing of the testator's intention until after his death. Upon the face of the will, the parties take indisputably for their own benefit.'
>
> (Wood VC)

10.4.2 Terms of trust not communicated

If the transferee agreed to hold the property on trust, but the terms of the trust have not been communicated during the testator's lifetime, the transferee will hold the property on resulting trust for the testator's heirs. The intended secret trust fails because there has been a failure to communicate the terms of the trust to the legatee during the lifetime of the testator. But, since the legatee is aware that he is required to hold on trust and acquires the property on the basis of this understanding, he holds the same on resulting trust for the testator. This principle was applied in *Re Boyes* (1884) 26 Ch D 531.

CASE EXAMPLE

Re Boyes; Boyes v Carritt (1884) 26 Ch D 531

A testator, by will, transferred property to a legatee, having secured an agreement from the legatee to hold on trust. The testator died before he communicated the terms to the legatee. The court decided that the intended secret trust failed but a resulting trust was created for the testator's heirs.

> **J** 'If the trust was not declared when the will was made, it is essential, in order to make it binding, that it should be communicated to the devisee or legatee in the testator's lifetime and that he should accept that particular trust.'
>
> (Kay J)

The fully secret trust obligation normally takes the form of the legatee (trustee) holding the property on trust for the secret beneficiary. Alternatively, the obligation may involve the legatee executing a will in favour of the secret beneficiary. In this event, the legatee may enjoy the property beneficially during his lifetime, but the obligation undertaken requires him to transfer the relevant property by his will to the named beneficiary. Accordingly, there are two beneficiaries involved in the transaction – the 'primary beneficiary' who acquires an interest for life and the 'secondary beneficiary' who is entitled to acquire the property under the will of the primary beneficiary.

CASE EXAMPLE

Ottaway v Norman [1972] Ch 698

A testator, Harry Ottaway, by his will devised his bungalow (with fixtures, fittings and furniture) to his housekeeper, Miss Hodges, in fee simple and gave her a legacy of £1,500. It was alleged that Miss Hodges had verbally agreed with the testator to leave by her will the bungalow and fittings, etc, and whatever 'money' was left over at the time of her death to the claimants, Mr and Mrs William Ottaway (the testator's son and daughter-in-law). By her will, Miss Hodges left all her property to someone else. The claimants sued Mr Norman (Miss Hodges' executor) for a declaration that the relevant parts of Miss Hodges' estate were held upon trust for the claimants. The court decided that there was clear evidence that a fully secret trust was created only in respect of the bungalow and fittings, etc, but not in respect of the 'money'. The intended trust of the money was uncertain and void. Mr Norman as her executor therefore held the bungalow on trust for Mr and Mrs William Ottaway.

CONTINUED ▸

> **J** 'I am content to assume for present purposes but without so deciding that if property is given to the primary donee on the understanding that the primary donee will dispose by his will of such assets, if any, as he may have at his command at his death in favour of the secondary donee, a valid trust is created in favour of the secondary donee which is in suspense during the lifetime of the primary donee, but attaches to the estate of the primary donee at the moment of the latter's death. There would seem to be at least some support for this proposition in an Australian case *Birmingham v Renfrew* (1937) 57 CLR 666.'
>
> (Brightman J)

10.4.3 Two or more legatees

Where a testator leaves property to two or more legatees but informs one or some of them (but not all of them) of the terms of the trust, the issue arises as to whether the uninformed legatees are bound by the communication to the informed legatees. The solution here depends on the timing of the communication and the status of the legatees. If (a) the communication was made to the legatees before or at the time of the execution of the will and (b) they take as joint tenants, the uninformed legatees are bound to hold for the purposes communicated to the informed legatees. The reason commonly ascribed to this principle is that no one is allowed to take property beneficially under a fraud committed by another. But if any of the above conditions is not satisfied, the uninformed legatees are entitled to take the property beneficially; the reason stated for this aspect of the rule is that the gift is not tainted with any fraud in procuring the execution of the will. Thus, if some of the legatees were told of the terms of the trust after the execution of the will but during the lifetime of the testator, the uninformed legatees will take part of the property beneficially. The informed legatees, of course, will hold on trust. In *Re Stead* [1900] 1 Ch 237, Farwell J reviewed the authorities and the justification for the rule, and confessed that he was unable to see any difference between a gift made on the faith of an antecedent promise and a gift left unrevoked on the faith of a subsequent promise to carry out the testator's wishes. He added, however, that he was bound by the principle.

This rule, by its nature, may not be extended to half-secret trusts for the trustee on the face of the will is not entitled to the property beneficially.

10.5 Requirements for the creation of half-secret trusts

This classification arises where the legatee or devisee takes as trustee on the face of the will but the terms of the trust are not specified in the will: for instance, T, a testator, transfers property to L, a legatee, to 'hold upon trust for purposes that have been communicated to him'. The will acknowledges the existence of the trust but the terms have been concealed.

The following points are relevant in order to establish a half-secret trust.

The will is irrevocable and sacrosanct on the death of the testator

Accordingly, evidence is not admissible to contradict the terms of the will. To adduce such evidence would have the potential to perpetrate a fraud: for instance, if the will points to a past communication (ie a communication of the terms of the trust before the will was made), evidence is not admissible to prove a future communication. Similarly, since the will names the legatee as trustee, evidence is not admissible to prove that he is a beneficiary, even of part of the property. This is the position even though the testator may wish the legatee to receive part of the property beneficially. If the testator wishes to benefit the legatee (trustee) he is required to express his intention in a separate disposition under the will.

CASE EXAMPLE

Re Rees [1950] Ch 204

A testator, by his will, appointed his friend H and his solicitor W to be executors and trustees and he devised and bequeathed all his property to 'my trustees absolutely, they well knowing my wishes concerning the same'. The testator told the executors and trustees at the time of making the will that he wished them to make certain payments out of the estate and retain the remainder for their own use. After the payments were made, there was a substantial surplus remaining. The executors claimed that they were entitled to keep the surplus in that there was no secret trust but a conditional gift in their favour. The court held that the surplus could not be taken by the executors and trustees beneficially. The relevant clause in the will created a half-secret trust and the trustees were not entitled to adduce evidence to show that they were entitled beneficially. The surplus funds passed on intestacy to the next of kin.

Communication before or at time of execution of the will

It is imperative that the testator communicate the terms of the trust before or at the time of the execution of the will and the intended trustees are required to accept (expressly or acquiescence) the obligation to hold on trust before or at the time of the execution of the will. Thus, an agreement between the parties is required to be made at the time of the execution of the will. On this basis the terms of the trust may be proved and the equitable obligation will be effective.

CASE EXAMPLE

Blackwell v Blackwell [1929] AC 318

A testator, by a codicil (an alteration of a will executed in accordance with the Wills Act 1837), bequeathed a legacy of £12,000 to five persons 'to apply for the purposes indicated by me to them'. Before the execution of the codicil, the terms of the trust were communicated to the legatees and the trust was accepted by them all. The beneficiaries were the testator's mistress and her illegitimate son. The claimant asked the court for a declaration that no valid trust in favour of the objects had been created, on the ground that parol evidence (oral evidence) was inadmissible to establish the trust. The court held that the trust was valid. Parol evidence was admissible to establish the terms of a half-secret trust in order to prevent the testator's intention being fraudulently avoided. The evidence did not vary the will; it merely gave effect to the intention of the testator.

> **J** 'Why should equity forbid an honest trustee to give effect to his promise, made to a deceased testator, and compel him to pay another legatee, about whom it is quite certain that the testator did not mean to make him the object of his bounty? ... the testator's wishes are incompletely expressed in his will.'
>
> (Lord Sumner)

Communication after the execution of the will

If the agreement between the testator and the trustees is made **after** the execution of the will, even if this is made in accordance with the will and during the lifetime of the testator, it is settled law that such evidence may not be adduced to prove the terms of the trust. The reason given for this controversial principle was stated by Viscount Sumner in *Blackwell v Blackwell* [1929] AC 318:

> **J** 'A testator cannot reserve to himself a power of making future unwitnessed dispositions by merely naming a trustee and leaving the purposes of the trust to be supplied afterwards, nor can a legatee give testamentary validity to an unexecuted codicil by accepting an indefinite trust, never communicated to him in the testator's lifetime ... To hold otherwise would indeed be to enable the testator to "give the go-by" to the requirements of the Wills Act, because he did not choose to comply with them. It is communication of the purpose to the legatee coupled with acquiescence or promise on his part, that removes the matter from the provision of the Wills Act and brings it within the law of trusts ... '.

CASE EXAMPLE

Re Keen [1937] Ch 236

A testator bequeathed a legacy to two legatees, A and B, 'to be held upon trust and disposed of by them among such persons or charities as may be notified by me to them or either of them during my lifetime'. Prior to the execution of the will, A had been given a sealed envelope subject to the direction, 'Not to be opened before my death'. A considered himself bound to hold the legacy subject to the terms declared in the envelope. The envelope contained the name of the beneficiary under the intended trust. Subsequently, the testator revoked the original will and executed a new will which contained an identical bequest. No fresh directions were issued to A, who was still prepared to carry out the testator's wishes. After the testator's death, an application was made to the court to determine whether the executors were required to distribute the property to A and B as trustees for the specified beneficiary or, alternatively, for the residuary estate. The Court of Appeal held that the trust failed and the property fell into residue on the grounds that:

(a) the delivery of the envelope constituted communication of the terms of the trust at the time of delivery. Since this was made prior to the execution of the will and was inconsistent with the terms of the will (which referred to a future communication), the letter was not admissible

(b) the provision in the will contained a power to declare trusts in the future. This power was not enforceable and the terms of the intended trust were not admissible.

But the theory underlying a secret trust (even a half-secret trust) is that it operates outside the will. The will merely transfers the property to the trustees who then hold subject to the obligation undertaken during the lifetime of the testator. The agreement between the testator and the trustees does not contradict the will but merely complements it, in that the will acknowledges a trust and the agreement supplies evidence of the trust. It is highly probable that the prohibition of post-will communications amounts to a confused or corrupt version of the probate doctrine of 'incorporation by reference'. In accordance with this doctrine an unattested document (eg a letter) may be joined and read with an attested document (eg a will). The conditions are that the former document is executed before, or at the time of, and is specifically referred to in, the attested document. In these circumstances, in probate law, the unattested document becomes public in much the same way as the will. In half-secret trusts there is no general requirement that the communication of the terms of the trust to the trustees be made in writing as is required under the probate doctrine.

In the context of fully secret trusts, it will be recalled, there is no equivalent to this rule. The terms of the fully secret trust may be agreed either before or after the execution of the will, provided that it was done during the lifetime of the testator.

Trustees not entitled to take property beneficially

The persons named as trustees on the face of the will are not entitled to take any part of the property beneficially. The reason is that to admit such evidence would have the effect of contradicting the will. Accordingly, it is immaterial that the testator made such an arrangement with the trustees before the execution of the will, see *Re Rees* (1950) (above). Likewise, on a failure, wholly or partly, of the secret trust, the trustee holds the property on resulting trust for the testator's estate or next of kin.

It should be noted that this principle does not apply to fully secret trusts. In such cases there is no objection to the intended trustees leading evidence to prove that they were intended to benefit in accordance with the intention of the testator, for the will does not name them as trustees but as apparent beneficiaries. There will be no contradiction of the will.

Testator adding further property

If the testator wishes to add further property he is required to make an agreement with the trustees to that effect. This may involve the testator executing a new will or codicil. If the testator fails to take the trustees into his confidence regarding the additional amount the trust of this amount will fail and a resulting trust will arise.

CASE EXAMPLE

Re Colin Cooper [1939] Ch 811

A testator bequeathed the sum of £5,000 to two trustees upon trust for purposes 'already communicated to them'. Shortly before his death he executed a codicil giving the same trustees the sum of £10,000, declaring that 'they knowing my wishes regarding that sum'. The testator failed to inform the trustees of this new bequest. On the question of the validity of the trust of the additional bequest. The Court of Appeal held that the gift failed and a resulting trust of the additional £5,000 was created. In respect of the £5,000 which the trustees had agreed to hold upon trust, a valid secret trust was created.

Although *Re Colin Cooper* (1939) involved a half-secret trust there is no reason, in principle, why this rule should not be extended to fully secret trusts. The consequence of failure, however, may be different. When a fully secret trust fails, the legatee takes the property beneficially. Thus, if there has been no agreement between the testator and the legatee (intended trustee) concerning the additional amount the legatee may be entitled to take this sum beneficially. The conscience of the legatee may not be affected.

10.6 Unresolved issues connected with secret trusts

10.6.1 Standard of proof

The traditional rule regarding the standard of proof applicable to fully and half-secret trusts is 'clear evidence', ie the quality of evidence that is required to rectify an instrument. In other words, the standard of proof to establish a secret trust exceeds the ordinary civil standard of a balance of probabilities but it is not as high as the criminal standard of proof.

> J
>
> '... if a will contains a gift which is in terms absolute, clear evidence is needed before the court will assume that the testator did not mean what he said. It is perhaps analogous to the standard of proof which this court requires before it will rectify a written instrument, for there again a party is saying that neither meant what they have written ...'
>
> Brightman J in *Ottaway v Norman* [1972] Ch 698

More recently, Megarry VC in *Re Snowden* [1979] Ch 528 introduced a more flexible standard of proof which is dependent on whether an allegation of fraud exists or not. In cases involving an allegation of fraud the standard of proof is higher. This exceeds a balance of probabilities. In other cases the ordinary civil standard of proof on a balance of probabilities is required to be established.

> J
>
> 'I am not sure that it is right to assume that there is a single, uniform standard of proof for all secret trusts ... If a secret trust can be held to exist in a particular case only by holding the legatee guilty of fraud, then no secret trust should be found unless the standard of proof suffices for fraud. On the other hand, if there is no question of fraud, why should so high a standard apply? In accordance with the general rule of evidence the standard of proof should vary with the nature of the issue and its gravity, see *Hornal v Neuberger* [1956] 3 All ER 970. I therefore hold that in order to establish a secret trust where no question of fraud arises, the standard of proof is the ordinary civil standard of proof that is required to establish an ordinary trust.'
>
> (Megarry VC)

On the question of what constitutes an allegation of fraud, which will import a higher standard of proof? Megarry VC in *Re Snowden* (1979) decided that these are cases when the legatee denies the existence of a trust, with the effect that he may be entitled to the property beneficially under the will:

> **J** 'It seems to me that fraud comes into the matter in two ways. First, it provides an historical explanation of the doctrine of secret trusts: the doctrine was evolved as a means of preventing fraud. That, however, does not mean that fraud is an essential ingredient for the application of the doctrine: the reason for the rule is not part of the rule itself. Second, there are some cases within the doctrine where fraud is indeed involved. *There are cases where for the legatee to assert that he is a beneficial owner, free from any trust, would be a fraud on his part.*'
>
> (Megarry VC)

The effect of this description of fraud is that it is restricted to allegations of fully secret trusts when the legatee denies the existence of an agreement with the testator to hold on trust. If the legatee acknowledges the existence of a trust but disputes a term of the trust, such as the identity of the beneficiary, the higher standard of proof may not be applicable. On the other hand, if the allegation concerns the existence of a half-secret trust, the lower standard of proof is applicable because the named trustee cannot adduce evidence that he is entitled beneficially.

10.6.2 Death of a secret beneficiary

If an intended secret beneficiary dies during the lifetime of the testator without a variation of the agreement, in principle, his interest under the intended trust ought to lapse. The reason is that the trust is created after the death of the testator or the latest moment in time when the trustees acquire the property. This can only happen after the death of the testator. However, in *Re Gardner (No 2)* (1923), Romer J came to the absurd conclusion that the secret beneficiary's interest did not lapse and his heirs were entitled to the property. It is generally recognised that this view cannot be supported in both trusts law and probate law. In the law of trusts, as explained above, the trust may be created at the earliest moment on the death of the testator. During the testator's lifetime a trust cannot exist because the trustees do not acquire the trust property and the intended beneficiaries obtain merely a *spes* or hope of enjoying the property. It is trite law that a *spes* cannot become the subject-matter of a trust. In any event, in probate law a disposition by will takes effect only on the death of the testator.

It is unlikely that the *Re Gardner (No 2)* (1923) solution will be extended to half-secret trusts where the intended secret beneficiary predeceases the testator. In principle, the trust will fail and a resulting trust for the testator's estate may arise.

10.6.3 Death of a secret trustee

The effect of an intended secret trustee predeceasing the testator varies with the type of secret trust intended by the testator. If a fully secret trust was intended by the testator but the trustee dies before the testator without a new agreement being reached with a different trustee, the intended trust will fail, the reason being that in probate law a legatee's interest in these circumstances will lapse. The effect is that the property will revert to the testator's estate. Cozens-Hardy MR in *Re Maddock* [1902] 2 Ch 220, in an *obiter* pronouncement, enunciated this view:

J ' ... the so-called trust does not affect property except by reason of a personal obligation binding the individual devisee or legatee. If he renounces and disclaims, or dies in the lifetime of the testator, the persons claiming under memorandum can take nothing against the heir at law or next of kin or residuary devisee or legatee.'

In the context of a half-secret trust, if the terms can be ascertained, the trust may remain valid. The court may appoint new trustees, for the maxim is 'Equity will not allow a trust to fail for want of a trustee'. The will names the legatee as a trustee and the probate rule involving lapse may not be relevant.

10.6.4 Classification of secret trusts

It is not clear whether fully secret trusts are 'express' or 'constructive'. The issue was left open in *Ottaway v Norman* (1972). The importance of the classification concerns the extent to which the formalities are applicable to the agreement between the testator and the trustee. In *Re Baillie* (1886) 2 TLR 660, it was decided that half-secret trusts are express, for the trust is apparent on the face of the will, and furthermore that s 53(1)(b) of the Law of Property Act 1925 (or its equivalent) was required to be complied with. Thus, an oral agreement between the testator and the intended trustee concerning land was unenforceable.

With regard to intended fully secret trusts, the original basis for enforcement was to prevent fraud and this was consistent with the constructive trust theory. The fraud that the trustee was prevented from perpetrating was to allege that the agreement did not comply with s 9 of the Wills Act 1837: see earlier. Section 53(2) of the Law of Property Act 1925 exempts constructive trusts from the requirements of writing under s 53(1)(b). Thus, fully secret trusts of land may be enforced despite not being evidenced in writing.

■ Key facts on secret trusts

KEY FACTS

General

The idea is to create a trust without revealing the identity of the beneficiaries on the face of a will – possibly because of moral obligations to the beneficiary.

Courts accept them if:

(i)   there is an intention to create a trust and the 'three certainties' are satisfied

(ii)   the trust is communicated to the legatee

CONTINUED ▶

KEY FACTS

(iii) the trust is accepted by the legatee.

Fully secret trusts are an apparent gift to the ostensible beneficiary.

Half-secret trusts are apparent as trusts on the face of the will.

Theoretical basis of secret trusts	Case
• Both secret and half-secret trusts fail to comply fully with Wills Act requirements. • So the testator is 'opting out'. • The fraud argument cannot apply to half-secret trusts. • So an 'independent trust' theory has been applied to both. • But has caused anomalies. • Uncertainty whether they are express or constructive.	*McCormick v Grogan* (1869); *Blackwell v Blackwell* (1929); *Re Young* (1951) *Re Snowden* (1979); *Re Gardner* (1923); *Ottaway v Norman* (1972); *Re Baillie* (1886)
Fully secret trusts	*Case*
• Ostensible beneficiary must be told of trust and agree to be bound before testator's death – or ostensible beneficiary takes absolutely. • Acquiescence is sufficient for acceptance. • They cannot be changed so are clearly inconsistent with the Wills Act. • Traditional reason they are enforced is to prevent fraud on the beneficiary.	*Wallgrave v Tebbs* (1855) *Moss v Cooper* (1861) *Ottaway v Norman* (1972)
Half-secret trusts:	*Case*
• Traditionally not enforced – because fraud on beneficiary not possible. • But were accepted in: • But, to be valid, must be communicated before making of will – not before death of testator as in fully secret.	*McCormick v Grogan* (1869); *Blackwell v Blackwell* (1929) *Re Keen* (1937)

ACTIVITY

> By his will made in 2001, Albert devised all his realty to Bertha 'in the sure and
> certain hope that she will carry out my wishes relating thereto'. In 2002, Albert
> informed Bertha verbally that she was to hold any property left to her by his will
> upon trust for Charles, David and herself in equal shares. Bertha remained silent.
> David died in January 2003. Albert has just died and his realty is worth £600,000.
>
> Advise Bertha, Charles and David's executors on the distribution of the estate.
>
> Would your advice differ if:
>
> (i) the communication of the terms of the trust to Bertha had been by unattested, but
> signed, writing handed to her in 2001, just prior to the execution of the will
>
> (ii) Charles had witnessed Albert's will?

10.7 Mutual wills

Where two or more testators wish to pool their resources together for the benefit of the ultimate
beneficiary and to give the survivor an interest, such as a life interest in the property of the first
testator to die, the 'mutual will' doctrine may be adopted by the parties. Mutual wills arise out of
an agreement between two or more persons that they will make substantially similar testamentary
dispositions in favour of a particular beneficiary. For example, A and B decide that after their death
their joint property will be transferred to Cancer Research. They may each make separate wills
transferring their property to the named charity. This does not involve mutual wills. Assume,
further, that the parties agree that the survivor ought to enjoy a life interest in the deceased's estate
and then transfer their joint resources to the specified charity. Each testator makes a will in
substantially identical terms, transferring his estate to the survivor, on the understanding that the
inter vivos agreement is binding. Each testator's will may spell out the terms of the trust, that is, to
the survivor for life with remainder to Cancer Research. Alternatively, each testator may transfer his
entire estate to the survivor. When the first testator dies (say, A) his will is required to be probated,
a trust will be created and B will enjoy a life interest in accordance with the agreement. When B
dies his entire estate (including the property taken under A's will) will be held upon trust for
Cancer Research in accordance with the *inter vivos* agreement.

10.7.1 The agreement

The agreement may be express or implied, written or oral, but it is essential that it is intended to
be binding on the survivor of the first to die. In other words, the intention of the parties must be
sufficient to amount to a contract. The parties to the agreement need not be married, although, in
practice, this is usually the case. This also makes proof of a contractual intention difficult. The basis
of the agreement and the consideration for the promise is that each party will make specific
testamentary dispositions in return for the other party doing the same. The nature and extent of

the property subject to the agreement varies with each case. The parties may limit the agreement to a specific fund or item of property (eg '50,000 Marks and Spencer plc shares') so that the survivor acquires a life interest in the property with remainder to another. But it is common for the agreement to cover the entirety of the parties' estates.

The agreement is required to be proved by clear and satisfactory evidence that, on a balance of probabilities, there had been an irrevocable agreement between the parties to dispose of their property by mutual wills. The mere fact that the wills were in identical terms and executed on the same date is not sufficient, by itself, to establish the agreement, although it will be a relevant factor to be taken into account along with the other evidence.

CASE EXAMPLE

Re Oldham [1925] Ch 75

A married couple made substantially similar wills. There was no direct evidence of an agreement that the wills were irrevocable. The husband was the first to die, leaving his estate to his widow. She later remarried and made a new will that was substantially different from the original will. On her death the claimant sought to make the widow's executor a trustee for the original purpose. The court rejected this claim and decided that there was no evidence of an irrevocable agreement between the original married couple.

J '... the fact that two wills were made in identical terms does not necessarily connote any agreement beyond that of so making them. There is no evidence that there was an agreement that the trust should in all circumstances be irrevocable. In order to enforce the trust I must be satisfied that its terms are certain and unequivocal and such as in the circumstances I am bound to give effect.'

(Astbury J)

A similar result was reached in *Re Goodchild (Decd)* [1997] 3 All ER 63, where identical wills between a husband and wife did not import the existence of an irrevocable agreement not to revoke the will.

J

'Two wills may be in the same form as each other. Each testator may leave his or her estate to the other with a view to the survivor leaving both estates to their heir. But there is no presumption that a present plan will be immutable in future. A key feature of the concept of mutual wills is the irrevocability of the mutual intentions. Not only must they be binding when made, but the testators must have undertaken, and so must be bound, not to change their intentions after the death of the first testator. The test must always be: suppose that during the lifetime of the surviving testator the intended beneficiary did something which the survivor regarded as unpardonable, would he or she be free not to leave the combined estate to him? The answer must be that the survivor is so entitled unless the testators agreed otherwise when they executed their wills. Hence the need for a clear agreement.'

(Leggatt L)

10.7.2 The effect of the agreement

An analysis of the operation of the agreement may be conducted in two stages: during the lifetime of both parties and on the death of the first to die.

During the lifetime of both parties

The agreement between the parties making mutual wills not to revoke the wills amounts to a contract and is binding on both parties from the date of the agreement. If one party, in breach of the agreement, revokes his will, the other party is entitled to sue for damages for breach of contract. The amount of loss may be nominal, for it would be difficult to quantify the loss suffered by a claimant who is aware that the other party has changed his will. The same will be the case if the ultimate beneficiary brings the claim under the Contracts (Rights of Third Parties) Act 1999. In addition, the breach of the contract by one party has the effect of releasing the other party from the agreement: see *Re Hobley*, *The Times*, 16th June 1997.

CASE EXAMPLE

Re Hobley, *The Times*, 16th June, 1997

On 4th December 1975, Mr and Mrs Hobley executed mutual wills in favour of each other, whosoever might survive, with substitutionary gifts to common beneficiaries. The house at No 65 Russel Terrace was devised to Mr Blyth and there were 11 pecuniary legatees, eight of whom were entitled to the residue. Some time later, Mr Hobley executed a codicil revoking the devise of No 65 Russel Terrace to Mr Blyth and left it as part of the residuary estate. There was no evidence as to the reason for the change or whether Mrs Hobley

CONTINUED ▶

knew of or consented to it. Mr Hobley died on 13th January 1980 and Mrs Hobley inherited his entire estate, including No 65 Russel Terrace. On 13th March 1992, Mrs Hobley executed a will which was substantially different from the 1975 will. She died on 23rd May 1993. The National Westminster Bank plc was appointed executor of Mrs Hobley's will and commenced the application to the court. The question in issue concerned the effect on the mutual will arrangement of the alteration of Mr Hobley's will. Counsel for the original beneficiaries, relying on *Hong Kong Fir Shipping Co v Kawasaki Kisen Kaisha Ltd* [1962] 2 QB 26, argued that Mr Hobley's codicil did not amount to a fundamental breach of the 1975 agreement so as to discharge Mrs Hobley from the agreement.

The High Court decided that the principles on which the court acted in order to impose a constructive trust, so as to give effect to an agreement to make and not revoke mutual wills, were not precisely the same as applied in the law of contract. The court could not evaluate the significance to the parties of any alteration in the terms of the will of the first testator, nor their subjective intentions. Moreover, it is irrelevant that the alteration did not personally disadvantage the survivor. Accordingly, the unilateral alteration of Mr Hobley's will had the effect of discharging Mrs Hobley from the agreement in 1975. She was, therefore, free to dispose of her estate as she wished.

A revocation of the agreement for these purposes is required to be intentional in the sense that it involves a positive act on the part of the party in breach. Section 18 of the Wills Act 1837 enacts that remarriage has the effect of revoking a will. This is the effect by operation of law. However, the better view is that this section is not applicable in the mutual wills context.

CASE EXAMPLE

Re Marsland [1939] Ch 820

A husband executed a deed of separation and covenanted in the same deed not to revoke a will previously made. The husband later obtained a divorce and expressed his wishes to remarry. The wife brought an action against him claiming damages for breach of covenant. The court held that remarriage does not have the effect of revoking the contract. To be actionable, a revocation of the agreement is required to be intentional.

On the death of the first testator

On the first death of one of the parties to the irrevocable agreement a trust is created by the courts in favour of the beneficiaries and is imposed on the survivor. If the survivor alters or executes another will, as he is entitled to do in accordance with probate rules, this adjusted or new will will be admitted to probate but his personal representatives will hold his property upon trust to perform the agreement.

CASE EXAMPLE

Re Hagger [1930] 2 Ch 190

A married couple made an irrevocable agreement not to revoke a joint will that transferred property to the surviving partner for life and in remainder to specified beneficiaries. The husband survived his wife and changed his will. The heirs of one of the beneficiaries, who died after the wife but before the husband, brought a successful claim to a share of the estate.

'... on the death of the first testator the position as regards that part of the property which belongs to the survivor is that the survivor will be treated in this court as holding the property on trust to apply it so as to carry out the effect of the joint will.'

(Clauson J)

The constructive trust created by the courts is imposed on the survivor, irrespective of whether or not he takes an interest in accordance with the agreement made between the two testators. The reason for this rule is to prevent the survivor committing a fraud on the beneficiaries by attempting to withdraw from the agreement.

'... I see no reason why the doctrine [of mutual wills] should be confined to cases where the second testator benefits when the aim of the principle is to prevent the first testator from being defrauded. A fraud on the first testator will include cases where the second testator benefits, but I see no reason why the principle should be confined to such cases.'

(Morritt J: *Re Dale* [1993] 3 WLR 652)

10.7.3 The scope of the agreement

It is a question of construction to determine the scope and extent of the property subject to the agreement and thus the trust. If the agreement is expressed to bind the whole of the interest owned by each party, the trust will bind the entire property owned by each party and the surviving testator may be unable to deal with his own property during his lifetime. Each case is determined on its own facts. In *Re Green* [1951] Ch 148, the constructive trust attached to half of the estate of the surviving testator in accordance with the agreement.

■Key facts on mutual wills

Similar wills made by two or more testators or joint wills on the death of the first to die	Insufficient on their own to create trusts	*Re Oldham* (1925)
PLUS agreement intended to bind the survivor of the first to die	During the lifetime of both testators (law of contract)	*Re Hobley* (1997)
	Death of the first testator (creation of constructive trust)	*Re Hagger* (1930)
	Scope of trust (construction of the agreement to ascertain the extent of the trust)	*Re Green* (1951)

ACTIVITY

Two years ago, John and his sister, Jane (both unmarried) decided that they would like to leave all their property by way of absolute gift to whoever survived the other, but with a view to the survivor leaving everything to their two nieces, Anna and Barbara. They consulted solicitors and, pursuant to their advice, John and Jane executed wills in similar terms under which each left his or her property to the other absolutely if she or he should be the survivor and in the event of her or his predeceasing the testator or testatrix then to Anna and Barbara absolutely.

John died last year, leaving a net estate worth £200,000 which passed under his will and in consequence Jane's total assets are now worth £500,000.

Jane has recently been befriended by Jasper and she is proposing:

(i) to provide the purchase price of a house of £150,000 to be vested in the joint names of herself and Jasper and

(ii) to make a fresh will leaving all her property to Jasper.

Advise Anna and Barbara as to their positions in regard to each of these proposals.

Further reading

Gratton, S, 'Mutual wills and remarriage' [1997] Conv 153.

Kincaid, D, 'The Tangled Web: The Relationship between a Secret Trust and the Will' (2000) 64 Conv 421.

Perrins, B, 'Can you keep half a secret?' (1972) 88 LQR 225.

Richardson, N, 'Floating trusts and mutual wills' (1996) 10 Tru LI 88.

Wilde, D, 'Secret and semi-secret trusts: justifying distinctions between the two' [1995] Conv 366.

chapter 11 PRIVATE PURPOSE TRUSTS ■

11.1 Introduction

An additional requirement concerning express private trusts is the need to identify beneficiaries who are capable of enforcing the trust. A purpose, as expressed by the settlor, is incapable of enforcing a trust. Alternatively, a public purpose trust, or charitable trust, is capable of being enforced by the Attorney-General. One of the duties of the Attorney-General is to act as a representative of the Crown on behalf of charitable bodies. In this context a charitable trust is designed to relieve poverty or advance education or religion or to promote other purposes beneficial to society.

An intended private purpose trust is void. A purpose trust is designed to promote a purpose as an end in itself, such as the discovery of an alphabet of 40 letters, to provide a cup for a yacht race, or the boarding up of certain rooms in a house. The effect is that such intended trusts are void, for the court is incapable of supervising the proper administration of such trusts. As there is no beneficiary with a *locus standi* capable of enforcing such trust, there is a real fear that improper behaviour by the trustees could go unnoticed. In consequence, a resulting trust arises in favour of the donor or settlor on the failure of a non-charitable purpose trust.

CASE EXAMPLE

Morice v Bishop of Durham (1804) 9 Ves 399

A bequest was made to the Bishop of Durham on trust for 'such objects of benevolence and liberality as the Bishop of Durham shall in his own discretion most approve of'. The court decided that this bequest failed as a charity because the objects were not exclusively charitable, and was invalid as a private trust, for there were no ascertainable beneficiaries.

> J '… it is a maxim, that the execution of a trust shall be under the control of the court, it must of such a nature, that it can be under that control; so that the administration of it can be reviewed by the court; or, if the trustee dies, the court itself can execute the trust; a trust therefore, which, in case of maladministration could be reformed; and a due administration directed; and then, unless the subject and objects can be ascertained, upon principles, familiar in other cases, it must be decided, that the court can neither reform maladministration, nor direct a due administration.'
>
> (Lord Eldon)

The court came to a similar conclusion in *Re Astor's Settlement Trust* [1952] Ch 534:

CASE EXAMPLE

Re Astor's Settlement Trust [1952] Ch 534

Lord Astor purported to create a trust for 'the maintenance of good understanding between nations and the preservation of the independence and integrity of newspapers'. The court held that the trust was void for uncertainty on the grounds that the means by which the trustees were to attain the stated aims were unspecified and the person who was entitled, as of right, to enforce the trust was unnamed. In other words, a trust creates rights in favour of beneficiaries and imposes correlative duties on the trustees. If there are no persons with the power to enforce such rights, then equally there can be no duties imposed on trustees.

> **J** '... the only beneficiaries are purposes and at present unascertainable persons, it is difficult to see who could initiate proceedings. If the purposes are valid trusts, the settlors have retained no beneficial interest and could not initiate them. It was suggested that the trustees might proceed *ex parte* to enforce the trusts against themselves. I doubt that, but at any rate nobody could enforce the trusts against them.'
>
> (Roxburgh J)

11.2 Reasons for failure of a private purpose trust

There are a number of common reasons why private purpose trusts fail. The list is not exhaustive but pitfalls which a settlor should avoid are:

* the lack of a beneficiary principle
* uncertainty of objects and
* the infringement of the perpetuity rule.

11.2.1 Lack of beneficiaries

A trust is mandatory in nature and imposes enforceable obligations on the trustees. Those capable of enforcing such obligations are the beneficiaries. These persons are granted rights *in rem* in the subject-matter of the trust. The courts have always jealously guarded the rights and interests of the beneficiaries under trusts. But such rights may be protected only if the beneficiary has a *locus standi* to enforce the same. Purposes cannot initiate proceedings against the trustees. Accordingly, a purported trust for private purposes is void because it lacks a beneficiary. In effect, in trusts law the courts regard two features of primary importance, namely ownership of property and the fiduciary office of trusteeship. The beneficiary, as an equitable owner, has the capacity of ensuring that the trustees carry out their duties in a responsible manner.

In other jurisdictions, such as the Cayman Islands, an alternative philosophy has been adopted whereby a settlor may expressly nominate a person to be obliged to enforce a private purpose trust against the trustees. In this context the focus of attention is not ownership but enforcement. The 'enforcer' has a public duty to enforce the trust which is followed up with severe penalties for breaches. On analogy, the English equivalent of such a third person is the Attorney-General, but only in respect of charities.

11.2.2 Uncertainty

As a corollary to the above-mentioned rule, it is obvious that the rights of the beneficiaries will be illusory unless the court is capable of ascertaining to whom those rights belong. Thus, as a second ground for the decision in *Re Astor* (1952), the trust failed for uncertainty:

> J
>
> 'If an enumeration of purposes outside the realm of charities can take the place of an enumeration of beneficiaries, the purposes must be stated in phrases which embody definite concepts and the means by which the trustees are to try to attain them must also be prescribed with a sufficient degree of certainty.'
>
> (Roxburgh J)

A case which illustrates this principle is *Re Endacott* [1960] Ch 232:

CASE EXAMPLE

Re Endacott [1960] Ch 232

A testator transferred his residuary estate to the Devon Parish Council 'for the purpose of providing some useful memorial to myself'. Lord Evershed MR held that no out-and-out gift to the Council was created, but the testator intended to impose an obligation in the nature of a trust on the Council, which failed for uncertainty of objects.

> J
>
> '… no principle has greater sanctity of authority behind it than the general proposition that a trust by English law, not being a charitable trust, in order to be effective must have ascertained or ascertainable beneficiaries'.
>
> (Lord Evershed MR)

Charitable trusts, on the other hand, are subject to a special test for certainty of objects, namely whether the objects are exclusively charitable: see later.

11.2.3 Perpetuity rule

The perpetuity rule is a common law principle (as modified by statute) which restricts the maximum period in which the vesting of property, real or personal, may be postponed (the rule against remote vesting). In addition, if the property has vested in the beneficiary the rule specifies the maximum period in which the property is required to be retained (the rule against excessive duration).

At common law, this period was measured in terms of a life or lives in being, plus 21 years. Time begins to run from the date that the instrument creating the gift takes effect (a will takes effect on the date of the death of the testator or testatrix; a deed takes effect on the date of execution). Only human lives may be chosen and not the lives of animals, some of which are noted for their longevity (such as tortoises and elephants). An embryonic child (*en ventre sa mère*) constitutes a life in being if this is relevant in measuring the period. A life or lives in being, whether connected with the gift or not, may be chosen expressly by the donor or settlor in order to extend the perpetuity period. Any number of lives may be selected. The test is whether the group of lives selected is certain and identifiable to such an extent that it is practicable to ascertain the date of death of the last survivor. This test was clearly incapable of being satisfied in *Re Moore* [1901] 1 Ch 936, where a testator defined the period as '21 years from the death of the last survivor of all persons who shall be living at my death'. The gift was considered void for uncertainty.

Indeed, the settlor may even select lives which have no connection with the trust. It became the practice to select Royal lives, such as 'the lineal descendants of Queen Elizabeth II living at my death', with the objective of ascertaining the date of death of the last survivor.

Alternatively, a life or lives in being may be implied in the circumstances if the life or lives is or are so related to the gift or settlement that it is or they are capable of being used to measure the date of the vesting of the interest. If no lives are selected or are implied, the perpetuity period at common law is 21 years from the date of the creation of the gift.

The common law approach to the perpetuity rule was based on the assumption that if there was a mere possibility, however slight, that a future interest may vest outside the perpetuity period, the grant of the interest is void *ab initio*. This was the approach of the courts before 1964. For example, if S, a settlor, during his lifetime transfers a portfolio of shares to T1 and T2 as trustees, on trust contingently for his first child to marry and S has unmarried children, this gift, before the Perpetuities and Accumulations Act 1964, would be void. S would be treated impliedly as the life in being and it was possible that none of his children may marry within 21 years after his death. Thus, there was a possibility that the gift may not vest within the perpetuity period.

The Perpetuities and Accumulations Act 1964 introduced three major reforms to the law. Under the Act, a future interest is no longer void on the ground that it 'might' vest outside the perpetuity period. It is void if, in the circumstances, the interest does not vest within the perpetuity period. In the meantime, the court will 'wait and see' whether or not the gift vests. Moreover, the Act introduced a certain and fixed period not exceeding 80 years which the grantor may expressly nominate as the perpetuity period. In addition, s 3(5) of the Act introduced a variety of persons who may be treated as a 'statutory life'. These are: the grantor, the beneficiary or potential beneficiary, the donee of a power, option or other right, parents and grandparents of the grantor and any person entitled in default. Where there are no lives within any of these categories, the 'wait and see' period is 21 years from the date the instrument takes effect.

Closely related to the perpetuity rule is the rule against excessive duration. This rule renders void any obligation to retain property for longer than the perpetuity period. The issue here is not whether the property or interest is, in fact, tied up forever but whether the owner is capable of disposing of the same within the perpetuity period. The question concerns merely the power to dispose of the capital. Thus, property may be owned perpetually by persons, companies or unincorporated associations if these bodies are entitled to dispose of the same at any time.

ASE EXAMPLE

Re Chardon [1928] Ch 464

A testator gave a fund to a cemetery company subject to the income being required to be used for the maintenance of two specified graves, with a gift over. The court held that the gift was valid, for the company was capable of alienating the property.

Charitable trusts, because of their public nature, are exempt from this principle.

11.3 Exceptions to the *Astor* principle

There are a number of private purpose trusts which are exceptionally considered to be valid. Despite the objections to the validity of purpose trusts as stated above, a number of anomalous exceptions exist. These trusts are created as concessions to human weakness. But it must be emphasised that the only concession granted by the courts is that it is unnecessary for the beneficiaries (purposes) to enforce the trust. The other rules applicable to express trusts are equally applied to these anomalous trusts (see *Re Endacott* (1960), above). Accordingly, such gifts are required to satisfy the test for certainty of objects and the perpetuity rule. These exceptionally valid trusts are not mandatory in effect but are merely 'directory' in the sense that the trustees are entitled to refuse to carry out the wishes of the settlor and the courts will not force them to do otherwise. At the same time, the courts will not forbid the trustees from carrying out the terms of the trust, if they express an intention to do so. In the latter event the traditional fiduciary duties attach to the trustees. These anomalous trusts are called 'hybrid trusts' or 'trusts for imperfect obligations'.

11.3.1 Trusts for the maintenance of animals

Gifts for the maintenance of animals generally are charitable, but trusts for the maintenance of specific animals, such as pets, are treated as valid private purpose trusts.

ASE EXAMPLE

Pettingall v Pettingall (1842) 11 LJ Ch 176

The testator's executor was given a fund in order to spend £50 per annum for the benefit of the testator's black mare. On her death, any surplus funds were to be taken by the executor. The court held that in view of the willingness of the executor to carry out the testator's wishes, a valid trust in favour of the animal was created. The residuary legatees were entitled to supervise the performance of the trust but they were not the primary beneficiaries. They were interested not in the validity of the gift but in its failure.

In *Re Dean* (1889) 41 Ch D 552, the testator directed his trustees to use £750 per annum for the maintenance of his horses and hounds should they live so long. It was held that the trust was valid. The difficulty with this case is the possible infringement of the perpetuity rule. The court treated the horses and hounds as the lives in being for the purpose of the perpetuity rule. It was stated earlier that for the purpose of the perpetuity rule a 'life' is treated as a human life. In any event, it was unclear who was entitled to enforce the trust against the trustees. In *Re Kelly* [1932] IR 255, the court took the view that lives in being were required to be human lives. In any event the court is entitled to take judicial notice of the lifetime of animals. In *Re Haines*, *The Times*, 7th November, 1952, the court took notice that a cat could not live for longer than 21 years.

In *Re Thompson* [1934] Ch 342, the *Pettingall* (1842) principle was unjustifiably extended to uphold a trust for the promotion and furtherance of fox hunting.

11.3.2 Monument cases

A trust for the building of a memorial or monument in memory of an individual is not charitable, but may exist as a valid purpose trust if the trustees express a desire to perform the task.

In *Mussett v Bingle* [1876] WN 170, a testator bequeathed £300 to his executors to be used to erect a monument to the testator's wife's first husband. The court held that the gift was valid. Similarly, a gift for the maintenance of a specific grave or particular graves may be valid as private purpose trusts but additionally, the donor is required to restrict the gift within the perpetuity period, otherwise the gift may be invalidated. In *Re Hooper* [1932] 1 Ch 38, a bequest to trustees on trust to provide 'so far as they can legally do so' for the care and upkeep of specified graves in a churchyard was upheld as a private trust. The perpetuity period was satisfied by the phrase 'so far as they can legally do so'.

On the other hand, a gift for the maintenance of all the graves in a churchyard may be charitable.

11.3.3 Saying of masses

In *Bourne v Keane* [1919] AC 815, the House of Lords decided that the saying of masses was valid. Prior to this decision the courts had adopted the view that such trusts were void, not because of the lack of a human beneficiary, but because they were superstitious activities. It should be noted that the *Bourne* (1919) principle is now restricted to masses to be said in private, for public masses may be treated as charitable events (see later). In *Khoo Cheng Teow* [1932] Straits Settlement Reports 226, a trust for the performance of non-Christian ceremonies was upheld as a valid private purpose trust.

11.4 The *Denley* approach

The approach adopted by the courts is to ascertain whether a gift or trust is for the promotion of a purpose *simpliciter* (within the *Astor* (1952) principle) which is void, or alternatively whether the trust is for the benefit of persons who are capable of enforcing the trust. This is a question for the courts to decide, on construction of the relevant trust instrument. The promotion of virtually all purposes affect persons. The settlor may, in form, create what appears to be a purpose trust but, in substance, the trust may be considered to be for the benefit of human beneficiaries.

In this respect, there is a distinction between a form of gift remotely in favour of individuals, to such an extent that those individuals do not have a *locus standi* to enforce the trust. On the other hand, a gift may appear to propagate a purpose which is directly or indirectly for the benefit of individuals. In this event, if the beneficiaries satisfy the test for certainty of objects, the gift may be valid. The courts are required to consider each gift prior to classification.

CASE EXAMPLE

Re Bowes [1896] 1 Ch 507

A testator bequeathed a fund for the planting of a clump of trees on land settled for the benefit of A and B. A and B did not want the money to be used for the planting of the trees but instead claimed the money for their benefit. North J held in favour of A and B on the ground that, on construction of the will, the money was intended for the benefit of the individuals and not for the benefit of the estate. The expressed purpose of planting trees was not intended to be imperative, but merely indicated the testator's motive for creating a trust for the benefit of A and B.

A similar approach was adopted in *Re Denley's Trust Deed* [1969] 1 Ch 373:

CASE EXAMPLE

Re Denley's Trust Deed [1969] 1 Ch 373

A plot of land was conveyed to trustees for use, subject to the perpetuity rule, as a sports ground primarily for the benefit of employees of a company and secondarily for the benefit of such other person or persons as the trustees may allow to use the same. The question in issue was whether the trust was void as a purpose trust. Goff J held that the trust was valid in favour of human beneficiaries. The test for certainty of objects and the perpetuity rule were satisfied. The court stated that the objection to purpose trusts was not that they sought to achieve a purpose but that they lacked any human beneficiary to enforce them. Thus, the 'lack of beneficiary principle' applied only where the trust was abstract or impersonal as opposed to where the trust, though expressed as a purpose, was directly or indirectly for ascertainable beneficiaries, within the perpetuity rule and was not otherwise uncertain.

> **J**
>
> 'Where the trust, though expressed as a purpose, is directly or indirectly for the benefit of an individual or individuals, it seems to me that it is in general outside the mischief of the beneficiary principle ... In my judgment, however, it would not be right to hold the trust void on this ground [lack of beneficiary]. The court can, as it seems to me, execute the trust both negatively by restraining any improper disposition or use of the land, and positively by ordering the trustees to allow the employees and such other persons (if any) as they may admit to use the land for the purpose of a recreation or sports ground.'
>
> (Goff J)

■Key facts on private purpose trusts

<table>
<tr><td colspan="4" align="center">KEY FACTS</td></tr>
<tr>
<td>Trusts to promote private purposes trusts</td>
<td>Void</td>
<td>Lack of a beneficiary with a locus standi to enforce</td>
<td>Morice v Bishop of Durham (1804); Leahy v A-G for NS Wales (1959) (see below); Re Astor (1952)</td>
</tr>
<tr>
<td>Alternatively, on construction (subject to the tests of certainty and perpetuity) the court may decide that a gift for a purpose may be treated as a gift for persons</td>
<td>Valid</td>
<td>Enforcement by beneficiaries</td>
<td>Re Bowes (1896); Re Denley (1969)</td>
</tr>
<tr>
<td colspan="4">EXCEPTIONS</td>
</tr>
<tr>
<td>Maintenance of animals</td>
<td>Valid</td>
<td>Subject to the tests of certainty and perpetuity</td>
<td>Pettingall v Pettingall (1842); Re Haines</td>
</tr>
<tr>
<td>Erection of monuments</td>
<td>Valid</td>
<td>Subject to the tests of certainty and perpetuity</td>
<td>Musset v Bingle (1876)</td>
</tr>
<tr>
<td>Maintenance of monuments</td>
<td>Valid</td>
<td>Subject to the tests of certainty and perpetuity</td>
<td>Re Hooper (1932)</td>
</tr>
<tr>
<td>Saying of masses (NB could be charitable)</td>
<td>Valid</td>
<td>Subject to the test of perpetuity</td>
<td>Bourne v Kean (1919)</td>
</tr>
</table>

ACTIVITY

> John, who has recently died, by his will bequeathed the following legacies:
>
> (1) £5,000 to use the income each year to provide a trophy for the winner of the Utopia Yacht Racing Competition, an annual event organised by the Utopia Yacht Club
>
> (2) £600 to my executors to maintain my pet cat, Tiddles, for the rest of her life
>
> (3) £15,000 to erect and maintain a tombstone, for a period not exceeding 21 years, in memory of my late wife, Ophelia
>
> (4) £500 to the vicar of my Parish Church in Utopia for the saying of private masses for my soul.
>
> Consider the validity of these bequests.

11.5 Gifts to unincorporated associations

There is some difficulty in deciding whether a gift to an unincorporated association creates a trust for a purpose which fails for want of a beneficiary to enforce the trust (under the *Astor* (1952) principle) or whether the gift will be construed in favour of human beneficiaries, the members of the association. This involves a question of construction of the circumstances surrounding the gift and the rules of the association.

For instance, a gift to the National Anti-Vivisection Society (an unincorporated non-charitable body) may be construed as a gift on trust for the work or purpose of such association and not for the benefit of its members. Accordingly, the gift may be considered void under the *Astor* (1952) principle.

> **J**
>
> 'A gift can be made to persons (including a corporation) but it cannot be made to a purpose or to an object. So also, a trust may be created for the benefit of persons as *cestuis que trust* but not for a purpose or object unless the purpose or object be charitable. For a purpose or object cannot sue, but if it be charitable, the Attorney-General can sue to enforce it.'
>
> (Viscount Simonds: *Leahy v A-G for New South Wales* [1959] AC 457)

An unincorporated association (as distinct from an incorporated association) is not a legal person but may take the form of a group of individuals joined together with common aims usually laid down in its constitution. The association was defined by Lawton LJ in *Conservative and Unionist Central Office v Burrell* [1982] 1 WLR 522. In this case the Court of Appeal decided that the Conservative Party was not an unincorporated association but an amorphous combination of various elements. The legal rights created in favour of donors and contributors exists on the basis of a mandate or agency.

'[An unincorporated association means] ... two or more persons bound together for one or more common purposes, not being business purposes, by mutual undertakings each having mutual duties and obligations, in an organisation which has rules which identify in whom control of it and its funds rests and on what terms and which can be joined or left at will.'

(Lawton LJ)

In *Neville Estates Ltd v Madden* [1962] Ch 832, Cross J, in an *obiter* pronouncement, outlined various constructions concerning gifts or trusts in favour of unincorporated associations:

'The position, as I understand it, is as follows. Such a gift may take effect in one or other of three quite different ways. In the first place, it may, on its true construction, be a gift to the members of the association at the relevant date as joint tenants, so that any member can sever his share and claim it whether or not he continues to be a member of the association. Secondly, it may be a gift to the existing members not as joint tenants, but subject to their respective contractual rights and liabilities towards one another as members of the association. In such a case a member cannot sever his share. It would accrue to the other members on his death or resignation, even though such members include persons who become members after the gift took effect. If this is the effect of the gift, it will not be open to objection on the score of perpetuity or uncertainty unless there is something in its terms or circumstances or in the rules of the association which precludes the members at any given time from dividing the subject of the gift between them on the footing that they are solely entitled to it in equity. Thirdly, the terms or circumstances of the gift or the rules of the association may show that the property in question is not to be at the disposal of the members of the time being, but is to be held in trust for or applied for the purposes of the association as a quasi-corporate entity. In this case the gift will fail unless the association is a charitable body. If the gift is of the second class, ie one which the members of the association for the time being are entitled to divide among themselves, then, even if the objects of the association are in themselves charitable, the gift would not, I think, be a charitable gift.'

(Cross J)

The following solutions have been adopted from time to time by the courts in respect of gifts to unincorporated associations. Although the courts have a wide discretion in construing the intention of the donor or settlor and the function and purpose of the association, the adoption of any of these solutions will vary with the facts of each case.

Gift to members as joint trustees

A settlor may make a gift to an unincorporated association which, on a true construction, is a gift to the members of that association who take as joint tenants free from any contractual fetter. Any member is entitled to sever his share and may claim it beneficially. In these circumstances, the association is used as a label or definition of the class which is intended to take. For instance, a testator might give a legacy to a dining or social club of which he is a member with the intention of giving a joint interest, which is capable of being severed, to the members. Such cases are extremely uncommon.

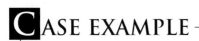ASE EXAMPLE

> *Cocks v Manners* (1871) LR 12 Eq 574
>
> The testatrix left part of her estate to the Dominican Convent at Carisbrooke, 'payable to the supervisor for the time being'. The court held that the gift was not charitable but was valid in favour of the individual members of the stated community as joint tenants.

Gift to members (subsisting) as an accretion to the funds

More frequently, the gift to the association may be construed as a gift to the members of the association on the date of the gift, not beneficially, but as an accretion to the funds of the society which is regulated by the contract (evidenced by the rules of the association) made by the members *inter se*. Thus, a subsisting member on the date of the gift is not entitled *qua* member to claim an interest in the property but takes the property by reference to the rules of the society. A member who leaves the association by death or resignation, will have no claim to the property, in the absence of any rules to the contrary. This approach was supported in an *obiter* pronouncement by Brightman J in *Re Recher's Will Trusts* [1972] Ch 526:

ASE EXAMPLE

> *Re Recher's Will Trusts* [1972] Ch 526
>
> A testatrix gave her residuary estate to the 'Anti-Vivisection Society, 76 Victoria Street, London SW1'. The London and Provincial Anti-Vivisection Society had carried on its activities at this address but, shortly before the will was made, the society ceased to exist (it was amalgamated with other societies) and it gave up its premises in Victoria Street. The question in issue was whether the gift could be taken by the amalgamated society, or failed and was subject to a resulting trust. The court held that, on construction of the will, the testator intended to benefit the Society at Victoria Street and not the larger body. Accordingly, the gift failed and a resulting trust was set up.

CONTINUED ▶

J '… it appears to me that the life members, the ordinary members and the associate members of the London Provincial Society were bound together by a contract *inter se*, with the result that the society represented an organisation of individuals bound together by a contract. Now just as two parties to a bi-partite bargain can vary or terminate their contract by mutual assent, so it must follow that the members of the society could, at any moment of time by agreement, authorised by its constitution, vary or terminate their multi-partite contract. There is no private trust or trust for charitable purposes or other trust to hinder the process. The funds of such an association may, of course, be derived not only from the subscriptions of contracting parties but also from donations from non-contracting parties and legacies from persons who have died. In the case of a donation which is not accompanied by any words which purport to impose a trust, it seems that the gift takes effect in favour of the existing members of the association not as joint tenants or tenants-in-common so as to entitle each member to an immediate share, but as an accretion to the funds of the organisation.'

(Brightman J)

The effect of the approach in *Re Recher* (1972) is that if a donor transfers property to the association for its general purposes, the gift may be construed as intended for the benefit of the members of the association to be enjoyed collectively.

Gift to subsisting members beneficially

Moreover, a gift to an association for a particular purpose may be construed as a gift to the members of the association for the time being for their own use. Where the association exists solely for the benefit of its members the gift will be valid. In this respect, the members of the association would be both trustees and beneficiaries. The purpose stated by the settlor may be construed as not imposing an obligation on the officers of the society to carry out such stated purpose but merely a manifestation of the motive of the settlor concerning a suggested use to which the property may be put.

 CASE EXAMPLE

Re Turkington [1937] 4 All ER 501

A gift was made in favour of a masonic lodge 'as a fund to build a suitable temple in Stafford'. The members of the lodge were both the trustees and the beneficiaries. The court held that the gift was absolute in favour of the members of the lodge for the time being. The purpose stipulated was construed by Luxmoore J as '… simply an indication by the testator of the purpose for which he would like the money to be expended, without imposing any trust on the beneficiaries'.

Gift to present and future members

Alternatively, the court may construe a gift to an association as a gift for the benefit of the members of the association, both present and future. In coming to this conclusion, the courts are required to consider the rules of the association, its function, in addition to the intention of the donor. Moreover, if the members of the society (in accordance with its constitution) are incapable of disposing of the assets of the society or are incapable of altering the rules of the association, the gift will fail for infringing the perpetuity rule.

CASE EXAMPLE

Re Drummond [1914] 2 Ch 90

A testator transferred his residuary estate to the 'Old Bradfordians Club to be utilised as the Committee of the Club should think best in the interests of the Club'. On the issue of the validity of the gift, the court held that the gift was valid since the committee was free to spend the capital in any manner it might consider fit.

However, in *Re Grant's Will Trusts* [1980] 1 WLR 360, the gift failed for infringing the perpetuity rule.

CASE EXAMPLE

Re Grant's Will Trusts [1980] 1 WLR 360

A gift for the purposes of the Chertsey Labour Party Headquarters (non-charitable unincorporated association) failed for infringing the perpetuity rule because the members of the local association did not control the society's property nor could they change the rules and obtain control, for the rules were subject to the approval of the National Executive Committee. Accordingly, the members of the local Labour Party did not have the power to liquidate the association and distribute its assets among themselves.

Gift on trust to promote the purpose of the association

If a settlor transfers property on trust for an association, it is possible for the court to decide that on construction, the transfer is made on trust for the function or operation of the society and not for its members. If this construction is adopted the court may decide that the trust fails under the *Astor* (1952) principle, because of the intention to promote a purpose. Such a construction would be exceptional. In addition, if the intention of the settlor is to set up an endowment in favour of the beneficiary, the gift may fail on the separate ground of the infringement of the perpetuity rule.

CASE EXAMPLE

Leahy v Attorney-General for New South Wales [1959] AC 457

A testator devised a plot of land of 730 acres on trust for 'such order of nuns of the Catholic church or the Christian brothers as my trustees shall select'. This transfer was not wholly charitable, as it permitted the trustees to select cloistered nuns. Under Australian law the trust was capable of being saved as a charitable donation by confining the gift to non-cloistered orders. The trustees, however, wanted to retain the freedom to give to cloistered nuns if possible. The question in issue was whether the trust in its existing form was valid as a non-charitable trust. The court held that, as a non-charitable gift, the trust failed as the testator's intention was clearly to create an endowment for the order of nuns (both present and future) and not for the benefit of individuals.

> **J** '... it seems reasonably clear that the testator's intention was to create a trust, not merely for the benefit of the existing members of the selected Order, but for its benefit as a continuing society and for the furtherance of its work.'
>
> (Viscount Simonds)

Gift on trust for the subsisting members of the association

A transfer of property or trust for an association may be construed as a transfer of property on trust for the current members of the association, and not on trust for purposes. In this event, provided that the rules of the association empower the members to liquidate and distribute the assets of the association, the perpetuity rule will not be infringed and the trust will be valid. The position remains the same even though the settlor may specify a purpose for which the fund may be used. Such stipulation may not be sufficient to prevent the members (beneficiaries) disposing of the property in any way they consider appropriate within the rules of the society.

CASE EXAMPLE

Re Lipinski's Will Trust [1977] 1 All ER 33

A testator transferred one-half of his residuary estate to the Hull Judeans (Maccabi) Association, an unincorporated, non-charitable association, 'in memory of my late wife to be used *solely* in the work of constructing new buildings for the association and/or improvements to the said buildings'. The question in issue was whether the trust was valid. The court held that the trust was for the benefit of ascertainable beneficiaries (the members at the date of the gift). On construction, the expression 'in memory of my late

CONTINUED ▸

wife' was not intended as a permanent endowment but merely a tribute which the testator paid to his wife. The stipulation concerning the use of the funds ('solely') was not intended to reduce the power of the members to dispose of the assets of the association in accordance with the rules of the association. For the same reason, the perpetuity rule was not infringed.

> J
>
> 'The beneficiaries, the members of the association for the time being, are the persons who could enforce the purpose and they must, as it seems to me, be entitled not to enforce it or, indeed, to vary it ... Thus, it seems to me that whether one treats the gift as a "purpose" trust or as an absolute gift with a superadded direction or, on the analogy of *Re Turkington* [1937] 4 All ER 501 as a gift where the trustees and the beneficiaries are the same persons, all roads lead to the same conclusion. The gift is a valid gift.'
>
> (Oliver J)

It should be noted that in *Re Lipinski* (1977), the court adopted a benevolent construction of the terms of the will. Oliver J stated that, as a matter of common sense, a clear distinction ought to be drawn between cases where a purpose is prescribed clearly for the benefit of ascertainable beneficiaries, particularly where those beneficiaries have the power to make the capital their own, and cases where no beneficiary is intended or where the beneficiaries are unascertainable. He went on to say that if a valid gift may be made to an unincorporated association as a simple accretion to the funds that are the subject matter of the contract which the members have made *inter se*, then there is no reason why such a gift, which specifies a purpose that is within the powers of the association and of which the members of the association are the beneficiaries, should fail. He then decided that there were three alternative bases for holding the transfer by will valid. First, the will could be construed as creating a valid gift to the present members of the association. Second, a trust for the present and future members could be spelt out (which did not infringe the perpetuity rule) on construction of the will. Third, a trust for the present members of the association could be ascertained.

ACTIVITY

1. 'The objection [to non-charitable purpose trusts] is not that the trust is for a purpose or an object *per se*, but that there is no beneficiary or *cestui que trust*.' (Goff J in *Re Denley's Trust Deed* (1969)).

   Discuss.

CONTINUED ▸

ACTIVITY

2. Consider the validity of the following testamentary dispositions:

   (i) £50,000 to the Dealing Bowls Club (an unincorporated association) for the purpose of constructing a new club house

   (ii) Blackacre (a five-acre plot of land) to my trustees for the purpose of maintaining and using the same as a recreation ground for the benefit of the employees of Monkey Business plc.

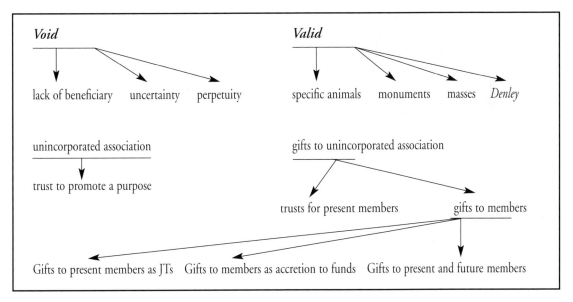

■ *Figure 11.1 Private purpose trusts*

Further reading

Emery, C, 'Do we need a rule against perpetuities?' (1994) 57 MLR 602.

Gardner, S, 'A detail in the construction of gifts to unincorporated associations' [1998] Conv 8.

Gravells, N, 'Gifts to unincorporated associations: where there is a will there is a way' (1977) 40 MLR 231.

Lovell, P, 'Non-charitable purpose trusts – further reflection' [1970] Conv 77.

Matthews, P, 'Gifts to unincorporated associations' [1995] Conv 302.

McKay, L, 'Trusts for purposes' [1973] Conv 420.

Rickett, C, 'Unincorporated associations and their dissolution' [1980] CLJ 88.

chapter 12 # CHARITABLE TRUSTS ■

A charitable trust is a type of purpose trust in that it promotes a purpose and does not primarily benefit specific individuals. However, in furthering a purpose the performance of the trust may result in individuals or members of the public deriving direct benefits. Even so, the trust remains one for a purpose and not for the benefit of those individuals. The purpose of the trust is to benefit society as a whole or a sufficiently large section of the community so that it may be considered public. Thus, a charitable trust is a public purpose trust and is enforceable by the Attorney-General on behalf of the Crown.

Private trusts, on the other hand, seek to benefit defined persons or narrower sections of society than charitable trusts and, as we saw, a private purpose trust is void for lack of a person to enforce the trust.

Generally, charitable trusts are subject to the same rules as private trusts but, as a result of the public nature of such bodies, they enjoy a number of advantages over private trusts in respect of:

(a) certainty of objects

(b) the perpetuity rule

(c) the *cy-près* rule and

(d) fiscal privileges.

12.1 Certainty of objects

A charitable trust is subject to a unique test for certainty of objects, namely whether the objects are exclusively charitable. In other words, if the trust funds may be used solely for charitable purposes, the test will be satisfied. Indeed, it is unnecessary for the settlor or testator to specify the charitable objects which are intended to take the trust property: provided that the trust instrument manifests a clear intention to devote the funds for 'charitable purposes' the test will be satisfied. Thus, a gift 'on trust for charitable purposes' will satisfy this test. The Charity Commissioners and the court have the jurisdiction to establish a scheme for the application of the funds (ie the court will make an order indicating the specific charitable objects which will benefit). In *Moggridge v Thackwell* (1807) 13 Ves 416, a bequest to 'such charities as the trustee sees fit' was valid as a gift for charitable purposes.

On the other hand, if the trust funds are capable of being devoted to both charitable and non-charitable purposes the gift will be invalid as a charity for uncertainty of objects. In *IRC v City of Glasgow Police Athletic Association* [1953] 1 All ER 747, the association promoted both a charitable purpose (efficiency of the police force) and a non-charitable purpose (promotion of sport). The

244

court decided that the association was not charitable. Similarly, where the draftsman of the objects clause uses words such as 'charitable or benevolent purposes', the court may, on construction of the clause, decide that the word 'or' ought to be interpreted **disjunctively**, with the effect that benevolent purposes which are not charitable are capable of taking thereby invalidating the charitable gift. The conjunction 'and' may exceptionally be construed disjunctively. In *A-G of the Bahamas v Royal Trust Co* [1986] I WLR 1001, a bequest to provide education 'and' welfare for Bahamian children failed as a charitable bequest.

In two circumstances, an objects clause which seeks to benefit both charitable and non-charitable purposes will not fail as a charity if:

(i) the non-charitable purpose is construed as being incidental to the main charitable purpose. This involves a question of construction for the courts to evaluate the importance of each class of objects. In *Re Coxen* [1948] Ch 747, the court construed the relevant clause and concluded that the gift was valid

(ii) the court is able to apportion the fund and devote the charitable portion of the fund for charitable purposes. An apportionment will be ordered where part only of the fund is payable for charitable purposes and the other part for non-charitable purposes. In the absence of circumstances requiring a different division, the court will apply the maxim 'Equality is equity' and order an equal division of the fund. In *Salusbury v Denton* (1857) 3 K&J 529, severance was permitted where an unspecified part of a fund was made for charitable purposes (the relief of poverty) and the remainder for a private purpose (the testator's relatives).

12.2 Perpetuity

Charities are not subject to the rule against excessive duration. Indeed, many charities (schools and universities) continue indefinitely and rely heavily on donations. But charitable gifts, like private gifts, are subject to the rule against remote vesting, ie the subject-matter of the gift is required to vest in the charity within the perpetuity period. But even in this respect the courts have introduced a concession for charities, namely **charitable unity**. Once a gift has vested in a specific charity, then, subject to any express declarations to the contrary, it vests forever for charitable purposes. Accordingly, a gift which vests in one charity (A) with a gift over in favour of another charity (B) on the occurrence of an event will be valid even if the event occurs outside the perpetuity period. This concessionary rule does not apply to a gift over to a charity after a gift in favour of a non-charity. The normal rules as to vesting apply. Similarly, a gift over from a charity to a non-charity is caught by the rules as to remote vesting.

12.3 The *cy-près* doctrine

The advantage over private trusts is that when a gift vests in a charity then, subject to express provisions to the contrary, the gift vests for charitable purposes. Accordingly, the settlor (and his estate) is excluded from any implied reversionary interests by way of a resulting trust in the event of a failure of the charitable trust. Thus, the *cy-près* doctrine is an alternative to the resulting trust principle.

12.4 Fiscal advantages

A variety of tax reliefs are enjoyed by both charitable bodies and members of the public (including companies) who donate funds for charitable purposes. A detailed analysis of such concessions is outside the scope of this book.

12.5 Charitable purposes

There is no statutory or judicial definition of a 'charity'. It has been recognised that a statutory definition of charities would create the undesirable effect of restricting the flexibility which currently exists in permitting the law to keep abreast with the changing needs of society. In s 96 of the Charities Act 1993 the expression 'charity' is defined as 'any institution, corporate or not (including a trust), which is established for charitable purposes'.

Most charitable bodies are required, under s 3 of the Charities Act 1993, to be registered with the Charity Commission. The effect of registration creates a conclusive presumption of charitable status: see s 4(1) of the Charities Act 1993.

Ever since the passing of the Charitable Uses Act 1601 (sometimes referred to as the Statute of Elizabeth I) the courts have developed the practice of referring to the preamble for guidance as to charitable purposes. The preamble contained a catalogue of purposes which at that time were regarded as charitable. It was not intended to constitute a definition of charities. The preamble has been expressly preserved by the Charities Act 1960 and s 38(4) endorses the purposes as stated in the preamble as charitable purposes. Thus, 'a reference to charity within the preamble shall be construed as a reference to charity within the UK law'.

The purposes included in the preamble to the 1601 Act are:

S 'Preamble

The relief of aged, impotent and poor people; the maintenance of sick and maimed soldiers and mariners, schools of learning, free schools and scholars of universities; the repair of bridges, ports, havens, causeways, churches, sea banks and highways; the education and preferment of orphans; the relief, stock or maintenance of houses of correction; the marriages of poor maids; the supportation, aid and help of young tradesmen, handicapped men and persons decayed; the relief or redemption of prisoners or captives; and the aid or care of any poor inhabitants concerning the payments of fifteens, setting out of soldiers and other taxes.'

Admittedly, the above-mentioned purposes were of limited effect, but Lord Macnaghten in *IRC v Pemsel* [1891] AC 531 classified charitable purposes within four categories, thus:

> **J** 'charity in its legal sense comprises four principal divisions:
>
> • trusts for relief of poverty;
>
> • trusts for the advancement of education;
>
> • trusts for the advancement of religion;
>
> • trusts for other purposes beneficial to the community'.

The approach of the courts is to treat the examples as stated in the preamble as a means of guidance in deciding on the validity of the relevant purpose. Two approaches have been adopted by the courts, namely:

• **reasoning by analogy**: the approach here is to ascertain whether a purpose has some resemblance to an example as stated in the preamble or to an earlier decided case which was considered charitable, eg the provision of a crematorium was considered charitable by analogy with the repair of churches as stated in the preamble in the following case:

> **J** 'What must be regarded is not the wording of the preamble, but the effect of decisions given by the Courts as to its scope, decisions which have endeavoured to keep the law as to charities moving according as new social needs arise or old ones become obsolete or satisfied.'
>
> (Lord Wilberforce in *Scottish Burial Reform and Cremation Society v City of Glasgow Corporation* [1968] AC 138)

• **the spirit and intendment of the preamble**: this approach is much wider than the previous approach. The courts decide if the purpose of the organisation is 'within the spirit and intendment' or 'within the equity' of the statute, unhindered by the specific purposes as stated in the preamble. In other words, the examples enumerated in the preamble are treated as the context or 'flavour' against which the purpose under scrutiny may be determined. In this respect it has been suggested that purposes beneficial to the community are *prima facie* charitable, unless they could not have been intended by the draftsman of the Statute of Elizabeth, assuming that he was aware of the changes in society.

'... if a purpose is shown to be so beneficial or of such utility it is *prima facie* charitable in law, but the courts have left open a line of retreat based on the equity of the statute in case they are faced with a purpose (eg a political purpose) which could not have been within the contemplation of the statute even if the then legislators had been endowed with the gift of foresight into the circumstances of later centuries.'

(Russell LJ in *Incorporated Council of Law Reporting v A-G* [1972] Ch 73)

CASE EXAMPLE

Incorporated Council of Law Reporting v A-G [1972] Ch 73

The court decided that the Incorporated Council of Law Reporting was a charitable body, on the grounds that it advanced education and other purposes beneficial to society. The fact that the reports may be used by members of the legal profession for their 'personal gain' was incidental to the main charitable purposes.

'In a case such as the present in which the object cannot be thought otherwise than beneficial to the community and of general public utility, I believe the proper question to ask is whether there are any grounds for holding it to be outside the equity of the statute; and I think the answer to that is here in the negative.'

(Russell LJ)

12.6 Public element

It must not be assumed that all public trusts will be treated as charitable: see *Chichester Diocesan Fund v Simpson* [1944] AC 341, where a gift for charitable or benevolent purposes failed as a charity because benevolent purposes which were not charitable were capable of benefiting. The criteria for charitable status are:

(i) the compliance with the 'public benefit' test and

(ii) the purpose is required to be within the 'spirit and intendment' of the preamble to the Charitable Uses Act 1601.

12.6.1 Public benefit

The 'public benefit' test is used to distinguish a public trust from a private trust. A public trust is required to exist for the benefit of the public (the community) or an appreciable section of society, with the exception of trusts for the relief of poverty. The satisfaction of the test is a question of law for the judge to decide on the evidence submitted to him. The policy which underpins the test was laid down by Lord Simonds in *IRC v Baddeley* [1955] AC 572. In this case, a trust in favour of Methodists in West Ham and Leyton failed the public element test because the beneficiaries were composed of a class within a class

J
> '[There is a] distinction between a form of relief accorded to the whole community yet by its very nature advantageous only to a few and a form of relief accorded to a selected few out of a larger number equally willing and able to take advantage of it … for example, a bridge which is available for all the public may undoubtedly be a charity and it is indifferent how many people use it. But confine its use to a selected number of persons, however numerous and important; it is then clearly not a charity. It is not of general public utility; for it does not serve the public purpose which its nature qualifies it to serve'.
>
> (Lord Simonds in *IRC v Baddeley* [1955] AC 572)

The public element test will not be satisfied if there is a personal *nexus* between the donor and the beneficiaries or between the beneficiaries themselves. The *nexus* may take the form of a 'blood' relationship. In *Re Compton* [1945] I All ER 198, the Court of Appeal decided that the test was not satisfied where the gift was on trust for the education of the children of three named relatives.

This test was approved and extended to a personal *nexus* by way of contract in *Oppenheim v Tobacco Securities Trust Co Ltd* [1951] AC 297, HL.

CASE EXAMPLE

Oppenheim v Tobacco Securities Trust Co Ltd [1951] AC 297, HL

Trustees were directed to apply monies in providing for the education of employees or ex-employees of British American tobacco or any of its subsidiary companies. The employees numbered 110,000. The court held that in view of the personal *nexus* between the employees themselves (being employed by the same employer), the public element test was not satisfied.

Lord MacDermott dissented and expressed the view that although the 'common link' test was of some value, it should not be an overriding consideration, as the majority believed.

CONTINUED ▶

> **J** 'If the bond between those employed by a particular railway is purely personal, why should the bond between those who are employed as railwaymen be essentially different? ... Are miners in the service of the National Coal Board now in one category and miners in a particular pit or of a particular district in another? Is the relationship between those in the service of the Crown to be distinguished from that obtaining between those of some other employer?'
>
> (Lord MacDermott)

More recently, in *Dingle v Turner* [1972] AC 601, Lord Cross of Chelsea gave his support to this view.

There is some support for the view that if the donor sets up a trust for the benefit of the public or a large section of the public, but expresses a preference (not amounting to an obligation) in favour of specified individuals, the gift is capable of satisfying the public element test.

CASE EXAMPLE

Re Koettgen's Will Trust [1954] Ch 252

A trust was created for the promotion and furtherance of the commercial education of British-born subjects, subject to a direction that preference be given to the employees of a company. The court decided that, on construction, the preference was intended as permitting, without obliging, the trustees to consider distributing the property in favour of the employees.

This decision has been criticised by the Privy Council in *Caffoor v Commissioners of Income Tax, Colombo* [1961] AC 584 as being in essence an 'employee trust' and 'had edged very near to being inconsistent with *Oppenheim's* case'.

In *IRC v Educational-Grants Association Ltd* [1967] 3 WLR 341, the Court of Appeal refused to follow *Re Koettgen's Will Trust* (1954).

> **J** 'I find considerable difficulty in the *Re Koettgen* decision. I should have thought that a trust for the public with reference for a private class comprised in the public might be regarded as a trust for the application of income at the discretion of the trustees between charitable and non-charitable objects.'
>
> (Pennycuick J)

In essence, the public element test will be satisfied if:

(i) the beneficiaries are not numerically negligible and

(ii) the beneficiaries have no 'link' in contract or in blood between themselves or with a narrow group of individuals.

> **J** 'To constitute a section of the public, the possible beneficiaries must not be numerically negligible and secondly, the quality which distinguishes them from other members of the community so that they form by themselves a section of it must be a quality which does not depend on their relationship to a particular individual ... A group of persons may be numerous but, if the nexus between them is their personal relationship to a single propositions or to several propositus they are neither the community nor a section of the community for charitable purposes.'
>
> (Lord Simonds in *Oppenheim v Tobacco Securities Trust Co* (1951))

Subject to the absence of a personal *nexus* between the beneficiaries and/or a limited class of individuals, the issue of whether or not the beneficiaries constitute a section of the public in order to satisfy the public element test is a question of degree. There are many decisions which appear to be inconsistent with each other. In *Gilmour v Coats* [1949] 1 All ER 848, HL, the court decided that a gift to a community of 20 cloistered nuns who devoted themselves to prayer and contemplation did not satisfy the public element test. On the other hand, the members of the Catford Synagogue were treated as an appreciable section of the public and satisfied the public element test because they integrated with the rest of society. In *Re Lewis* [1954] 3 All ER 257, a gift to 10 blind boys and 10 blind girls in Totteham was charitable. But in *Williams' Trustees v IRC* [1947] AC 447, HL, a gift in order to create an institute in London for the promotion of Welsh culture failed as a charity.

> **J** 'I doubt whether the "public benefit" test could be satisfied if the beneficiaries are a class of persons not only confined to a particular area but selected from within the area by reference to a particular creed ... the persons to be benefited must be the whole community, or all the inhabitants of a particular area. Not a class within a class.'
>
> (Lord Simonds in *Williams' Trustees v IRC* [1947] AC 447, HL)

The same principle was applied in *IRC v Baddeley* (1955).

There is also a presumption to the effect that purposes within the first three classifications of Lord Macnaghten in *IRC v Pensel* (1891) are beneficial to society. Purposes within the fourth classification are required to be proved positively to be beneficial to society.

12.6.2 Poverty exception

Trusts for the relief of poverty are charitable even though the beneficiaries are linked *inter se* or with an individual or small group of individuals. In short, trusts for the relief of poverty are not subject to the public element test. The practice of the courts has always been to exclude such trusts from the public element test. Accordingly, in *Gibson v South American Stores Ltd* [1950] Ch 177 and *Dingle v Turner* [1972] AC 601, the courts decided that gifts in order to relieve the poverty of employees of a company were charitable.

At the same time, the courts have drawn a subtle distinction between private trusts for the relief of poverty and public trusts for the same purpose, eg a gift for the settlor's poor relations, A, B and C, may not be charitable but may exist as a private trust, whereas a gift for the benefit of the settlor's poor relations without identifying them may be charitable. It appears that the distinction between the two types of trusts lies in the degree of precision in which the objects have been identified. The more precise the language used by the settlor in identifying the poor relations, the stronger the risk of failure as a charitable trust. This is a question of degree.

Re Scarisbrick [1951] Ch 622, CA

A bequest was made on trust 'for such relations of my said son and daughters as in the opinion of the survivor shall be in needy circumstances'. The court held that the gift was charitable.

> **J** 'It should be added that the class of beneficiaries falls to be ascertained at the death of the survivor of the three children, not at the testatrix's death. Thus, the class of beneficiaries is so extensive as to be incapable of being exhaustively ascertained and includes persons who the testatrix may never have seen or heard of.'
>
> (Jenkins LJ)

12.6.3 Classification of charitable purposes

Lord Macnaghten in *IRC v Pemsel* (1891) classified the charitable purposes, as stated in the preamble to the Charitable Uses Act 1601, as follows:

(a) the relief of poverty

(b) the advancement of education

(c) the advancement of religion and

(d) other purposes beneficial to the community.

The relief of poverty

'Poverty' includes destitution but is not interpreted so narrowly as to mean destitution. It connotes that the beneficiaries are in straitened circumstances and unable to maintain a modest standard of living (determined objectively).

> **J** 'Poverty does not mean destitution; it is a word of wide and somewhat indefinite import; it may not unfairly be paraphrased for present purposes as meaning persons who have to "go short" in the ordinary acceptation of that term, due regard being had to their status in life and so forth.'
>
> (Evershed MR in *Re Coulthurst* [1951] Ch 661)

In addition, the gift is required to relieve the misery of poverty by providing the basic necessities of human existence – food, shelter and clothing. The expression 'relief' signifies that the beneficiaries have a need attributable to their condition which requires alleviating and which the beneficiaries may find difficulty in alleviating from their own resources.

In *Biscoe v Jackson* [1887] 25 Ch D 460, a gift to establish a soup kitchen in Shoreditch was construed as a valid charitable trust for the relief of poverty. Likewise, in *Shaw v Halifax Corporation* [1915] 2 KB 170 it was decided that a home for ladies in reduced circumstances was charitable. Similarly, in *Re Clarke* [1923] 2 Ch 407 a gift to provide a nursing home for persons of moderate means was charitable. But a gift for the 'working classes' does not connote poverty: see *Re Saunders' Will Trust* [1954] Ch 265, although a gift for the construction of a 'working men's hostel' was construed as charitable under this head: see *Re Niyazi's Will Trust* [1978] 1 WLR 910.

Under this head, it is essential that all the objects fall within the designation 'poor'. If someone who is not poor is able to benefit from the funds, the gift will fail as not being one for the relief of poverty. In *Re Gwyon* [1930] 1 Ch 225, a trust to provide free trousers for boys resident in Farnham was not charitable because there was no restriction to the effect that the boys were required to be poor.

The advancement of education

This classification originates from the preamble to the 1601 Act which refers to 'the maintenance of schools of learning, free schools and scholars in universities'. 'Education' has been interpreted generously and is not restricted to the classroom mode of disseminating knowledge but requires some element of instruction or supervision. Thus, research is capable of being construed as the provision of education.

CASE EXAMPLE

Re Hopkins' Will Trust [1964] 3 All ER 46

Money was bequeathed to the Francis Bacon Society, to be used to search for the manuscripts of plays commonly ascribed to Shakespeare but believed by the Society to have been written by Bacon. The court decided that the gift was for the advancement of education. The discovery of such manuscripts would be of the highest value to history and literature.

> **J** 'The word "education" must be used in a wide sense, certainly extending beyond teaching, and the requirement is that, in order to be charitable, research must either be of educational value to the researcher or must be so directed as to lead to something which will pass into the store of educational material, or so as to improve the sum of communicable knowledge in an area which education may cover – education in this last context extending to the formation of literary taste and appreciation.'
>
> (Wilberforce J)

More recently, Slade J in *McGovern v A-G* [1981] 3 All ER 493 summarised the principles:

> **J** '(i) A trust will ordinarily qualify as a charitable trust if, but only if, (a) the subject matter of the proposed research is a useful object of study; and (b) it is contemplated that the knowledge acquired as a result of the research will be disseminated to others; and (c) the trust is for the benefit of the public, or a sufficiently important section of the public.
>
> (ii) In the absence of a contrary context, however, the court will be readily inclined to construe a trust for research as importing subsequent dissemination of the results thereof.
>
> (iii) Furthermore, if a trust for research is to constitute a valid trust for the advancement of education, it is not necessary either (a) that the teacher/pupil relationship should be in contemplation, or (b) that the persons to benefit from the knowledge to be acquired should be persons who are already in the course of receiving "education" in the conventional sense.'
>
> (Slade J)

On the other hand, the mere acquisition of knowledge without dissemination or advancement will not be charitable:

CASE EXAMPLE

Re Shaw; Public Trustee v Day [1957] 1 All ER 745

The testator, George Bernard Shaw, bequeathed money to be used to develop a 40-letter alphabet and translate his play *Androcles and the Lion* into this alphabet. The court held that the gift was not charitable as it was aimed merely at the increase of knowledge.

Gifts which have been upheld as charitable under this head have included trusts for choral singing in London (*Royal Choral Society v IRC* [1943] 2 All ER 101); the diffusion of knowledge of Egyptology and the training of students in Egyptology (*Re British School of Egyptian Archaeology* [1954] 1 All ER 887); the encouragement of chess playing by boys or young men resident in the city of Portsmouth (*Re Dupree's Trusts* [1944] 2 All ER 443); the furtherance of the Boy Scout movement by helping to purchase sites for camping (*Re Webber* [1954] 3 All ER 712); the promotion of the education of the Irish by teaching self-control, elocution, oratory, deportment and the arts of personal contact and social intercourse (*Re Shaw's Will Trust* [1952] 1 All ER 712); the publication of law reports which record the development of judge-made law (*Incorporated Council of Law Reporting for England and Wales v A-G* [1971] 3 All ER 1029); the promotion of the works of a famous composer (*Re Delius' Will Trust* [1957] 1 All ER 854) or celebrated writer (*Re Shakespeare Memorial Trust* [1923] 2 Ch 389); the students' union of a university (*Baldry v Feintuck* [1972] 2 All ER 81); the furtherance of the Wilton Park project, ie a conference centre for discussion of matters of international importance (*Re Koeppler's Will Trust* [1986] Ch 423); the provision of facilities at schools and universities to play association football or other games (*IRC v McMullen* [1981] AC 1); and professional bodies which exist for the promotion of the arts or sciences (*Royal College of Surgeons of England v National Provincial Bank Ltd* [1952] 1 All ER 984).

Before deciding whether the gifts are charitable or not, the courts are required to take into account the usefulness of the gifts to the public. This may be effected by judicial notice of the value of the gift to society. In the event of doubt, the courts may take into account the opinions of experts. The opinions of the donors are inconclusive. In *Re Pinion* [1965] Ch 85, a gift to the National Trust of a studio and contents to be maintained as a collection failed as a charity. The collection as a whole lacked any artistic merit. The judge could conceive of no useful purpose in foisting on the public this 'mass of junk'.

The advancement of religion

The preamble to the 1601 Statute refers to 'the repair of churches'. English law steers a neutral course between all forms of religions. 'Religion' is defined in the *Oxford Dictionary* as a 'recognition on the part of man of some higher unseen power as having control of his destiny and as being entitled to obedience, reverence and worship' or 'a particular system of faith and worship'. There is not a great deal of authority recognising non-Christian religions (although Judaism has been recognised in *Strauss v Goldsmith* [1837] 8 Sim 614 and *Neville Estates v Madden* [1962] Ch 832) but regulations made under the Charities Act 1993 (and its predecessor) assume that non-Christian religions are charitable. The Goodman Report (1976) declared that account must be taken of all religions whether monotheistic or not. This would include a polytheistic religion such as Hinduism. Buddhism, which does not involve a belief in God, is universally regarded as a religion and may be treated as an exception to the rule that a religion involves a faith or spiritual belief in a supreme being. On the other hand, in *Re South Place Ethical Society* [1980] 1 WLR 1565, it was decided that the study and dissemination of ethical principles but which did not involve faith in a deity could not constitute religion although the society was charitable on the ground of advancement of education:

> **J** ' "Religion", as I see it, is concerned with man's relations with God and "ethics" is concerned with man's relation with man. The two are not the same and are not made the same by sincere inquiry into the question: What is God? If reason leads people not to accept Christianity or any known religion, but they do believe in the excellence of qualities such as truth, beauty and love, their beliefs may be to them the equivalent of a religion but viewed objectively they are not religion.'
>
> (Dillon J)

Similarly, a body, such as the Freemasons Society, whose rules demand the highest personal and social standards, does not constitute a religion: see *United Grand Lodge of Freemasons in England and Wales v Holborn Borough Council* [1957] 1 WLR 1090. Likewise, in principle, a trust to promote atheism or to demonstrate that religious belief is erroneous will not be charitable under this head.

Unlike trusts for the advancement of education, the courts do not evaluate the merit of one religion as opposed to another or indeed the benefit to the public of religious instruction. Provided that the religious gift is not subversive of all morality, the gift will be charitable.

CASE EXAMPLE

Thornton v Howe [1862] 31 Beav 14

A trust was created for the publication of the writings of Joanna Southcote who believed that she would miraculously conceive and give birth, at an advanced age, to the second Messiah. Although the judge though that she was foolish, deluded and confused, he held that the gift was charitable.

Similarly, in *Re Watson* [1973] 3 All ER 678, the court decided that a gift to publish the religious works of Hobbs (which had no intrinsic value) was charitable:

'... provided that the purposes are not immoral, then, even though the courts might consider the relevant opinions as foolish and devoid of foundation, or not capable of leading to moral improvement, the gift remains charitable as being for the advancement of religion.'

(Plowman J)

The institution or association is required to promote or advance religion. This was considered by Donovan J in *United Grand Lodge of Freemasons in England and Wales v Holborn Borough Council* (1957):

 'To advance religion means to promote it, to spread its message ever wider among mankind; to take some positive steps to sustain and increase religious belief; and these things are done in a variety of ways which may be comprehensively described as pastoral and missionary. It should include religious instruction, a programme for the persuasion of unbelievers, religious supervision to see that its members remain active and constant in the various religions they may profess.'

(Donovan J)

Religion may be advanced in a variety of ways, such as the maintenance of places of worship including the upkeep of churchyards, gifts for the clergy, the provision of an organ or maintenance of a choir and the active spread of religion at home and abroad, although a gift for 'parish work' will be void as including many objects which are not charitable (*Farley v Westminster Bank* [1939] 3 All ER 491). A gift to an officer of the church in his official capacity (the vicar), to be applied in his absolute discretion, may be construed as imposing an implied limitation for ecclesiastical purposes (*Re Garrard* [1907] 1 Ch 382). A gift for the saying of masses in public is charitable because *inter alia* the gift increases the stipend of priests (*Re Hetherington* [1989] 2 All ER 129).

Other purposes beneficial to the community

The preamble refers to a list of miscellaneous purposes which are charitable. The approach of the courts to novel purposes capable of being decided under this head has already been mentioned. It does not follow that every purpose which is beneficial to the community will be charitable. Thus, a gift for 'charitable or benevolent purposes' is not charitable (*Chichester Diocesan Fund v Simpson* (1944)). In order to establish that a purpose is charitable under this head, it must be shown that the purpose is beneficial to the community in a way that the law considers charitable, ie the purpose is within the spirit and intendment of the preamble.

> J 'Lord Macnaghten did not mean that all trusts for purposes beneficial to the community are charitable, but that there are certain beneficial trusts which fall within that category; and accordingly, to argue that because a trust is for a purpose beneficial to the community, it is therefore a charitable trust, is to turn his sentence round and to give it a different meaning … it is not enough to say that the trust in question is for public purposes beneficial to the community, or for the public welfare; you must also show that it is a charitable trust.'
>
> (Viscount Cave LC in *A-G v National Provincial and Union Bank of England* [1924] AC 262)

Illustrations of charitable purposes under this head:

Animals

A trust which promotes the welfare of animals generally or even a species of animals (as opposed to benefiting specific animals) is a valid charitable trust because it is calculated to promote public morality by checking an inborn tendency in humans towards cruelty. In *Re Wedgwood* [1915] 1 Ch 113 CA, a trust for the protection and benefit of animals was charitable. Similarly, in *University of London v Yarrow* (1857) 1 De G & J 72, a hospital for sick animals was charitable. In *Re Moss* [1949] 1 All ER 495, a home for unwanted or stray cats was charitable.

It is essential to establish that the welfare of the animals provides some benefit to mankind, albeit indirect. Failure to establish such benefit was fatal in *Re Grove-Grady* [1929] 1 Ch 557. An animal sanctuary (game reserve) where all animals were allowed to live free from 'molestation or destruction by man' was not charitable because there were no safeguards against the destruction of the weaker animals by the stronger.

> J 'It is not a trust directed to ensure absence or diminution of pain or cruelty in the destruction of animal life. If this trust is carried out according to its tenor, no animal within the area may be destroyed by man no matter how necessary that destruction may be in the interests of mankind or in the interests of the other denizens of the area or in the interests of the animal itself; and no matter how painlessly such destruction may be brought about. It seems to be impossible to say that the carrying out of such a trust necessarily involves benefit to the public. Consistently with the trust the public could be excluded from entering the area or even looking into it. All that the public need know about the matter would be that one or more areas existed in which all animals were allowed to live free from any risk of being molested or killed by man, though liable to be molested and killed by other denizens of the area.'
>
> (Russell LJ in *Re Grove-Grady* (1929))

Moreover, where the welfare of animals (anti-vivisection) conflicts with the interests of mankind (scientific research) the latter prevails and the animal welfare association will not be charitable: see *National Anti-Vivisection Society v IRC* [1948] AC 31.

The relief of the aged and impotent

The preamble specifically refers to 'the relief of the aged, impotent and poor people'. The words have been construed disjunctively and objects need not qualify on all three grounds.

In *Joseph Rowntree Memorial Trust Housing Association v A-G* [1983] 1 All ER 288 the provision of housing for the elderly was held to be charitable.

> **J** 'The first set of charitable purposes contained in the preamble is 'the relief of aged, impotent and poor people'. Looking at those words, I would have thought that two inferences were tolerably clear. First, the words must be read disjunctively. It would be absurd to require that the aged must be impotent and poor … Second, the gift should relieve aged, impotent and poor people. The word 'relief' implies that the persons in question have a need attributable to their condition as aged, impotent and poor people requires alleviating and which those persons could not alleviate or would find difficulty in alleviating from their own resources.'
>
> (Gibson J in *Joseph Rowntree Memorial Trust Housing Association v A-G* (1983))

Likewise, in *Re Robinson* [1951] Ch 198, the provision of housing for persons over the age of 60 was charitable.

Recreational facilities

The promotion of sport *simpliciter* is not charitable, illustrated by *IRC v City of Glasgow Police Athletic Association* (1953). But in appropriate cases such gifts may be included under the heading advancement of education (see *IRC v McMullen* (1981)).

The provision of recreational facilities has been regarded as a charitable purpose and many village and town halls are used in part for recreational purposes. The decision of the House of Lords in *IRC v Baddeley* (1955) created doubts as to whether a number of bodies created for recreational purposes were charitable and the Recreational Charities Act 1958 was passed in order to clarify the law. Section 1(1) of the 1958 Act stipulates that the provision of recreational facilities shall be charitable if two criteria are fulfilled, namely:

(1) the public benefit test is satisfied and

(2) the facilities are provided in the interests of social welfare.

Section 1(2) of the 1958 Act declares that the requirement that the facilities are provided in the interests of social welfare will be satisfied only if:

's 1(2)(a) they are provided with the object of improving the conditions of life of those for whom they are primarily intended and

(b) either –

(i)   those persons have need for such facilities by reason of their youth, age, infirmity or disablement, poverty or social and economic circumstances; or

(ii) the facilities are available to the members or female members of the public at large.'

Under the 1958 Act, the social welfare test will be complied with if two conditions are satisfied as enacted in s 1(2). The first requirement is continuous, as stipulated in s 1(2)(a). The second requirement may be satisfied in alternative ways either by proving that the facilities are available to a limited class of objects who have a need for such facilities by virtue of one or more of the factors enumerated within s 1(2)(b)(i) (such as a youth club or an organised outing for orphaned children) or the facilities are available to the entire public (such as a public swimming pool or a public park) or female members of the public (Women's Institutes etc).

The House of Lords in *Guild v IRC* [1992] 2 All ER 10, HL construed the requirements under s 1(2)(a) liberally and rejected the view that it is necessary to prove that the beneficiaries were deprived of the relevant facilities. The test today is whether the facilities are provided with the purpose of improving the conditions of life of the beneficiaries, irrespective of whether the participating members of society are disadvantaged or not. In short, the material issue concerns the nature of the facilities rather than the status of the participants.

CASE EXAMPLE

Guild v IRC [1992] 2 All ER 10, HL

The Inland Revenue opposed a claim by an executor for exemption from capital transfer tax, on the ground that the gift was not for the promotion of charitable purposes. The House of Lords held in favour of the executor and decided that the gift was charitable under the Recreational Charities Act 1958 and, on construction of the second part of the residuary clause, the gift was exclusively in favour of charitable purposes

' "Hyde Park improves the conditions of life for residents in Mayfair and Belgravia as much as those in Pimlico or the Portobello Road, and the village hall may improve the conditions of life for residents for the squire and his family as well as the cottagers".'

(Bridge LJ, cited by Lord Keith)

In this case, a testator by his will disposed of the residue of his estate to the Town Council of North Berwick '(i) for the use in connection with the Sports Centre in North Berwick and (ii) some similar purpose in connection with sport'. The court held that the gift was charitable under the 1958 Act.

Section 1(3) of the 1958 Act declares that, subject to the provision of social welfare, the Act applies:

's 1(3) ... in particular to the provision of facilities at village halls, community centres and women's institutes, and to the provision and maintenance of grounds and buildings to be used for purposes of recreation or leisure-time occupation, and extends to the provision of facilities for those purposes by the organising of any activity.'

Miscellaneous examples

Other charitable purposes decided under Lord Macnaghten's fourth heading include the encouragement and advancement of choral singing (*Royal Choral Society v IRC* [1943] 2 All ER 101); gifts for the promotion of the defence of the United Kingdom (*Re Good* [1905] 2 Ch 60); gifts for the production of better organists and better organ music (*Re Levien* [1955] 3 All ER 35); a gift to provide a local fire brigade (*Re Wokingham Fire Brigade Trusts* [1951] 1 All ER 454); and a trust to relieve hardship and suffering by the local people as a result of a disaster (*Re North Devon and West Somerset Relief Fund Trusts* [1953] 2 All ER 1032), but it is imperative that the size of the class of beneficiaries be sufficiently large to satisfy the public element test; the publication and dissemination of law reports (*Incorporated Council for Law Reporting v A-G* (1971)); the promotion of industry, commerce and art (*Crystal Palace Trustees v Minister of Town and Country Planning* [1950] 2 All ER 857); the general improvement of agriculture (*IRC v Yorkshire Agricultural Society* [1928] 1 KB 611); the promotion of inexpensive and sanitary methods of disposal of the dead, in particular, cremation (*Scottish Burial Reform and Cremation Society Ltd v Glasgow City Corporation* [1968] AC 138); 'a gift unto my country, England' (*Re Smith* [1932 1 Ch 153); a gift to the inhabitants of a town or village (*Goodman v Saltash Corporation* [1882] 7 AC 633); and the study and dissemination of ethical principles and the cultivation of a national religious sentiment (*Re South Place Ethical Society* [1980] 1 WLR 1565).

Political purposes

Political purposes include attempts to change the law and gifts to further the objects of political parties. A trust for political purposes is incapable of subsisting as a charity: see *National Anti-Vivisection Society v IRC* [1948] AC 31. In this case, the general rule was stated by Lord Parker:

> 'A trust for the attainment of political objects has always been held invalid, not because it is illegal, for everyone is at liberty to advocate or promote by any lawful means a change in the law, but because the court has no means of judging whether a proposed change in the law will or will not be for the public benefit, and therefore cannot say that a gift to secure the change is a charitable gift.'
>
> (Lord Parker in *National Anti-Vivisection Society v IRC* (1948))

Accordingly, an educational trust along the lines of the Labour Party failed in *Re Hopkinson* [1949] 1 All ER 346. Similarly, a gift to Amnesty International failed in *McGovern v A-G* [1981] 3 All ER 493. Alternatively, a trust may be treated as charitable if its political purpose, on construction, is purely incidental to its main charitable purpose. A borderline case is *Re Scowrcroft* [1898] 2 Ch 638, where the gift for the maintenance of a village club and reading room was construed as charitable, for the advancement of education, even though the reading room was 'to be used for the furtherance of conservative principles'.

12.7 Charitable activities outside the United Kingdom

A number of British registered charities carry on their activities abroad. There is little judicial authority on the attitude of the courts to such overseas activities. In 1963, the Charity Commissioners issued guidelines on the way they would approach this problem. Their view is that activities of trusts within the first three heads of Lord Macnaghten's classification (trusts for the relief of poverty, for the advancement of education and for religion) are charitable wherever such operations are conducted. In respect of the fourth head, such purposes would be charitable only if carried on for the benefit (direct or reasonably direct) of the UK community, such as medical research. The Commissioners added that it may be easier to establish this benefit in relation to the Commonwealth (although this link has become weaker since this statement was made).

The limited number of authorities in this field seem to make no distinction between activities conducted abroad as opposed to UK activities.

CASE EXAMPLE

Keren Kayemeth Le Jisroel Ltd v IRC [1932] AC 650

A company was formed with the main object of purchasing land in Palestine, Syria and parts of Turkey for the purpose of settling Jews in such lands. It was argued that the company was established for charitable purposes, namely the advancement of religion, the relief of poverty and other purposes beneficial to the community. The court held that the company was not charitable because of the lack of evidence of religion and poverty. In addition, the company was not charitable under the fourth head because of the uncertainty of identifying the community.

In *Re Jacobs* [1970] 114 SJ 515, a trust for the planting of a clump of trees in Israel was held to be charitable because soil conservation in arid parts of Israel is of essential importance to the Israeli community. The court relied on *IRC v Yorkshire Agricultural Society* [1928] 1 KB 611: the promotion of agriculture is a charitable purpose.

However, if the organisation is not registered in the United Kingdom but abroad, and carries on its activities substantially abroad, the connection with the UK may be so insignificant that the English courts may reject jurisdiction. In *Gaudiya Mission v Brahmachary* [1997] 4 All ER 957, the Court of Appeal refused jurisdiction on the ground that the Charities Act 1993 could not be extended to such institutions.

■Key facts on charitable trusts

KEY FACTS

Advantages enjoyed by charitable trusts:

• Certainty of objects – private trusts are subject to strict tests for certainty of objects. The test for certainty of charitable objects is whether the objects are exclusively charitable.

• Enforcement – a private trust is ultimately required to be enforced by the beneficiaries, but charitable trusts are enforced by the Attorney-General on behalf of the Crown.

• Perpetuities – the perpetuities rule has a modified application to charitable trusts.

• Tax privileges – charities enjoy a number of tax privileges not enjoyed by private trusts.

• *Cy-près* – on a failure of a private trust, a resulting trust may arise, but when a charitable trust fails the property may be applied *cy-près* (to the nearest alternative).

In private trusts, trustees are required to act unanimously, but in administering charitable trusts, trustees act by a majority

Requirements of a charitable trust:

In order for a trust to be considered to be charitable, the following three requirements must be satisfied:

• the purposes are required to be, in law, charitable

CONTINUED ▸

KEY FACTS

- the trust is required to promote a public benefit and

- the objects of the trust must be exclusively charitable.

Definition of a charity?

- There is no statutory definition of 'charity'.

- Section 96 of the Charities Act 1993: 'charity' is described as any institution, corporate or not (including a trust), which is established for charitable purposes.

- What is a charity is a question of law.

- In novel cases, the approach adopted by the courts has been:

  (1) to treat as charitable any purpose which clearly falls within the preamble and

s 38(4) Charities Act 1960

  (2) to include, by analogy, any purpose which has been treated as charitable in the past

Scottish Burial Reform and Cremation Society v City of Glasgow Corporation (1968)

  (3) to declare that a purpose which falls within the spirit and intendment of the preamble is charitable

ICLR v A-G (1972)

- The purposes laid down in the preamble have been classified by Lord Macnaghten in *IRC v Pemsel* (1891) into the following four categories:

IRC v Pemsel (1891)

  trusts for the relief of poverty;

  trusts for the advancement of education;

  trusts for the advancement of religion; and

  trusts for other purposes beneficial to the community.

CONTINUED ▸

KEY FACTS

• The public benefit test is two-fold:	
– the purposes are required to provide some useful benefit to members of the community in accordance with the preamble or spirit of the preamble	*Re Compton* (1945); *IRC v Baddeley* (1955); *Williams' Trustees v IRC* (1947); *Gilmour v Coats* (1949); *Re Lewis* (1954)
– the class of persons who are entitled to enjoy the property must not be numerically negligible and connected in blood or contract to the donor. This condition does not apply to trusts for the relief of poverty.	
• Trusts for the relief of poverty.	*Re Saunders* (1954); *Re Niyazi* (1978); *Re Scarisbrick* (1951); *Dingle v Turner* (1972)
• Trusts for the advancement of education.	*Re Shaw* (1957); *Re Hopkins* (1964); *Re British School of Egyptian Archaeology* (1954); *Royal Choral Society v IRC* (1943); *Re Delius* (1957); *Re Pinion* (1965)
• The encouragement of sport is charitable if carried out as part of the activities of a school or university.	*IRC v McMullen* (1981); *Re Dupree* (1944)
• Recreational Charities Act 1958.	*Guild v IRC* (1992)

CONTINUED ▶

KEY FACTS

• Trusts for the advancement of religion.	*Bowman v Secular Society* (1917); *Neville Estates v Madden* (1962); *Re South Place Ethical Society* (1980); *United Grand Lodge of Freemasons v Holborn BC* (1957); *Gilmour v Coats* (1949); *Re Garrard* (1907); *Re Simson* (1946); *Farley v Westminster Bank* (1939); *Thornton v Howe* (1862); *Re Watson* (1973); *Re Hetherington* (1989)
• Other purposes beneficial to the community.	*ICLR v A-G* (1972); *National Anti-Vivisection Society v IRC* (1948); *Re Wedgwood* (1915); *Re Grove-Grady* (1929); *IRC v City of Glasgow Police Athletic Association* (1953); *IRC v Baddeley* (1955)
• Political purposes are not charitable.	*Re Shaw* (1957); *McGovern v A-G* (1981); *Re Koeppler* (1986)

CONTINUED ▸

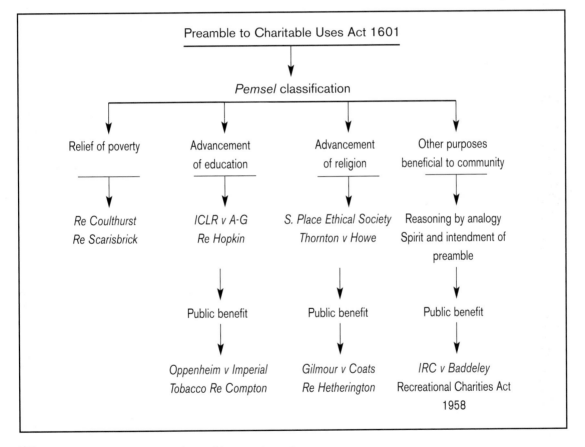

■ *Figure 12.1 Preamble to Charitable Uses Act 1601*

12.8 The *cy-près* doctrine examined

The expression '*cy-près*' originates from Norman French, meaning 'near this'. Over the centuries the expression has been taken to mean 'as near as possible'. The *cy-près* doctrine is a principle applicable to gifts for charitable purposes which fail (initially or subsequently) because of the impossibility or impracticality of giving effect to the donor's intention. Schemes may be approved by the Charity Commissioners and the courts for the application of the funds as nearly as possible to the original purposes as stated by the settlor. When the *cy-près* doctrine is adopted the donor or his estate is excluded from benefiting by way of a resulting trust.

There are only two conditions to be satisfied for a *cy-près* application, namely:

(1) the impossibility or impracticality of carrying out the original charitable purpose or the existence of a surplus of funds after the charitable purpose has been fulfilled and

(2) the manifestation of a general charitable intention by the donor as opposed to a specific charitable intention.

12.8.1 Impossibility

Prior to the introduction of the Charities Act 1960, the courts approached this question by considering whether the purposes, as stated by the settlor, were capable of being achieved as distinct from merely being undesirable.

CASE EXAMPLE

Attorney-General v City of London [1790] 3 Bro CC 171

Trust funds to be used for the advancement and propagation of the Christian religion among the infidels in Virginia were applied *cy-près* when it became clear that there were no longer any infidels in Virginia.

Similarly, in *A-G v Ironmongers Company* [1834] 2 My & K 567, funds devoted to the redemption of British slaves in Turkey and Barbary were applied *cy-près* when the purpose subsequently became impossible to achieve.

The test of 'impossibility' was construed broadly in *Re Dominion Students' Hall Trust* [1947] 1 Ch 183, where a limited company was formed for charitable purposes.

CASE EXAMPLE

Re Dominion Students' Hall Trust [1947] 1 Ch 183

The memorandum of association declared its object as being to maintain a hostel for students 'of European origin' from the overseas dominions of the British Empire. The company proposed a scheme, for approval of the court, whereby the offensive words 'of European origin' would be deleted so that the company would be better equipped to administer the funds for the benefit of all students from the dominions regardless of racial origin. The court approved the scheme because the retention of the colour bar had the effect of defeating the main object of the charity.

> **J** 'It is true that the word "impossible" should be given a wide significance. It is not necessary to go to the length of saying that the original scheme is absolutely impracticable. ... it is said that to retain the condition, so far from furthering the charity's main object might defeat it and would be liable to antagonise those students, both white and coloured, whose support and goodwill it is the purpose of the charity to sustain. The case, therefore, can be said to fall within the broad description of impossibility.'
>
> (Evershed J)

On the other hand, the test of impossibility was not satisfied in *Re Weir Hospital* [1910] 2 Ch 124.

CASE EXAMPLE

Re Weir Hospital [1910] 2 Ch 124

The testator devised property to be used as the site for a hospital. Expert evidence was admitted to the effect that the site was not suitable for a hospital and a scheme was proposed for the building of a nurses' home instead. The court refused to approve the scheme on the ground that it was not impossible to carry out the testator's wishes but simply inadvisable.

12.8.2 Section 13 of the Charities Act 1993

This consolidates to some extent and substantially extends the powers of the Charity Commissioners and the courts to apply property *cy-près*. The circumstances when the purposes of the charity will become impractical or impossible are enacted in s 13(1)(a)–(e) of the Charities Act 1993.

's 13(1)(a) where the original purposes wholly or partly have been as far as may be fulfilled, or cannot be carried out according the directions given and to the spirit of the gift'.

This paragraph gives the court the jurisdiction to decide that the original purposes of the gift have been fulfilled or have become impractical. The only restriction on the discretion of the court is in regard to the construction of 'the spirit of the gift'. This phrase has been interpreted by Pennycuick VC in *Re Lepton's Charity* [1972] Ch 276 as meaning 'the basic intention underlying the gift, as ascertained from its terms in the light of admissible evidence'.

CASE EXAMPLE

Re Lepton's Charity [1972] Ch 276

A testator who died in 1716 devised specific property to trustees on trust to pay an annual sum of £3 to the Protestant Minister in Pudsey, and the surplus income to the poor and aged people of Pudsey. In 1716, the total income was £5. On the date of the application to the court that income was £790 *per annum*. Two questions arose for the determination of the court, namely:

(i)   whether, on a true construction of the will, the minister ought to be paid a fixed sum of £3 or three-fifths of the annual income and

(ii)   whether the court would approve a *cy-près* scheme increasing the minister's entitlement to £100 per annum.

The court held that on a construction of the will the minister was not entitled to three-fifths of the annual income but only a fixed sum of £3 *per annum*, but having regard to the spirit of the gift a *cy-près* scheme would be approved entitling the minister to £100 *per annum*.

CASE EXAMPLE

Oldham Borough Council v A-G, The Times, 20th August 1992

The Court of Appeal was required to consider the original purpose of a devise of land to the Oldham Borough Council 'on trust to preserve and manage the same as playing fields known as the "Clayton Playing Fields" for the benefit of inhabitants of Oldham, Chatterton and Royton'. The Court of Appeal, reversing the decision of the High Court, held that, on construction, the original purpose of the devise was not intended to impose an obligation on the council to retain the site in perpetuity, for use only as playing fields for the local community, but to make provision for playing fields for the benefit of the local community. Accordingly, the council was entitled to sell the site to developers and use the proceeds to acquire a new site for playing fields for the local community.

In *Re Laing Trust* [1984] Ch 143, the court drew a distinction between the 'original purposes' of the trust under s 13 which may be reviewed by the court on a *cy-près* application, and a direction to distribute within a specific period of time, which is treated as an administrative provision outside of s 13. Under the inherent jurisdiction of the court a scheme may be approved even though the court has no jurisdiction within s 13.

CASE EXAMPLE

Re Laing Trust [1984] Ch 143

In 1922, a settlor transferred shares to the plaintiff company as trustee to hold for charitable purposes. Both capital and income were to be wholly distributed during the lifetime of the settlor or within 10 years of his death. The settlor died in 1978. By 1982 the capital which was undistributed was worth £24 million. The plaintiff company applied to the court to sanction a scheme dispensing with the obligation to distribute the capital within 10 years of the settlor's death. The court decided that it had no jurisdiction under s 13, as the 'original purposes' of the charitable gift did not include an administrative provision concerning the date of distribution, but in the exercise of its inherent jurisdiction the court would approve the proposed scheme.

J

'I would regard it as an abuse of language to describe the requirement as to distribution as a purpose of the gift ... I remain unpersuaded that such a gift is capable of being applied *cy-près* and, in particular, I am not persuaded that the requirement as to distribution is a purpose within the meaning of section 13. Rather, it seems to me to fall on the administrative side of the line, going, as it does, to the mechanics of how the property devoted to charitable purposes is to be distributed. Accordingly, I must refuse the application so far as it is based on section 13 ... I have no hesitation in reaching the conclusion that the court should, in the exercise of its inherent jurisdiction, approve a scheme under which the trustees for the time being of the charity will be discharged from the obligation to distribute the capital within 10 years of the death of the settlor.'

(Peter Gibson J)

's 13(1)(b) where the original purposes provide a use for part only of the property available by virtue of the gift'.

The approval of the court may be granted under this paragraph where a surplus of funds are left over after the original charitable purposes have been carried out. This paragraph merely declares the law that existed before 1960.

CASE EXAMPLE

Re North Devon and West Somerset Relief Fund [1953] 2 All ER 1032

A public appeal was launched following extensive flooding in North Devon and West Somerset. There was an overwhelming response and the question arose whether the surplus ought to be applied *cy-près* or be repayable to the donors. The court decided that the surplus funds would be applied *cy-près*.

 's 13(1)(c) where the property available by virtue of the gift and other property applicable for similar purposes can be more effectively used in conjunction with property held for common purposes, regard being had to the spirit of the gift'.

This provision enables a number of small charities with common purposes to be amalgamated in order to create larger funds.

CASE EXAMPLE

Re Faraker [1912] 2 Ch 488

A testatrix, who died in 1911, left a legacy to 'Mrs Bailey's Charity, Rotherhithe'. A charity was founded by Mrs Hannah Bayly in 1756 for poor widows in Rotherhithe. In 1905 the charity was consolidated with a number of local charities under a scheme, approved by the Charity Commissioners, for the benefit of the poor in Rotherhithe. The court decided that the legacy was taken by the consolidated charities.

 's 13(1)(d) where the original purposes were laid down by reference to an area which has ceased to be a unit, or by reference to a class of persons or to an area which has ceased to be suitable or practicable, regard being had to the spirit of the gift'.

Under this paragraph, the court is entitled to consider that, because of local government boundary changes, the original class of beneficiaries has become difficult to identify or the class of beneficiaries has dwindled over the years. See *A-G v City of London* (1790) and *Ironmongers Co v A-G* (1844).

CASE EXAMPLE

Peggs and Others v Lamb, The Times, 19th March 1993

The court considered a *cy-près* scheme under s 13(1)(d) of the Charities Act 1960. Freemen and their widows in the Ancient Borough of Huntingdon were entitled to the income from specific plots of land. In 1992 the number of beneficiaries had dwindled to 15 and the income available for distribution had risen to £550,000. The court decided, under s 13(1)(d), that the original purposes of the gift was to benefit the freemen and widows in the Huntingdon Borough but the class of beneficiaries had dwindled to such an extent that they ceased to be a suitable class for the deployment of the funds (due consideration being paid to the spirit of the gift). Accordingly, a scheme would be approved whereby the class of beneficiaries would be enlarged to include the inhabitants of the borough as a whole.

's 13(1)(e) where the original purposes, in whole or in part, have since they were laid down:

(i) been adequately provided for by other reasons; or

(ii) ceased, as being useless or harmful to the community, or, for other reasons, to be in law charitable; or

(iii) ceased in any other way to provide a suitable and effective method of using the property given, regard being had to the spirit of the gift.'

Subsection 13(1)(e)(i) empowers the court to modify the original purposes as stated by the donor, in view of the charitable purposes being provided for by other bodies such as central and local government, eg the repair of roads and bridges may not be an appropriate mode of utilising charitable resources.

Subsection 13(1)(e)(ii) will rarely be used. It assumes that a purpose was once charitable but because of changed circumstances the purpose ceases to be charitable, eg anti-vivisection in the early nineteenth century was considered a charitable purpose (see *Re Fouveaux* [1895] 2 Ch 501), but with the advance of medical research, anti-vivisection is no longer treated as a charitable purpose. At the time when the Anti-Vivisection Society was removed from the Charities Register its funds could have been applied *cy-près*. Subsection 13(1)(e)(ii) merely confirms this approach.

Subsection 13(1)(e)(iii) enacts a wide-ranging provision giving the courts the power to consider whether the original purposes selected by the donor represent an effective method of using the property. In *Re Lepton's Charity* (1972) the court assumed jurisdiction *inter alia*, under s 13(1)(e)(iii), to sanction the scheme.

CASE EXAMPLE

Varsani v Jesani [1983] 3 All ER 273

A charitable trust had been established for the purpose of promoting the faith of a particular Hindu sect. The sect split into two groups. The majority brought proceedings seeking a scheme for the administration of the property of the charity. The court decided that it had jurisdiction under s 13(1)(e)(iii) of the 1993 Act. The original purpose had ceased to be a suitable and effective method of using the available property. The scheme involved dividing the property between the two groups.

12.8.2 General charitable intention

This is the second condition which is required to be fulfilled before the charitable funds may be applied *cy-près*.

Subsequent failure

But there is one type of event where the courts have dispensed with the need to prove a general charitable intention. These are cases of 'subsequent failure', ie occasions when the charitable bodies exist at the appropriate date of vesting but cease to exist subsequently. The appropriate date of vesting varies with the nature of the instrument creating the gift. An *inter vivos* transfer by deed takes effect on the date of the execution of the deed and a transfer by will takes effect on the date of death of the donor. Once the gift vests in the charity the donor and his heirs are excluded from benefiting on a subsequent liquidation of the charity, irrespective of whether the gift was made subject to a general or specific charitable intention.

CASE EXAMPLE

Re Wright [1954] Ch 347

A testatrix, who died in 1933, gave her residuary estate to trustees on trust for a tenant for life, Mr Webb (who died in 1942), with the remainder to found and maintain a convalescent home for 'impecunious gentlewomen'. On the date of the testatrix's death the residuary estate was sufficient to implement her wishes, but at the time of Webb's death, the fund was insufficient to carry out the charitable purpose. It was argued that the appropriate date for deciding whether the charitable purpose was practical or not was on the date of Webb's death. The court rejected this argument and decided that the date for deciding whether the funds were applicable *cy-près* was on the date of vesting, namely the date of death of the testatrix.

CONTINUED ▶

> J
>
> 'Once money is effectually dedicated to charity, whether in pursuance of a general
> or a particular charitable intent, the testator's next of kin or residuary legatees are
> forever excluded and no question of subsequent lapse, or of anything analogous to
> lapse, between the date of the testator's death and the time when the money
> becomes available for actual application to the testator's purpose can affect the
> matter so far as they are concerned.'
>
> (Romer LJ)

The same principle applies where the charity existed at the testator's death but was liquidated before the gift took effect. This arose in *Re Slevin* [1891] 2 Ch 236; the testator left money to St Dominic's orphanage in Newcastle. The orphanage existed at the date of the death but closed down soon afterwards, before it received the legacy. The court held that the fund was applied *cy-près*.

However, it is essential that an absolute and perpetual gift be made to the charity at the time of vesting. If, alternatively, a limited gift (for a number of years) is made to the charity which existed on the date of vesting, but it ceases to exist at the time the gift purported to take effect, on construction, the court may decide that a resulting trust in favour of the settlor's estate may take effect. This was decided in *Re Cooper's Conveyance Trusts* [1956] 3 All ER 28.

Initial failure

In the event of an initial failure of the charitable institution, it is essential to prove a general charitable intention before the funds are applied *cy-près*. In other words, if, at the time of the vesting of the gift, the charitable body, specified by the donor, did not exist, the fund may only be applied *cy-près* on proof of a general charitable intention as opposed to a specific charitable intention.

General/specific charitable intention

The intention of the donor is essentially a question of fact. The courts are required to consider all the circumstances in order to determine whether the donor intended to benefit a charitable 'purpose' simpliciter identified by reference to a charitable institution (paramount charitable intention), or whether the settlor's intention was to benefit a specific charitable body identified by him.

The court adopted a broad approach to this question in *Re Lysaght* [1966] Ch 191.

CASE EXAMPLE

Re Lysaght [1966] Ch 191

A testatrix bequeathed £5,000 to the Royal College of Surgeons (trustees) on trust to apply the income in establishing studentships, with disqualifications in respect of Jews and Roman Catholics. The College declined to accept the gift but declared that if the religious bar was excised it would be willing to accept the gift. The court decided that in accordance with the paramount charitable intention of the testatrix the religious bar would be deleted. On construction, the court decided that the paramount charitable intention of the testatrix was to make the College a trustee of the fund and since this paramount intention was capable of being defeated if the religious bar was upheld, the court was entitled to delete the offending clause in order to give effect to the paramount intention of the settlor.

Buckley J distinguished a general charitable intention from a specific charitable intention:

> **J** 'A general charitable intention may be said to be a paramount intention on the part of the donor to effect some charitable purpose which the court can find a method of putting into operation, notwithstanding that it is impracticable to give effect to some direction by the donor which is not an essential part of his true intention – not, that is to say, part of his paramount intention. In contrast, a particular charitable intention exists where the donor means his charitable disposition to take effect if, but only if, it can be carried into effect in a particular specified way.'
>
> (Buckley J)

The court came to a similar conclusion in *Re Woodhams* [1981] 1 All ER 202.

CASE EXAMPLE

Re Woodhams [1981] 1 All ER 202

A limitation attached to scholarships to two music colleges, restricting applicants to boys from Dr Barnardo's Homes and the Church of England Children's Society Homes, was deleted because the colleges would otherwise have declined the gifts on the ground that the limitation was impractical.

Form/substance

The classic statement of the distinction between a general charitable intention and a specific charitable intention was issued by Parker J in *Re Wilson* [1913] 1 Ch 314.

> J
>
> 'The authorities must be divided into two classes. First of all we have a class of cases where, in form, the gift is given for a particular charitable purpose, but it is possible, taking the gift as a whole, to say that, notwithstanding the form of the gift, the paramount intention is to give property in the first instance for a general charitable purpose rather than a particular charitable purpose, and to graft into the general gift a direction as to the desires or intentions of the donor as to the manner in which the general gift is to be carried into effect. Then there is the second class of cases where, on the true construction of the gift, no such paramount general intention can be inferred, and where the gift being in form a particular gift – a gift for a particular purpose, and it being impossible to carry out that particular purpose, the whole gift is held to fail.'
>
> (Parker J)

Examples of cases within the first class are *Re Lysaght* (1966) and *Re Woodhams* (1981). In *Biscoe v Jackson* [1887] 35 Ch D 460, a legacy for the establishment of a soup kitchen and a cottage hospital in the parish of Shoreditch disclosed, on construction of the will, a general charitable intention to benefit the poor in Shoreditch.

Within the second category of cases, the courts are entitled to draw the inference that the donor has manifested a specific charitable intention if he has described the charitable purpose with precision. Indeed, the clearer the description of the charitable objective which the donor has in mind, the stronger the inference that the intention is specific.

CASE EXAMPLE

Re Wilson [1913] 1 Ch 314

A testator gave property upon trust to pay the salary of a schoolmaster (whose duties were specified) who was expected to teach in a school which he expected would be built with funds raised from the public. Detailed directions were given as to the expected location of the school and the running of the school. There was no possibility of carrying out these instructions and on construction the court decided that the testator manifested a specific charitable intention.

ASE EXAMPLE

> *Re Good* [1950] 2 All ER 653
>
> A legacy to provide rest homes in Hull was subject to a detailed scheme as to the types of homes to be provided, the types of inmates to be admitted and the management powers of the trustees. When the scheme proved impracticable because the funds were insufficient the court decided that the testator did not manifest a general charitable intention. Accordingly, the funds resulted to the residuary legatees.

Existent/non-existent charitable body

A factor which may influence the judge in deciding the question of the intention of the donor is the fact that the charitable body selected by the donor has never been in existence. The approach here is that the specification by the donor of a named charitable institution which never existed may be construed as a reference to the purpose to which the donor intended to devote his funds and is evidence of a general charitable intention.

ASE EXAMPLE

> *Re Harwood* [1936] Ch 285
>
> A testatrix bequeathed legacies to (a) the 'Wisbech Peace Society, Cambridge' (a society which had existed at one time but had ceased to exist before the testatrix's death) and (b) the 'Peace Society of Belfast' (which had never existed). The court held that the gift to the Wisbech Peace Society manifested a specific charitable intention for the object of the testatrix's bounty was carefully selected and identified and that portion of the estate was held on resulting trust. But the legacy to the Belfast Society was applicable *cy-près* because her intention must have been to benefit any charitable society which promoted peace in Belfast.

A similar approach was adopted by the Court of Appeal in the following case:

CASE EXAMPLE

Re Satterthwaite's Will Trust [1966] 1 WLR 277

A testatrix who announced to a bank official that she hated the whole human race and wished to leave her estate to animal charities made her will in December 1952 and died in 1962 leaving her residuary estate equally to nine animal welfare organisations selected from a telephone directory. Seven of these bodies were animal charities but the remaining two were an anti-vivisection society and the London Animal Hospital. The question in issue concerned the one-ninth share bequeathed in favour of the London Animal Hospital. This share was claimed *inter alia* by a veterinary surgeon who had carried on his profession under that name from 1943 to July 1952 when, following the Veterinary Surgeons Act 1948, the name was withdrawn from the Register of Animal Hospitals. At all material times this hospital was private and not charitable. There was no evidence that the testatrix had any knowledge of the surgeon's establishment or that she knew that it was a private hospital. The court decided that the one-ninth share was applicable *cy-près*. The evidence suggested that the testatrix meant to benefit a purpose and not an individual. The other bequests taken as a whole (despite the one-ninth share to the anti-vivisection society) showed a general charitable intention to benefit animals.

> J 'I have already indicated that the testatrix is to be taken as intending to benefit a charitable activity. But the organisation picked by name was not such ... any assumption is that the testatrix was pointing to a particular charitable application of this one-ninth of residue. If a particular mode of charitable application is incapable of being performed as such, but it can be discerned from her will that the testatrix has a charitable intention (commonly referred to as a general charitable intention) which transcends the particular mode of application indicated, the court has jurisdiction to direct application of the bequest to charitable purposes *cy-près*. Here I have no doubt from the nature of the other dispositions by this testatrix of her residuary estate that a general intention can be discerned in favour of charity through the medium of kindness to animals. I am not in any way deterred from this conclusion by the fact that one-ninth was given to an anti-vivisection society which in law – unknown to the average testator – is not charitable.'
>
> (Russell LJ)

Incorporated and unincorporated associations

Another factor which has found favour with the courts in deciding the intention of the settlor concerns the distinction between charitable corporations and unincorporated associations. An incorporated association, as distinct from an unincorporated association, has an independent legal existence distinct from its members. In *Re Vernon's Will Trust* [1972] Ch 300, Buckley J expressed the view that a gift to a corporate charity is *prima facie* intended to take effect as a beneficial gift to the named body and will lapse if the charity ceases to exist before the testator's death. It will only be possible to apply the funds *cy-près* if the court, on construction, finds a general charitable intention. On the other hand, where the gift is to an unincorporated association, the gift *prima facie* takes effect for the purposes of the association. The named unincorporated association is treated as the trustee to carry out the charitable purpose. Accordingly, if the association ceases to exist the court is entitled to use its inherent jurisdiction to ensure that the trust will not fail for want of a trustee and may appoint new trustees to continue the charitable purposes. (This *prima facie* rule may be rebutted by evidence which shows that the gift was dependent upon the continued existence of the particular trustees.) This approach appealed to Goff J in the following case.

CASE EXAMPLE

Re Finger's Will Trust [1972] Ch 286

A testatrix who died in 1965, by her will made in 1930, transferred her residuary estate on trust in favour of 11 charitable institutions equally. One share was given to the 'National Radium Commission'. No institution by that name existed, although an unincorporated body called the 'Radium Commission' had existed since 1929 but was liquidated in 1947 when the National Health Service was set up. The work previously undertaken by the Commission was carried on by the Minister of Health. The court construed the bequest as intended for the Radium Commission. Another share of the bequest was given to the National Council for Maternity and Child Welfare. This was a corporate body which was in existence at the time of the execution of the will but was wound up in 1948. The bulk of its assets were transferred to the National Association for Maternity and Child Welfare, an association similar to the Council and which continued the Council's activities. The question in issue was whether both shares might be applied *cy-près*.

The court held that the testatrix exhibited a general charitable intention in respect of both gifts. The gift to the unincorporated association (the Radium Commission) was construed as intended for the purposes of the Commission which was not dependent on the continued existence of the Commission. The gift to the incorporated association which ceased to exist on the date of vesting was treated *prima facie* as a gift to the body (see *Re Harwood* (1936)) but was still capable of being construed as a general charitable gift since virtually the whole estate was devoted for charitable purposes, the testatrix regarded herself as having no relatives and the Council had merely a co-ordinating function.

CONTINUED ▶

J

(distinguishing *Re Harwood* (1936)) 'In the present case the circumstances are very special … First, virtually the whole estate is devoted to charity and again the nature of the Council was mainly, if not exclusively, a co-ordinating body. I cannot believe that this testatrix meant to benefit that organisation and that alone. Finally, I am entitled to place myself in "the armchair of the testatrix" and I have evidence that she regarded herself as having no relatives. Taking all these matters into account, in my judgement I can and ought to distinguish *Re Harwood* and find, as I do, a general charitable intent.'

(Goff J)

This basis of distinguishing *Re Harwood* (1936) was doubted by Megarry VC in the following case:

CASE EXAMPLE

Re Spence [1979] Ch 483

A testatrix who died in 1972, by her will dated 4th December 1968, bequeathed part of her estate to the 'Old Folks Home at Hillworth Lodge, Keighley, for the benefit of the patients'. Hillworth Lodge was built as a workhouse in 1858 and was closed in 1939. In 1948, it became an aged persons' home under the National Assistance Act 1948 but was closed down in 1971. Since then the building had been used as government offices. The question in issue was whether the testatrix had manifested a general or specific charitable intention.

The court held (applying *Re Harwood* (1936) and refusing to follow *Re Finger's Will Trust* (1972)) that the testatrix had manifested a specific charitable intention by identifying a particular charitable purpose which on the date of the will was capable of being carried out but was incapable of being fulfilled at the time of death.

J

'This is a fairly plain case of a will which made a gift for a particular purpose in fairly specific terms. The gift was for the benefit of the patients at a particular home. At the date of the will there were several patients at that home, but when the testatrix died, there was no longer any home there, but offices instead; and so there were no longer any patients there, or any possibility of them … if a particular purpose is specified, then it is that purpose and no other, that is the object of the benefaction. The specific displaces the general. I am not sure that I have been able to appreciate to the full the cogency of the special circumstances that appealed to Goff J. in *Re Finger*.'

(Megarry J)

12.8.3 Section 14 of the Charities Act 1993

The general rule, as detailed above, is that property given for a specific charitable purpose which fails from the outset cannot be applied *cy-près* if no general charitable intention can be imputed to the donor. Such property will be held on resulting trust for the donor.

By the way of exception to the general rule, s 14 of the Charities Act 1993 enacts that property given for specific charitable purposes which fail shall be applicable *cy-près* as if given for charitable purposes generally where the property belongs to a donor who cannot be identified or found after reasonable enquiries and advertisements have been made or who disclaims his right to the property in writing. In *Re Henry Wood National Memorial Trusts* [1965] 109 SJ 876, in the case of a nationwide appeal, notices in *The Times*, *The Telegraph* and *The Scotsman* newspapers and letters to addresses of donors noted in the appeal records constituted reasonable advertisements and enquiries.

The section continues (s 14(3)) to the effect that in the case of cash collections by use of collecting boxes or where it is not possible to distinguish one gift from another or in the case of money raised by lotteries, entertainment and similar money-raising activities, the property will be conclusively presumed to belong to unidentifiable donors without a need for advertisement and enquiry.

Moreover, s14(4) enacts that, in any other cases, the court may order that property may be treated as belonging to donors who cannot be identified (without an advertisement or enquiry) if the amounts are so small that it would be unreasonable to incur the expense of returning the property to the donors, or it would otherwise be unreasonable to do so, having regard to the nature and circumstances of the gift or the lapse of time since the gifts were made.

■Key facts on the *cy-près* doctrine

KEY FACTS

Introduction

The *cy-près* doctrine enables the court (and the Charity Commissioners) to make a scheme for the application of the property for other charitable purposes, as close as possible to those intended by the donor. There are two conditions to be satisfied before a *cy-près* scheme is made. These are impossibility or impracticality in carrying out the charitable purpose and the manifestation of a general charitable intention by the settlor.

CONTINUED ▸

KEY FACTS

Impossibility

Prior to the Charities Act 1960 (predecessor to the Charities Act 1993) this question was approached as to whether the charitable purposes were capable of being achieved as opposed to merely being undesirable.	*A-G v City of London* (1790); *A-G v Ironmongers Co* (1834); *Re Dominion Students' Hall* (1947)
s 13 Charities Act 1993	*Re Lepton* (1972); *Oldham BC v A-G* (1992); *North Devon and West Somerset Relief Fund* (1953); *Re Faraker* (1912); *Peggs v Lamb* (1993); *Re Fouveaux* (1895); *Varsani v Jesani* (1983)

General charitable intention

Subsequent failure

• Where a gift made to a charity ceases to exist after the gift has taken effect, there is no need to demonstrate a general charitable intention in order to apply the gift *cy-près*.	*Re Wright* (1954); *Re Wokingham Fire Brigade Trusts* (1951)

Initial failure

• A general charitable intention may not be inferred if the gift was for a particular, specified charity which once existed but no longer does at the date of vesting of the gift.	*Re Spence* (1979)
• Where the institution has never existed it is easier to find a general charitable intention.	*Re Harwood* (1936)

CONTINUED ▸

KEY FACTS

• If the institution subsequently fails to exist in Its original form (merger with other bodies) a general charitable intention may be inferred if the original purposes of the institution are promoted by the new body.	*Re Faraker* (1912); *Re Vernon* (1972)
• A gift to an unincorporated charity by name *prima facie* takes effect as a gift for charitable purposes (as a trust). If the charitable body ceased to exist, the gift may be applied *cy-près* if the purposes of the association are carried out by the new entity.	*Re Finger* (1972); *Re Harwood* (1936)
• A gift to an incorporated charity takes effect simply as a gift to that body beneficially. If the charity has ceased to exist *prima facie* the gift will fail unless, exceptionally, a general charitable intention is found.	*Re Finger* (1972); *Re Spence* (1979)
• A gift to a non-charitable institution is not made charitable by being included in a list of charitable gifts, even if the purposes are similar.	*Re Jenkins* (1966); *Re Satterthwaite* (1966)
• s 14 Charities Act 1993	

12.9 The Charity Commissioners

The Charity Commissioners for England and Wales are a statutory body regulated by the Charities Act 1993, with functions under that Act and others. The Commissioners have the general function of promoting the effective use of charitable resources by encouraging the development of better methods of administration, by giving charity trustees advice and information on any matter affecting the charity and by investigating and checking abuses. The Commissioners also have the power to mediate informally in charity disputes but not to arbitrate or adjudicate.

12.10 The Attorney-General

The role of the Attorney-General is to represent the beneficial interests or objects of the charity. His duty is to protect the interests of charity generally, and in so doing he contributes to a framework of supervision and control over charities in which the Charity Commission plays a significant role. The Attorney-General is generally a necessary party to all claims relating to charities.

12.11 Litigation by charities

Section 32(1) of the Charities Act 1993 confers on the Commissioners the same powers with respect to the taking of legal proceedings or the compromise of claims as are exercisable by the Attorney-General acting *ex officio*.

Section 33(1) of the 1993 Act authorises 'charity proceedings' (as defined) to be taken with reference to a charity either by the charity, or by any of the charity trustees, or by any person interested in the charity, or by two or more inhabitants of the area if it is a local charity, but not by any other person.

In *Gunning v Buckfast*, *The Times*, 9th June 1994, the High Court decided that parents of children at a school possessed a sufficient standing to bring proceedings opposing the closure of the school.

Section 33(2) provides that no charity proceedings shall be entertained or proceeded with in any court unless the taking of the proceedings is authorised by order of the Commissioners. If the Commissioners refuse to authorise the taking of proceedings, leave can be obtained from a High Court judge. Section 33(8) defines 'charity proceedings' as proceedings in any court in England and Wales brought under the court's jurisdiction with respect to charities.

12.12 Reform of charities

12.12.1 The Charities Bill 2004

The Charities Bill was published on 20th December 2004. It was a culmination of a number of reports. In 2001 the Prime Minister's Strategy Unit commissioned a review of the law and regulation of charities and not-for-profit organisations. The review was carried out and in September 2002 a document entitled 'Private Action, Public Benefit' was published. This involved an analysis of the strengths and weaknesses of the current legal framework of charities. In July 2003 the Government published a report entitled 'Charities and Not-for-Profits: a Modern Legal Framework' which summarised the results of the Strategy Unit's recommendations. The Charities Bill reflects the majority of these recommendations. The Bill contains 72 clauses and is divided into four Parts. Part 1 deals with the definition of a 'charity', including the 'public benefit' test. Part 2 deals with the regulation of charities, including the objectives, functions and the constitution of the Charities Commission and an amendment regarding schemes that may be applied *cy-près*. Part 3 regulates the fund-raising activities of charities and Part 4 deals with miscellaneous, incidental matters. This brief note is in respect of Part 1 of the Bill.

Clause 1(1) adopts a general definition of a 'charity' which endorses the principle laid down in s 96(1) of the Charities Act 1993. This is that 'charity'

> 'means a body or trust which –
>
> (a) is established for charitable purposes *only*, and
>
> (b) falls to be subject to the control of the High Court in the exercise of its jurisdiction with respect to charities.'

This broad definition preserves the current approach to charities by reference to the identification of the objects as exclusively charitable. The policy of cl 1(1)(b) involves the jurisdictional aspect of the definition. For all practical purposes, a charity needs to be under the control of the High Court.

Clause 2 adopts a statutory definition by reference to a two-step approach – the listing of a variety of charitable purposes and the 'public benefit' test. Clause 2(2) contains a list of 12 charitable purposes. This is intended to be a comprehensive list of charitable activities. In any event, most of these purposes were charitable before the Bill was introduced. These purposes are:

(a)   the prevention or relief of poverty

(b)   the advancement of education

(c)   the advancement of religion

(d)   the advancement of health [including the prevention or relief of sickness, disease or human suffering]

(e)   the advancement of citizenship or community development

(f)   the advancement of the arts, heritage or science

(g)   the advancement of amateur sport [involving physical skill and exertion]

(h)   the advancement of human rights, conflict resolution or reconciliation

(i)   the advancement of environmental protection or improvement

(j)   the relief of those in need, by reason of youth, age, ill-health, disability, financial hardship or other disadvantage [including the provision of accommodation and care to the beneficiaries mentioned within this clause]

(k)   the advancement of animal welfare

(l)   any other purpose within sub-clause (4).

With the exception of amateur sport, all of these purposes are charitable under current law.

Clause 2(4) endorses the common-law approach to charitable objects by reference to the purposes declared in paras (a)–(k) above. This affirms the common-law approach by considering the 'spirit and intendment' of the preamble and reasoning by analogy by reference to decided cases.

Clause 3 lays down the second part of the definition of a 'charity' namely the 'public benefit' test. Clause 3(1) stipulates that each of the listed purposes indicated above is required in order to satisfy the 'public benefit' test. Clause 3(2) declares that **no presumption** will be made to the effect that a purpose satisfies the 'public element' test. Thus, if there is a dispute as to the validity of a charitable purpose, the trustees of the organisation are required positively to establish that the purpose has a real and substantial benefit to society.

Clause 3(3) consolidates the case law meaning of 'public benefit'. This involves a two-step test of demonstrating a benefit to society (as mentioned above) and that those eligible to receive benefits comprise a large enough group to be considered as the public and without a personal or private relationship being used to limit those who may benefit.

In summary, the legal re-definition of a 'charity' in terms of classifying the objects into 12 purposes, coupled with the statutory test of public benefit, has done little more than consolidate the law. The courts will continue to adapt the law to keep abreast with the changing needs of society.

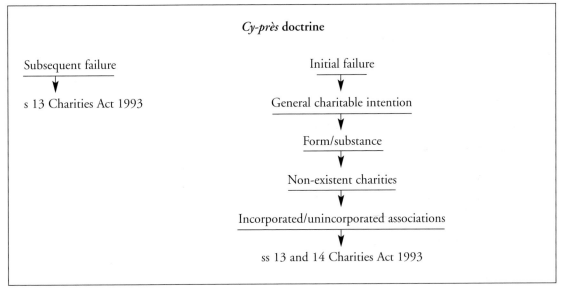

Figure 12.2 The cy-près *doctrine*

ACTIVITY

1. 'There is a distinction between a form of relief accorded to the whole community yet, by its very nature, advantageous only to a few and a form of relief accorded to a selected few out of a larger number equally willing and able to take advantage of it … for example a bridge which is available for all the public may undoubtedly be a charity and it is indifferent how many people use it. But confine its use to a selected number of persons … it is then clearly not a charity.'

   Explain and discuss.

2. By his will, a testator, who died last year, made the following gifts:

   '(a) £10,000 to A upon trust to distribute it among such persons or charitable objects as he shall select;

   (b) £200,000 to B upon trust to purchase a suitable site near Birmingham for a football field for use of all inhabitants of Birmingham;

   (c) £50,000 to C to hold upon trust to promote such activities as will further the spread of socialist principles in Great Britain;

   (d) £100,000 to the University of London upon trust to establish and maintain in perpetuity a School for Law Reform.'

   Consider the validity of these gifts as charitable trusts.

3. By his will made in 2003 John bequeaths £150,000 to his trustees, Sarah and Susan, directing them to invest the same and to apply the income arising therefrom for the following purposes:

   (a) one-third to be used to further the education of the children of employees and ex-employees of AB Co Ltd

   (b) one-third to be used to relieve poverty among ex-employees of YZ Co Ltd and

   (c) one-third to be given to the vicar of Littleacre for him to use for such benevolent purposes as to him seem suitable.

   John has recently died and Sarah and Susan seek your advice as to whether all or any of these purposes are of a charitable nature.

4. In 2001 a public appeal for funds to establish a community centre for young persons of the Baptist faith living in Greater London was launched.

   (a) £50,000 was raised by street collections

   (b) £80,000 was donated anonymously

   (c) £90,000 was bequeathed by the late Mrs Tremble

   (d) £70,000 was realised from various entertainments held in aid of the appeal.

CONTINUED ▸

ACTIVITY

It is impossible to obtain a suitable site for the community centre and the trustees seek your advice as to what is to be done with the funds raised.

5. A testator bequeathed the following legacies:

   (a) 'I leave £200, 000 for the Methodist Church at [*X address*].'

   (b) 'I leave £50,000 to such charitable institutions or public purposes as my trustees may select.'

   (c) 'I leave £100,000 to the Central Hospital at [*Y address*], provided that if at any time it ceases to be a free hospital the legacy shall pass to John Smith.'

   There has never been a Methodist Church at *X address*.

   Consider what will happen to these gifts.

Further reading

Atiyah, P S, 'Public benefit in charities' (1958) 21 MLR 138.

Bright, S, 'Charity and trusts for the public benefit: time for a rethink' [1981] Conv 28.

Chesterman, M, ' Foundations of Charity Law in the New Welfare State' (1999) 62 MLR 333.

Cotterell, R, 'Gifts to Charitable Institutions: A Note on Recent Developments' [1972] Conv 198.

Hopkins, J, 'Trusts for the advancement of sport – Recreational Charities Act 1958' [1992] CLJ 429.

Norman, H, 'Sporting charities – social welfare defined: Guild v IRC' [1992] Conv 361.

Warburton, J, 'Charitable Trusts – Unique' (1999) Conv 20.

chapter 13 APPOINTMENT, RETIREMENT AND REMOVAL OF TRUSTEES ∎

13.1 Appointment

There are only two occasions when it may be necessary to appoint trustees:

- on the creation of a new trust – whether *inter vivos* or by will and

- during the continuance of an existing trust, either in replacement of a trustee or as an additional trustee.

13.1.1 Creation of a new trust

The settlor or testator who creates a trust usually appoints the first trustees. If, in purported creation of a trust *inter vivos*, the settlor fails to nominate trustees, the intended trust will be imperfect. This principle, however, does not extend to trusts created by wills because, on the death of the testator, the trust becomes completely constituted. The deceased would have managed to part with the trust property. On the assumption that the trust is completely constituted, but the testator does not name trustees in his will or the trustees named are unwilling or unable to act, a replacement trustee will be appointed as on a continuance of the trust (see below). The principle applied here is that 'Equity will not allow a trust to fail for want of a trustee'.

13.1.2 Continuance of the trust

When a trust is created (whether *inter vivos* or by will) the trust property (real or personal) vests in all the trustees as joint tenants. The effect is that on the death of a trustee the property devolves on the survivors. This is the effect of s 18(1) of the Trustee Act 1925.

On the death of the sole or surviving trustee, the property vests in his personal representatives, subject to the trust, until replacement trustees are appointed. This principle is enacted in s 18(2) of the Trustee Act 1925.

The authority to appoint replacement trustees is derived from three sources, namely:

- an express power

- a statutory power

- the court.

This hierarchical order of authority to appoint trustees is required to be followed strictly. It is only when there is no person in one group willing to make an appointment that the power can be exercised by a person in a different group: see *Re Higginbottom* [1892] 3 Ch 132, where the majority of the beneficiaries under a trust were not able to prevent the sole executrix of the sole surviving trustee from appointing new trustees.

Express power

The trust instrument may confer the authority to appoint a trustee. This is exceptional because the statutory power to appoint is generally regarded as adequate. The express authority may be 'general' or 'special'. A general authority is one which confers an authority to appoint trustees in any circumstances. If the person named in the instrument is willing to exercise the power, this will be decisive as to the authority to appoint trustees provided that the power is exercised in good faith. If the authority is special (ie exercisable in limited circumstances) it would be strictly construed by the courts.

CASE EXAMPLE

Re Wheeler and De Rochow [1896] 1 Ch 315

A nominee was entitled to appoint trustees in specified circumstances, including the occasion when a trustee became 'incapable' of acting. One of the trustees became bankrupt. The court decided that this made him 'unfit' but not incapable of acting as a trustee. Thus, the nominee did not have the authority to appoint.

Similarly, where two or more persons have the power to appoint new trustees, they are required to exercise the authority jointly, unless there are express provisions to the contrary. It follows that such a joint power cannot be exercised where one of the appointors dies or cannot agree on the candidate to be appointed as trustee. This was decided in *Re Harding* [1923] 1 Ch 182.

Statutory power (s 36 of the Trustee Act 1925)

The statutory power to appoint trustees is contained in s 36 of the Trustee Act 1925 (replacing the Trustee Act 1893). The occasions giving rise to the need to appoint trustees are enacted in s 36(1) (replacement trustees) and s 36(6) (additional trustees).

Replacement trustees (s 36(1))

There are seven circumstances listed in s 36(1) when a replacement trustee may be appointed. These are:

(1) When a trustee is **dead**. Under s 36(8), this includes a person nominated as trustee under a will but predeceasing the testator.

(2) Where a trustee remains **outside the United Kingdom** for a continuous period of 12 months or more. The United Kingdom includes England, Wales, Scotland and Northern Ireland but does not include the Channel Islands or the Isle of Man. The motive for remaining outside the UK is irrelevant; this condition will be satisfied even if the trustee remains outside the UK against his will.

(3) Where a trustee desires to be **discharged** from all or any of the trusts or powers reposed in or conferred on him. Thus, a trustee may retire from part only of the trust.

(4) Where a trustee **refuses** to act. This includes the occasion when the trustee disclaims his office. It is advisable that the disclaimer be executed by deed.

(5) Where a trustee is **unfit** to act. Unfitness refers to some defect in the character of the trustee which suggests an element of risk in leaving the property in the hands of the individual, eg a conviction for an offence involving dishonesty or bankruptcy (see *Re Wheeler and De Rochow* (1896)).

(6) Where a trustee is **incapable** of acting. Incapacity refers to some physical or mental inability to administer the trust adequately, but does not include bankruptcy (see *Re Wheeler and De Rochow* (1896)). Under s 36(3), a corporation becomes incapable of acting on the date of the dissolution.

(7) Where the trustee is an **infant**, ie a person under the age of 18. Such a person may become a trustee under an implied trust (resulting or constructive). An infant is incapable of becoming an express trustee.

<u>Persons who may exercise the statutory power</u>: Section 36(1) lists, in chronological order, the persons who are entitled to exercise the statutory power of appointing replacement trustees. These are:

- the person or persons **nominated** in the trust instrument for the purpose of appointing new trustees (see the discussion earlier)

- the **surviving or continuing** trustee, if willing to act. This subsection was enacted to empower a sole retiring trustee to appoint his successor. It enables a 'retiring' or 'refusing' trustee to participate with the surviving trustees in appointing a successor (s 36(8) of the Trustee Act 1925). But there is no obligation on such a 'retiring' trustee to concur in making the appointment. An appointment by the remaining trustees would be valid if the retiring trustee did not participate in the appointment: see *Re Coates* (1886) 34 Ch D 370.
  A trustee who is legitimately removed as a trustee is not a 'continuing' or 'refusing' or 'retiring' trustee for the purposes of s 36(8). He is a removed trustee. This was decided in *Re Stoneham's Settlement Trust* [1953] Ch 59

- the **personal representatives of the last surviving or continuing trustee**. In order to become a surviving or continuing trustee, the property is required to vest in the individual. Accordingly, if all the persons, entitled as trustees under a will predecease the testator, the personal representative of the last to die would not be empowered to appoint new trustees. The personal representative of the testator will become the trustee and, subject to provisions to the contrary, will be entitled to appoint new trustees.

Section 36(4) provides that the personal representative of the last surviving or continuing trustee, includes those who have proved the will of the testator or the administrator of a person dying intestate.

Section 36(5) provides that a sole or last surviving executor intending to renounce probate shall have the power of appointment of trustees at any time before renouncing probate.

Additional trustees (s 36(6) of the Trustee Act 1925)

Section 36(6) authorises the appointment of additional trustees although no trustee needs to be replaced.

Section 36(6) provides:

's 36(6) Where a sole trustee, other than a trust corporation, is or has been originally appointed to act in a trust, or where, in the case of any trust, there are not more than three trustees (none of them being a trust corporation) either original or substituted and whether appointed by the court or otherwise, then and in any such case –

(a) the person or persons nominated for the purpose of appointing new trustees by the instrument, if any, creating the trust; or

(b) if there is no such person, or no such person able and willing to act, then the trustee or trustees for the time being

may, by writing, appoint another person or other persons to be an additional trustee or additional trustees, but it shall not be obligatory to appoint any additional trustee, unless the instrument, if any, creating the trust, or any statutory enactment provides to the contrary, nor shall the number of trustees be increased beyond four by virtue of any appointment.'

The subsection is self-explanatory but it may be observed that a trust corporation (corporate professional trustee, such as a bank or an insurance company) has the power of two or more individual trustees. No power exists under s 36(6) to increase the number of trustees beyond four.

Direction of the beneficiaries

Sections 19–21 of the Trusts of Land and Appointment of Trustees Act 1996 (TOLATA 1996) invested new powers in the beneficiaries to direct a retirement of trustees and/or appointment of trustees. These provisions relate to trusts of all types of property (whether land or personalty). But the provisions may be excluded in whole or in part by the trust.

Section 19 of TOLATA 1996 applies where there is no person nominated under the trust instrument to appoint new trustees, and all the beneficiaries are of full age and capacity and collectively are absolutely entitled to the trust property. The beneficiaries have either one or both of the following rights. A right to direct in writing that one or more of the trustees shall retire from the trust, and/or that a named person or persons be appointed, in writing, as new trustee or trustees. The direction may be by way of substitution for a trustee or trustees directed to retire or as an additional trustee or trustees.

If a direction to retire is given, the trustee concerned *shall* execute a deed effecting his retirement if:

(a) reasonable arrangements have been made to protect his rights under the trust

(b) after retirement, there will be either a trust corporation or at least two persons to act as trustees and

(c) either a replacement trustee is to be appointed on his retirement or the continuing trustees, by deed, consent to his retirement.

The section contains no provision compelling the trustees (or the personal representative of the last surviving trustee) to act on a direction to appoint a person as a new trustee. On a practical level, the trustee is unlikely to refuse to make the appointment without good reason.

Section 20 of TOLATA 1996 applies where:

(a) a trustee becomes mentally incapable of exercising his functions as trustee and

(b) no person entitled to appoint new trustees is willing and able to do so and

(c) the beneficiaries are of full age and capacity and are collectively entitled to the trust property,

then, the beneficiaries may give a written direction to the trustee's receiver or his attorney under a registered enduring power or to a person authorised under the Mental Health Act 1983 to appoint a particular person to be a new trustee. The Act is silent on the consequences of a failure to act on the direction.

Section 21(1) of TOLATA 1996 declares that a direction for the purposes of s 19 or s 20 may take one of two forms:

• either a single direction collectively executed by all the beneficiaries or

• a number of directions, whether solely or jointly with one or more, but not all, of the beneficiaries,

identifying the same person or persons for retirement or appointment.

Section 21(3) of TOLATA 1996 enacts that the effect of an appointment of a new trustee under s 19 or s 20 is the same as if he were appointed under s 36(7) of the Trustee Act 1925, ie he shall have the same powers and discretions as if he was appointed under the trust.

Section 36(7) of the 1925 Act (as amended by TOLATA 1996) enacts that the effect of an appointment under s 36 or s 19 or s 20 of TOLATA 1996 shall have the same consequences 'as if he had been originally appointed a trustee by the instrument, if any, creating the trust'.

The number of trustees

- **Realty**: s 34 of the Trustee Act 1925 (as amended by TOLATA 1996) provides that where land is held on trust there may not be more than four trustees. If the instrument purports to appoint more than four trustees, only the first four named as trustees will take the property.

On the other hand, while a sole trusteeship is not forbidden, s 14(2) of the Trustee Act 1925, enacts that a sole trustee (other than a trust corporation) may not give a valid receipt for the proceeds of sale arising under a disposition of a trust of land or capital money arising under the Settled Land Act 1925.

- **Personalty**: in theory, there is no restriction on the number of persons who may be appointed trustees of personalty.

In practice, it may be inconvenient and cumbersome to have too many trustees. The office of trusteeship requires unanimous approval of all the trustees (charities are treated as an exception). The law does not recognise a 'sleeping' or inactive trustee. A breach may be committed by a 'sleeping' trustee in failing to oppose a decision taken by his colleagues. This was decided in *Bahin v Hughes* (1886) 31 Ch D 390.

There are rarely more than four trustees and if the appointment is made under s 36 of the Trustee Act 1925 there will be not more than four trustees.

Alternatively, a sole trustee is most unsatisfactory because of the danger or risks of fraud or misconduct in administering the trust.

Vesting of trust property in trustees

On an appointment of replacement or additional trustees, the trust property is required to be vested in the new trustee or trustees to enable him or them to carry out his or their duties. Trustees hold the property as joint tenants so that the right of survivorship applies.

The vesting of the property in new trustees may be effected in one of two ways, namely:

(1) by a **conveyance** or **transfer** effective to vest the property in the transferee. The relevant formalities that are required to be complied with vary with the nature of the property involved. The legal title to unregistered land requires a conveyance, whereas registered land requires a deed to be executed in order to register the new owner. Shares require registration in the share register of the company

(2) s 40(1) and (2) of the Trustee Act 1925 create short-form and inexpensive methods of vesting the trust property in the new trustee or trustees. By virtue of s 40(1)(a) if the deed merely declares that the property vests in the new trustee this would be sufficient without a conveyance etc. Section 40(1)(b) enacts that if the deed of appointment omits to include a vesting declaration, it will be treated as if it had contained the same.

Exceptions: Section 40(4) of the Trustee Act 1925 excludes certain types of properties from the general provisions in s 40(1) and (2). These include:

- land held by trustees on a mortgage as security for a loan of trust money
- leases containing a condition prohibiting dispositions without consent unless the consent has already been obtained
- stocks and shares.

In these circumstances the property is required to be transferred in accordance with the appropriate formalities for that type of property.

Appointment by the court

Section 41 of the 1925 Act enacts the sweeping power of the court to appoint new trustees either as replacement or as additional trustees.

Section 41(1) enacts:

'The court may, whenever it is expedient to appoint a new trustee or new trustees, and it is found inexpedient, difficult or impracticable so to do without the assistance of the court, make an order appointing a new trustee or new trustees either in substitution for or in addition to any existing trustee or trustees, or although there is no existing trustee …'

The most popular occasions when the court's discretion may be exercised are where a sole surviving trustee dies intestate, or where an appointor is incapable of making an appointment because of infancy, or where all the trustees of a testamentary trust predecease the testator or where there is friction between the trustees.

The court will only exercise its power to appoint trustees when all other avenues have been exhausted. Thus, the court will not exercise its power where an express or statutory power can be exercised.

In exercising its discretion under s 41, the court will have regard to the wishes of the settlor, the interests of the beneficiaries and the efficient administration of the trust. This was decided in *Re Tempest* (1866) 1 Ch App 485, where the court decided that a nominated person was unsuitable to be appointed as trustee in order to avoid family dissension.

Section 43 of the Trustee Act 1925 enacts that the effect of an appointment by the court will be treated 'as if the appointee had been originally appointed a trustee by the instrument, if any, creating the trust'.

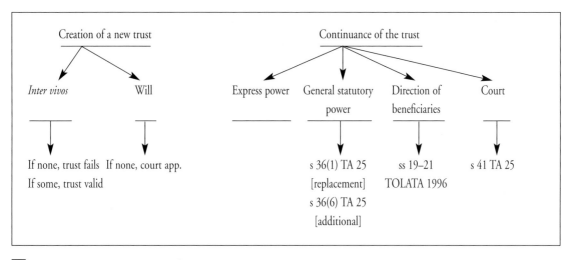

■ *Figure 13.1 Appointment of trustees*

13.2 Retirement

A trustee may retire from the trust in one of five ways:

- by taking advantage of a power in the trust instrument or
- by taking advantage of a statutory power under:

    (a) s 36(1) of the Trustee Act 1925 when a new trustee is appointed or

    (b) s 39 of the Trustee Act 1925 where no new trustee is appointed or

- by obtaining the consent of all the beneficiaries who are *sui juris* and absolutely entitled to the trust property under the principle in *Saunders v Vautier* (1841) or
- by direction from the relevant beneficiaries under s 19 of TOLATA 1996 or
- by obtaining the authority of the court.

13.2.1 Retirement procedure under s 39

Unlike a retirement under s 36(1), a trustee is not allowed to retire from part of a trust under s 39 of the Trustee Act 1925. He is required to retire from the trust as a whole or not at all. The procedure for retirement under s 39 is as follows:

(1) at least two individuals will continue to act as trustees or a trust corporation and

(2) the remaining trustees (or trustee) and other persons empowered to appoint trustees consent to the retirement by deed and

(3) the retiring trustee makes such a declaration by deed.

It should be noted that a retiring trustee remains liable for breaches of trust committed while he was a trustee. He is absolved from liability in respect of subsequent breaches, unless he retired in order to facilitate a breach of trust. This was decided in *Head v Gould* [1898] 1 Ch 250.

13.2.2 Retirement under a court order

Generally speaking, the court will not discharge a trustee under its statutory jurisdiction under s 41 of the 1925 Act unless it appoints a replacement trustee. However, the court has an inherent jurisdiction to discharge a trustee without replacement, in accordance with its responsibility to administer the trust. This will be the position when s 39 is not applicable because the appropriate consent cannot be obtained.

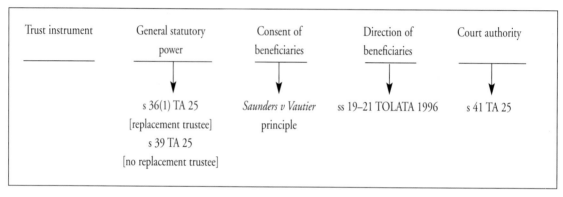

Figure 13.2 Retirement of trustees

13.3 Removal

A trustee may be removed from office in one of the following four ways:

- by virtue of a **power** contained in the trust instrument: this is highly unusual, but if such power exists the court is required to construe the instrument to ascertain whether the circumstances have arisen which give rise to the exercise of the power
- under **s 36 of the Trustee Act 1925**: this involves the removal of the existing trustee and appointment of a replacement trustee in circumstances laid down in s 36(1)
- in the circumstances specified in ss 19 and 20 of TOLATA 1996
- under a court order under s 41 of the Trustee Act 1925 or the inherent jurisdiction of the court.

13.3.1 Court order

Under s 41 of the Trustee Act 1925, the court has the jurisdiction to remove an existing trustee and appoint a replacement trustee.

Under its inherent jurisdiction to secure the proper administration of the trust, the court has the power to remove a trustee without appointing a replacement trustee.

CASE EXAMPLE

Letterstedt v Broers (1884) 9 AC 371

The Privy Council declared that the court had a general duty to ensure that trusts were properly executed and their main guide was the welfare of the beneficiaries. Accordingly, friction and hostility between the trustees and the beneficiaries which is likely to prejudice the proper administration of the trust may be a ground for the removal of trustees. In this case, a beneficiary made allegations of misconduct against a trustee concerning the administration of the trust. The court decided that, notwithstanding the allegations were not substantiated, it would exercise its jurisdiction to remove the trustees.

Trust instrument	General statutory power	Direction of the beneficiaries	Court order	
	s 36(1) TA 25	ss 19–21 TOLATA 96	s 41 TA 25	Inherent
	[replacement trustee]			[jurisdiction]

■ *Figure 13.3 Removal of trustees*

ACTIVITY

1. In what circumstances and by whom may a trustee of a personalty settlement be removed from his trusteeship?

2. Is it necessary or useful for a new trustee to be appointed by deed rather than by writing under hand?

3. Can a trustee who retires ever be made liable for breaches of trust which take place after his retirement and, if so, in what circumstances?

4. Does the notion of a 'sleeping' trustee have any legal significance?

Further reading

Bell, C, 'Some reflections on choosing trustees' (1988) *Trust Law and Practice* 86.

Hopkins, N, 'The Trusts of Land and Appointment of Trustees Act 1996' [1996] Conv 411.

chapter 14 DUTIES AND POWERS OF TRUSTEES ■

14.1 Duties of trustees

The duties of a trustee are varied and extremely onerous. They are required to be executed with the utmost diligence and good faith. Otherwise he will be liable for breach of trust. The primary duty of the trustee is to comply with the terms of the trust and, subject thereto, to act in the best interests of the beneficiaries. In order to carry out these duties, the trustee is invested with a variety of powers and discretions which are required to be exercised for the benefit of the beneficiaries.

14.1.1 Duty and standard of care at common law

Throughout the administration of the trust the trustee is required to exhibit an objective standard of skill as would be expected from an ordinary prudent man of business. In the case of a power of investment the duty would be exercised so as to yield the best return for all the beneficiaries, judged in relation to the risks inherent in the investments and the prospects of the yield of income and capital appreciation. The classical statement of the rule was laid down by Lord Watson in *Learoyd v Whiteley* (1887) 12 AC 727.

> J
>
> 'As a general rule the law requires of a trustee no higher degree of diligence in the execution of his office than a man of ordinary prudence would exercise in the management of his own private affairs.'
>
> (Lord Watson)

The courts will have regard to all the circumstances of each case in order to ascertain whether the trustees' conduct fell below the standard imposed on such persons.

In considering the investment policy of the trust, the trustees are required to put on one side their own personal interests and views. They may have strongly held social or political views. They may be firmly opposed to any investments in companies connected with alcohol, tobacco, armaments or many other things. In the conduct of their own affairs, trustees are free to abstain from making any such investments. However, in performance of their fiduciary duties, if investments of the morally reprehensible type would be more beneficial to the beneficiaries than other investments, the trustees must not refrain from making the investments by reason of the views that they hold. Trustees may even act dishonourably (though not illegally) if the interests of their beneficiaries require it.

CASE EXAMPLE

Buttle v Saunders [1950] 2 All ER 193

Trustees struck a bargain for the sale of trust property. This was not legally binding, but the court held that they were under a duty to consider and explore a better offer received by them.

CASE EXAMPLE

Cowan v Scargill and others [1984] 3 WLR 501

The defendants were trustees of the Mineworkers' Pension Scheme who raised an objection to a new investment plan of trust funds in competing forms of energy. The court decided that the plan would yield the best return for the beneficiaries and refused the application for objection.

In an action for breach of trust the claimant is required to establish that the trust has suffered a loss which is attributable to the conduct or omission of the trustees. If the trustee's conduct or omission fell below the required standard imposed on trustees, he becomes personally liable whether he acted in good faith or not.

CASE EXAMPLE

Re Lucking's Will Trust [1968] 1 WLR 866

A trustee-director of a company was liable to the trust when he allowed the managing director and (a friend) to appropriate £15,000 of the company funds through the delivery of blank cheques to the managing director which were signed by the trustee.

With regard to professional trustees such as banks and insurance companies, the standard of care imposed on such bodies is higher than the degree of diligence expected from a non-professional trustee. The professional trustee is required to administer the trust with such a degree of expertise as would be expected from a specialist in trust administration. This objective standard is applied by the courts after due consideration of the facts of each case.

CASE EXAMPLE

Bartlett v Barclays Bank [1980] Ch 515

The trust estate was the majority shareholder in a property company and the trustee was a professional trust company. The board of directors, for good commercial reasons, decided to restructure the investment portfolio and invest in land development. The trustee did not actively participate in the company's deliberations nor was he provided with regular information concerning the company's activities, but was content to rely on the annual balance sheet and profit and loss account. One of the schemes pursued by the company proved to be disastrous. In an action brought against the trustee the court held that the trustee was liable because it (the trust corporation) had not acted reasonably in the administration of the trust.

On the other hand, the claimant failed in her action in *Nestlé v National Westminster Bank* [1993] 1 WLR 1260 on the ground that she failed to prove positively that the defendant's action or inaction resulted in a loss to the trust.

But while the duties imposed on trustees are onerous, there is no liability for an error of judgement.

> **J** 'A trustee who is honest and reasonably competent is not to be held responsible for a mere error in judgment when the question he has to consider is whether a security of a class authorised, but depreciated in value should be retained or realised, provided he acts with reasonable care, prudence and circumspection.'
>
> (Lopes J in *Re Chapman* [1896] 2 Ch 763)

Section 61 of the Trustee Act 1925 may also apply to relieve a trustee from liability. This section applies where a trustee has acted honestly and reasonably, and ought fairly to be excused for the breach of trust. In these circumstances the court may relieve him either wholly or partly from personal liability.

14.1.2 Duty and standard of care under the Trustee Act 2000

The Trustee Act 2000 describes the duty of care which is applicable to trustees. Section 1(1) provides that whenever the duty under the sub-section applies to a trustee, he must exercise such care and skill as is reasonable in the circumstances, having regard in particular:

(a) to any special knowledge or experience he has or holds himself out as having and

(b) if he acts as a trustee in the course of a business or profession, to any special knowledge or experience that it is reasonable to expect of a person acting in the course of that kind of business or profession.

Thus, a solicitor who is a trustee will be under a more stringent duty of care and skill as opposed to a lay trustee.

Schedule 1 specifies when the duty of care applies to trustees. These are in the *exercise* of the statutory and express powers of investment, including the duty to have regard to the standard investment criteria and the duty to obtain and consider proper advice. In addition, the duty applies to the trustees' power to acquire land. Moreover, the duty of care applies when trustees enter into arrangements in order to delegate functions to agents, nominees and custodians as well as the review of their actions. The duty of care also applies to trustees when exercising their power under s 19 of the Trustee Act 1925 to insure property. However, para 7 of the Schedule enacts that the duty of care does not apply if, or in so far as, it appears from the trust instrument that the duty is not meant to apply. Thus, a settlor may expressly restrict the application of the statutory duty (or the common-law duty of care).

14.2 Duty to act unanimously

Trustees are required to act unanimously, subject to any provision in the trust instrument to the contrary. The settlor has given all of his trustees the responsibility to act on behalf of the trust. Subject to provisions to the contrary in the trust instrument, the acts and decisions of some of the trustees (even a majority of trustees) are not binding on others. Thus, once a trust decision is made, the trustees become jointly and severally liable to the beneficiaries in the event of a breach of trust. In practice, it may be that one trustee is active or dominant, but nevertheless all the trustees must agree on a particular course of action concerning the trust. In *Bahin v Hughes* [1886] 31 Ch D 390, 'passive' trustees were liable to the beneficiaries for breach of trust along with an 'active' trustee.

A claim by one trustee against his co-trustee is now subject to the Civil Liability (Contribution) Act 1978. Briefly, a trustee who is sued for breach of trust may claim a contribution from his co-trustee. The court has a discretion to make a contribution order if such 'is just and equitable having regard to the extent of the [co-trustee's] responsibility for the damage in question'.

14.3 Duty to act personally

Generally speaking, a trustee is appointed by a settlor because of his personal qualities. It is expected that the trustee will act personally in the execution of his duties. The general rule is *Delegatus non potest delegare*.

However, in the contemporary commercial climate the functions and needs for the proper administration of a trust have become increasingly complex, requiring specialised skill and knowledge. Accordingly, it is unrealistic to expect trustees to act personally in all matters relating to the trust. Trustees are entitled to appoint agents to perform acts in respect of the trust.

Part IV of the Trustee Act 2000 has reformed the law as to the trustees' powers of delegation. It repeals ss 23 and 30 of the Trustee Act 1925 (which created some confusion regarding the duties of trustees) and introduces provisions with a clearer framework for delegation. Generally, the new provisions deal with the appointment of agents, nominees and custodians and the liability of the trustees for such persons.

Sections 11–20 of the Trustee Act 2000 deal with the appointment of agents, nominees and custodians. Sections 21–23 deal with the review of acts of the agents, nominees and custodians and the question of liability for their acts.

Section 11(1) enacts that the trustees of a trust 'may authorise any person to exercise any or all of their *delegable functions* as their agent'. Section 11(2) defines 'delegable functions' as *any function* of the trustee, subject to four exceptions. These are:

(a) functions relating to the distribution of assets in favour of beneficiaries, ie dispositive functions

(b) any power to allocate fees and other payments to capital or income

(c) any power to appoint trustees and

(d) any power conferred by the trust instrument or any enactment which allows trustees to delegate their administrative functions to another person.

Thus, the trustees cannot delegate their discretion under a discretionary trust to distribute the funds or to select beneficiaries from a group of objects. But they may delegate their investment decision-making power and thereby obtain skilled professional advice from an investment manager.

In the case of charitable trusts, the trustees' *delegable functions* are set out in s 11(3). These are:

's 11(3)(a) any function consisting of carrying out a decision that the trustees have taken;

(b) any function concerning investment of assets subject to the trust;

(c) any function relating to the raising of funds for the trust otherwise than by means of profits of a trade which is an integral part of carrying out the trust's charitable purpose;

(d) any other function prescribed by order of the Secretary of State.'

Section 12 provides who may or may not be appointed an agent of the trustees. The trustees may appoint one of their number to act as an agent but cannot appoint a beneficiary to carry out that function. If more than one person is appointed to exercise the same function, they are required to act jointly.

Section 14 authorises the trustees to appoint agents on such terms as to remuneration and other matters as they may determine. But certain terms of the agency contract are subject to a test of reasonableness. These are terms permitting the agent to sub-delegate to another agent, or to restrict his liability to the trustees or the beneficiaries, or to allow the agent to carry out functions that are capable of giving rise to a conflict of interest. Thus, sub-delegation to another trustee or the insertion of an exclusion clause in the contract appointing the agent is subject to a test of reasonableness.

Section 15 imposes special restrictions within certain types of agency contracts. With regard to asset management functions the agreement is required to be evidenced in writing. In addition, the trustees are required to include a 'policy statement' in the agreement, giving the agent guidance as to how the functions ought to be exercised, and should seek an undertaking from the agent that he will secure compliance with the policy statement. In the ordinary course of events, the policy statement will refer to the 'standard investment criteria' and, in the case of beneficiaries entitled in succession, require the agent to provide investments with a balance between income and capital.

Section 24 provides that a failure to observe these limits does not invalidate the authorisation or appointment.

14.3.1 Power to appoint nominees

Section 16 of the Act of 2000 authorises trustees to appoint nominees in relation to such of the trust assets as they may determine (other than settled land). In addition, the trustees may take steps to ensure the vesting of those assets in the nominee. Such appointment is required to be evidenced in writing.

14.3.2 Power to appoint custodians

Section 17 of the Trustee Act 2000 authorises the trustees to appoint a person to act as custodian in relation to specified assets. A custodian is a person who undertakes the safe custody of the assets or any documents or records concerning the assets. The appointment is required to be evidenced in writing.

14.3.3 Persons who may be appointed as nominees or custodians

Section 19 of the Trustee Act 2000 provides that a person may not be appointed as a nominee or custodian unless he carries on a business which consists of or includes acting as a nominee or custodian, or is a body corporate controlled by the trustees. The trustees may appoint as a nominee or custodian one of their number if that is a trust corporation, or two (or more) of their number if they act jointly.

14.3.4 Review of acts of agents, nominees and custodians

Provided that the agent, nominee or custodian continues to act for the trust, the trustees are required to:

- keep under review the arrangements under which they act, and how those arrangements are put into effect

- *consider* whether to exercise any powers of intervention, if the circumstances are appropriate
- intervene if they consider that a need has arisen for such action.

14.3.5 Liability for the acts of agents, nominees and custodians

Section 23 of the Trustee Act 2000 provides that a trustee will not be liable for the acts of agents, nominees and custodians provided that he complies with the general duty of care laid down in s 1 and Schedule 1, both in respect of the initial appointment of the agent etc. and when carrying out his duties under s 22 (review of acts of agents etc). The effect of this provision is that it lays to rest the eccentric principles that were applied under the 1925 Act, and introduces one standard objective test concerning the trustees' duty of care.

14.4 Other statutory provisions permitting delegation of discretions

Trustees may delegate their discretions under the following statutory provisions:

- Part IV of the Trustee Act 2000 (see above)
- s 25 of the Trustee Act 1925 (as amended by the Trustee Delegation Act 1999) or
- s 9 of the Trusts of Land and Appointment of Trustees Act 1996 (see below).

Individual delegation

Section 25 of the Trustee Act 1925 (as re-enacted by s 5 of the Trustee Delegation Act 1999) enables a trustee to delegate, by a power of attorney, 'the execution or exercise of all or any of the trusts, powers and discretions vested in him either alone or jointly with any other person or persons'. The delegation of the powers commences on the date of execution or such time as stated in the instrument, and continues for a period of 12 months or such shorter period as mentioned in the instrument. Written notice is required to be given by the donor of the power to each nominee under the trust instrument who is entitled to appoint trustees, and each other trustee within seven days after its creation. The donor of the power remains liable for the acts or defaults of the donee.

14.4.1 Delegation under the Trusts of Land and Appointment of Trustees Act 1996

Section 9 of the 1996 Act enacts that trustees of land may delegate any of their powers in relation to the land by a power of attorney to adult beneficiaries who are currently entitled to interests in possession. In exercising their powers, the trustees are required to have regard to the rights of the beneficiaries and are obliged to observe any rules of law and equity. Thus, the trustees may not favour or prejudice the interest of any beneficiary when exercising their powers. It should be noted that the powers included in s 6 relate only to a trust of land and not to any personal property. In addition, the s 6 powers may be amended or excluded by the settlement, or made subject to obtaining the consent of any person (s 8). Thus, the settlor may prevent any dealing with the land (although this could be challenged under s 14: see above). In the case of charitable trusts, the trustees' powers may not be amended or excluded, but they may be made subject to obtaining consent.

Protection of purchasers from delegate

In respect of land, where a person deals with the delegate in good faith in the belief that the trustees were entitled to delegate to that person, it is presumed that the trustees were entitled to delegate to that person, unless the purchaser had knowledge at the time of the transaction that the trustees were not entitled to delegate to that person (s 9(2)). 'Knowledge' for these purposes has not been defined in the legislation, but it is submitted that since we are concerned here with a proprietary interest, any type of cognisance will suffice for these purposes, even constructive knowledge.

14.5 Exclusion clauses

Exclusion clauses which are validly inserted into trust instruments may have the effect of limiting the liability of trustees. Such clauses are not, without more, void on public policy grounds. Moreover, provided that the clause does not purport to exclude the basic minimum duties ordinarily imposed on trustees, it may be valid. Some of the minimum duties which cannot be excluded are the duties of honesty, good faith and acting for the benefit of the beneficiaries: see *Armitage v Nurse* [1997] 3 WLR 1046. In this case, Millett LJ made the following observations:

> J
>
> 'I accept the submission … that there is an irreducible core of obligations owed by the trustees to the beneficiaries and enforceable by them which is fundamental to the concept of a trust. If the beneficiaries have no rights enforceable against the trustees there are no trusts. But I do not accept the further submission that these core obligations include the duties of skill and care, prudence and diligence. *The duty of the trustees to perform the trusts honestly and in good faith for the benefit of the beneficiaries is the minimum necessary to give substance to the trusts,* but in my opinion it is sufficient.'
>
> (Millett LJ)

Much depends on the wording of such clauses. *Prima facie* any ambiguities are construed against the trustees.

CASE EXAMPLE

Wight v Olswang, The Times, 18th May 1999

A trust settlement incorporated two conflicting exemption clauses, one protecting all trustees from liability for breach of trust (a general exemption clause) and the other which applied only to unpaid trustees. The court decided that the paid trustees could not rely on the general exemption clause.

14.6 Duty to provide accounts and information

Because of the nature of the fiduciary relationship of trustees, a duty is imposed on them to keep proper accounts for the trust. In pursuance of this objective, the trustees may employ an agent (an accountant) to draw up the trust accounts. The beneficiaries are entitled to inspect the accounts but if they need copies they are required to pay for these from their own resources.

In *O'Rourke v Darbishire* [1920] AC 581, Lord Wrenbury declared that the beneficiary's right to disclosure of trust documents is proprietary because they belong to him. He also drew a distinction between disclosure and discoveries.

> **J** 'The beneficiary is entitled to see all trust documents because they are trust documents and because he is a beneficiary. They are in this sense his own. Action or no action, he is entitled to access to them. This has nothing to do with discovery. The right to discovery is a right to see someone else's documents. The proprietary right is a right to access to documents which are your own.'
>
> (Lord Wrenbury)

In *Re Londonderry's Settlement* [1964] 3 All ER 855, Salmon LJ adopted the principle laid down by Lord Wrenbury and decided that the beneficiaries are entitled to inspect documents created in the course of the administration of the trust. These are trust documents and are *prima facie* the property of the beneficiaries. Indeed, 'trust documents' were described by Salmon LJ in *Re Marquess of Londonderry's Settlement* [1965] Ch 918 as possessing the following characteristics:

> **J** '(i)   they are documents in the possession of the trustees as trustees;
>
> (ii)   they contain information about the trust, which the beneficiaries are entitled to know;
>
> (iii)   the beneficiaries have a proprietary interest in the documents, and, accordingly, are entitled to see them.'

However, in *Schmidt v Rosewood Trust Ltd* [2003] 3 All ER 76, the Privy Council rejected the statement of the principle in *O'Rourke v Darbishire* (1920), and decided that the more principled approach to the issue is to regard the right to seek disclosure of trust documents as one aspect of the court's inherent jurisdiction to supervise, and if necessary to intervene in, the administration of trusts. Accordingly, the beneficiary's right to inspect trust documents is founded not on an equitable proprietary right in respect of those documents, but upon the trustee's fiduciary duty to inform the beneficiary and to render accounts. This right to seek the court's intervention is not restricted to beneficiaries with fixed interests in the trust, but also extends to objects under a discretionary trust. The power to seek disclosure may be restricted by the court in the exercise of its discretion. The court is required to balance the competing interests of the different beneficiaries, the trustees and third parties.

CASE EXAMPLE

Schmidt v Rosewood Trust Ltd [2003] 3 All ER 76

The settlor executed two Isle of Man trust settlements which created a discretionary trust in favour of a group of objects, including the claimant. The defendant company became the sole trustee of the two settlements. The settlor died intestate. The claimant alleged that he devoted considerable time and resources to trace his father's assets and believed that his efforts had been frustrated by some of his father's co-directors. He applied in his personal capacity as a member of a class of objects, and as administrator for disclosure of trust accounts and information about the trust assets. The defendant contended that a beneficiary's right of disclosure of trust documents is treated as a proprietary right, and that an object of a discretionary power does not have such a right, but merely a hope of acquiring a benefit. The Isle of Man court held in favour of the defendant and the claimant appealed to the Privy Council.

The Court allowed the appeal and decided that:

(a) the right to seek the court's intervention does not depend on entitlement to an interest under the trust. An object of a discretionary trust (including a mere power of appointment) may also be entitled to protection from a court, although the circumstances concerning protection and the nature of the protection would depend on the court's discretion

(b) no beneficiary has an entitlement, as of right, to disclosure of trust documents. Where there are issues of personal and commercial confidentiality, the court will have to balance the competing interests of the beneficiaries, the trustees and third parties and limitations or safeguards may be imposed.

14.7 Duty to distribute to the correct beneficiaries

It is an elementary principle of trusts law that the trustees are required to distribute the trust property (income and/or capital) to the beneficiaries properly entitled to receive the same. Failure to distribute to the correct beneficiary subjects the trustees to liability for breach of trust, although in appropriate cases they may apply to the court for relief under s 61 of the Trustee Act 1925. Thus, in *Eaves v Hickson* (1861) 30 Beav 136, trustees were liable to make good sums wrongly paid to a beneficiary in reliance on a forged marriage certificate. Likewise, in *Re Hulkes* (1886) 33 Ch D 552, the trustees were liable for sums paid to the wrong beneficiaries based on an honest, but incorrect, construction of the trust instrument.

Where the trustee makes an overpayment of income or instalment of capital, he may recover the amount of the overpayment by adjusting the payments subsequently made to the same beneficiary. Where the payment is made to a person who is not entitled to receive the sum, the trustee has the right to recover the amount based on a quasi-contractual claim of money paid under a mistake of fact. Such claim will not succeed if the mistake is one of law. This was illustrated in *Re Diplock* [1947] Ch 716 (see below).

CASE EXAMPLE

Woolwich Building Society v IRC (No 2) [1992] 3 All ER 737

The House of Lords decided that money paid by a member of the public to a public authority in the form of taxes paid, pursuant to an *ultra vires* demand by the authority, is *prima facie* recoverable by the member of the public as of right. An aggrieved beneficiary may, in addition to his right to sue the trustee, trace his property in the hands of the wrongly paid person.

Where the trustees have a reasonable doubt as to the validity of claims of the beneficiaries, they may apply to the court for directions, and will be protected, provided that they act in accordance with those directions. The court has the power to make a *Benjamin* order (derived from the case *Re Benjamin* [1902] 1 Ch 723), authorising the distribution of the trust property without identifying all the beneficiaries and creditors.

In addition, where the trustees cannot identify all the beneficiaries, they are entitled to pay the trust funds into court as a last resort: see *Re Gillingham Bus Disaster Fund* [1959] Ch 62. Where there is no good reason for a payment into court, the trustees may personally have to pay the costs of such an application.

By virtue of s 27 of the Trustee Act 1925, a simplified form of distribution is allowed and, at the same time, the trustees or personal representatives are given protection from claims for breach of trust. The section permits the trustees (or personal representatives) to advertise for beneficiaries in an appropriate newspaper or gazette, and after the expiration of a period of time, not being less than two months, they are entitled to distribute the property to the beneficiaries of whom the trustees are aware. If the trustees comply with the requirements of s 27, they will not be liable for breach of trust at the instance of beneficiaries, of whom the trustees were unaware. However, the ignored beneficiaries are entitled to trace their property in the hands of the recipient. Finally, the section is incapable of being excluded or modified by the trust instrument.

14.8 Duty not to make profits from the trust

This duty was referred to earlier in Chapter 9. The duty is sometimes referred to as the rule in *Keech v Sandford* (1726) 2 Eq Cas Abr 7419 (see above). The court decided that the trustee held the renewed lease on trust for the infant beneficiary. The duty is of wide application. It attaches to any property added to the trust: see *Boardman v Phipps* [1967] 2 AC 46, and also the interests of the beneficiaries. In the latter case, the purchase is voidable at the instance of the beneficiary, even if the market price was paid for the property.

The approach of the courts is to consider whether an unfair advantage had been obtained by or on behalf of the trustee. Thus, the rule extends to purchases by the spouses of trustees and to purchases by companies in which the trustee has an interest. The rule will also apply to a sale to a third party if there is an understanding that the trustee will then purchase the property.

There are various exceptions to this rule. Firstly, the settlement or will may expressly permit a trustee to purchase the trust property. Secondly, if all the beneficiaries are of full age and sound mind and absolutely entitled to the property they may agree to the sale. The questions would be whether the trustees had made full disclosure of all the material facts to the beneficiaries and whether the beneficiaries exercised an independent judgement. In this event, the beneficiaries may need separate legal advice.

14.9 Powers of investment

Trustees have an obligation to maintain the real value of trust funds and may need to consider investing the trust property. An 'investment' for these purposes refers to property which will produce an income yield. This was decided in *Re Wragg* [1918–19] All ER 233. The trustees are required to consider the investment policy of the trust with the standard of care expected from an ordinary prudent man of business (see above). The powers of investment may exist in the trust instrument or may be implied by statute or the court may enlarge the power of the trustees.

14.9.1 Express power

A prudent settlor will include a wide investment clause in the trust instrument in order to give the trustees the maximum flexibility in the selection of investments. The modern approach of the courts is to construe investment clauses liberally.

CASE EXAMPLE

Re Harari's Settlement [1949] 1 All ER 430

The issue concerned the effect of a clause in the trust instrument, to make 'such investments as the trustees may think fit'. The court decided that the words will be given their ordinary meaning without any restriction.

14.9.2 Statutory power under the Trustee Act 2000

The Trustee Act 2000 (which came into force on 1st February 2001) repeals and replaces the out-of-date Trustee Investment Act 1961. The new statutory power of investment is found in s 3(1) of the Trustee Act 2000.

Section 3(1) of the Trustee Act 2000 enacts:

's 3(1) ... a trustee may make any kind of investment that he could make if he were absolutely entitled to the assets of the trust'.

The trustee must, of course, comply with the general duty of care as stated in s 1 of the 2000 Act (see above). This new power is required to be considered in the light of the new powers of delegation (see above). As will be seen trustees will be able to delegate their discretion as well as their duty to invest.

The new power is treated as a **default provision** and will only operate in so far as there is no contrary provision in the trust instrument. It should be noted that restrictions imposed by the trust instrument prior to 3rd August 1961 are treated as void (see s 7(2) of the Trustee Act 2000). This new power operates retrospectively in the sense that trusts existing before or after the commencement of the 2000 Act are subject to this default provision. However, the new regime does not apply to occupational pensions schemes, authorised unit trusts and schemes under the Charities Act 1993.

Section 4 of the 2000 Act requires trustees to have regard to the 'standard investment criteria' when investing. This is defined in s 4(3) to mean the suitability of the investment to the trust and the need for diversification as is appropriate in the circumstances. Thus, trustees are no longer restricted as to the type of investments they make but are restricted by reference to the standard investment criteria. The standard investment criteria are important because the suitability of investments vary from trust to trust. Having exercised the power of investment the trustees are required to review the trust investments periodically by reference to the standard investment criteria (s 4(2)). The purpose of this provision is to require the trustees to determine whether the trust fund ought to be re-invested or not.

By virtue of s 5 of the Trustee Act 2000, trustees are required to obtain and consider proper advice before investing, unless in the circumstances they reasonably conclude that it is unnecessary to do so, eg if funds are paid in to an interest bearing account pending investment by the trustees, it may be unnecessary to take advice regarding the interim account, or one or more of the trustees may be suitably qualified to give proper advice.

Section 5(4) defines 'proper advice' as follows:

's 5(4) ... advice of a person who is *reasonably believed* by the trustee to be qualified to give it by his ability in and practical experience of financial and other matters relating to the proposed investment'.

This is an objective issue and the test is not restricted to individuals with paper qualifications but includes those with practical experience. Although the provision does not require the advice to be in writing a prudent trustee will require advice to be in such form.

Mortgages

Prior to the Trustee Act 2000, the trustees' powers to invest in mortgages were laid down in the Trustee Investment Act 1961 and s 8 of the Trustee Act 1925. The effect of these provisions was that trustees were authorised to invest in mortgages of freehold or leasehold property provided that in the latter case the lease had at least 60 years to run. Section 8 of the Trustee Act 1925 provided that a trustee was not impeachable for breach of trust if the amount of the loan did not exceed two-thirds of the value of the property, and he acted on the written advice of a suitable and independent valuer.

The Trustee Act 2000 repeals and replaces these provisions. Section 3 of the Act of 2000 authorises the trustees to invest by way of a loan secured on land. Although the point is far from clear, it is generally advisable for the trustees to invest in a legal estate by way of a legal mortgage as under the previous law. In addition, the security is restricted to land in the UK.

Acquisition of land

Before the passing of the Trustee Act 2000, trustees had no general power to purchase land as an investment. There were two exceptions to this rule. First, the trust instrument may authorise trustees to purchase land as an investment. For these purposes and subject to any contrary provision, the land was required to be bought in order to generate an income. Second, s 6(4) of the Trusts of Land and Appointment of Trustees Act 1996 empowered trustees of land to purchase land as an investment, or for the occupation by a beneficiary or for other purposes. The trustees may sell all of the land subject to the trust and purchase further land with the proceeds of sale (s 17 of the 1996 Act). The trustees of land have wide powers to mortgage or lease the land, though not to make a gift of the property, or sale at an undervalue (for such action will involve a loss to the trust, but may be lawful if all the beneficiaries, being of full age and capacity consent to such action). The trustees under s 6 are subject to the statutory duty of care under s 1 of the Trustee Act 2000 and will be in breach of trust if they enter into a dealing for less than the full market value of the land. In exercising their powers under s 6, the trustees are required to have regard to the rights of the beneficiaries and any rule of law or equity or statute. The trustees are required to consult the beneficiaries entitled to possession and give effect to the wishes of the majority, measured by reference to the value of their interest (if consistent with the general interests of the trust). Moreover, the trust deed may impose an obligation on the trustees to obtain the consent of any person prior to a dealing. Failure to consult such a person may not necessarily invalidate the transaction, but will give rise to liability for breach of trust, unless the court dispenses with the need to obtain consent by an order under s 14 of the 1996 Act.

By virtue of s 8 of the Trustee Act 2000, trustees are now entitled to purchase freehold or leasehold land in the UK:

- as an investment or

- for the occupation by a beneficiary or

- for any other purpose.

Thus, the new power mirrors the power of trustees under s 6(4) of the Trusts of Land and Appointment of Trustees Act 1996, which has been repealed and replaced by s 8 of the 2000 Act. Once trustees have acquired the relevant land they will be vested with the same powers as an absolute owner of land. Accordingly, the trustees will be able to sell, lease and mortgage the land. This new power is a **default** provision which may be excluded by a contrary intention in the trust instrument.

Duty of care

Section 1 of the Trustee Act 2000 reformulates the duty of care applicable to powers exercisable by trustees under the Act. This provision replaces the common law standard of care as indicated above. The section enacts that the trustees are required to exercise such care and skill as is reasonable in the circumstances:

(a) having regard to any special knowledge or experience he has or holds himself out as having and

(b) if he acts as a trustee in the course of a business or profession, to any special knowledge or experience that it is reasonable to expect of a person acting in the course of that kind of business or profession.

Thus, the section has created a combined objective and subjective test of the standard of care required from the trustees. The minimum degree of care and skill expected from a trustee is to be determined objectively by the court. But this standard of care may be increased by reference to the trustees' special knowledge or experience acquired personally or held out by him. This provision echoes the view of Brightman J in *Bartlett v Barclays Bank* [1980] Ch 515.

Schedule 1 to the Trustee Act 2000 lists the occasions when the duty of care arises. These are in the **exercise** of the statutory and express powers of investment, including the duty to have regard to the standard investment criteria and the duty to obtain and consider proper advice. In addition, the duty applies to the trustees' power to acquire land. Moreover, the duty of care applies when trustees enter into arrangements in order to delegate functions to agents, nominees, custodians as well as the review of their actions.

14.9.3 Enlargement of investment powers

Trustees are entitled to apply to the court under s 57 of the Trustee Act 1925 or under the Variation of Trusts Act 1958 in order to widen these investment powers. The approach of the courts has been encouraging in granting its approval in order to update the investment policy of trusts beyond the scope of the Trustee Investments Act 1961. In *Mason v Farbrother* [1983] 2 All ER 1078, the court approved a scheme to widen the investment powers of trustees of the employees of the Co-operative Society's pension fund because of the effects of inflation and the size of the funds (some £127 million).

14.10 The right of beneficiaries to occupy land

Section 12 of the Trusts of Land and Appointment of Trustees Act 1996 confers on a beneficiary entitled to an interest in possession under a trust of land the right to occupy the land. But this right does not apply where the land is not available or is unsuitable for occupation by the beneficiary.

Where a number of beneficiaries are entitled under s 12, the trustees are entitled under s 13 to exclude or restrict, on reasonable grounds, the right of some of the beneficiaries to occupy. Moreover, the trustees are entitled to impose reasonable conditions on an occupying beneficiary and, if appropriate, to compensate a beneficiary whose right of occupation has been excluded or restricted.

14.11 Powers of maintenance and advancement

14.11.1 Power of maintenance

A power of maintenance is a discretion granted to the trustees to pay or apply income for the benefit of an infant beneficiary at a time prior to the beneficiary acquiring a right to the income or capital of the trust. Maintenance payments are expenditure incurred out of the income of a fund for routine recurring purposes such as food, clothing, rent and education.

The issues that are required to be considered by the trustees are:

(1) whether they have a power to maintain an infant beneficiary

(2) whether there is any income available for maintenance

(3) whether the trustees are prepared to exercise their discretion to maintain the beneficiary.

Power to maintain

Express power

A settlor may expressly include a power of maintenance in the trust instrument. Most professionally drafted settlements will include this power. If this is the case the trustees' duties will be encapsulated in the clause.

Inherent power

The court has an inherent power to authorise the trustees to maintain beneficiaries. The underlying unexpressed intention of the settlor must have been consistent with the maintenance payments in favour of infant beneficiary or beneficiaries.

Statutory power

Section 31 of the Trustee Act 1925 authorises the trustees in their discretion, to pay the whole or part of the income from the trust to the parent or guardian of an infant beneficiary, or otherwise apply the relevant amount towards the maintenance, education or benefit of the infant beneficiary, during his infancy or until his interest fails.

But this statutory power may be modified or excluded by the settlor in the trust instrument (see s 69(2) of the 1925 Act).

An exclusion of the power may be express or implied in the settlement. Section 31 was intended to be implied into every settlement subject to any contrary intention expressed by the terms of the instrument. A contrary intention will be established if the settlor has specifically disposed of the income, eg a payment of the income to another or has directed an accumulation of income.

Availability of income

The issue here is whether the income of the trust is available to maintain the infant beneficiary. The effect of complex rules of case law, s 175 of the Law of Property Act 1925 and s 31(3) Trustee Act 1925, is that a vested interest carries the intermediate income, unless someone else is entitled to it or the income is required to be accumulated. Contingent interests created *inter vivos* or by will carry the intermediate income (save in so far as the settlor or testator has otherwise disposed of the income). A contingent pecuniary legacy does not carry the income, except where the gift was made by the infant's father or a person standing *in loco parentis*, and the contingency is attaining the age of majority and no other fund is set aside for the maintenance of the legatee.

Exercise of power during infancy

The trustees have a discretion to maintain infant beneficiaries. This discretion is required to be exercised responsibly and objectively, as ordinary prudent men of business. Thus, in *Wilson v Turner* (1883) 22 Ch 521, trustees who applied the income automatically to the infant's father without consciously exercising their discretion, were liable to the beneficiaries for breach of trust when the father used the sums for his own benefit.

Under the proviso to s 31(1) of the Trustee Act 1925, the trustees are required to take a number of factors into account such as the age and requirements of the infant and whether other income is applicable for the same purpose and generally all the surrounding circumstances. The exercise of the power will vary with the facts of each case.

Accumulations

Alternatively, the trustees may accumulate the income instead of maintaining the infant with the fund. Such accumulations (or capitalised income) will produce further income if invested in authorised investments. The additional income as well as accumulations of income become available for maintenance of the infant beneficiary in the future, should the need arise (proviso to s 31(2)).

If, in accordance with the express terms of the trust instrument, the beneficiary attains a vested interest in the income on attaining the age of majority (18) or marries under that age, he becomes entitled to the accumulated income (s 31(2)(i)(a)).

Where the beneficiary acquires a vested interest in capital on attaining the age of majority or earlier marriage, he also becomes entitled to the accumulated income (s 31(2)(i)(b)), eg 'shares are held on trust for A provided that he attains the age of 18'. On attaining the age of majority A becomes entitled to the accumulated dividends from the shares in addition to the capital.

Attaining the age of majority

If the beneficiary attains the age of majority without attaining a vested interest under the terms of the trust, the trustees are required to pay the income to the beneficiary until he acquires a vested interest or dies or his interest fails (s 31(1)(ii)). The payment includes accumulated income. Accordingly, a beneficiary acquires a vested interest in the income of the trust by statute on attaining the age of majority even though under the trust he does not enjoy a vested interest in the capital, eg 'On trust for A provided he attains the age of 25'. On attaining the age of 18, the beneficiary becomes entitled to an interest in possession.

However, this provision is subject to any contrary intention stipulated by the settlor. In *Re Turner's Will Trust* [1937] Ch 15, it was decided that such contrary intention may be manifested by the settlor directing the income to be accumulated beyond the age of majority.

14.11.2 Power of advancement

An advancement is a payment from the capital funds of a trust to, or on behalf of, a beneficiary in respect of some long term commitment, such as the purchase of a house or establishment of a business. A potential beneficiary may be in need of capital from the trust fund prior to becoming entitled, as of right, to the capital from the fund. In such a case the trustees may be entitled to accelerate the enjoyment of his interest by an advance payment of capital, eg S, a settlor, transfers £50,000 to T(1) and T(2) on trust for B contingently on attaining the age of 25. Assuming that while B is only 14 years old, a legitimate need for capital arises. But for special provisions to the contrary, the trustees would be prevented from making an advancement to B on the grounds that the contingency entitling B to the capital has not taken place and in any event B, as a minor, is incapable of giving a valid receipt for the payment of capital. If, on the other hand, the trustees validly exercise their power of advancement, capital may be released in favour of B before the satisfaction of the contingency and B will be prevented from claiming the capital a second time.

Authority to advance

The authority to exercise a power of advancement may originate from a variety of sources such as the trust instrument, the inherent jurisdiction of the courts or statutory power. Only the statutory power is considered below.

Statutory power

Section 32 of the Trustee Act 1925 creates a statutory power of advancement, which is not limited to minors, but empowers the trustees with a discretion to distribute an amount not exceeding one half of the beneficiary's presumptive share capital in favour of any beneficiary, who may become entitled to the whole or part of the capital in the future.

However, this statutory power may be excluded expressly or impliedly by the settlor. An implied exclusion involves any power of advancement which is inconsistent with the statutory power. In *IRC v Bernstein* [1961] Ch 399, it was decided that an express power which exceeded the statutory maximum amount that may be used to advance to the beneficiaries amounted to an implied exclusion.

Advancement or benefit

Under s 32, the trustees are entitled to pay or apply capital in their discretion for the 'advancement or benefit' of a beneficiary. The expression has been considered liberally by the courts and 'benefit' has been interpreted as extending the wide ambit of 'advancement':

'The word "advancement" itself meant … the establishment in life of the beneficiary…
The expression ["benefit"] means any use of the money which will improve the
material situation of the beneficiary.'

(Viscount Radcliffe in *Pilkington v IRC* [1964] AC 612)

Thus, the phrase includes the use of money not only for the immediate personal benefit of the beneficiary but also an indirect 'benefit'. In *Re Clore's Settlement* [1966] 2 All ER 272, the phrase included a moral obligation to donate funds to a charity. Similarly, in *Re Kershaw* (1868) LR 6 Eq 322, it was held that the power may be exercised by making a loan to the beneficiary's husband to facilitate him to set up a business in England in order to keep the family together.

Scope of s 32

The policy of s 32 is to invest trustees with a discretion to appoint up to one-half of the presumptive share of the capital of the beneficiary for his advancement or benefit.

The value of the presumptive share of the beneficiary is measured on the date of the advancement. If the ceiling concerning the statutory power of advancement has been reached (ie half of the presumptive share of capital) the statutory power of advancement would be exhausted even if the value of the capital increases subsequently. This was the position in *Marquess of Abergavenny v Ram* [1981] 2 All ER 643.

However, the settlor may increase the ceiling of sums which may be advanced, but this may only be done expressly.

The sum (or sums) advanced is (or are) credited to the prospective share of the beneficiary (or beneficiaries), so that if a beneficiary becomes absolutely entitled to a share as of right, the sum advanced is taken into account (s 32(1)(b)).

Prior interests

If a beneficiary is entitled to a prior interest (life interest), whether vested or contingent, the consent in writing of such beneficiary is required to be obtained prior to the exercise of the power of advancement. The reason being that an advancement reduces the income available to other beneficiaries (s 32(1)(c)).

Trustees' duties

The trustees are required to exercise their power of advancement in a fiduciary manner. In *Molyneux v Fletcher* [1898] 1 QB 648, the court decided that the exercise will not be *bona fide* and will be void if the trustees advance funds to a beneficiary on condition that the sum is used to repay a loan made by one of the trustees. Moreover, the trustees may transfer the capital to the beneficiary directly if they reasonably believe that he may be trusted with the money. If the trustees specify a particular purpose which they reasonably believe the beneficiary is capable of fulfilling, they (trustees) may pay the fund over to him. But in *Re Pauling Settlement Trust* [1964] Ch 303, the court decided that the trustees are under an obligation to ensure that the beneficiary, recipient of the fund, expends the sum for the specific purpose.

14.12 Power of trustees to give receipts

Section 14(1) of the Trustee Act 1925 provides that the receipt in writing of a trustee for any money, securities, investments or other personal property or effects payable, transferable or deliverable to him under any trust or power shall be a sufficient discharge to the person paying, transferring or delivering the same and shall effectually exonerate him.

Section 14(2) provides that the section does not, except where the trustee is a trust corporation, enable a sole trustee to give a valid receipt for:

(a) the proceeds of sale or other capital money arising under a trust of land

(b) capital money arising under the Settled Land Act 1925.

14.13 Power to partition land under a trust of land

Section 7 of the Trusts of Land and Appointment of Trustees 1996, which repeals s 28 of the Law of Property Act 1925, confers on trustees of land the power to partition the land, or part of it, among adult beneficiaries who are absolutely entitled in undivided shares, subject to their consent. If an infant is absolutely entitled to a share, partition may still take place, but the trustees will hold his share on trust for him. This may end the co-ownership of the whole or part of the land subject to the trust. This section may be excluded or varied by the settlement, except in the case of trusts for ecclesiastical, public or charitable trusts.

The trust settlement may require the trustees to obtain the consent of any person before exercising any of their powers as trustees of land. If the consent of more than two persons are required, and have not been obtained, the purchaser is protected if, at least, two consents are obtained (s 10). But, this is without prejudice to the liability of the trustees for breach of trust. In the case of land held on ecclesiastical, charitable or public purposes, the purchaser is required to ensure that all necessary consents have been obtained. The consent of an infant is not required, but in such a case the trustees are duty bound to obtain the consent of the person with parental responsibility for the infant or his guardian.

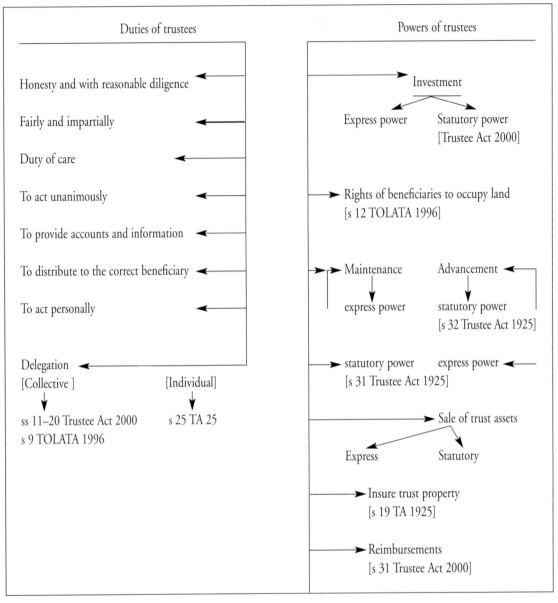

Duties of trustees

Honesty and with reasonable diligence

Fairly and impartially

Duty of care

To act unanimously

To provide accounts and information

To distribute to the correct beneficiary

To act personally

Delegation
[Collective]   [Individual]

ss 11–20 Trustee Act 2000   s 25 TA 25
s 9 TOLATA 1996

Powers of trustees

Investment

Express power   Statutory power
                     [Trustee Act 2000]

Rights of beneficiaries to occupy land
[s 12 TOLATA 1996]

Maintenance   Advancement

express power   statutory power
                       [s 32 Trustee Act 1925]

statutory power   express power
[s 31 Trustee Act 1925]

Sale of trust assets

Express   Statutory

Insure trust property
[s 19 TA 1925]

Reimbursements
[s 31 Trustee Act 2000]

■ *Figure 14.1 Duties and powers of trustees*

ACTIVITY

1. Under the trusts of a settlement, a personalty fund worth £150,000 is held by the trustees upon trust for such of the settlor's grandchildren, Tom, Dick and Harriet, as attain the age of 25 and in equal shares absolutely. Tom is now 25, Dick is 18 and Harriet is 13. Advise the trustees:

   (i)   Whether they may now distribute one-third of the capital of the trust fund to Tom.

   (ii) Whether they should distribute any, and if so what, trust income and to whom.

   (iii) Whether they may advance the sum of £25,000 out of capital to enable Dick to train for a commercial pilot's licence.

   (iv) Whether they may pay out of trust monies the school fees of Harriet who is about to go to a boarding school.

2. David is a solicitor to a trust. The trustees are Margaret and Norman and the beneficiaries Edward and Francis. The assets of the trust included a painting which David wished to buy. David informed the trustees of his wish and, upon David's suggestion, the trustees approached a valuer, Tony, from whom they sought a valuation of the painting. David was aware that Tony had previously been convicted of an offence involving fraud but did not reveal that fact to the trustees. The trustees themselves made no enquiry as to Tony's character and merely accepted David's nomination of him.

   Having been told by David of his wish to buy the painting, Tony put its value at £100,000, approximately one-half of its true market value, and David bought it from the trustees at that price. He has just sold it for £210,000.

   Discuss the possible liabilities of Margaret, Norman, David and Tony to the beneficiaries.

Further reading

Clements, L, 'The changing face of trusts: the Trusts of Land and Appointment of Trustees Act 1996' (1998) 61 MLR 56.

Hochberg, D and Norris, W, 'The Rights of Beneficiaries to Information concerning a Trust' (1999) PCB 292.

Megarry, R, 'The ambit of a trustee's duty of disclosure' (1965) 81 LQR 192.

Nicholls of Birkenhead, Lord, 'Trustees and their broader community: where duty, morality and ethics converge' (1995) 9 Tru LI 71.

Panesar, S, 'The Trustee Act' (2001) ICCLR 151.

Watt, G, 'Escaping s 8(1) provisions in "new style" trusts of land' [1997] Conv 263.

VARIATION OF TRUSTS

Trustees are required to administer the trust in accordance with its terms. They have a primary duty to obey the instructions as detailed by the settlor or implied by law. Any deviation from the terms of the trust is a breach making them personally liable, irrespective of how well intentioned the trustees may have been. But circumstances may arise, since the setting up of the trust, which indicate that the trust might be more advantageously administered if the terms were altered.

For example, authority may be needed to use funds from the trust to maintain an infant beneficiary, an investment or the impact of a potential liability to taxation may have the effect of depreciating the trust assets if no action is taken. A partitioning of the trust property between the life tenant and remainderman may have the effect of avoiding inheritance tax if the life tenant survives for seven years or more, whereas, if no action is taken the entire capital may suffer inheritance tax on the death of the life tenant and a second time on the death of the remainder.

In these circumstances the trustees are in need of some mechanism whereby authority may be conferred on them to depart from or vary the terms of the trust. Such authority may be conferred in a variety of ways:

15.1 The rule in *Saunders v Vautier*

Where the beneficiaries are of full age and of sound mind and are absolutely entitled to the trust property, they may deal with the equitable interest in any way they wish. They may sell, exchange or gift away their interest. As a corollary to this rule, such beneficiaries acting in unison are entitled to terminate the trust. Equally, such beneficiaries acting in concert are entitled to empower the trustees to perform such acts as they (the beneficiaries) consider appropriate. In short, the beneficiaries, collectively, are entitled to rewrite the terms of the trust.

ASE EXAMPLE

Saunders v Vautier (1841) 4 Beav 115

Stock was bequeathed upon trust to accumulate the dividends until Vautier (V) attained the age of 25. At this age, the trustees were required to transfer the capital and accumulated income to V. V attained the age of majority (21) and claimed the fund at this age. The question in issue was whether the trustees were required to transfer the fund to V. Lord Langdale MR decided that since the fund had vested in V, the sole beneficiary, subject to the enjoyment being postponed, and he was of full age, he was entitled to claim the entire fund. The beneficiary had a vested interest in the income, and the accumulations were for his sole benefit, which he was entitled to waive.

 'I think that principle has been repeatedly acted upon; and where a legacy is directed to accumulate for a certain period, or where the payment is postponed the legatee, if he has an absolute indefeasible interest in the legacy, is not bound to wait until the expiration of that period, but may require payment the moment he is competent to give a valid discharge.'

(Lord Langdale MR)

But where minors or persons under a disability or persons unborn are beneficiaries (or potential beneficiaries) there cannot be a departure from the terms of the trust without the court's approval.

The courts drew a distinction between

- a variation concerning the management and administration of trusts and

- a variation of the beneficial interests under the trusts.

We shall now consider the first of these.

15.2 Variation of the management powers of trustees

15.2.1 Inherent jurisdiction of the court

The court has an inherent jurisdiction to depart from the terms of a trust in the case of an 'emergency', ie an occasion when no provision was made in the trust instrument and the event could not have been foreseen by the settlor. This power is very narrow and arises in order to 'salvage' the trust property, such as effecting essential repairs to buildings.

The power was exercised in *Re New* [1901] 2 Ch 534, which was described as the 'high water mark' of the emergency jurisdiction.

CASE EXAMPLE

Re New [1901] 2 Ch 534

The trust property consisted of shares in a company divided into £100 units. The court approved a scheme of capital reconstruction on behalf of minors and unborn persons by splitting the shares into smaller units so that they could be more easily realised.

In *Re Tollemache* [1903] 1 Ch 955, the court refused to sanction a scheme authorising the mortgage of the life tenant's beneficial interest in order to increase her income. There was no emergency.

15.2.2 Section 57 of the Trustee Act 1925

The section is drafted in fairly wide terms and empowers the court to confer the authority on the trustees to perform functions whenever it is expedient to do so.

Section 57(1) provides:

S 's 57(1) where in the management or administration of any property ..., any sale, lease, mortgage, surrender, release or other disposition or any purchase, investment, acquisition, expenditure or other transaction is in the opinion of the court expedient, but the same cannot be effected by reason of the absence of any power ... the court may by order confer on the trustees, either generally or in any particular instance the necessary power ...'.

The policy of s 57 is to secure that the trust property is managed as advantageously as possible in the interests of the beneficiaries and to authorise specific dealings with the trust property outside the scope of the inherent jurisdiction of the court. It may not be possible to establish an emergency or that the settlor could not reasonably have foreseen the circumstances which have arisen. In these circumstances the court may sanction the scheme presented for its approval.

However, there are a number of limitations within s 57. First, the scheme proposed by the trustees is required to be for the benefit of the trust as a whole and not only for an individual beneficiary. In *Re Craven's Estate (No 2)* [1937] Ch 431, the court refused to sanction a scheme authorising an advancement to a beneficiary for the purpose of becoming a Lloyd's underwriter. The scheme would not have been expedient for the trust as a whole. Second, additional powers may only be conferred on the trustees with regard to the 'management or administration' of the trust. No power exists under s 57 to alter the beneficial interest or to re-write the trust administration clause as opposed to merely authorising specific dispositions or transactions. This distinction is one of degree. In *Re Coates' Trusts* [1959] 1 WLR 375 and *Re Byng's Will Trusts* [1959] 1 WLR 375, orders were made approving arrangements to confer wider powers of investment on the trustees. Orders approving such arrangements were frequently made between the passing of the Variation of Trusts Act in 1958 and the passing of the Trustee Investment Act 1961.

Under s 57 the courts have sanctioned schemes for the partition of land (*Re Thomas* [1939] 1 Ch 194); a sale of land where the necessary consent could not be obtained (*Re Beale's Settlement Trust* [1932] 2 Ch 15); the sale of a reversionary interest which the trustees had no power to sell until it fell into possession (*Re Heyworth's Contingent Reversionary Interest* [1956] Ch 364); blended two charitable trusts into one (*Re Shipwrecked Fishermen's and Mariners' Benevolent Fund* [1959] Ch 220); and extended investment powers of pension fund trustees (*Mason v Farbrother* [1983] 2 All ER 1078).

On a variation of beneficial interests, the court has the jurisdiction to approve schemes which go beyond an alteration of the management powers of trustees and to effect arrangements which vary the beneficial interests under a trust.

15.3 Variation of beneficial interests

15.3.1 Section 53 of the Trustee Act 1925

Where an infant is beneficially entitled to real or personal property and the property does not produce income which may be used for the infant's maintenance and education or benefit, the court may adopt a proposal authorising a 'conveyance' of the infant's interest with a view to the application of the capital or income for his maintenance, education or benefit.

The section may not be used simply to terminate a settlement without making some new trust provision for the infant.

ASE EXAMPLE

Re Meux [1958] Ch 154

The claimant was a life tenant of a trust fund and his infant son was entitled to a contingent reversionary interest. The court sanctioned a scheme on behalf of the infant whereby a person was appointed to convey the infant's interest to the claimant in consideration of a purchase price which was paid to the trustees for the benefit of the infant.

15.3.2 Section 64 of the Settled Land Act 1925

This section applies where land is settled. The court has the power to sanction 'any transaction … which in the opinion of the court would be for the benefit of the settled land or the persons interested under the settlement'.

This section has a wider application than s 57 of the Trustee Act 1925, because it is not limited to managerial or administrative matters but allows alterations to be made to the beneficial interests. Moreover, it extends to both settled land and land held under a trust for sale. In *Raikes v Lygon* [1988] 1 All ER 884, the court decided that s 64 was wide enough to permit the creation of a second settlement.

This statutory provision was recently considered in the following case:

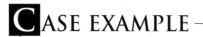

CASE EXAMPLE

Hambro v Duke of Marlborough, The Times, 25th March 1994

The court decided that it had jurisdiction under s 64 of the Settled Land Act 1925 to authorise the tenant for life to vary the beneficial interest of a beneficiary under the 1706 parliamentary settlement of Blenheim Palace, without that beneficiary's consent. However, this is subject to the condition that the variation is either for the benefit of the settled land or all the beneficiaries under the settlement.

15.3.3 Sections 23 and 24 of the Matrimonial Causes Act 1973

This section gives the court power to make property adjustment orders between spouses on divorce, separation or nullity, and this includes a power to make orders extinguishing or reducing the interest of either of the parties to the marriage.

15.3.4 Section 96 of the Mental Health Act 1983

This section gives the Court of Protection wide powers to authorise the making and variation of settlements of the property of mental patients.

15.3.5 Compromise (inherent jurisdiction)

The court has an inherent jurisdiction to approve compromise arrangements governing the rights of beneficiaries including infants and unborn persons under trusts. Before the House of Lords' decision in *Chapman v Chapman* [1954] AC 429, there was some doubt as to whether the jurisdiction existed if there was not a genuine dispute between the beneficiaries. The House of Lords in that case clarified the meaning of the expression 'compromise', by deciding that its jurisdiction concerned cases of genuine disputes about the existence of rights.

Chapman v Chapman [1954] AC 429

The trustees applied for leave to execute a scheme releasing certain properties from the trust in order to avoid estate duty. Some of the interests were enjoyed by infants and might be enjoyed by unborn persons, so that any re-arrangement of interests required the consent of the court. The House of Lords held that the scheme would not be approved because the court had no jurisdiction to sanction a re-arrangement of beneficial interests on behalf of infants and unborn persons where there was no real dispute.

15.3.6 The Variation of Trusts Act 1958

The Variation of Trusts Act 1958 was passed in order to reverse the decision of the House of Lords in *Chapman v Chapman* (1954) and to introduce sweeping changes in the law. The jurisdiction of the courts was extended in order to approve variations of trusts (in respect of both administrative matters and beneficial interests) on behalf of infants, unborn persons and others who lacked the capacity to consent to an arrangement. The court is entitled to sanction 'any arrangement varying or revoking all or any trusts or enlarging the powers of the trustees of managing or administering any of the property subject to the trusts'.

The court in its discretion may make an order approving a scheme, provided that the following four conditions are satisfied:

1. property, whether real or personal, is held on trust and

2. the trust was created by will or *inter vivos* settlement or other disposition and

3. the four categories as enumerated in s 1(1) of the 1958 Act, namely:

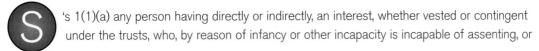

   's 1(1)(a) any person having directly or indirectly, an interest, whether vested or contingent under the trusts, who, by reason of infancy or other incapacity is incapable of assenting, or

   (b) any person (whether ascertained or not) who may become entitled, directly or indirectly, to an interest at a future date or on the happening of a future event, a person of any specified description or a member of any specified class of persons, but not including any person who would be of that description or a member of that class if the said date had fallen or the said event had happened at the date of the application to the court, or

   (c) any person unborn, or

   (d) any person in respect of any discretionary interest of his under protective trusts where the interest of the principal beneficiary has not failed or determined' and

4. provided that, with the exception of para (d) above, the arrangement was carried out for the benefit of that person.

The purpose of the 1958 Act is to permit the court to approve arrangements on behalf of beneficiaries who cannot give their consent by virtue of infancy or other incapacity or because their identity is unascertained, such as a future spouse. It follows, therefore, that the court has no jurisdiction to approve arrangements on behalf of beneficiaries who are *sui juris*, adult and ascertained. Thus, the consent of all adult, ascertained beneficiaries must be obtained before the court may grant its approval to a scheme.

APPLYING THE LAW

T1 and T2 hold property on trust for A (adult) for life, with the remainder to B (an infant) for life, with the remainder to C (adult) absolutely. A scheme of equal division is proposed. The court may approve the scheme on behalf of B (the infant) but not in respect of A and C. Their consent will be required.

The only exception to the above rule is to be found in s 1(1)(d) of the 1958 Act, namely the court may consent on behalf of an adult 'beneficiary' who may become entitled to an interest on the failure of the principal beneficiary's interest under a protective trust.

APPLYING THE LAW

Trustees hold property on protective trust for M for life. A scheme is submitted for the approval of the court to grant M's wife, W, a one-fifth share of the capital. The court may approve the arrangement on behalf of W, but M is required to consent to the scheme.

In *Allen v Distillers Co (Biochemicals) Ltd* [1974] QB 384, the court decided that the Act was not applicable to an out-of-court settlement of litigation.

CASE EXAMPLE

Allen v Distillers Co (Biochemicals) Ltd [1974] QB 384

The trust funds were received pursuant to a negotiated settlement of the Thalidomide litigation. The desire of many of the parents of children affected was to ensure that the sums held for their children should not become their absolute property at the age of 18. Eveleigh J decided that he had the power to achieve the objective of the parents under the court's inherent jurisdiction, but he had no power under the 1958 Act because that Act did not apply to the payment out to trustees under an out-of-court settlement of litigation. This was not the type of trust contemplated in the 1958 Act.

> **J**
>
> 'The Act contemplates a situation where a beneficial interest is created which did not previously exist and probably one which is related to *at least one other beneficial interest*. Moreover, the Act is designed to deal with a situation where the original disposition was intended to endure according to its terms but which in the light of changed attitudes and circumstances it is fair and reasonable to vary.'
>
> (Eveleigh J)

Section 1(1)(b) of the 1958 Act

Generally, the court may consent on behalf of potential beneficiaries who have a contingent interest in the trust (see s 1(1)(b)). But the proviso to s 1(1)(b) prevents the court from approving on behalf of adult beneficiaries who stand only one step removed from entitlement under the trust. It was the intention of Parliament that such persons should be allowed to consent for themselves.

APPLYING THE LAW ☐☐☐

Trustees hold property on trust for A for life with an ultimate remainder for his next-of-kin. A is a widower with one son, B (adult). A scheme is proposed in order to divide the fund equally between A and B. In such a case B is required to consent to the arrangement under the proviso to s 1(1)(b), on the ground that B is only one step removed from acquiring a vested interest, namely the death of A. This principle may be illustrated by the following case.

☐☐☐

CASE EXAMPLE

Re Suffert's Settlement [1961] Ch 1

Under a settlement, B was granted a protected life interest with a power to appoint the capital and income on trust for her children. The settlement provided that if B had no children the property was to be transferred to anyone in respect of whom B may appoint (ie a general power) with a gift over in default of appointment in favour of B's statutory next-of-kin. B was 61 years of age, unmarried and without issue. She had three first cousins (next-of-kin) all of whom had attained the age of majority. B and one of her cousins sought to vary the settlement. The other two cousins had not consented and were not joined as parties. The court was asked to approve the arrangement on behalf of any unborn or unascertained persons and the two adult cousins. The court held that it had jurisdiction to approve on behalf of unborn and unascertained persons, but could not approve on behalf of the two cousins. Their consent was required.

> **J** 'What the subsection required was that the applicant should be treated as having died at the date of the issue of the summons, to find out who in that event would have been her statutory next-of-kin, and any persons who are within that class are persons whose interest the section provides that the court cannot bind. It is impossible to say who are the statutory next-of-kin of somebody who is alive, but it is not impossible to say who are the persons who would fill that description on the hypothesis that the propositus is already dead.'
>
> (Buckley J)

Variation or re-settlement?

Although the 1958 Act gives the court a wide discretion to approve a scheme varying the terms of a trust, there appears to be a limitation on this discretion. The courts have adopted the policy of not 're-writing' the trust. Accordingly, a distinction is drawn between a 'variation' and a 're-settlement'. A 'variation' retains the basic fundamental purpose of the trust but alters some important characteristic of the trust, whereas a 're-settlement' destroys the foundation or substance of the original design or purpose of the trust. Whether a scheme amounts to a variation or a re-settlement will vary with the facts of each case.

CASE EXAMPLE

Re Ball's Settlement [1968] 1 WLR 899

A settlement conferred a life interest on the settlor, with the remainder, subject to a power of appointment, in favour of his sons and grandchildren. In default of appointment the fund was to be divided between the two sons of the settlor or their issue *per stirpes* (ie to the son's issue if either predeceased the settlor). A scheme was proposed for approval by the court whereby the original settlement would be revoked and replaced by new provisions in which the fund would be split into two equal portions each held on trust for each of the sons for life and subject thereto, for such of each of the son's children equally as were born before 1st October 1977. The court approved the scheme.

> 'The test is if the arrangement changes the whole substratum of the trust, then it may well be that it cannot be regarded merely as varying that trust. But if an arrangement, while leaving the substratum, effectuates the purpose of the original trusts by other means, it may still be possible to regard that arrangement as merely varying the original trusts, even though the means employed are wholly different and even though the form is completely changed ... In this case, it seems to me that the substratum of the original trust remains. True, the settlor's life interest disappears; but the remaining trusts are still in essence trusts of half the fund for each of the two named sons and their families ... The differences between the old and new provisions lie in detail rather than substance.'
>
> (Megarry J)

Settlor's intention

The 1958 Act makes no mention of the settlor or testator. Rules of Court (RSC Ord 93 r 6(2)) have been made requiring the joinder of the settlor, if living, as a defendant to an application under the Act. In exercising its discretion whether to approve an arrangement or not, the function of the court is to determine, by reference to all the circumstances, whether the arrangement as a whole is beneficial to the stipulated class of beneficiaries. However, in the context of deciding whether to approve an arrangement or not, the intention of the settlor or testator is only a factor (if relevant) to be taken into consideration by the court. But the settlor's or testator's intention is certainly not an overriding factor, nor even a weighty consideration in determining how the discretion of the court is to be exercised. The role of the court is not to act as a representative of the settlor or testator in varying the trusts.

In *Re Steed's Will Trust* [1960] Ch 407, the court took into consideration the testator's intention and refused to approve the proposed arrangement.

In *Goulding v James* [1997] 2 All ER 239, Mummery LJ reviewed *Re Steed* (1960) and decided that the latter case did not lay down 'any rule, principle or guideline of general application on the importance of the intentions and wishes of the settlor or testator to applications to approve arrangements under the 1958 Act'. In other words, the settlor's wishes coincided with, but were not a cause for, the court's refusal to vary the trust.

CASE EXAMPLE

Goulding v James [1997] 2 All ER 239

The court decided that, in the exercise of its discretion, it would approve a scheme of variation of a trust, despite the contradiction of the clear intention of a testatrix concerning adult, ascertained beneficiaries. In this case June and Marcus Goulding – the beneficiaries under will trusts – applied to the court for a variation under s 1(1)(c) of the 1958 Act. The proposed variation was partly in favour of a grandchildren's trust fund, and would benefit unborn great-grandchildren of the testatrix. However, the variation was contrary to the wishes of the testatrix. Despite the testatrix's wishes, the court approved the scheme. Mummery LJ summarised the court's approach.

'In my judgment, the legal position is as follows:

(1) The court has a discretion whether or not to approve a proposed arrangement.

(2) That discretion is fettered by only one express restriction. The proviso to s 1 prohibits the court from approving an arrangement which is not for the benefit of the classes referred to in (a), (b) or (c). The approval of this arrangement is not prevented by that proviso, since it is plainly the case that it is greatly for the benefit of the class specified in s 1(1)(c).

(3) It does not follow from the fact of benefit to unborns that the arrangement must be approved …

(4) That overall discretion … is to be exercised with regard to all relevant factors properly considered in the statutory context. The context is that the court is empowered to approve an arrangement 'on behalf of' the members of the specified class …

(5) Viewed in that context, an important factor in this case is that Mrs June Goulding and Mr Marcus Goulding are sui juris and Mrs Froud's [the testatrix's] intentions and wishes related to their beneficial interests under the testamentary trusts rather than to the contingent interests of her unborn great-grandchildren whom the court is concerned to protect. Mrs Froud's contrary non-testamentary wishes could not inhibit Mrs June Goulding's proprietary rights, as a person beneficially entitled to the life interest in residue.

CONTINUED ▶

J

(6) In these circumstances, the critical question is: what relevance, if any, can Mrs Froud's intentions and wishes with regard to the interests in residue taken under the will by her daughter and grandson and with regard to the exclusion of her son in law from direct or indirect benefit, have to the exercise of the court's jurisdiction on behalf of unborn great-grandchildren of Mrs Froud?

(7) [The judge reviewed the principle in *Re Steed's Will Trust* (1960), distinguished that case and continued:] …

(8) The fact that the rules of court require a living settlor to be joined as a party to proceedings under the 1958 Act does not mean that the court attaches any overbearing or special significance to the wishes of the settlor. The court has a discretion to approve an arrangement under the Act, even though the settlement or will may make it crystal clear that the settlor or testator does not want any departure from any of the strict terms of the trust.'

(Mummery LJ)

Benefit (proviso to s 1(1))

The scheme of variation is required to display some benefit for the persons as stated in s 1(1)(a)–(c) of the Variation of Trusts Act 1958. No such requirement exists for persons in category (d) of s 1(1) of the Act. The statute does not list the factors which the court is required to take into account in deciding the issue. It seems that all the circumstances are required to be considered and the court must weigh up the possible advantages against the disadvantages of adopting a scheme of variation of the trust and decide accordingly.

CASE EXAMPLE

D (a child) v O [2004] 3 All ER 780

An application to vary a settlement under the Variation of Trusts Act 1958 was made in writing, in chambers and without a hearing, but subject to written submissions. The application was made to increase the ceiling of 50 per cent of the presumptive share of an infant beneficiary's capital (imposed by s 32 of the Trustee Act 1925) in order to make an advancement for school fees. The court decided that it had the jurisdiction under the Variation of Trusts Act 1958 to modify the statutory power of advancement and that it was for the claimant's benefit that the limit imposed by s 32 of the Trustee Act 1925 be lifted.

A wide variety of factors have been prominent in either approving or rejecting schemes of variations. Some of these include tax avoidance, moral benefits and the avoidance of family dissension.

Tax avoidance

The majority of applications have been made with a view to reducing the tax which would otherwise have been payable if the variation was not made.

APPLYING THE LAW

Property was settled on trust for A for life, with the remainder to B absolutely. Inheritance tax would be payable on the entire estate on A's death and a second time on B's death. If the settlement was varied so that the fund is divided between A and B equally, inheritance tax would be payable on only half of the trust fund on the death of each of the beneficiaries.

The courts are required to be satisfied that the scheme as a whole is advantageous to the objects. It follows that the court will not approve a scheme if the overall effect is detrimental to the objects, even though there may be financial rewards inherent in the scheme. Tax avoidance is merely one factor to be taken into account by the courts.

CASE EXAMPLE

Re Weston's Settlement [1969] 1 Ch 223

The settlor created two settlements in 1964 for the benefit of his two sons. A total of 500,000 shares were transferred to the trustees. In 1965 capital gains tax was introduced. The shares rose in value and at the time of hearing the tax due on a disposal of the shares was £163,000. The settlor lived in England until 1967. He made three short visits to Jersey in 1967 and then in August 1967 purchased a house there in which he intended to live. In November 1967 an application was made to the court under the Variation of Trusts Act 1958 to appoint two trustees in Jersey as trustees of the two English settlements. In addition, the plaintiff sought the court's sanction to 'export' the trust to Jersey on identical terms. The motive was to save capital gains tax and estate duty. The Court of Appeal decided that the scheme would not be approved because it would have been morally and socially detrimental to the beneficiaries despite being financially advantageous.

CONTINUED ▸

J   'The Court should not consider merely the financial benefit to the infants and unborn children but also their educational and social benefit. There are many things in life more worthwhile than money. One of these things is to be brought up in this our England, which is still the envy of less happier lands. I do not believe it is for the benefit of children to be uprooted from England and transported to another country simply to avoid tax. I should imagine that even if they had stayed in this country they would have had a very considerable fortune at their disposal even after paying tax. The only thing that Jersey can do for them is to give them a greater fortune. Many a child has been ruined by being given too much. The avoidance of tax may be lawful, but it is not yet a virtue. The children may well change their minds and come back to this country to enjoy their untaxed gains. Are they to be wanderers over the face of the earth, moving from this country to that according to where they can best avoid tax? Children are like trees, they grow stronger with firm roots.'

(Lord Denning)

On the other hand, where the applicants have a long-standing connection with the foreign country concerned in the proposed scheme, the court may grant its approval.

CASE EXAMPLE

Re Windeatt's Will Trust [1969] 1 WLR 692

The settlor was domiciled in England. He created a trust for the benefit of his children, who had lived in Jersey for 19 years prior to the application to transfer the trust to Jersey. The court approved the scheme because the beneficiaries were permanently resident in Jersey.

Moral benefit

The court may have regard to evidence which establishes the financial instability of infant beneficiaries and adopt a scheme which has the effect of postponing the vesting of such a beneficiary's interest in capital.

CASE EXAMPLE

Re T's Settlement [1964] Ch 158

An infant was entitled absolutely to one-quarter of a trust fund on attaining the age of 21 years (age of majority at this time) and a further one-quarter on the death of her mother. Eighteen days before she reached the age of majority her mother asked the court to approve a transfer to new trustees of the infant's share, to be held either:

(i)   on protective trust for her life or

(ii)   to postpone the vesting of capital until she reached the age of 25,

but in the meantime the property would be held on protective trusts. It was conceded that the infant was alarmingly immature and irresponsible in respect of financial matters. The court held that:

(a)   the protective trust for life would have amounted to a 're-settlement' of property which was outside the jurisdiction of the court and in any event would not be beneficial to the child but

(b)   the postponement of the capital until a later date and the interim protective trust were approved.

> J   '... it appears to me to be a definite benefit for this infant for a period during which it is to be hoped that independence may bring her to maturity and responsibility to be protected against creditors ... And this is the kind of benefit which seems to be within the spirit of the Act.'
>
> (Wilberforce J)

In *Re Holt's Settlement* [1969] 1 Ch 100, the court approved the decision in *Re T's Settlement* (1964) but postponed the vesting of an infant's benefit without evidence of financial immaturity.

CASE EXAMPLE

Re Holt's Settlement [1969] 1 Ch 100

Personal property was settled on Mrs Wilson for life with remainder to such of her children as would reach the age of 21 years and, if more than one, in equal shares. She wanted to surrender her life interest in half of the income for the benefit of the children (in order to reduce the impact of income tax on her husband and her) and to re-arrange the trusts so that the interest of the children would vest at the age of 30 years. The court sanctioned the scheme because, on the whole, it was for the benefit of the children.

CONTINUED ▶

> **J** 'It seems to me that the arrangement proposed is for the benefit of each of the beneficiaries contemplated by s 1(1) of the 1958 Act. The financial detriment to the children is that the absolute vesting of their interests will be postponed from age 21 to 30. As against this, they will obtain very substantial financial benefits, both in the acceleration of their interests in a moiety [half] of the trust fund and in the savings of estate duty ... it is also most important that young children should be reasonably advanced in a career and settled in life before they are in receipt of an income sufficient to make them independent of the need to work. The word "benefit" in the proviso to s 1(1) is plainly not confined to financial benefit, but may extend to moral and social benefit as is shown in *Re T's Settlement*.'
>
> (Megarry J)

Avoidance of family dissension

The court may approve an arrangement if its effect would be to prevent real or potential conflict within a family. In this respect, although the intention of the settlor carries a great deal of weight, it is not conclusive.

CASE EXAMPLE

Re Remnant's Settlement Trust [1970] Ch 560

A trust gave contingent interests to the children of two sisters, Dawn and Merrial, and contained a forfeiture clause if they practised Roman Catholicism or married or lived with a Roman Catholic. The children of Dawn were Protestants, whereas the children of Merrial were Roman Catholics. The sisters sought the court's approval of a scheme which deleted the forfeiture clause. The court gave its approval in order to prevent a family conflict. Although Dawn's children did not benefit financially from the deletion of the clause, the court decided that on the whole they would be better off because the religious bar could have deterred them from selecting a spouse.

> **J** 'Obviously a forfeiture provision of this kind might well cause very serious dissension between the families of two sisters ... I am entitled to take a broad view of what is meant by "benefit", and so taking it, I think this arrangement can fairly be said to be for their "benefit" ... It remains to be considered whether the arrangement is a fair and proper one. As far as I can see, there is the reason for saying otherwise, except that the arrangement defeats this testator's intention. That is a serious but by no

CONTINUED ▶

> J means conclusive consideration. I have reached the clear conclusion that these forfeiture provisions are undesirable in the circumstances of this case and that an arrangement involving their deletion is a fair and proper one.'
>
> (Pennycuick J)

Effect of variation

The variation takes effect as soon as the order is made by the court and without the necessity of any further instrument. As equitable interests are being dealt with, one would have thought that compliance with s 53(1)(c) of the Law of Property Act 1925 (requiring the written consent of adult beneficiaries) would be necessary. However, in *Re Holt's Settlement* (1969) Megarry J concluded that it is not necessary to satisfy this requirement, declaring that s 53(1)(c) had been impliedly excluded by the Variation of Trusts Act 1958. Alternatively, where the variation was made for consideration, the consenting adults could be compelled to perform the contract. They therefore held their original interests on constructive trusts, which did not require fulfilment of s 53(1)(c).

Figure 15.1 Variation of trusts

ACTIVITY

1. What differences are apparent in the law's attitude to variations of administrative provisions and dispositive provisions?

2. Under the trusts of a settlement of personalty, a trust fund currently worth £250,000 is held by the trustees upon trust to pay the income thereof to Amy during her life upon a s 33 Trustee Act 1925 protective trust for her life and, subject thereto, upon trust for such of Amy's children as she shall by deed appoint, and in default of appointment upon trust for such of Amy's children as shall attain the age of 21 and if more than one in equal shares.

   Amy is 56 years of age and has two children: Janet (aged 20) and John (aged 18). Amy, Janet and John would like to divide up the capital of the trust fund among themselves.

   Advise them as to whether this may be done and, if so, as to the legal steps that would need to be taken.

Further reading

Cotterell, R, 'The requirement of "benefit" under the Variation of Trusts Act 1958' (1971) 34 MLR 96.

Hayes, M, 'Breaking and varying trusts painlessly' (1998) 4 MLR 17.

Luxton, P, 'An unascertainable problem in variation of trusts' (1986) 136 NLJ 1057.

Riddall, J, 'Does it or doesn't it? Contingent interests and Variation of Trusts Act 1958' [1987] Conv 144.

chapter 16 · BREACH OF TRUST ■

A trustee is liable for breach of trust if he fails to perform his duties, either by omitting to do any act which he ought to do, or by doing an act which he ought not to do. Such duties may be created by the settlor in the trust instrument (such as the duty to distribute both income and capital) or may be imposed generally in accordance with trust law (eg duties of care and impartiality). A breach of trust may range from a fraudulent disposal of trust property to an innocent dereliction of duties by investing trust monies in unauthorised investments. The beneficiary is required to establish a causal connection between the breach of trust and the loss suffered either directly or indirectly by the trust. Indeed, even if the trust suffers no loss, the beneficiary is entitled to claim any profit occurring to the trustees as a result of a breach.

16.1 Measure of liability

Trustees' liability for breach of trust is based on principles of restitution to the trust estate. The trust is required to be compensated fully for any loss caused by the breach. The extent of this liability is not restricted by common principles governing remoteness of damage in actions in tort or breach of contract. Once a breach has been committed the trustees become liable to place the trust estate in the same position as it would have been in if no breach had been committed. Considerations of causation, foreseeability and remoteness do not readily feature in this question.

CASE EXAMPLE

Caffrey v Darby (1801) 6 Ves 488

Trustees, because of their negligence, failed to recover possession of part of the trust assets and later still the assets became lost. The trustees argued that the loss was not attributable to their neglect. The court rejected this argument and decided that once the trustees had committed a breach of trust, they were responsible for compensating the estate in respect of any loss, whether consequential on the breach or not.

CONTINUED ▶

> 'if they have already been guilty of negligence they must be responsible for any loss in any way to that property, for whatever may be the immediate cause, the property would not have been in a situation to sustain that loss if it had not been for their negligence. If the loss had happened by fire, lightning, or any other accident, that would not be an excuse for them if guilty of previous negligence.'
>
> (Lord Eldon)

The effect of this strict rule is that the liability of the trustees to account for losses suffered by the trust estate is absolute. Accordingly, it may be possible to obtain damages for breach of trust in cases where it is not possible to recover damages at common law in actions for breach of contract and tort.

> 'The obligation of a trustee who is held liable for breach of trust is fundamentally different from the obligation of a contractual or tortious wrongdoer. The trustee's obligation is to restore to the trust estate the assets of which he has deprived it.'
>
> (Brightman J in *Bartlett v Barclays Bank Trust Co Ltd (No 2)* [1980] 2 All ER 92)

The same sentiments were expressed by Lord Browne-Wilkinson in the House of Lords' decision in *Target Holdings v Redferns* [1995] 3 All ER 785:

> '... the basic rule is that a trustee in breach of trust must restore or pay to the trust estate either the assets which have been lost ... or compensation for such loss ... the common law rules of remoteness ... and causation do not apply.'
>
> (Lord Browne-Wilkinson)

It appears that in equity, although the strict common-law test of foreseeability is not applicable in assessing damages for breach of trust, it is essential that the compensation awarded is linked to the breach of trust. The House of Lords in *Target Holdings v Redferns* (1995) decided that in assessing compensation for loss arising from a breach of trust, the nature of the breach of duty and whether the trust is a traditional or commercial trust are important. Their Lordships declared that in the case of a trust arising out of a commercial transaction, the basis of compensation is similar to that applied in the case of common-law damages, ie that the beneficiary is put into the position he would have been in had the breach not occurred. In such a case the common-law rules of remoteness and causation would apply. However, where the breach occurs in a traditional type of trust (eg a family trust) the trustee has to account for and restore all that which has been lost by the trust.

343

CASE EXAMPLE

Target Holdings v Redferns [1995] 3 All ER 785

The claimants, mortgagees, loaned a company £1.525 million, to be secured by way of a mortgage on property which was fraudulently made to appear to be worth £2 million, but in reality was worth only £775,000. The defendants, a firm of solicitors, were not parties to this fraud and acted for the purchasers and the mortgagees. The purchasers became insolvent and the claimants repossessed the property and sold it for £500,000. The claimants sued the firm of solicitors. The firm conceded that it acted in breach of trust by paying out the mortgage funds without authority, but argued that it was not liable to compensate the claimant for the loss suffered because its breach did not cause the loss sustained by the claimant. The firm of solicitors alleged that the claimants' loss was wholly caused by the fraud of the third parties. The House of Lords decided in favour of the firm of solicitors. The claimant company advanced the same amount of money, obtained the same security and received the same amount on the realisation of that security, with or without the breach of trust committed by the defendant.

In *Nationwide Building Society v Various Solicitors (No 3)* [1999] PNLR 52, the High Court applied the principles laid down by Lord Browne-Wilkinson in the *Target* case (1995) in assessing damages for breach of fiduciary duties. The court decided that the correct approach in such a claim is to put the beneficiary in the position he would have been in if the fiduciary had performed his duty.

The following examples illustrate the principles that are applied by the courts:

Where the trustees make an unauthorised investment they are liable for any loss incurred on the sale of the assets. The position remains the same even if the sale is ordered by the courts and, but for the order of sale within a specified time, the investments would have produced a profit had they been retained for a longer period. The loss is measured by deducting the proceeds of sale of the unauthorised investment (accruing to the trust) from the amount improperly invested.

CASE EXAMPLE

Knott v Cottee (1852) 16 Beav 77

A testator, who died in 1844, directed his trustee to invest in government stocks and land in England and Wales. In 1845 and 1846 the executor-trustee invested part of the estate in Exchequer bills which in 1846 were ordered into court and sold at a loss. In 1848, the court declared that the investment was improper. If, however, the investment had been

CONTINUED ▶

retained its realisation at the time of the declaration in 1848 would have resulted in a profit. The court held that the trustee was liable to compensate the estate for the difference in value of the assets in 1848 and the sale proceeds in 1846.

J   'The case must either be treated as if these investments had not been made, or had been made for his own benefit out of his own monies, and that he had at the same time retained monies of the testator in his hands.'

(Romilly MR)

Where the trustees, in breach of their duties, fail to dispose of unauthorised investments and improperly retain the assets, they will be liable for the difference between the current value of the assets and the value at the time when they should have been sold.

CASE EXAMPLE

Fry v Fry (1859) 28 LJ Ch 591

A testator, who died March 1834, directed his trustees to sell a house 'as soon as convenient after [his death] … for the most money that could be normally obtained'. In April 1836 the trustees advertised the house for £1,000. In 1837 they refused an offer of £900. In 1843 a railway was built near the property which caused it to depreciate in value. The property remained unsold in 1856, by which time both the original trustees had died. The court held that their estates were liable for the difference between £900 and the sum receivable for the house when it was eventually sold.

Where the trustees retain an authorised investment they will not be liable for breach of trust unless their conduct falls short of the ordinary prudence required of trustees. This was decided in *Re Chapman* [1896] 2 Ch 763. Under s 6 of the Trustee Investment Act 1961 (now repealed), the trustees, from time to time, were required to obtain and consider advice on whether the retention of the investment is satisfactory, having regard to the need for diversification and suitability of the investment.

Where the trustees improperly sell authorised investments and re-invest the proceeds in unauthorised investments, they will be liable to replace the authorised investments if these have risen in value, or the proceeds of sale of the authorised investments.

CASE EXAMPLE

Re Massingberd's Settlement (1890) 63 LT 296

The trustees of a settlement had power to invest in government securities. In 1875 they sold Consols (authorised investments) and re-invested in unauthorised mortgages. The mortgages were called in and the whole of the money invested was recovered. At this time the Consols had risen in value. In an action for an account the court held that the trustees were required to replace the stock sold or its money equivalent.

Where the trustees are directed by the settlor to invest in an identified or specific investment (eg shares in British Telecom plc) and the trustees fail to acquire the stipulated investments, they will be required to purchase the same at the proper time. If the specified investments have fallen in value, the trustees may be ordered to pay compensation to the trust equivalent to the difference between the values of the investments at the time the investments should have been made, and the value of the investments at the time of the judgment.

On the other hand, where the trustees retain a discretion to invest in a specified range of investments and they fail to invest, they are chargeable with the trust fund itself and not with the amount of one or other of the investments which might have been purchased. In *Shepherd v Mouls* (1845) 4 Hare 500, it was decided that there is no one specific investment which may be used to measure the loss suffered by the trust.

Where the trustees in breach of trust make a profit on one transaction and a loss on another they are not allowed to set off the loss against the profit, unless the profit and loss are treated as part of one transaction.

CASE EXAMPLE

Bartlett v Barclays Bank Trust Co (No 2) [1980] Ch 515

The trust estate consisted of a majority shareholding in a property company and the trustees were a professional trust company. For a number of years the property company maintained traditional investments and these were sufficient to maintain large dividends. As a result of inflation, the board resolved to re-structure the investment portfolio into land developments. The new investments, known as the 'Old Bailey' project and the 'Guildford' project, were not completely successful and resulted in a loss to the trust. The court found that the new investments were in breach of trust and *inter alia* the trustees attempted to set off a loss made in the 'Old Bailey' project against a gain made in the 'Guildford' scheme. The court allowed the set-off as the mixed fortunes originated from the same transaction.

CONTINUED ▶

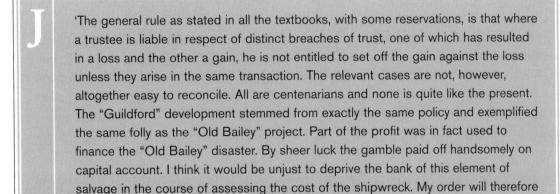

'The general rule as stated in all the textbooks, with some reservations, is that where a trustee is liable in respect of distinct breaches of trust, one of which has resulted in a loss and the other a gain, he is not entitled to set off the gain against the loss unless they arise in the same transaction. The relevant cases are not, however, altogether easy to reconcile. All are centenarians and none is quite like the present. The "Guildford" development stemmed from exactly the same policy and exemplified the same folly as the "Old Bailey" project. Part of the profit was in fact used to finance the "Old Bailey" disaster. By sheer luck the gamble paid off handsomely on capital account. I think it would be unjust to deprive the bank of this element of salvage in the course of assessing the cost of the shipwreck. My order will therefore reflect the bank's right to an appropriate set off.'

(Brightman J)

The principles of restitution which govern the computation of the loss to the trust are concerned with the gross loss suffered by the estate. The tax position of the beneficiaries is irrelevant in the assessment of the loss to the estate. Accordingly, compensation to the trust will not be reduced by an equivalent amount of tax which the beneficiaries would have paid, had the trustees not committed a breach of trust (the principle in *British Tax Commission v Gourley* [1956] AC 185 is excluded).

'I have reached the conclusion that tax ought not to be taken into account ... but I do not feel that the established principles on which equitable relief is granted enable me to apply the *Gourley* principles to this case.'

(Brightman J in *Bartlett v Barclays Bank Trust Co Ltd (No 2)* (1980))

16.1.1 Interest

As a general rule, the court is entitled to award simple interest under s 35A of the Supreme Court Act 1981 on monetary sums payable by the trustees. The rate of interest that may be charged is 1 per cent above the banks' base rate. The court has a discretion to award compound interest against the trustees. The purpose of such an order is not designed to punish the trustees, but to require them to disgorge the benefit of the use of the trust funds. The principle here stems from the policy of preventing the trustees profiting from their breach. The Law Lords, in *Westdeutsche Landesbank Girozentrale v Islington Borough Council* [1996] 2 All ER 961, considered that the jurisdiction to award compound interest originated exclusively in equity. In the absence of fraud, this jurisdiction is exercised against a defendant who is a trustee or otherwise stands in a fiduciary position, and makes an unauthorised profit or is assumed to have made an unauthorised profit. The majority of the Law Lords decided that, since the defendant did not owe fiduciary duties to the bank in relation to the payments made, compound interest would not be awarded. To award compound interest in the circumstances of this case would be tantamount to the courts usurping the function of Parliament. However, simple interest would be awarded on the balance of the fund remaining outstanding, calculated from the date of the original payment by the bank to the local authority.

■Key facts on measure of liability of trustees

KEY FACTS

• The measure of the trustees' liability for breach of trust is restitution based.	*Bartlett v Barclays Bank* (1980); *Target Holdings v Redferns* (1995); *Nationwide BS v Various Solicitors* (1999)
• Unauthorised investment.	*Knott v Cottee* (1852)
• Failure to dispose of unauthorised investments.	*Fry v Fry* (1859)
• Trustees improperly sell authorised investments and invest the proceeds in unauthorised investments.	*Re Massingberd* (1890)
• In breach of trust the trustees make a profit on one transaction and a loss on another.	*Bartlett v Barclays Bank* (1980)
• Tax is not deductible from the damages payable by trustees under the *BTC v Gourley* (1956) rule.	*Bartlett v Barclays Bank* (1980)
• Interest on damages.	*Westdeutsche Landesbank v Islington BC* (1996)

16.2 Contribution and indemnity between trustees

Trustees are under a duty to act jointly and unanimously. In principle, each trustee has an equal role and standing in the administration of the trust. Accordingly, if a breach of trust has occurred each trustee is equally liable or the trustees are collectively liable to the beneficiary. Thus, the liability of the trustees is joint and several. The innocent beneficiary may sue one or more or all of the trustees.

If a successful action is brought against one trustee he has a right of contribution against his co-trustees, with the effect that each trustee will contribute equally to the damages awarded in favour of the claimant, unless the court decides otherwise. The position today is that the right of contribution is governed by the Civil Liability (Contribution) Act 1978. The court has a discretion concerning the amount of the contribution which may be recoverable from any other person liable in respect of the same damage. The discretion is enacted in s 2 of the 1978 Act, thus:

's 2 ... the amount of contribution shall be such as may be found by the court to be just and equitable having regard to the extent of that person's responsibility for the damage in question.'

The Act does not apply to an indemnity which is governed entirely by case law. There are three circumstances when a trustee is required to indemnify his co-trustees in respect of their liability to the beneficiaries.

16.2.1 Fraudulent benefit from breach of trust

Where one trustee has fraudulently obtained a benefit from a breach of trust. Such a claim for indemnity failed in *Bahin v Hughes* (1886) 31 Ch D 390.

CASE EXAMPLE

Bahin v Hughes (1886) 31 Ch D 390

A testator bequeathed a legacy of £2,000 to his three daughters, Miss Hughes, Mrs Edwards and Mrs Burden, on specified trusts. Miss Hughes did all the administration of the trust. The trust money was invested in unauthorised investments, resulting in a loss. Miss Hughes and Mrs Burden (in whose name the money was entered) selected the investment and by letter told Mrs Edwards, who failed to give her consent. The trustees were liable to the beneficiaries for breach of trust. Mr Edwards (whose wife had died) claimed that Miss Hughes, as an active trustee, ought to indemnify him against his late wife's liability. The court decided that the defendants were jointly and severally liable to replace the £2,000 and Mr Edwards had no right of indemnity against Miss Hughes.

CONTINUED ▶

> J '… where one trustee has got the money into his own hands, and made use of it, he will be liable to his co-trustee to give him an indemnity … relief has only been granted against a trustee who has himself got the benefit of the breach of trust, or between whom and his co-trustees there has existed a relation which will justify the court in treating him solely liable for the breach of trust … Miss Hughes was the active trustee and Mrs Edwards did nothing, and in my opinion it would be laying down a wrong rule that where one trustee acts honestly, though erroneously, the other trustee is to be held entitled to an indemnity who by doing nothing neglects his duty more than the acting trustee … In my opinion the money was lost just as much by the default of Mrs Edwards as by the innocent though erroneous action of her co-trustee, Miss Hughes.'
>
> (Cotton LJ)

16.2.2 Breach committed on advice of a solicitor-trustee

The requirements here, in addition to a breach of trust, are:

(1) a co-trustee is a solicitor and

(2) the breach of trust was committed in respect of his advice and

(3) the co-trustees had relied solely on his advice and did not exercise an independent judgement.

CASE EXAMPLE

Re Partington (1887) 57 LT 654

Mrs Partington and Mr Allen, a solicitor, were trustees who were liable for a breach of trust. The trust fund was invested in an improper mortgage which resulted in a loss. Mr Allen had assured Mrs Partington that he would find a good investment on behalf of the trust. He failed in his duties to verify statements by the borrower, he failed to give proper instructions to the valuers and he did not give sufficient information to Mrs Partington to enable her to exercise an independent judgement. The court held that Mrs Partington was entitled to claim an indemnity from Mr Allen.

CASE EXAMPLE

Head v Gould [1898] 2 Ch 250

The claim for an indemnity against a solicitor-trustee failed because the co-trustee actively encouraged the solicitor-trustee to commit the breach of trust. The mere fact that the co-trustee is a solicitor is insufficient to establish the claim.

> **J** 'I do not think that a man is bound to indemnify his co-trustee against any loss merely because he was a solicitor, when that co-trustee was an active participator in the breach of trust complained of, and is not proved to have participated merely in consequence of the advice and control of the solicitor.'
>
> (Kekewich J)

16.2.3 The rule in *Chillingworth v Chambers*

This rule is to the effect that where a trustee is also a beneficiary (whether he receives a benefit or not is immaterial) the beneficiary trustee is required to indemnify his co-trustee to the extent of his beneficial interest. If the loss exceeds the beneficial interest, the trustees will share the surplus loss equally in so far as it exceeds the beneficial interest.

■Key facts on contribution and indemnity

KEY FACTS

Contribution	Civil Liability (Contribution) Act 1978
Indemnity	
• Where a trustee has fraudulently obtained a benefit from a breach of trust.	*Bahin v Hughes* (1886)
• Where the breach of trust was committed on the advice of a solicitor/trustee.	*Re Partington* (1887); *Head v Gould* (1898)
• Trustee/beneficiary who instigates a breach indemnifies co-trustee up to the amount of his beneficial interest.	*Chillingworth v Chambers* (1896)

16.3 Defences to an action for breach of trust

In pursuance of an action against trustees for breach of trust, there are a number of defences which the trustees are entitled to raise. These are:

16.3.1 Knowledge and consent of the beneficiaries

A beneficiary who has freely consented to or concurred in a breach of trust is not entitled to renege on his promise and sue the trustees.

In order to be prevented from bringing an action against the trustees, the beneficiary is required to be of full age and sound mind, with full knowledge of all the relevant facts, and to exercise an independent judgement. The burden of proof of establishing these elements will be on the trustees.

CASE EXAMPLE

Nail v Punter (1832) 5 Sim 555

The husband of a life tenant under a trust encouraged the trustees to pay him money from the trust fund, in breach of trust. The life tenant commenced proceedings against the trustees but died shortly afterwards. The husband became a beneficiary and continued the action against the trustees for breach of trust. The court held that the action could not succeed because the husband was a party to the breach.

The trustees are required to prove that the consent was not obtained as a result of undue influence. In *Re Pauling's Settlement Trust* [1964] Ch 303 (see above), the trustees claimed that the children were not entitled to bring an action because they had consented to the advancements. The court rejected this argument and decided that the consent was not freely obtained from the children because they were under the influence of their parents who benefited from the advancements. The statement of the principle by Wilberforce J (below) was approved by the Court of Appeal.

> J
> 'The court has to consider all the circumstances in which the concurrence of the beneficiary was given with a view to seeing whether it is fair and equitable that, having given his concurrence, he should afterwards turn around and sue the trustees … subject to this, it is not necessary that he should know that what he is concurring in is a breach of trust, provided that he fully understands what he is concurring in, and … it is not necessary that he should himself have directly benefited by the breach of trust.'
>
> (Wilberforce J in *Re Pauling's Settlement Trust* (1964))

16.3.2 Impounding the interest of a beneficiary

In the above section the beneficiary who concurs or acquiesces in a breach of trust will not be allowed to bring an action against the trustees. But this principle does not prevent other beneficiaries from bringing an action against the trustees. In these circumstances the court has a power to impound the interest of the beneficiary who instigated the breach.

Under the inherent jurisdiction of the court a beneficiary who instigated the breach of trust may be required to indemnify the trustees. The rule was extended in s 62 of the Trustee Act 1925, which declares:

's 62 Where a trustee commits a breach of trust at the instigation or request or with the consent in writing of a beneficiary, the court may if it thinks fit make such order as the court seems just for impounding all or any part of the interest of the beneficiary in the trust estate by way of indemnity to the trustee or persons claiming through him.'

It is clear from the section that the court has a discretion which it will not exercise if the beneficiary was not aware of the full facts. Section 62 is applicable irrespective of an intention, on the part of the beneficiary, to receive a personal benefit or not. The beneficiary's consent is required to be in writing.

16.3.3 Relief under s 61 of the Trustee Act 1925

Section 61 of the Trustee Act 1925 provides:

's 61 If it appears to the court that a trustee … is or may be personally liable for any breach of trust … but has acted honestly and reasonably, and ought fairly to be excused for the breach of trust and for omitting to obtain the directions of the court in the matter in which he committed such breach, then the court may relieve him either wholly or partly from personal liability for the same.'

This section re-enacted, with slight modifications, s 3 of the Judicial Trustees Act 1896.

The section provides three main ingredients for granting relief, namely:

(a) the trustee acted honestly and

(b) the trustee acted reasonably and

(c) the trustee ought fairly to be excused in respect of the breach and omitting to obtain directions of the court.

These ingredients are cumulative and the trustee has the burden of proof.

The expression 'honestly' means that the trustee acted in good faith. This is a question of fact. The word 'reasonably' indicates that the trustee acted prudently. If these two criteria are satisfied the court has a discretion on whether to excuse the trustee or not. The test in exercising the discretion is to have regard to the interests of both the trustees and the beneficiaries and to decide whether the breach of trust ought to be forgiven in whole or in part. In the absence of special circumstances, a trustee who has acted honestly and reasonably ought to be relieved.

CASE EXAMPLE

Perrins v Bellamy [1899] 1 Ch 797

The trustees of a settlement were erroneously advised by their solicitor that they had a power of sale. They sold the leaseholds comprised in the settlement, thereby diminishing the income of the plaintiff, the tenant for life. The plaintiff brought an action against the trustees for breach of trust. The trustees claimed relief under the predecessor to s 61 of the Trustee Act 1925. The court, in its discretion, granted relief.

> **J** 'I venture, however, to think that, in general and in the absence of special circumstances, a trustee who has acted "reasonably" ought to be relieved, and it is not incumbent on the court to consider whether he ought 'fairly' to be excused, unless there is evidence of a special character showing that the provisions of the section ought not to be applied in his favour.'
>
> (Kekewich J)

But each case is decided on its own facts. A factor which is capable of influencing the court is whether the trustee is an expert, professional trustee or not.

In *National Trustee Co of Australia Ltd v General Finance Co* [1905] AC 373, the court refused relief to professional trustees who had acted honestly and reasonably and on the advice of a solicitor in committing a breach of trust.

A similar view was echoed by Brightman J in *Bartlett v Barclays Bank* (1980): the professional trustee company was refused relief under s 61 of the Trustee Act 1925 because it acted unreasonably in failing to keep abreast or informed of the changes in the activities of the investment company.

> **J** 'A trust corporation holds itself out in its advertising literature as being above ordinary mortals. With a specialist staff of trained trust officers and managers, with ready access to financial information and professional advice, dealing with and solving trust problems day after day, the trust corporation holds itself out, and rightly, as capable of providing an expertise which it would be unrealistic to expect and unjust to demand from the ordinary prudent man or woman who accepts, probably unpaid and sometimes reluctantly from a sense of family duty, the burden of trusteeship. Just as, under the law of contract, a professional person possessed a particular skill is liable for breach of contract if he neglects to use the skill and experience which he professes, so I think that a professional corporate trustee is liable for breach of trust if loss is caused to the trust fund, because it neglects to exercise the special care and skill which it professes to have.'
>
> (Brightman J)

Other factors that have been taken into account by the courts include the status of the adviser to the trust and the size of the trust estate. It has been suggested that nothing less than the advice of a Queen's Counsel should be taken by the trustees in respect of a large estate. The circumstances regarding the breach of trust may be considered by the courts, in particular, whether the breach of trust originated from a complicated rule of law and whether the trustees acted on erroneous belief that the beneficiaries had consented.

16.3.4 Limitation and laches

The limitation periods concern the time limits during which a beneficiary is entitled to pursue a cause of action in respect of trust property. The remarks of Kekewich J in *Re Timmins* [1902] 1 Ch 176 refer to the rationale concerning an earlier limitation statute.

> **J** 'The intention of the statute was to give a trustee the benefit of the lapse of time when, although he had done something legally or technically wrong, he had done nothing morally wrong or dishonest, but it was not intended to protect him where, if he pleaded the statute, he would come off with something he ought not to have i.e. money of the trust received by him and converted to his own use.'
>
> (Kekewich J)

Six-year limitation period

By virtue of s 21(3) of the Limitation Act 1980, the general rule concerning the limitation period for actions for breach of trust is six years from the date on which the cause of action accrued. A cause of action does not accrue in respect of future interests (remainders and reversions) until the interest falls into possession. Thus, a life tenant under a trust is required to bring an action within six years of the breach of trust but a remainderman has up to six years from the death of the life tenant before his cause of action becomes time-barred. In addition, time does not begin to run against a beneficiary suffering from a disability (infancy or mental incapacity) at the time of the breach until the disability ends. For these purposes a trustee includes a personal representative and no distinction is drawn between express, implied or constructive trustees.

Section 23 of the Limitation Act 1980 enacts that in an action for an account, the same limitation period will apply as is applicable to the claim which is the basis for the account. The purpose of this provision is to restrict the period in which claims may be brought for an account by reference to the underlying nature and substance of the claim. Thus a claim for an account for breach of a simple contract is required to be brought within six years from the date of the breach of contract.

In *Paragon Finance Ltd v Thakerar* [1999] 1 All ER 400, the Court of Appeal refused to grant leave to amend a claim that was brought more than six years after the cause of action had accrued. In doing so, the court overruled *Nelson v Rye* [1996] 2 All ER 186. Likewise, in *Coulthard v Disco Mix Club* [2000] 1 WLR 707, the High Court decided that the six-year limitation period was applicable to an action for an account arising out of a contractual claim.

Exceptions to the six-year rule

Under s 21(1), where a beneficiary brings a claim in respect of any fraud by the trustee or to recover trust property or the proceeds of sale from trust property (ie actions *in rem* (see below)), the fixed limitation periods shall not apply. A transferee from a trustee is in the same position as the trustee, unless he is a *bona fide* transferee of the legal estate for value without notice.

Where the right of action has been concealed by fraud or where the action is for relief from the consequences of a mistake, time does not begin to run until the claimant discovers the fraud or mistake or ought with reasonable diligence to have discovered it (s 32).

In accordance with s 22, the limitation period in respect of any claim to the estate of a deceased person is 12 years.

Furthermore, the limitation periods mentioned above do not apply to an action for an account brought by the Attorney-General against a charitable trust, because charitable trusts do not have beneficiaries in a way similar to private trusts: *A-G v Cocke* [1988] Ch 414.

Laches

Where no period of limitation has been specified under the Act (see s 21(1)), the doctrine of laches will apply to equitable claims. Section 36 of the Limitation Act 1980 enacts that nothing in the Act affects any equitable jurisdiction to refuse relief on the grounds of acquiescence or otherwise.

The doctrine of laches consists of a substantial lapse of time coupled with the existence of circumstances which make it inequitable to enforce the claim of the claimant. The doctrine is summarised in the maxim 'Equity aids the vigilant and not the indolent'. The rationale behind the doctrine was stated by Lord Camden LC in *Smith v Clay* (1767) 3 Bro CC 639, thus:

> 'A court of equity has always refused its aid to stale demands, where a party has slept upon his rights and acquiesced for a great length of time. Nothing can call forth this court into activity, but conscience, good faith and reasonable diligence; where these are wanting, the court is passive and does nothing.'

It may be treated as inequitable to enforce the claimant's cause of action where the delay has led the defendant to change his position to his detriment in the reasonable belief that the claim has been abandoned, or the delay has led to the loss of evidence which might assist the defence or if the claim is to a business (for the claimant should not be allowed to wait and see if it prospers).

The jurisdiction of the court in respect of laches was summarised by Lord Selborne in *Lindsay Petroleum Co v Hurd* (1874) LR 5.

> 'Now the doctrine of laches in courts of equity is not an arbitrary or technical doctrine. Where it could be practically unjust to give a remedy either because the party has, by his conduct, done that which might fairly be regarded as equivalent to a waiver of it or where by his conduct the neglect he has, though perhaps not waiving that remedy, yet put the other party in a situation in which it would not be reasonable to place him if the remedy were afterwards to be asserted, in either of these cases lapse of time and delay are most material.'

The applicability of the equitable doctrines of laches and acquiescence depend on the facts of each case. Unreasonable delay by the claimant, substantial prejudice and manifest injustice to the defendant are significant factors to be taken into consideration by the court. In order to raise a successful defence, the defendant is required to establish the following three elements:

(1) that there has been unreasonable delay in bringing the action by the claimant

(2) that there has been consequent substantial prejudice or detriment to the defendant

(3) that the balance of justice requires the claimant's cause of action to be withheld.

16.4 Proprietary remedies (tracing or the claim *in rem*)

The claimant beneficiary who suffers a loss as a result of a breach of trust is entitled to claim restitution of the trust estate in an action for an account against the wrongdoers, the trustees. Such an action is a claim against the trustees and is referred to as a claim *in personam*, ie the claim is against the trustees personally, who are required to satisfy the claim from their personal assets. Provided that the trustees are solvent and have sufficient assets to satisfy the claim of the innocent beneficiary, the claimant will not be out of pocket. But if the trustees are insolvent, the claimant's cause of action will rank with the claims of the trustees' other unsecured creditors. This may result in the order of the court remaining unsatisfied. An alternative remedy available to the beneficiary is to 'trace' the trust assets in the hands of the trustees or third parties, not being *bona fide* transferees of the legal estate for value without notice, and recover such property or obtain a charging order in priority over the trustees' creditors. This is known as a proprietary remedy or a claim *in rem* or a 'tracing order'.

A tracing order is a remedy whereby the claimant establishes and protects his title to assets in the hands of another. The remedy is 'proprietary' in the sense that the order is attached to specific property under the control of another or may take the form of a charging order thereby treating the claimant as a secured creditor. The remedies at common law and equity are mainly 'personal' in the sense that they are remedies which force the defendant to do or refrain from doing something in order to compensate the claimant for the wrong suffered. But the proprietary remedy exists as a right to proceed against a particular asset in the hands of the defendant.

16.4.1 Advantages of the proprietary remedy over personal remedies

The proprietary remedy has a number of advantages over the personal remedy, namely:

- the effectiveness of the claimant's action is not dependent on the solvency of the defendant. Indeed, the claimant's action is based on an assertion of ownership of the asset in question

- the claimant may be able to take advantage of increases in the value of the property in appropriate cases

- on a proprietary claim, interest accrues from the date the property was acquired by the defendant while claims *in personam* carry interest only from the date of the judgment

- the limitation periods for commencing claims are not applicable to claimants who seek to trace their property in the hands of the defendant.

16.4.2 Tracing at common law

To a limited extent the right to trace exists at common law. The approach here is that provided that the claimant's property is 'identifiable', the process of tracing may continue through any number of transformations. The form which the property takes is irrelevant, provided that the claimant shows a direct connection between his property in its original form and the property in its altered form in the hands of the defendant.

The main restriction in the common-law right to trace is that the property ceased to be 'identifiable' when it became comprised in a mixed fund or when the asset ceases to be wholly owned by the claimant.

CASE EXAMPLE

Taylor v Plumer (1815) 3 M & S 562

The defendant, Sir Thomas Plumer (later Master of the Rolls), had given money to Walsh, his stockbroker, in order to purchase Exchequer bills. Walsh, without authority, purchased American investments and bullion and attempted to abscond to America. There was a dramatic chase by the defendant's attorney and a police officer who caught up with Walsh at Falmouth where he was waiting for a boat bound for Lisbon. Walsh handed the property over to the defendant's agents and was later adjudicated bankrupt. His assignee in bankruptcy claimed to recover the property from the defendant. The court held in favour of the defendant because the property had belonged to him.

> J 'It makes no difference in reason or in law into what other form, different from the original, the change may have been made ... for the product of or substitute for the original thing still follows the nature of the thing itself, as long as it can be ascertained to be such and the right only ceases when the means of ascertainment fail which is the case when the subject is turned into money and mixed and confounded in a general mass of the same description.'
>
> (Lord Ellesborough CJ)

More recently, in *Lipkin Gorman (a firm) v Karpnale Ltd* [1991] 3 WLR 10, Lord Goff said:

> **J** 'It is well established that a legal owner is entitled to trace his property into its product, provided that the latter is indeed identifiable as the product of his property ... Of course, "tracing" or "following" property into its product involves a decision by the owner of the original property to assert his title to the product in place of his original property ... the bank was the debtor and the solicitors were its creditors. Such a debt constitutes a choice in action, which is a species of property; and since the debt was enforceable at common law, the choice in action was legal property belonging to the solicitors at common law. There is in my opinion no reason why the solicitors should not be able to trace their property at common law in that choice in action, or in any part of it, into its product ie cash drawn by loss from their client account at the bank. Such a claim is consistent with their assertion that the money so obtained by loss was their property at common law.'
>
> (Lord Goff)

In *Trustee of the Property of F C Jones and Sons v Jones* [1996] 3 WLR 703, the Court of Appeal allowed the Official Receiver of a bankrupt firm to trace at law and recover the profits derived from the claimant's property.

16.4.3 Tracing in equity

Equity had developed a more realistic approach to tracing as opposed to the common law. Equity had conceived the notion that once property was identifiable, recognition of the claimant's right could be given by attaching the order:

*   to specific property or
*   by charging the asset for the amount of the claim.

Unmixed fund

Equity followed the common law and declared that where the trust property has been transformed into property of a different form by the trustees and has been kept separate and distinct from the trustees' resources, the beneficiary may take the proceeds. If the proceeds of sale have been used to acquire further property, the beneficiary may elect:

(i) to take the property which has been acquired wholly with the trust property or

(ii) to charge the property for the amount belonging to the trust.

> **J** 'The modern doctrine of Equity as regards property disposed of by persons in a fiduciary position is a very clear and well established doctrine. There is no distinction between a rightful or wrongful disposition of the property so far as the right of the beneficial owner to follow the "proceeds". You can take the proceeds of sale if you can identify them. But it very often happens that you cannot identify the proceeds. The proceeds may have been invested together with money belonging to the person standing in a fiduciary position, in a purchase. He may have bought land with it. In that case, according to the now well established doctrine of Equity, the beneficial owner has a right to elect either to take the property purchased, or to hold it as security for the amount of the purchase money, or, as we generally express it, he is entitled at his election either to take the property or to have a charge on the property for the amount of the trust money ...'
>
> (Jessel MR in *Re Hallett's Estate* (1880) 13 Ch D 696)

ASE EXAMPLE

Banque Belge pour L'Etranger v Hambrouck [1921] 1 KB 321

The defendant drew cheques from his employer's bank account which were paid into his own account. Sums were drawn out of this account and paid into the account of his mistress, Mlle Spanoghe. A claim to trace and recover the sum from her account succeeded.

Mixed fund

Where the trustee or fiduciary has mixed his funds with that of the beneficiary or has purchased further property with the mixed fund, the beneficiary loses his right to elect to take the property acquired. The reason is that the property would not have been bought with the beneficiary's money pure and simple but with the mixed fund. However, in the exercise of the exclusive jurisdiction of equity, the beneficiary would be entitled to have the property charged for the amount of the trust money.

> **J** 'But where the trustee has mixed the money with his own the beneficiary can no longer elect to take the property, because it is no longer bought with the trust money but with a mixed fund. He is, however, still entitled to a charge on the property purchased for the amount of the trust money laid out in the purchase ... That is the modern doctrine of Equity ...'
>
> (Jessel MR in *Re Hallett's Estate* (1880))

CASE EXAMPLE

Mr Hallett was a solicitor and a trustee of his own marriage settlement in favour of his wife for life and subject thereto for himself for life with remainder to the issue of the marriage. He paid the trust monies into his bank account. As a solicitor he acted on behalf of Mrs Cotterill and paid a sum of money received on her behalf into his account. He made various payments into and out of the account. At the time of his death the account had sufficient funds to meet the claims of the trust and Mrs Cotterill but not, in addition, the claims of the general creditors. The personal representatives of Hallett sued to ascertain whether or not the trustees and Mrs Cotterill (collectively) had priority in satisfaction of their claim over the general creditors. The Court of Appeal held that the trustees and Mrs Cotterill had priority and were entitled to a charge on the bank account to the extent of their claim. The personal representatives had argued that the amounts withdrawn from the account were primarily trust monies so that the balance remaining in the account belonged to the personal representatives. This argument was rejected by the Court of Appeal on the ground that an individual who controls funds belonging to an innocent person which have been mixed with his own and withdraws part of the fund which is dissipated is assessed to have withdrawn his own funds before depleting the innocent person's balance in the account.

J

'Where a man does an act which may be rightfully performed, he cannot say that that act was intentionally and in fact done wrongly. When we come to apply that principle to the case of a trustee who has blended trust monies with his own, it seems to me perfectly plain that he cannot be heard to say that he took away the trust money when he had a right to take away his own money. The simplest case put is the mingling of trust monies in a bag with money of the trustee's own. Suppose he had 100 sovereigns in a bag and he adds to them another 100 sovereigns of his own, so that they are co-mingled in such a way that they cannot be distinguished and the next day he draws out for his own purposes £100, is it tolerable for anybody to allege that what he drew out was the first £100 of trust monies and that he misappropriated it and left his own £100 in the bag? It is obvious he must have taken away that which he had a right to take away, his own £100.'

(Jessel MR)

The rule in *Re Hallett's Estate* (1880) seems to be that if a trustee or fiduciary mixes trust monies with his own:

* the beneficiary is entitled in the first place to a charge on the amalgam of the fund in order to satisfy his claim

- if the trustee or fiduciary withdraws monies for his own purposes, he is deemed to draw out his own monies so that the beneficiary may claim the balance of the fund as against the trustee's general creditors.

Where a trustee misappropriates trust funds in order to fund premiums on a life assurance policy, the beneficiaries (under the trust) become part owners of a chose in action, and thus the policy proceeds, and are entitled to a *pro rata* share of the sum assured.

CASE EXAMPLE

Foskett v McKeown [2001] 1 AC 102

Trustees held funds allegedly in pursuance of a land development deal which did not materialise. One of the trustees effected a whole life insurance policy in the sum of £1 million. The first two annual premiums were paid out of the trustee's funds, but the fourth and fifth premiums were paid out of the investors' funds. The trustee committed suicide and the insurance company duly paid the sum assured to the named beneficiaries under the policy. The claimant sued as a representative of the investors for a *pro rata* share of the policy proceeds. The House of Lords, by a majority, held in favour of the claimant on the ground that immediately before the payment of the fourth premium, the property, held in trust for the defendants, was a chose in action, ie the bundle of rights enforceable under the policy against the insurers. The trustee, by paying the fourth premium out of the monies of the claimants' trust fund, wrongly mixed the value of the premium with the value of the policy. Thereafter, the defendants held the same chose in action (ie the policy) but with the enhanced value of both contributions. The effect was that the proceeds of the policy were held in proportion to the contributions which the parties made to the five premiums.

Assets purchased

Since the beneficiaries are entitled to trace their property (including a charge) into a mixed fund, it follows that that right (to trace) may extend to property (assets) acquired with the mixed fund. Accordingly, if a part of the fund is used to purchase an asset which is identifiable and the remainder of the fund has been exhausted (the right to trace against the fund becoming otiose), the beneficiary may claim to trace against the asset acquired by the trustees.

In short, from the point of view of the beneficiary, the trustee and his successors in title are prevented from denying the interest deemed to be acquired with the mixed fund.

CASE EXAMPLE

Re Oatway [1903] 2 Ch 356

O, a trustee, paid trust monies of £3,000 into his private bank account containing his own monies. He later purchased shares in Oceana Ltd for £2,137. After this drawing out there was still more in the account than the amount of trust monies paid in. O paid further sums into the account but his subsequent drawings for his own purposes exhausted the entire amount standing to his credit. The shares were later sold for £2,474. O died insolvent. The beneficiaries claimed that the proceeds of sale of the shares represented their monies. The personal representatives claimed that as O had sufficient monies in his account to satisfy the claim of the beneficiaries at the time of the purchase of the shares, that purchase was met by the trustee's own funds. The court held in favour of the beneficiaries.

J

'It is clear that when any of the money drawn out has been invested and the investment remains in the name or under the control of the trustee, the balance having been dissipated by him, he cannot maintain that the investment which remains represents his own money and that what was spent and can no longer be recovered was the money belonging to the trust. In other words, when private money of the trustee and that which he held in a fiduciary capacity have been mixed in the same banking account from which various payments have been made, then, in order to determine to whom any remaining balance or any investment paid for out of the account ought to be deemed to belong, the trustee must be debited with all the sums that have been withdrawn and applied to his own use so as to be no longer recoverable, and the trust money in like manner debited with any sums taken out and duly invested in the names of the proper trustees. The personal representatives have contended that the trustees were entitled to withdraw from the account and rightly applied the fund for his own purposes; and accordingly the shares belong to his estate. To this I answer that he never was entitled to withdraw the £2,137 from the account or, at all events, that he could not be entitled to take that sum from the account and hold it or the investments made therewith, freed from the charge in favour of the trust, unless and until the trust money paid into the account had been first restored and the trust fund reinstated by due investment of the money in the joint names of the proper trustees, which was never done.'

(Joyce J)

Scope of the charge

After some hesitation, it appears that a beneficiary who has a right to trace into an asset bought by the trustees would be permitted to claim any increase in the asset purchased. It makes no difference whether the asset was bought with an unmixed or a mixed fund. No difficulty arises if the asset was bought with an unmixed fund because the claimant is the sole owner of such asset. But the difficulty surrounds the claim to any increase in the asset bought with a mixed fund. One argument which has been put forward is that the charge on the asset ought to be limited to the amount of the trust monies and no more because the claimant is only seeking to recover his money and not claiming the asset bought with his funds. Supporters of this view refer to Jessel MR's judgment in *Re Hallett's Estate* (1880) as advancing this argument. However, Ungoed-Thomas J in *Re Tilley's Will Trust* [1967] Ch 1179 distinguished the statement by Jessel MR in *Re Hallett* (1880) on the ground that the judge was not considering the question of the 'proportion' of the property that would have been subject to the charge, but was only considering whether the charge existed or not. Furthermore, Ungoed-Thomas J declared *obiter* that the beneficiary's charge on the asset would be in respect of a proportionate part of the increase in value, because otherwise the trustee (and his successors in title who ought to be in no better position) may profit from the breach of trust.

CASE EXAMPLE

Re Tilley's Will Trust [1967] Ch 1179

A testator, who died in 1932, left property to his widow, as sole trustee, on trust to his widow for life, with the remainder to Charles and Mabel (his children by a former marriage) in equal shares. The trust properties were realised between 1933 and 1952 for a total of £2,237 (trust monies). This amount was paid into the widow's bank account and was blended with her own monies. Until 1951, the widow's bank account was at various times substantially overdrawn (in 1945, overdraft of £23,536). Investments were purchased by the widow, financed by overdraft facilities at the bank. From 1951 her account was sufficiently in credit from her own personal contributions, ie without regard to any trust monies. In 1959, the widow died with an estate valued at £94,000. Mabel had predeceased the widow and her administrators sued the widow's personal representatives, claiming that Mabel's estate was entitled to one-half of the proportion of the profits made by the widow, ie on the assumption that the widow's personal representative failed to show that Mrs Tilley's investments were made out of her personal monies the claimant was entitled to a *pro rata* amount of the profits from the investments. The court held that the trust monies were not used to purchase the investments made by Mrs Tilley (the trustee) but were used only to reduce her overdraft which was the source of the purchase monies. In short, there was a *causa sine qua non* between the trust monies and the investments, but the trust monies were not the *causa causans* of the profit.

CONTINUED ▸

> **J** '... it seems to me, on a proper appraisal of all the facts of this case, that Mrs Tilley's breach halted at the mixing of the funds in her bank account. Although properties bought out of those funds would, like the bank account itself (at any rate if the monies in the bank account were inadequate) be charged with repayment of the trust monies which then would stand in the same position as the bank account, yet the trust monies were not invested in properties at all but merely went in reduction of Mrs Tilley's overdraft which was in reality the source of the purchase monies. The plaintiff's claim therefore failed and he was entitled to no more than repayment of half of £2,237 ...'
>
> (Ungoed-Thomas J)

However, Ungoed-Thomas J considered *obiter* the scope of the charge on the assets bought, had the claimant been entitled to trace into the investments, and reasoned thus:

> **J** 'In *Re Hallett* the claim was against a bank balance of mixed fiduciary and personal funds, and it is in the context of such a claim that it was held that the person in a fiduciary character drawing out money from the bank account must be taken to have drawn out his own money in preference to the trust money, so that the claim of the beneficiaries prevailed against the balance of the account.
>
> *Re Oatway* (1903) was the converse of the decision in *Re Hallett* (1880). In that case the claim was not against the balance left in the bank of such mixed monies, but against the proceeds of sale of shares which the trustee had purchased with monies which, as in *Re Hallett* (1880), he had drawn from the bank account. But, unlike the situation in *Re Hallett* (1880), his later drawings had exhausted the account so that it was useless to proceed against the account. It was held that the beneficiary was entitled to the proceeds of sale of the shares which were more than their purchase price but less than the trust monies paid into the account. Further, *Re Oatway* (1903) did not raise the question whether the beneficiary is entitled to any profit made out of the purchase of property by the trustee out of a fund consisting of his personal monies which he mixed with the trust monies and so the judgment was not directed to, and did not deal with that question ... Lord Parker in *Sinclair v Brougham* (1914) had considered *Re Hallett* (1880) but he did not address his mind to the question of whether the beneficiary could claim a proportion of the property corresponding to his own contribution to the purchase. In *Snell's Principles of Equity* (26th edn, 1966) the law is thus stated at p 315:

CONTINUED ▸

> **J** "Where the trustee purchases shares with part of a mixed fund and then dissipates the balance, the beneficiary's charge binds the shares; for although the trustee is presumed to have bought the shares out of his own money, the charge attaches to the entire fund and could be discharged only be restoring the trust monies. Where the property purchased has increased in value, the charge will not be merely for the amount of the trust monies but for a proportionate part of increased value."[1]

Lowest intermediate balance

The rule in *Re Hallett's Estate* (1880) (*vis-à-vis* the 'balance' in a blended bank account) is to the effect that withdrawals from a mixed fund are deemed to take the order of the trustee's monies before the beneficiary's funds. Accordingly, if the funds in the account fall below the amount of the trust funds originally paid in, that part of the trust fund (the depreciation) is presumed to have been spent. The right to trace into the balance held in the bank account will be depreciated to the extent of the lowest balance in the account. The lowest intermediate balance is presumed to be the trust property. Subsequent payments in are not *prima facie* treated as repayments to the trust fund in order to repair the breach unless the trustee earmarks such repayments as having that effect.

CASE EXAMPLE

Roscoe v Winder [1915] 1 Ch 62

The purchaser of the goodwill of a business, Wigham, had agreed to collect the debt and pay it over to the company. He collected the debt (£623.8s.5d) and paid £455.18s.1d into his personal bank account. The remainder of the debt was unaccounted for. He drew out funds which were dissipated until the credit balance in his account was only £25.18s. Later, he paid in more of his own monies and died leaving a balance in the account of £358.5s.5d. The question in issue was the extent to which the claimant could assert a charge under the rule in *Re Hallett's Estate* (1880). It was held that although Wigham had held the money as trustee, the charge was limited to £25.18s – the lowest intermediate balance subsequent to the appropriation.

CONTINUED ▶

J

'It appears that after the payment in by the debtor of a portion of the book debts which he had received, the balance at the bank was reduced by his drawings to a sum of £25.18s. So that, although the ultimate balance at the debtor's death was about £358, there had been an intermediate balance of only £25.18s. The result of that seems to me to be that the trust monies cannot possibly be traced into this common fund which was standing to the debtor's credit at his death to an extent of more than £25.1s because although *prima facie* under the second rule in *Re Hallett* any drawings out by the debtor ought to be attributed to the private monies which he had at the bank and not to the trust monies, yet, when the drawings out had revealed such an amount that the whole of his private money part had been exhausted, it necessarily followed that the rest of the drawings must have been against trust monies. Counsel for the plaintiff contended that the account ought to be treated as a whole and the balance from time to time standing to the credit of that account was subject to one continual charge or trust ... you must for the purpose of tracing put your finger on some definite fund which either remains in its original state or can be found in another shape. That is tracing and tracing seems to be excluded except as to £25.18s.

Certainly, after having heard *Re Hallett's Estate* stated over and over again, I should have thought that the general view of that decision was that it only applied to such an amount of the balance ultimately standing to the credit of the trustee as did not exceed the lowest balance of the account during the intervening period.'

(Sargant J)

The logical effect of this rule is that *prima facie* if the mixed account is left without funds after the appropriation by the trustee, the claimant will not be entitled to a charge under *Re Hallett* (1880). This is the position whether subsequent funds are paid in or not.

Conversely, if the trustees, after the appropriation, deliberately earmark a repayment or purchase as belonging to the trust, the beneficiaries will be entitled to trace into that fund or asset.

CASE EXAMPLE

Robertson v Morrice (1845) 4 LTOS 430

A trustee who held stock subject to a trust, and additionally similar stock of his own, mixed both sets of properties and treated them as one holding. He sold parts of the mixed stock from time to time, so that, shortly before his death, the amount left was less than what he should have been holding on trust. On his deathbed, he instructed the clerk to buy more stock of a similar nature in order to replace that which he had misappropriated from the trust. This was done by the clerk. The beneficiaries claimed to be entitled to the stock as trust property. It was held that the entire portfolio of stock was subject to the trust, on the following grounds:

(i) the balance of the original mixed holding was subject to the charge that attached on the mixing

(ii) the newly acquired holding was trust property because of the declaration by the trustee that such purchase was designed to replace the trust property.

Rule in *Clayton's case*

The rule in *Clayton's case* (*Devaynes v Noble* (1816 1 Mer 529)) is a rule of banking law and one of convenience which had been adopted in the early part of the nineteenth century to ascertain the respective interests in a bank account of two innocent parties *inter se*. Where a trustee mixes trust funds subsisting in an active current bank account belonging to two beneficiaries, the amount of the balance in the account is determined by attributing withdrawals in the order of sums paid in to the account ('first in first out' (FIFO)).

The rule is applied as between beneficiaries (or innocent parties) *inter se* in order to ascertain:

(a) ownership of the balance of the fund and

(b) ownership of specific items bought from funds withdrawn from the account.

The basis of the rule lies in the fact that as between the beneficiaries (or innocent parties) the 'equities are equal', ie there is no need to give one beneficiary any special treatment over the other. But it is worth noting that as between the trustee and beneficiary, the rule in *Re Hallett* (1880) and not *Clayton* (1816) applies. The wrongdoer may never take advantage of the FIFO rule.

CASE EXAMPLE

Clayton's case, Devaynes v Noble (1816) 1 Mer 529

Mr Clayton, a customer of a bank, had a balance of £1,713 in his favour at the time of the death of Devaynes, a partner in the bank. Clayton drew out more than £1,713 (thus creating an overdraft) and then paid in further sums totalling more. Later, the firm of bankers went bankrupt. Clayton sought to recover from Devaynes' estate. It was held that the sums withdrawn by Clayton, after Devaynes died, must have been appropriated to the earlier debt of £1,713 so that Devaynes' estate was free from liability. The sums which Clayton subsequently paid in constituted a 'new debt' for which the surviving partners alone were liable.

The rule in *Clayton's case* (1816), as originally formulated, was a rule in banking law applicable in determining ownership of funds in an account. However, the rule has been extended to ascertain the interests of

(a) beneficiaries *inter se* under two or more separate trusts and

(b) competing claimants or beneficiaries under the same trust.

In *Re Stenning* [1895] 2 Ch 433, the court considered the application of the rule in *Clayton's case* (1816) in an *obiter* pronouncement.

CASE EXAMPLE

Re Stenning [1895] 2 Ch 433

A solicitor paid monies belonging to a number of clients into his personal bank account. This money included £448.18s.6d due to Mrs Smith. There was often more than this amount in the account, but there was often less than the total of the clients' monies paid in. On a claim made by Mrs Smith alleging that she was a beneficiary under a trust, the court held that no trust had been created on the facts but only a loan has been made by agreement. But if £448.18s.6d had been trust monies, *Clayton's case* (1816) would have applied as between Mrs Smith and the other clients.

One criticism that has been levelled against the rule in *Clayton's case* (1816) is that it lacks justice as between claimants of equal standing. The rule exists as a rough and ready solution the outcome to which depends on a matter of chance, ie the application of the rule depends on the precise time when money from two trusts (or monies from the same trust but belonging to two or more beneficiaries) was paid into a current account. A more equitable solution would have been to allow the two groups of beneficiaries to share the balance in the account, rateably, in proportion to the

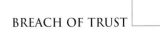

sums originally placed in the account from the two trusts, ie the beneficiaries ought to be entitled to an order ranking *in pari passu*.

In *Sinclair v Brougham* [1914] AC 398 the House of Lords adopted this equitable solution in respect of the claims of two innocent parties *inter se* to a fund, not being a current account, which had been mixed by a fiduciary.

CASE EXAMPLE

Sinclair v Brougham [1914] AC 398

The litigation arose when the Birkbeck Building Society, having borrowing power, established and developed, in addition to the legitimate business of a building society, a banking business which was admittedly *ultra vires*. In connection with this banking business, customers deposited sums of money. In 1911, the society was wound up. The assets were claimed *inter alia* by the ordinary shareholders and the depositors, each group claiming priority over the other. The House of Lords held that the two classes of claimants were entitled to the assets rateably, following the rule in *Re Hallett* (1880), ie an order was made entitling both groups of claimants to a charge ranking *in pari passu*, according to the proportion of their respective contribution.

> J
>
> 'My Lords, I agree that the principle on which *Hallett's* case is founded justifies an order allowing the appellants to follow the assets, not merely to the verge of actual identification, but even somewhat further in a case like the present, where after a process of exclusion only two classes or groups of persons, having equal claims, are left in and all superior classes have been eliminated. Tracing in a sense it is not, for we know that the money coming from A went into one security and that coming from B into another and that the two securities did not probably depreciate exactly in the same percentage and we know further that no-one will ever know anymore. Still I think this well within the 'tracing' equity, and that among persons making up these two groups the principle of rateable division of the assets is sound …'
>
> (Lord Sumner)

Re Hallett extended in *Sinclair v Brougham*

Sinclair v Brougham (1914) was overruled in *Westdeutsche Landesbank v Islington BC* [1996] AC 669 on the ground that no single *ratio* could be detected. However, *Sinclair v Brougham* (1914) is mentioned here in order to demonstrate the application of the *Re Hallett* (1880) principle and the court's reluctance to follow *Clayton's case* (1816).

The litigation in *Re Hallett* (1880) was between persons of unequal standing, namely the innocent claimant and the wrongdoer (or successor). The wrongdoer is prevented from denying the interest acquired by the innocent claimant to the mixed fund.

On the other hand, the litigation in *Sinclair v Brougham* (1914) was between two groups of innocent claimants (of equal standing) whose monies had been represented in assets available for distribution. Accordingly, the House of Lords extended the principle in *Re Hallett* (1880) in concluding that the claimants were entitled to the assets rateably.

> J 'Each of the two classes of contributors claimed priority over the other. Until the case reached the House of Lords, the possibility that they might rank *pari passu* does not appear to have been considered … The House of Lords held that on the principle on which *Hallett's* case was founded, the two classes shared rateably. In one respect, no doubt, this application of the principle is an extension of it since, although the right of individuals to trace their own money (if they could) was preserved in the order of the House, the order provided for tracing the aggregate contributions of the two classes as classes … the extension of the principle in *Sinclair v Brougham* was the obvious and, indeed on the facts, the only practical method of securing a first distribution of the assets …'
> (Lord Greene MR in *Re Diplock* [1948] Ch 465, CA)

In *Barlow Clowes v Vaughan* [1992] 4 All ER 22, the Court of Appeal favoured the *pari passu* charge where the claimants were investors in a common fund, as opposed to the 'rough and ready' solution in *Clayton's case* (1816). The Court of Appeal recognised that the rule in *Clayton's case* (1816) was to be applied when money belonging to several beneficiaries had been 'blended in one bank account'. The court was, however, satisfied that in the circumstances of the case, it was not appropriate to apply the rule because it was wholly inequitable to do so.

Innocent volunteers

In *Sinclair v Brougham* (1914), the mixing of the funds of the two innocent claimants was effected by a fiduciary, namely the directors of the building society. This was consistent with the principle in *Hallett* (1880).

But a controversial issue was whether the tracing remedy would be available to a claimant when the mixing was effected by an innocent volunteer and not by the fiduciary. The Court of Appeal in *Re Diplock* (1948) enunciated (*obiter*) that the remedy would be available.

APPLYING THE LAW

Trustees hold property on trust for A for life, with remainder to B absolutely. The trustees, without authority, distribute £2,000 of the trust income to the remainderman, B, who pays the same into a bank account containing £3,000 of his personal monies. The trust is later terminated (see *Saunders v Vautier* (1841)) and B becomes bankrupt. A may be entitled to a charge on B's bank account ranking *in pari passu*.

J 'Where an innocent volunteer (as distinct from a purchaser for value without notice) mixes "money" of his own with "money" which in equity belongs to another person, or is found in possession of such a mixture, although that other person cannot claim a charge on the mass superior to the claim of the volunteer ... it appears to us to be wrong to treat the principle which underlies *Hallett's* case as coming into operation only where the person who does the mixing is not only in a fiduciary position but is also a party to the tracing action. If he is a party to the action he is, of course, precluded from setting up a case inconsistent with the obligations of his fiduciary position. But supposing he is not a party? The result cannot surely depend on what equity would or would not have allowed him to say *if* he had been a party.'

(Lord Greene MR in *Re Diplock* (1948))

CASE EXAMPLE

Re Diplock [1948] Ch 465

Caleb Diplock, by his will, directed his executors to apply the residue of his estate 'for such charitable institutions or other charitable or benevolent objects in England as they may select in their absolute discretion'. The executors assumed that the will created a valid charitable trust and distributed £203,000 among 139 different charities before the validity of the distribution was challenged by the next-of-kin. In earlier litigation in *Chichester Diocesan Fund v Simpson* [1944] AC 341, the House of Lords decided that the clause in Caleb Diplock's will failed to create a charitable trust for uncertainty of charitable objects. The next-of-kin sued the executors and charities. The claim against the executors was eventually compromised. But the claimants persisted in their action against the wrongly paid charities on two grounds, namely:

CONTINUED ▸

(i) claims *in personam* against the recipient institutions – see *Ministry of Health v Simpson* [1951] AC 251, affirming the decision of the Court of Appeal, and

(ii) claims *in rem* against the assets held by the institutions.

It was held by the Court of Appeal that the action *in rem* would not succeed because the next-of-kin's monies were no longer identifiable and, in any event, the charge ranking *in pari passu* would have inflicted an injustice on the institutions in causing the institutions to sell such assets.

Limitations

The Court of Appeal in *Re Diplock* (1948) enunciated the limits surrounding the right to trace:

- the equitable remedy does not affect rights obtained by a *bona fide* transferee of the legal estate for value without notice. All equitable claims are extinguished against such persons

- tracing will not be permitted if the result will produce inequity because 'He who comes to equity must do equity'. Accordingly, if an innocent volunteer spends money improving his land there can be no declaration of charge because the method of enforcing the charge would be by way of sale, thus forcing the volunteer to convert his property.

Recently, in *Lipkin Gorman (a firm) v Karpnale* [1991] 3 WLR 10, Lord Goff advocated a defence of change of position which ought to be adopted in English law in respect of restitutionary claims. This defence will be developed on a case-by-case basis.

> **J** 'Whether change of position is, or should be, recognised as a defence to claims in restitution is a subject which has been much debated in the books. It is however a matter on which there is a remarkable unanimity of view, the consensus being to the effect that such a defence should be recognised in English law. I myself am under no doubt that this is right ... At present I do not wish to state the principle any less broadly than this: that the defence is available to a person whose position has so changed that it would be inequitable in all the circumstances to require him to make restitution or alternatively to make restitution in full.'
>
> (Lord Goff)

The usual approach adopted by the courts is based on estoppel, which has limitations that make it unsuitable to restitutionary claims. The estoppel is based upon a representation by the claimant, whether express or implied, that the defendant is entitled to treat the money as his own. The mere payment of money under a mistake cannot, by itself, constitute a representation which will estop the payer from asserting his right to receive his payment.

- The right to trace is extinguished if the claimant's property is no longer identifiable, eg the trust monies have been spent on a dinner or a cruise or in paying off a loan.

> **J**
>
> 'The equitable remedies presuppose the continued existence of the money either as a separate fund or as part of a mixed fund or as latent in property acquired by means of such a fund. If, on the facts of any individual case, such continued existence is not established, equity is as helpless as the common law itself ...'
>
> (Lord Greene MR in *Re Diplock* (1948))

- It is essential that the claimant proves that the property was held by another on his behalf in a fiduciary or quasi-fiduciary capacity in order to attract the jurisdiction of equity. This fiduciary need not be the person who mixes the funds or the assets. The mixture may be effected by an innocent volunteer, as in *Re Diplock* (1948).

CASE EXAMPLE

Agip (Africa) Ltd v Jackson and Others [1991] 3 WLR 116

The Court of Appeal decided that the claimant company was entitled to trace in equity a fraudulent payment of £518,822, which was received by the defendants.

> **J**
>
> '... in the present case, there is no difficulty about the mechanics of tracing in equity. The money can be traced through the various bank accounts to Baker Oil and onwards. It is, however a prerequisite to the operation of the remedy in equity that there must be a fiduciary relationship which calls the equitable jurisdiction into being. There is no difficulty about that in the present case since Mr Zdiri must have been in a fiduciary relationship with Agip. He was the chief accountant of Agip and was entrusted with the signed drafts or orders...'
>
> (Fox LJ)

CASE EXAMPLE

Chase Manhattan Bank v Israel–British Bank [1979] 3 All ER 1025

The court decided that a payment of funds, by mistake, from the claimant bank to the defendant bank affected the conscience of the latter to such an extent that the defendant bank became subject to a fiduciary duty to repay the fund to the claimant.

■Key facts on proprietary remedy (tracing)

KEY FACTS

Common-law tracing	
• The common law had recognised the right to trace to a limited extent, ie provided that the property had remained unmixed.	*Taylor v Plumer* (1815); *Banque Belge pour L'Etranger v Hambrouck* (1921); *Lipkin Gorman v Karpnale* (1991); *F C Jones v Jones* (1996)
Tracing in equity	
• This principle exists in both unmixed and mixed funds. However, it is crucial that the claimant establish the existence of a fiduciary relationship.	
• Mixed property.	*Re Hallett* (1880)
• Assets purchased by withdrawals from mixed fund.	*Re Oatway* (1903)
• Increases in the value of assets.	*Re Tilley* (1967); *F C Jones v Jones* (1996); *Foskett v McKeown* (2001)
• Lowest intermediate balance.	*Roscoe v Winder* (1915); *Robertson v Morrice* (1845)
• Tracing as between beneficiaries of two trusts.	*Clayton's case* (1816); *Sinclair v Brougham* (1914); *Barlow Clowes Int v Vaughan* (1992)

CONTINUED ▶

KEY FACTS

Limits regarding the right to trace in equity	*Re Diplock* (1948)
• Tracing cannot affect rights acquired by a *bona fide* purchaser of the legal estate for value without notice.	
• Tracing is extinguished where property cannot be identified, eg the fund has been spent on a holiday.	
• Tracing is not allowed where it would lead to inequitable consequences, now called a 'change of position defence'.	*Lipkin Gorman v Karpnale* (1991)
• It is essential that the claimant establish that the property was held by a trustee or fiduciary, even though the mixing need not be effected by the fiduciary.	*Chase Manhattan v Israel–British Bank* (1979); *Agip v Jackson* (1991) *Westdeutsche Landesbank Girozentrale v Islington Borough Council* (1996)

ACTIVITY

1. 'Equitable tracing claims are, in some respects too narrow in their scope and in other respects too wide.' Discuss.

2. In January of this year, Harold, a trustee, paid £2,000 into his private account (the balance then was £500). The sum paid into his account represented the proceeds of sale of assets belonging to the Church of Belvedere, of which he was a trustee. The following day he withdrew £900 and used it to pay his debts.

   In February of this year, Harold paid into his account £300 representing the half-yearly dividends of trustees' stock belonging to the estate of his father, Charles. Harold was the sole trustee of this estate.

   In March of this year, Harold withdrew £1,000 and again spent it on his own affairs.

   In April of this year, he paid into the account £500 of his own money. Shortly afterwards, Harold became bankrupt.

   Explain the rights of Harold's trustee in bankruptcy and of the beneficiaries of the two trusts.

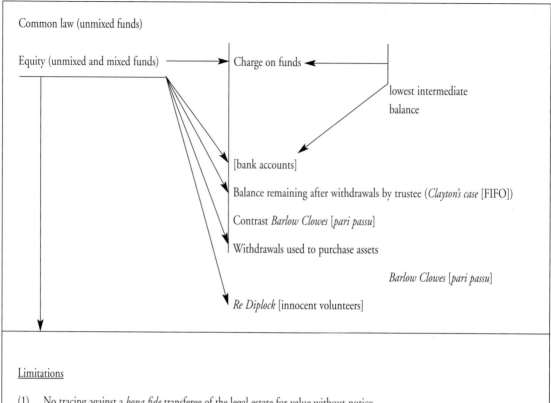

Common law (unmixed funds)

Equity (unmixed and mixed funds) ⟶ Charge on funds ◀

lowest intermediate
balance

[bank accounts]

Balance remaining after withdrawals by trustee (*Clayton's case* [FIFO])

Contrast *Barlow Clowes* [*pari passu*]

Withdrawals used to purchase assets

Barlow Clowes [*pari passu*]

Re Diplock [innocent volunteers]

Limitations

(1) No tracing against a *bona fide* transferee of the legal estate for value without notice.

(2) Defence of change of position.

(3) Property no longer identifiable.

(4) Existence of a fiduciary relationship.

 Figure 16.1 Tracing

Further reading

Birks, P, 'Proprietary restitution: an intelligible approach' (1995) 9 Tru LI 43.

Birks, P, 'Tracing, subrogation and change of position' (1996) 9 Tru LI 124.

Capper, D, 'Compensation for Breach of Trust' (1997) 61 Conv 14.

Chambers, R, 'Tracing, trusts and liens' (1997) 11 Tru LI 86.

Elliott, S, 'Remoteness criteria in equity' (2002) 65 MLR 588.

Hayton, D, 'Rights of creditors against trustees and trust funds' (1997) 11 Tru LI 58.

Halliwell, M, 'Restitutionary claims: a change of position defence?' [1992] Conv 124.

Maudsley, R, 'Proprietary remedies for the recovery of money' (1959) 75 LQR 234.

Oliver, P, 'The extent of equitable tracing' (1995) 9 Tru LI 78.

Stevens, J, 'Vindicating the Proprietary Nature of Tracing' (2001) Conv 94.

INDEX ■

Page numbers in *italics* refer to key facts summaries.
Page numbers followed by f, eg 204f, refer to figures.

MOHAMED RAMJOHN

UNLOCKING
TRUSTS

SERIES EDITORS:
JACQUELINE MARTIN & CHRIS TURNER

Hodder Arnold

A MEMBER OF THE HODDER HEADLINE GROUP

Orders: please contact Bookpoint Ltd, 130 Milton Park, Abingdon, Oxon OX14 4SB. Telephone: (44) 01235 827720. Fax: (44) 01235 400454. Lines are open from 9.00–5.00, Monday to Saturday, with a 24-hour message answering service. You can also order through our website www.hoddereducation.co.uk

If you have any comments to make about this, or any of our other titles, please send them to educationenquiries@hodder.co.uk

British Library Cataloguing in Publication Data
A catalogue record for this title is available from the British Library

ISBN-13: 978 0 340 886946

First Published 2005
Impression number   10 9 8 7 6 5 4 3
Year   2009 2008 2007

Hodder Headline's policy is to use papers that are natural, renewable and recyclable products and made from wood grown in sustainable forests. The logging and manufacturing processes are expected to conform to the environmental regulations of the country of origin.

Cover photo of Pound Sterling © David Aubrey/Corbis.
Typeset by Phoenix Photosetting, Chatham, Kent.
Printed in Malta for Hodder Arnold, an imprint of Hodder Education, a member of the Hodder Headline Group, 338 Euston Road, London NW1 3BH by Gutenberg Press.